'The *oikoumene* was the name the ancient Greeks gave to what they saw as the inhabited world. In *Age of Conquests*, Angelos Chaniotis tells the story of the Hellenistic *oikoumene* – its staggering cultural diversity, as well as the people, ideas, and events that unified it for centuries. Chaniotis boldly breaks with the traditional chronological divisions of ancient history and writes of the long Hellenistic era from the reign of Alexander to Hadrian. Anyone interested in the great cultural achievements of the ancient Greek world will profit greatly from this ambitious book by a leading historian.' Alain Bresson, author of *The Making of the Ancient Greek Economy: Institutions, Markets, and Growth in the City-States*

'A wide-ranging and lively history of the Greek East that offers a rare combination of erudition and accessibility.' Andrew Erskine, University of Edinburgh

'Angelos Chaniotis conveys all the richness and excitement of an extraordinary era in human history in this new work. The period of Greek history after the death of Alexander is the story of the rise and fall of empires and kingdoms, of a new global Greek world stretching from Cyrenaica to Afghanistan, and of the struggle of the cities of the 'old' Greek world to maintain their position. But it is also a period of intense cultural and scientific creativity, in which rulers were widely worshiped as gods, and where for the first time our sources reveal details of the lives of everyday Greeks and foreigners. There is no one who knows the evidence for the long Hellenistic Age better than Angelos Chaniotis – and in *Age of Conquests* he brings this canvas to life.' Tom Harrison, University of St Andrews

'The period that begins with the conquests of Alexander the Great and ends with the reign of the Roman emperor Hadrian is one of the most important and tumultuous in world history. Jesus Christ, Cleopatra, Julius Caesar, and Nero are only a few of the figures who lived during this era. Greeks and Greek-speakers played a crucial role during these years and bear witness to a number of astonishing phenomena – the emergence of Christianity, the consolidation of the Roman Empire, the founding of the library in Alexandria, and lasting developments in philosophy, literature, political thought, and technology. Angelos Chaniotis brings the Hellenistic age to life with remarkable learning, mastery of evidence, and sensitivity. His book offers a brilliant picture of the cosmopolitan Greek world and shows why it still matters to us today.' Phiroze Vasunia, author of *The Gift of the Nile: Hellenizing Egypt from Aeschylus to Alexander*

ALSO BY ANGELOS CHANIOTIS

War in the Hellenistic World: A Social and Cultural History

AGE OF
CONQUESTS

THE GREEK WORLD FROM ALEXANDER
TO HADRIAN (336 BC-AD 138)

ANGELOS CHANIOTIS

P

PROFILE BOOKS

First published in Great Britain in 2018 by
PROFILE BOOKS LTD
3 Holford Yard
Bevin Way
London
WC1X 9HD
www.profilebooks.com

1 3 5 7 9 10 8 6 4 2

Typeset in Garamond by MacGuru Ltd

Printed and bound in Great Britain by
Clays, St Ives plc

A CIP catalogue record for this book is available from the British Library.

ISBN 978 1 84668 296 4
eISBN 978 1 86765 421 2

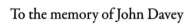
To the memory of John Davey

CONTENTS

priests to kings – The rise and fall of Greek kingdoms in central Asia – The Seleucid dynastic conflicts and the slow death of the Seleucid dynasty – Game of thrones: the civil wars of the Ptolemies prestige and political power – Voluntary associations – Agonistic culture and international stars in sport and entertainment – Shaping civic values and civic identity: the *ephebeia* and the gymnasium – New marriage patterns and the visibility of women – Shades of grey: slavery in the Hellenistic world and the Roman East

Global trends, individual experiences – What is 'Hellenistic' about the religions of the 'long Hellenistic Age'? – Festivals – Shifting popularities of the old gods – Egyptian and Egyptianising cults – Mithras – The Highest God, Jewish influences and monotheistic trends – An age of miracles – Lend me your ears: personal communication with the divine – Traditional mystery cults – Afterlife – Religious innovation: cult founders, missionaries and 'holy men' – Christianity and the beginnings of religious intolerance

Six degrees of separation: an ancient 'globalisation' – Connectivity: a small world – People on the move – Cultural convergence and local traditions

LIST OF MAPS

Greece and western Asia Minor

THRACE

Black Sea

Herakleia Pontike

Perinthos   Byzantion   Chalkedon

Nikomedeia

P r o p o n t i s

Lysimacheia

Kyzikos   BITHYNIA

Lampsakos

Abydos

Ilion   MYSIA

Skepsis

Alexandreia Troas

SBOS   Pergamon   Aizanoi

Mytilene

Kaikos   LYDIA   PHRYGIA

Thyateira

Ipsos

Kyme

Hermos

Phokaia   Magnesia by Sipylos

Erythrai   Sardis

Chios   Smyrna   Apameia

CHIOS   Teos   Kolophon

Kaystros

Ephesos   *Maeander*   Laodikeia

SAMOS   Magnesia on the Maeander

IKARIA   Priene

OS   Miletos   Herakleia under Latmos

Mylasa   CARIA

DELOS   Iasos   Stratonikeia

NAXOS   Halikarnassos   Attaleia   Aspendos

Kaunos

KOS   Telmessos   LYCIA

Knidos   Xanthos   Limyra

Rhodes   Patara

RHODES

KARPATHOS

M e d i t e r r a n e a n   S e a

Lyttos

Hieraptyna

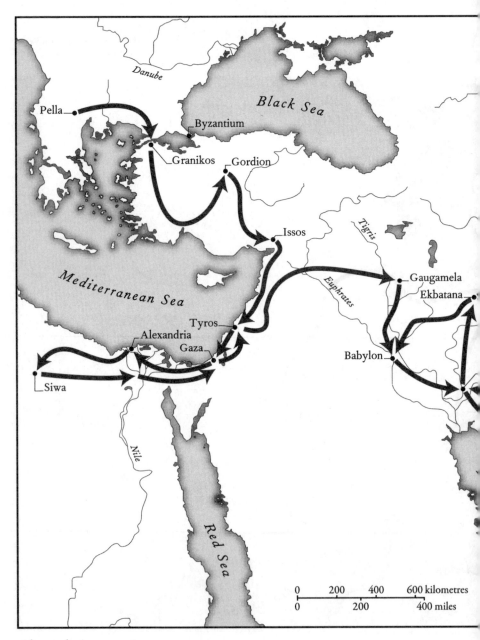

Alexander's campaign

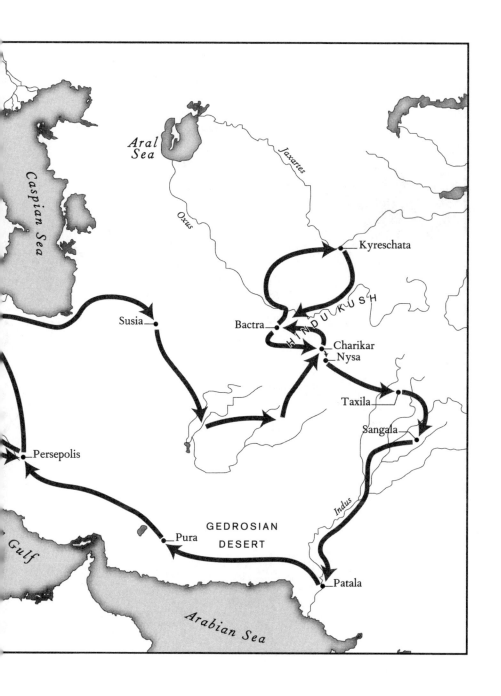

The Hellenistic world

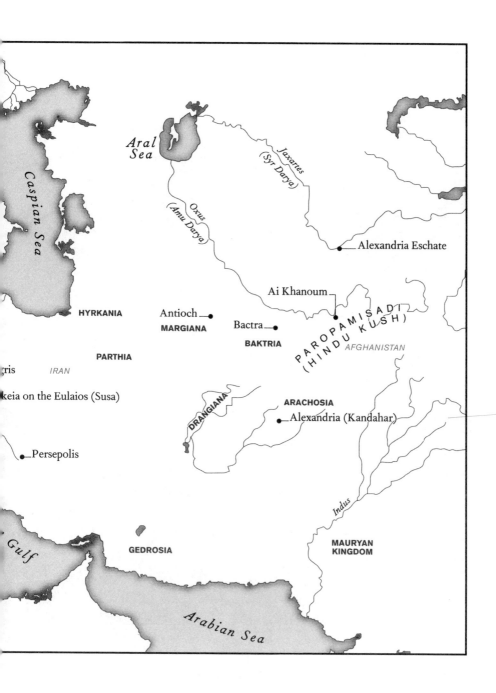

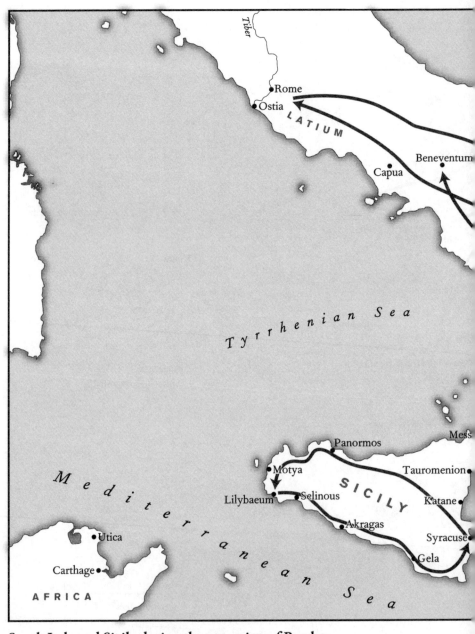

South Italy and Sicily during the campaign of Pyrrhos

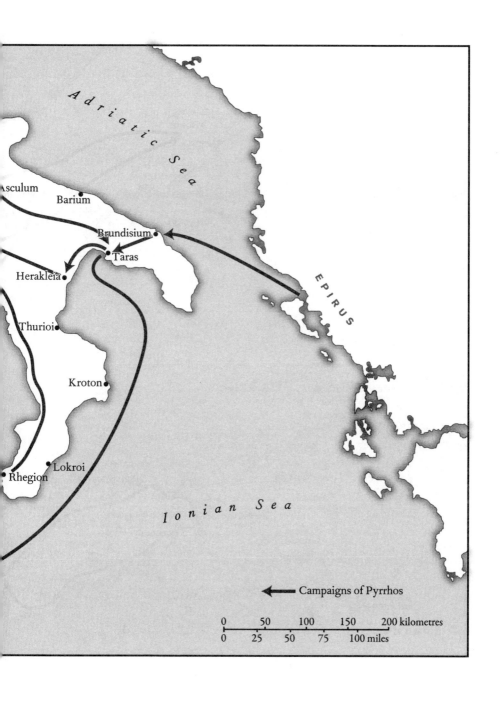

Campaigns of Pyrrhos

| 0 | 50 | 100 | 150 | 200 kilometres |
| 0 | 25 | 50 | 75 | 100 miles |

Asia Minor

Black Sea

0   50   100   150   200 kilometres
0   25   50   75   100 miles

Abonouteichos
Sinope

Amisos

...ios

Amnias

PAPHLAGONIA
Gangra

Amaseia

PONTOS

Kerassous

Trapezous

Komana

Iris

Lykos

Nikopolis

Halys

Zela

Karana

ARMENIA

Ankyra

Tavium

Halys

Euphrates

ARMENIA

Lake
Tatta

Mazaka

Archelais

Komana

Melitene

KAPPADOKIA

KOMMAGENE

Tyana

Samosata

TAUROS

Anazarbos

MESOPOTAMIA

Kastabala

CILICIA

Zeugma

Tarsos

Mopsuesta

...adnos

Olba

Aigeai

AMANOS

Soloi

CILICIA
TRACHEIA

Elaioussa
Korykos
Seleukeia

Antioch

SYRIA

ourion

The Seleucid kingdom and the Greco-Bactrian kingdoms

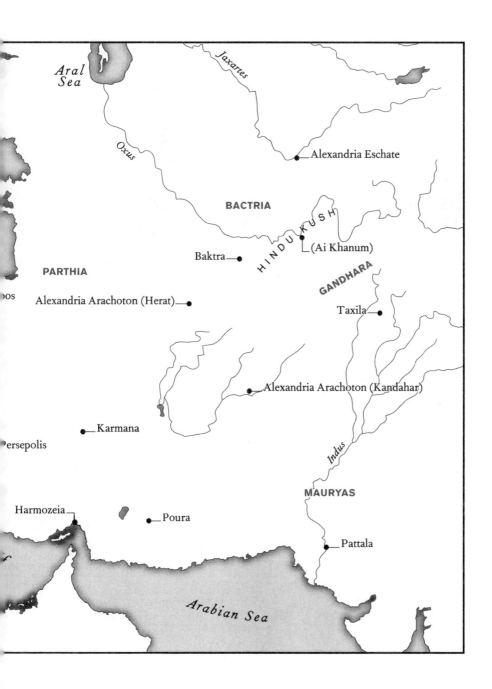

The empire of Augustus

The Roman Empire under Trajan and Hadrian

MOESIA
INFERIOR

Danube

THRACIA

Byzantium

ASIA

GALATIA

LYCIA ET
PAMPHYLIA

CILICIA

CYPRUS

CRETA

ET

CYRENAE

AEGYPTUS

Alexandria

Nile

Red Sea

Black Sea

BITHYNIA ET
PONTUS

CAPPADOCIA

ARMENIA

ASSYRIA

SYRIA

JUDAEA

ARABIA

Euphrates

Tigris

MESOPOTAMIA

PARTHIA

Caspian Sea

Aral Sea

LIST OF FIGURES

PREFACE

This book has been written for a non-specialised audience. It aims to provide general information about the main historical developments in politics, society and religion in the areas in which Greeks lived after the Classical period. The book covers two historical periods which are commonly treated separately: the Hellenistic period, which conventionally starts with the campaigns or the death of Alexander the Great (334 or 323 BC) and ends with the death of Cleopatra (30 BC), and the early Imperial period, from the establishment of Augustan monarchy (27 BC) to the death of Hadrian (AD 138). In the Introduction, I explain how the joint treatment of these two periods contributes to a better understanding of social and cultural developments. The title *Age of Conquests* does not only refer to the fact that the main turning points of these two periods are military conquests (of Philip and Alexander, the Hellenistic kings, Roman generals and emperors, the Parthians and other eastern states); it also metaphorically refers to an unprecedented expansion of knowledge, technical skills and intellectual horizons.

The narrative part presents, with inevitable brevity, the main political developments from the foundation of a Greek alliance by Philip II of Macedonia and the campaigns of Alexander the Great to the death of Hadrian. Because of the complexity of the relevant military and political events, the narrative must move back and forth to different theatres of events; the Chronology (pp. 427–35) will help the reader establish the synchronicity of the various episodes. It has been impossible to narrate in detail the history of individual kingdoms or cities, to describe battles or to present biographies of the protagonists. The narrative is selective, and the main criteria for the selection were the historical significance and the exemplary character of a given event. I interrupt the account of events at the end of the fourth chapter, when Rome enters the scene, in order to provide overviews of kingship, the administration of kingdoms, the institutions and political life of city-states, and the rise of federal states, an important innovation of the third century BC, in Chapters 5 and 6. The subsequent four chapters examine the Roman expansion into the East, from the first wars against the Illyrian pirates to the death of Cleopatra and the end of the Roman civil wars. Chapter 11 is a short overview of the major developments in the world of the Greeks under the first Roman emperors. Chapter 12 deals with the main institutions of the Imperial period from the perspective of the Greek and Hellenised provinces: the position of the emperor, provincial administration and the changed political systems of the cities and the Roman colonies. The next three chapters are dedicated to important changes in society, culture and religion. An adequate and differentiated discussion of philosophy, literature, science and technology, the visual arts and architecture would have required space that was not available in this book. Finally, in the last chapter, I briefly summarise how the 'long Hellenistic Age' changed the position of the Greeks in the *oecumene* (the inhabited earth), making their history an integral part of ancient 'global' history. Unavoidably, sometimes the depth of the analysis had to be sacrificed for the sake of the geographical breadth, exactly as the presentation of general features and trends left little space for an adequate discussion of local differences.

Until the late nineteenth century, Hellenistic history was primarily written on the basis of the surviving narratives of historians – especially Polybius, Diodorus and Appian – the information privided by the geographer Strabo, the *Lives of Plutarch* and a few other literary sources. The study of the Greek world under Roman rule was underdeveloped, with the exception of literature and art. Things changed in the course of the twentieth century, with the progress of archaeological research, especially in Macedonia, Asia Minor and central Asia (e.g. at Ai-Khanoum), the publication of inscriptions and the study of papyri and coins. New textual sources – inscriptions and papyri – are continually added to the known source material, answering some questions, confronting us with new ones and adding nuances to established knowledge. Today, the Hellenistic and the Imperial periods are extremely dynamic areas of research. New discoveries continually enhance scholarship, calling for revisions, usually small but sometimes dramatic.

If I were to list all the books, articles and corpora of inscriptions on which the content of this book is based, the bibliography would probably be much longer than the narrative part. In the notes, I have limited myself to references to sources that are quoted or mentioned in the text and to a small selection of articles and books which are recommended for further reading and which contain references to sources and further bibliography. The general bibliography is also very selective.

Neither the bibliography nor the notes do justice to the contribution of editors and interpreters of inscriptions to the study of the Hellenistic world and the Roman East. Among them I mention with great respect only those who are no longer alive, and on whose work our understanding of the post-Classical Greek world is based: Wilhelm Dittenberger, Philippe Gauthier, Peter Herrmann, Maurice Holleaux, Louis Robert, Frank Walbank and Adolph Wilhelm.

A note on the transcription of Greek names is required. Generally, I do not use the Latinised forms of Greek personal and geographical names – I use Miletos and not Miletus, Pyrrhos and not Pyrrhus – except for the cases in which the Latinised form is very common (e.g. Polybius and not Polybios) or the modern English form is familiar (Ptolemy and not Ptolemaios, Corinth and not Korinthos).

Tom Harrison and an anonymous referee offered invaluable advice. I am also very grateful to Michael Fowler, Roberta Gerdes, Henry Heitmann-Gordon, Kathryn Minogue and Matthew Peebles for improving my English prose, and to Emyr Dakin who assisted me in the proofreading process. I am especially grateful to Lesley Levene, who prepared with efficency and care the copy-edited version. Penny Daniel and Louisa Dunnigan at Profile Books competently supervised the publication process. John Davey invited me to write this book and accompanied its composition, often in difficult times, with good advise and patience. He did not live to see it published. It is dedicated to his memory in gratitude.

INTRODUCTION

Alexander the Macedonian, son of Philip ... defeated Darius king of Persia and Media and became king in his place ... He waged many wars, conquered strongholds, and slaughtered kings in the land. He marched to the ends of the earth, and seized plunder from a mass of peoples ... He reigned for twelve years and then died. His followers assumed power, each in his own province, and they all put on the diadem after his death; they were succeeded by their own children over a period of many years. The earth was filled with miseries.

This excerpt from the first book of the *Maccabees*, a Hebrew text from the late second century BC surviving in a Greek translation, is a subjective summary of what we traditionally call 'the Hellenistic Age' – the time between the campaigns of Alexander (334–324 BC) and the death of Cleopatra (30 BC). The author's perspective is that of a militant representative of a conquered province that took arms against Greek kings and their Hellenised Jewish supporters.

There are good reasons to begin a book on the history of the Greeks in a cosmopolitan era by quoting a Jewish text: first, because it shows the existence of different perspectives and contrasting views; second, because a book that challenged Greek cultural and political domination was diffused thanks to the use of Greek as a lingua franca; and third, because the Hellenistic Age owes its name to the 'Hellenisers', a Jewish group that adopted Greek ways. This text reflects some of the contrasts and contradictions of this period.

What is the Hellenistic period? Why do we study it? And is it appropriate to expand the traditional end date, the year 30 BC, and examine this period together with the first 150 years of the Imperial period, as a 'long

Hellenistic Age'? As for its beginnings, the death of Alexander the Great is indeed an important turning point in the history of ancient Greece. The creation of dynasties by his successors is perhaps the most visible and certainly the most novel aspect of the decades that followed his death. And the earth was undeniably filled with miseries, perhaps not the miseries that the Jewish author of the *Maccabees* had in mind – the religious and cultural oppression of the Jews – but certainly the miseries caused by never-ending wars, private and public indebtedness, and civil strife. Of course, to characterise the Hellenistic Age simply as an age of misery is one-sided and wrong. This historical period is more than just the sum of wars between the successors of Alexander, the dynasties that they founded, Rome, barbaric tribes, foreign kings, cities and federations. What else is worth considering about these three centuries?

In our everyday speech we say that someone made a *colossal* mistake or that a person *stoically* endures adversities in life. We may refer to *epicurean* delicacies, and while on holiday in a foreign place we may be tempted to visit a *museum.* Some who took *Euclidean* geometry at school hated it, others loved it. When we unexpectedly find the solution to a problem, we may exclaim, '*Eureka!*' And although we may not understand how they work, *hydraulic* pumps and cylinders are part of our life. What the words colossal, stoical, epicurean, museum, Euclidean, eureka and hydraulic have in common is that they originated in the Hellenistic Age. The philosophical schools of the Epicureans and the Stoics were founded in the late fourth century BC; '*Eureka!*' ('I have found it!') is what Archimedes allegedly exclaimed around 230 BC, when he realised that the volume of water displaced while stepping into a bath was equal to the volume of the part of his body he had submerged; and Euclid was a mathematician who lived in Alexandria in the early third century BC under Ptolemy I, the king who founded the Mouseion, 'the shrine of the Muses', a centre of learning attached to his palace. In the Mouseion, the mathematician and engineer Ktesibios applied his understanding of water power to create the first pipe organ (*hydraulis*), which operated through the pressure of water. The Colossus was a huge statue of the sun god erected in the harbour of Rhodes in 280 BC, regarded together with the Pharos – the huge lighthouse of Alexandria – as one of the Seven Wonders of the World. In order to assess the impact of a historical period, it is worth examining the words or expressions that it has bequeathed to posterity.

Scientific, artistic, intellectual and cultural achievements such as those above cannot and should not be studied out of their contexts. The Mouseion of Alexandria, the library attached to it, and the innumerable contributions of the scholars and scientists who worked there existed only because Alexander founded the eponymous city of Alexandria, and because the kings who ruled Hellenistic Egypt had huge resources and made them available for the advancement of knowledge. The shift of cultural leadership from Athens in Greece to Egypt and Asia was part of a process that was initiated with the settlement of Greek immigrants in newly founded cities in the territories conquered by Alexander. The Colossus commemorated a military victory; the Pharos of Alexandria was connected with the increased importance of traffic in the eastern Mediterranean; Stoic philosophy was set in a constant dialectic with political life and social developments. The history of the social conflicts, wars, political experiments and innovations in the cities and kingdoms of the Hellenistic Age is indispensable for understanding art and science, philosophy and literature, technology and religion. So, there are good reasons to study the Hellenistic Age, and more will be mentioned later. The campaigns of Alexander are a good place to start. But where do we stop?

The study of the Hellenistic Age traditionally ends with the suicide of Cleopatra in 30 BC and the annexation of her Egyptian kingdom by Rome. This certainly is an important turning point in political history. It marks the end of the last great Hellenistic kingdom and the beginning of the principate – a form of monarchical rule that took shape under Augustus and his successors. The year 30 BC, however, is not a turning point in the history of society, economy, religion and culture. Trends that we observe in the Hellenistic Age continued in the two centuries after Cleopatra's death. In order to fully understand them, we need to consider sources that postdate that year. And vice versa, we cannot understand the political institutions, the social organisation, the economy, the culture and the religion of the Graeco-Roman East in the first two centuries of the Imperial period without considering their Hellenistic roots. The period from Alexander's campaigns in the East to roughly the reign of Marcus Aurelius (AD 161–80) should be best studied as one single historical period, for which I introduce the term 'long Hellenistic Age'. One may recognise several distinct phases in this period of approximately 500 years – indicated by the division of chapters in this book – but the development was continuous.

The historical narrative of this book ends with the death of Hadrian in AD 138, although the conditions in the Greek-speaking provinces did not change under his successor, Antoninus Pius. Changes started to occur with the beginning of the wars of Marcus Aurelius against the Parthians in AD 161. If I have chosen Hadrian's reign to mark the end of this book, it is neither because he is better known to a general readership than his successor nor because he consolidated the borders of the Roman Empire, putting an end to the great offensive under his predecessor Trajan. Rather, it is because the foundation of the Panhellenion – a council that, at least in theory, united all cities of Hellenic origin – symbolically closes a circle that was opened with the effort of Philip II of Macedonia and his son Alexander to unite all the Greeks. Since the unity of the Greeks – or the lack thereof – is one of the broader themes of this book, it is appropriate that the Panhellenic alliance of Philip and Alexander and the Panhellenic council of Hadrian frame the narrative.

Alexander started the campaign against the Persian Empire as the leader of an alliance of the Greeks with the declared aim of liberating the Greek cities of Asia Minor that were under barbarian rule, and of avenging the destruction of Greek sanctuaries by the Persians in 480 BC. He could never forgive the Spartans, a great power that did not join the alliance, for preventing him from claiming that he was leading a campaign of *all* the Greeks. After his first victory at Granikos, he made a dedication to Athena in Athens. The short dedicatory inscription humiliated the only enemy that Alexander had failed to defeat in direct battle: 'Alexander, son of Philip, and the Greeks, except for the Lacedaemonians, from the barbarians who inhabit Asia.' Hadrian did not try to succeed where Alexander had failed; his Panhellenion had nothing in common with Alexander's military alliance. Precisely this contrast between two different versions of Greek unity – one addressed against a barbarian enemy, the other uniting the Greeks within the administrative framework of the Roman Empire – makes Hadrian's reign a suitable point of closure for this book.

Four and a half centuries after Alexander's campaign, Greek cities – this time, all Greek cities – were once again subject to an imperial power: the Roman Empire. Alexander's birthplace, Pella, was a Roman colony; his eponymous city in Egypt, Alexandria, remained the most important harbour in the Mediterranean, but had lost its significance as a centre of political power that it had held for the greater part of the third century BC. Despite the cataclysmic changes in political power that integrated almost all areas in which Greeks and Greek speakers lived into the Roman Empire, what did not change was a separate Greek identity that distinguished the Hellenes from the others. We have every justification to study a distinct Greek history within the empire, exactly as we can study the history of the Jews, the Germans, the Iberians, the Britons or any other subject group. Admittedly this 'Greek' identity was flexible and adaptable. Astute Greek authors could even declare the Romans to be descendants of a Greek tribe, if this helped them come to terms with Roman domination; Hellenised cities in Asia Minor could enter the Panhellenion by inventing evidence that they had been founded by Greek heroes or Greek colonists; almost anyone with a Greek education and citizenship in a city with real or invented Greek origin could be regarded as Greek, no matter whether his name was Greek, Thracian, Iranian or Roman.

Intellectuals in Athens, Ephesos and Alexandria may have looked with contempt upon Hellenised populations in Asia or the Balkans, but in the cosmopolitan world of the Roman Empire with its wide-ranging political, economic, cultural, social and religious networks a 'history of the Greeks' cannot be limited to the regions where Greek cities and colonies existed before Alexander's campaigns; it must also consider the areas in which Greeks settled in Alexander's empire and in the kingdoms of his successors. Accordingly, my approach to the history of the Greeks from Alexander to Hadrian is geographically inclusive. The main focus will be on the areas that are best represented in our sources and had the greatest concentration of Greek communities: mainland Greece, the Aegean, Asia Minor, Syria, Cyrenaica and the Nile Delta in Egypt. But I have tried, both in the narrative and in the overview of important political, social, religious and cultural developments, to include the western Greeks of Sicily and southern Italy, the Greek cities along the western and northern shores of the Black Sea, and the Greeks in central Asia – in Afghanistan, Pakistan and northern India.

The unifying factors in the 'long Hellenistic Age' that also distinguish it from the preceding periods are the importance of monarchy; the strong imperialist drive that characterised the policies of both Hellenistic kings and the Roman senate; the close interdependence of political developments in the Balkans, Italy, the Black Sea region, Asia Minor, the Near East and Egypt; the increased mobility of populations in these areas; the spread of urban life and culture; advanced technology; and the gradual homogenisation of language, culture, religion and institutions. Most of the above phenomena did not exist in similar dimensions before Alexander's campaigns.

This period is truly the cosmopolitan era of the Greeks in a way that no preceding period of Greek history was. Many of the phenomena that one observes in the 'long Hellenistic Age' find parallels in the modern world, and the 'modernity' of this historical period adds to its attractiveness for both historians and alert observers of our own day and age. I will briefly comment on four of them: globalisation, megacities, new religions and governance.

Because of the interconnection of vast areas in Europe, Asia and North Africa, the Hellenistic world and the Roman Empire have justly been considered as early examples of globalisation. Of course, the modern term globalisation can only be used within inverted commas. First, the Hellenistic and Roman networks did not cover the entire globe but only what the contemporaries regarded as the *oecumene*, and second, many people in that period did not think of the inhabited earth as a globe but as a disc surrounded by the Ocean. The breadth of the connectivity in the areas known to the Greeks and the Romans is nevertheless impressive. The conquests of Alexander did not create a lasting empire but they did engender a huge political network of kingdoms, semi-independent dynasts and *poleis* (city-states) extending from the Adriatic to Afghanistan and from Ukraine to Ethiopia. These states had relations with Italy, the Greek colonies in southern France, Carthage in North Africa and the Mauryan Empire in India, thus constituting a network that comprised the entire known world with the exception of China. The Roman expansion enlarged this interconnected world by adding central and western Europe and large parts of North Africa. Already in the mid-second century BC, Polybius, a statesman and historian who discussed the early phases of Roman expansion, was fully aware of the connectivity throughout the entire Mediterranean and introduced the term *symploke* (entanglement; see p. 84).

How this change affected people's lives and the institutions and cultures of very heterogeneous communities is a fascinating question. On the surface, one observes an increased homogeneity in various aspects of life. Greek became the lingua franca in the Hellenistic kingdoms in Asia and Africa and remained so in the eastern Roman provinces; it was often used in Italy and the western provinces, especially among intellectuals and immigrants from the East. Greek and Roman legal institutions reached remote areas. Most aspects of culture – from the appearance of cities to the dress and facial hair of men and the hairstyle of women, from the style of works of art to the form of the lamps that were used to light nocturnal activities, and from the techniques of rhetorical performance to the forms of entertainment – showed an astonishing level of conformity, following the trends that were developed in the major political and cultural centres.

To call these processes of cultural convergence 'Hellenisation' for the Hellenistic and 'Romanisation' for the Imperial periods, as has been traditional, would be misleading. While these terms imply a one-sided relationship between centre and periphery, the development of a cultural *koine* (a common form of expression) in the 'long Hellenistic Age' was the result of longer and far more complex processes. The chief players were not only people with political authority, but also itinerant artists, orators and poets, soldiers and slaves, and magicians and dream interpreters moving across borders. Increased mobility in the multi-ethnic kingdoms and the Roman Empire resulted in cultural convergence and a merging of religious ideas characterised as 'syncretism'. Therefore, when I use the term 'Hellenisation' and 'Hellenised' in this book, I refer only to the adoption of the Greek language and script by non-Greek populations, being aware of the fact that under the surface of a common language, local customs and distinct identities persevered. Bilingual and trilingual inscriptions in Greek and Latin, Greek and Egyptian, Greek and Hebrew, Latin and Aramaic, and so on, are visible expressions of the undying cultural complexity. A dynamic exchange between the Greeks, the local populations in Asia and Egypt, and later immigrants from Italy continually reshaped culture. The non-Greek element can most clearly be seen in religious practices and personal names, but it certainly also existed in a variety of phenomena that range from myths, historical memory and ideas about the afterlife to social customs, burial practices, garments, the preparation of food and the way the soil was cultivated.

Naturally, multiculturalism was a more prominent feature of the 'megacities' of this period. Cities such as Alexandria, Antioch, Athens, Ephesos, Thessalonike, Corinth and Pergamon, with populations of 100,000 to a million inhabitants, cannot be compared with the modern megacities of 10 million people or more. But they did appear oversized to contemporaries. In the early third century BC, the poet Theocritus presents the reactions of two women, immigrants from Syracuse to Alexandria, as they walk in a crowded street during a festival: 'Heavens, what a crowd! How and when are we to get through this plague? They're like ants – there's no numbering or counting them.' Big cities with a heterogeneous population, such as Alexandria, confronted their inhabitants with a number of problems that are familiar to us: safety, tensions between people of different origins, anonymity, the feeling of abandonment, the desire to belong to a group. The weaker the political participation of citizens in their communities became, the stronger grew the need to compensate for this loss with participation in another form of community – religious, professional or other.

Some of these needs, much as in our world, were answered by 'new religions' that promised protection in life and bliss after death. Exotic cults were imported and adapted to a Greek environment, organising their devotees in voluntary associations; these were both exclusive, inasmuch as they required initiation, and inclusive, since they were usually open to people independent of their origin, gender and social status. Voluntary associations, religious and other, gave members a sense of identity.

Despite the predominant position of kingdoms and large federal states, the *polis* remained the main stage of political, social and religious life. In no other period of Greek history, not even in the age of the great colonisation from the eighth to the sixth centuries BC, were so many new cities founded as in the late fourth and third centuries BC. Old and new *poleis*, and later the Roman colonies that were founded in Greece, Asia Minor and the Near East from the late first century BC to the early second century AD, all had some form of sovereignty and extensive self-administration. But this sovereignty was curtailed, first through royal interventions, after 146 BC through the establishment of Roman provincial administration and later through the overwhelming presence of the Roman emperor. Although the cities retained institutions that allowed for the citizens' participation in decision-making, such as the popular assembly, they were increasingly dependent on the contributions of wealthy benefactors. This, as well as the direct intervention of kings and Roman authorities in favour of oligarchic institutions, gradually transformed the cities from moderate democracies, in which wealthy men had to negotiate their power with the citizens, competed with their peers for offices and were subject to accountability, into oligarchies, in which political rights and power depended on property qualifications. This contrast between nominal people's sovereignty and participation and real power, not unknown to democracies of today, resulted in the adoption by the elite, but also by kings, of a theatrical behaviour that aimed at creating a balance between staged affability and appropriate distance – a behaviour that resembles modern populism. Occasional uprisings of the indebted, the dispossessed, the less privileged and those facing discrimination failed to generate reforms. The rule of the 'notables' was unchallenged as long as they were willing to spend part of their wealth on what we today call 'public spending'. Social relations in the 'long Hellenistic Age' were based on complex forms of reciprocity.

Such features of obvious topicality will no doubt seem, for the modern audience, a striking aspect of the historical period discussed in this book. An ancient readership would have been fascinated with two other elements that the Hellenistic and Imperial periods offer in abundance: *peripeteiai* (sudden turns of fortune) and *paradoxa* (unexpected phenomena). The 'long Hellenistic Age' confronts us with contrasts and contradictions: the persistence of traditions and technological revolutions, such as the development of the Antikythera mechanism, a complex device that displayed phenomena of the heavenly bodies and cycles of the Sun and the Moon; between rationality and superstition, monarchy and people's participation, the small world of the *polis* and the huge world of the kingdoms and the empire, the local and the universal. It provides the cultural context for the rise of Christianity. And it offers food for thought to alert observers of the modern world. Hopefully, these are sufficient reasons to delve into the pages of this book.

I

HOW IT ALL BEGAN

From Macedon to the *Oecumene*
(356–323 BC)

A father's legacy (c. 356–336 BC)

A visitor to Mieza, a small site at the foot of Mount Bermion, in 343 BC would have first admired the breathtaking beauty of the landscape: tree-covered slopes, streams of clear water and a series of grottoes on the face of a rock wall. It was the beauty of this location that had inspired the inhabitants to believe that it was a dwelling place of nymphs, a Nymphaion. Our imaginary visitor would have been surprised to see that the nymphs had received male company: a bearded teacher in his early forties and a group of teenagers and young men engaged in discussions about poetry, geography, myth and natural phenomena. Never would our imaginary visitor have thought that the people gathered in this idyllic place were destined to make a lasting impact on world history. One of these people, Aristotle, would lay the foundations of western philosophy and science; no other individual until Descartes was to exercise a stronger influence on European thought. He had been assigned by the Macedonian king, Philip, to educate his son Alexander and the offspring of the kingdom's elite. Aristotle's nephew, Kallisthenes, in his late twenties, was to write an influential history of Alexander that would later inspire the *Alexander Romance* that circulated in Greek, Latin, Syrian, Armenian and Slavonic adaptations and became one of the most widely read books before modern times. Alexander, thirteen years old, would launch less than ten years later a military campaign that would change the face of the known world; eleven years on, he would found Alexandria, a city destined to overshadow all other cities of the eastern Mediterranean in wealth, population size and culture. In this city, Ptolemy, another teenager, was to establish a dynasty that surpassed any other known dynasty of the ancient world in longevity; but more importantly, he would found the greatest centre of learning the world had ever known: the Mouseion, with its famous library.

Such constellations of extraordinary personalities present in the same place at the same time are uncommon in history. If they occur when the demand for change is strong, great things may happen, as during the Renaissance, the Enlightenment or the French Revolution. In 343 BC, demand for change was strong in Greece. The late fifth and the first half of the fourth centuries saw a succession of hegemonic powers that had only briefly succeeded in establishing their leadership in the world of free cities and federations. The continual wars between the hegemonic powers and their rebellious allies gave the Achaemenid kings of Persia the opportunity to take their revenge for the defeats that they had suffered in a series of wars with the Greeks (480–449 BC). In 387 BC, the Achaemenids reincorporated the Greek cities of Asia Minor into their empire. After the city-states of Athens, Sparta and Thebes had seen their leadership established, challenged and demolished, a new power emerged in the mid-fourth century on the fringes of the Greek world: the Macedonians (Makedones), ruled by the Argead king Philip II.

The royal house of the Argeads had ruled the Macedonians since the seventh century BC. The dynasty claimed its descent from Temenos, king of Argos, and, ultimately, from Heracles. The Makedones were a tribe with a Greek name, which most likely meant 'the Highlanders' – from *makednos* (high). They worshipped Greek gods, the Olympian Zeus in particular. Their most important settlements bore Greek names: Dion, 'the sanctuary of Zeus', and Aigai, 'the place of goats'. Their personal names had Greek etymologies: Philippos, 'the one who loves horses'; Ptolemaios, 'the warlike'; Perdikkas, 'the partridge'; Amyntas, 'the defender'; Alexandros, 'the protector of men'; Berenike, 'the woman who brings victory'; Kleopatra, 'the daughter of a glorious father'; Archelaos, 'leader of the

1. Miniature ivory head of Philip II of Macedon.

army'. And they spoke a Greek dialect. What distinguished them from the Greeks of mainland Greece and the colonies was not so much their dialect – probably as hard to understand for an Athenian as the English of the Deep South for an Oxford don – as their way of life. Until the fifth century BC, they were mainly pastoralists living in small settlements. Unlike the Greeks of the south, who had abolished hereditary royalty before the sixth century BC – Sparta's dual kingship is an exception – they were ruled by kings. The distinction that is sometimes made in public documents between 'the Hellenes and the Makedones' is not based on ethnicity but rather refers to different forms of communal organisation.

Until the beginning of the fourth century BC, the Macedonians lived in the shadow of the Achaemenid kings and then of Athens. King Archelaos (413–399 BC) invigorated the kingdom, advancing urban life and culture; it was in his court that Euripides composed his *Bacchae*. His death was, however, followed by dynastic struggles and wars. When King Perdikkas III was killed in battle in 359 BC, his brother Philip seized power at the expense of his nephew Amyntas, a minor. In the twenty-five years of his rule, Philip II (see Fig. 1) transformed Macedonia and the entire Greek world as dramatically as his son would later transform the rest of the known world. The second-century-AD historian Arrian puts in Alexander's mouth an appreciation of Philip's contribution to the Macedonians:

He found you wandering about and without means, most of you clothed with sheepskins, pasturing a few sheep and desperately fighting for them against Illyrians, Triballians, and Thracians, your neighbors. He gave you cloaks to wear instead of sheepskins; he brought you down from the mountains to the plains; he made you capable to fight against the neighboring enemies, so that you had the confidence to protect yourselves with your courage more than with the natural strength of your villages. He made you dwellers of cities and provided you with laws and good customs.

Although this image of Macedonia before Philip is certainly exaggerated, as archaeological research in Macedonia has shown, his achievements were remarkable. A military genius, a shrewd diplomat, a great organiser, eager to learn from others and keen in recognising challenges and opportunities, skilled at propaganda and with unlimited ambition, Philip II deserves the epithet 'the Great' no less than his son. Having spent some years of his youth as a hostage in Thebes, Philip had learned the new tactic of the Theban army, the oblique phalanx, in which the left wing was stronger than the centre and right wing. While the weaker right wing engaged the enemy, remaining stationary as long as possible or retreating, the left wing had the opportunity to advance against the traditionally strong right wing of the opponent, break it and encircle the enemy. Philip improved this tactic with an ingenious device. He equipped his infantry with a long spear (*sarissa*) that was lowered in unison and whose length of between fifteen and eighteen feet protected five rows of soldiers. He also improved the training of the cavalry. His military victories over the years, which enlarged his kingdom, were accompanied by administrative measures. The offspring of his noblemen were educated under the supervision of the court, cities were founded, the natural resources of the new territories – timber and silver – were exploited for the construction of a fleet, and land was granted to soldiers in exchange for military service.

That Philip invited Aristotle, a rising star in philosophy and science, to educate his son, who seemed to be a suitable successor, shows that Philip was more than a man of action. His recently excavated palace at Aigai (modern Vergina) reveals ideological sophistication. One of the courts was decorated with an emblematic theme, Zeus abducting the Phoenician princess Europa. Contemporary viewers would have recognised an allusion to the conflict between Europe and Asia. Herodotus begins his narrative of the Persian Wars with a reference to this myth in order to explain how the continual conflicts between Greeks and barbarians began. Philip was consciously preparing the Greeks for the next step in their conflict with the then weakened Persian Empire: a renewed campaign against Asia, under his command. While Philip's palace was being built and decorated, an Athenian intellectual, Isocrates, was urging him in an open letter in 346 BC 'to champion the cause of concord among the Hellenes and of a campaign against the barbarian': that is, against the Persian Empire.

In order to achieve his plan to invade the Persian Empire, Philip gradually secured a network of support, which culminated in the creation of an alliance in 337 BC, his most ingenious diplomatic move. The enlargement of Philip's influence outside the geographical confines of Macedonia, towards the south, had started much earlier, with the de facto annexation of Thessaly to his realm around 352 BC. Appointed as the highest magistrate of the Thessalian League (*archon*), he controlled a land rich in grain and horses and owned the revenues from the harbours and markets. Philip's success did not rely on military strength alone. He bribed statesmen in Athens, his competitor for leadership in Greece, and signed treaties of alliance whenever they seemed an opportune medium to neutralise an enemy – without, however, intending to respect them. Philip is often remembered as the elderly drunk father embroiled in a conflict with his talented son and ambitious wife. But Philip was a man who could silence the greatest orator of antiquity simply through his presence. When Demosthenes of Athens had his one and only chance to encounter Philip face to face as an ambassador in 347 BC, he was abandoned by his best weapon: his words. After uttering a few introductory words, he suddenly stopped speaking and collapsed.

Philip's greatest achievement is that he united the Greeks in an alliance for the first time since 477 BC. His army defeated the allied troops of Athenians and Boiotians in the Battle of Chaironeia in 338 BC. For historians in the nineteenth and early twentieth centuries, this battle spelled the end of the free city-states and, consequently, the end of Greek history – or at least the part of it worth studying. Seen from another perspective, the Battle of Chaironeia is the beginning of the end of Achaemenid history. Instead of destroying his defeated enemies, Philip invited them to a conference – one of his unexpected and ingenious diplomatic moves. The location was chosen carefully: Corinth. In the place where a narrow corridor of land joins central Greece with the Peloponnese was a sanctuary of Poseidon, the locus of one of the four traditional Panhellenic athletic festivals. More importantly, Corinth was the place where the Greeks had first agreed on an alliance against the Persians in 480 BC. It was this Corinthian Alliance that beat Xerxes at Salamis in 479 and Plataiai in 478 BC, to fall apart a year later. Philip placed himself in the tradition of these victors; he reminded the Greeks that they could defeat the Persians and protect their freedom only if they were united; and he reminded them of their duty to liberate the Greek cities of Asia Minor from Persian rule, as they had done in 478 BC. With the exception of Sparta and Epirus, most Greek cities and federations accepted the invitation. The delegates concluded a peace treaty guaranteeing what the Greeks valued most: their independence, exemption from tribute and freedom from garrisons. Those who swore the oath of the treaty obliged themselves to maintain the peace and not to attempt to overthrow the constitution of the members or the royal rule of Philip and his successors. The members of the alliance were represented in a council (*synhedrion*), presumably in proportion to the size of their population or their troops; small communities may have shared a delegate. In case of conflicts between members, the council functioned as a court of arbitration. An attack against the territory or the constitution of a member obliged the other members to declare war against the assailant. The alliance elected a leader (*hegemon*) who had command of the military in the event of war and determined the size of the contingents to be dispatched by each ally. As expected, Philip was elected *hegemon* and mobilised the Greeks in a war against the Persians. His ultimate aims were probably to expand his realm, liberate the Greek cities of Asia Minor from Persian rule and incorporate them into his alliance; he probably did not intend to destroy the Persian Empire. Although many details of this treaty escape us, its influence on future history was substantial. This Corinthian or Hellenic Alliance was the basis for Alexander's leadership in his campaign and was periodically resurrected by later kings who claimed leadership of the Greeks for themselves.

Philip may have successfully put the affairs of Greece in order, but he failed to ease tensions in his own family. That he took a new wife – his seventh – in 338 or 337 BC was not strange; Macedonian kings practised polygamy. But this new wife, Cleopatra, belonged to an elite Macedonian family, unlike his other wives; any sons she had would place Alexander's claim to succession in question. Relations between father and son became so strained that Alexander had to leave the court for a brief period. Shortly before the beginning of the Persian campaign, he reconciled himself with his father and returned to Aigai.

A son's vision: from Troy to Egypt (336–331 BC)

At the height of his power, on the day that Philip was celebrating the wedding of his daughter Cleopatra in the theatre of Aigai, he was murdered by one of his bodyguards, a former lover of his. Allegedly, the murderer's motive was that Philip had neglected to punish those who had raped him during one of the usual drinking parties in the court. Only minutes before the murder, images of the Twelve Gods had been carried into the theatre in procession, accompanied by a thirteenth image of Philip himself. With this image Philip assimilated his worldly power with that of the gods. Many Greeks would have regarded this as insolence, hubris, and his death as divine punishment. Indeed, the fact that his murder took place in the theatre was tragic irony. Audiences went to the theatre to see how the hubris of mythical heroes was punished without delay by the gods. This is precisely the spectacle that fate offered to the audience gathered in the theatre of Aigai on that day. Life imitated art.

But most contemporaries turned their thoughts elsewhere. Had Olympias, Philip's estranged wife and mother of Alexander, a powerful and passionate woman, encouraged the murderer? Was Alexander involved in the conspiracy that led his father to the grave and him to the throne? Did Persian gold change hands for this murder, in order to remove the threat of the imminent invasion? Rumours circulated; nothing was ever even remotely proved. In Athens, Demosthenes appeared publicly in glorious dress to rejoice in Philip's death, even though he was mourning for the death of his daughter. He wanted to demonstrate that his affection for his child was subordinate to his love of his fatherland and the freedom that he hoped Athens would obtain. Demosthenes' joy was in vain.

Alexander, now twenty years old, consolidated his position as king of the Macedonians. To this effect, his cousin Amyntas, the son of King Perdikkas, had to die, so Alexander had him killed. With a series of quick campaigns, the young king protected the borders in the north, defeated those who had thought that the Macedonian hegemony was over and demolished the city of Thebes. In 336 BC, he renewed the Hellenic Alliance and was elected its *hegemon*, in order to resume his father's work.

Philip had already sent troops to Asia Minor. Now Alexander mobilised the allied troops in a war against Darius III, the Great King.

He crossed over to Asia in May 334 BC. His first stop was Troy, where he performed a series of symbolic actions intended to assimilate his campaign with the Trojan War.

> At the tomb of Achilles, after anointing himself with oil and taking part in a nude race with his Companions, as is the custom, he deposited crowns and remarked upon how fortunate Achilles was to have had a faithful friend while he was alive [Patroclus] and a great herald of his fame after his death [Homer].

The declared aim of the campaign seems to have been the liberation of the Greek cities of Asia Minor and revenge for the destruction of sanctuaries by the Persians during the invasion of Greece in 480/479 BC. The first aim was achieved in less than two years. The second aim was – perhaps intentionally – vague. What constituted an appropriate requital could and should be a matter of interpretation.

Alexander's first moves following his victory in the first major battle at Granikos in 334 BC and the capture of Sardis, the Persian capital of Asia Minor, were more or less predictable (see Map 2). Apart from a strategically unnecessary but symbolically important diversion to Gordion – where he cut the Gordian knot and made clear that the rule of Asia, which the unbinding of the knot promised, was a matter for the sword – he continued his campaign along the coast. He persistently sought direct confrontation with the Persian army until he defeated the Great King himself at Issos in October or November 333 BC. It was also predictable that Darius would at this point make an offer in order to stop the war. But the offer, which ceded to Alexander all areas west of the Euphrates, was rejected. Although the authenticity of the letters allegedly exchanged between the two kings is disputable, it seems that by this point Alexander was already challenging the legitimacy of Darius' rule. His next move also makes sense: one of the weakest aspects of his strategy was that Greece and the Aegean were left vulnerable due to the operations of the Persian fleet in the Aegean; so Alexander's next targets were the most important Persian naval bases in Phoenicia. After a long, seven-month siege, the valuable harbour of Tyre fell. Whereas most generals would probably have pursued the defeated enemy, Alexander interrupted what seemed the normal course of the campaign and headed to Egypt in late 332 BC. This decision was an important turning point of his campaign.

Was this move justified? It was to be expected that a Persian province that had often revolted against the Achaemenids would be an easy target; and, indeed, Egypt offered no resistance. It is likewise reasonable that after two years of campaigning, and in particular after the hardships endured during the sieges of Tyre and later Gaza, the army needed some rest. Strategically, control of Egypt would mean that the entire eastern Mediterranean would be in Alexander's hands. However, Alexander's actions in Egypt show that he had not come there to give his army a holiday or to consolidate control of the eastern Mediterranean. In the few months of his stay in Egypt, Alexander proceeded with a series of measures that are paradigmatic of his understanding of his rule and indicative of his plans. He assumed the pharaoh's titles and powers; with his visit to Amun's oracle in the oasis of Siwa, he took the first step towards his worship as a god; and he founded a new city that was given his name.

Egyptian documents attribute to Alexander the official titles of the Egyptian pharaoh, although it is not certain that he was officially enthroned. A clear indication of how Alexander intended to rule his realm was his adoption of local traditions. He offered a sacrifice to the sacred bull in Memphis, restored the authority of the priests and initiated building projects at the sacred sites of Karnak and Luxor. He then crossed the Libyan Desert in order to visit the sanctuary of Amun (Ammon in Greek) in the Siwa Oasis. Why did Alexander decide to attempt the challenging task of crossing one of the most dangerous deserts? Was he attracted by yet another challenge, wanting to succeed where Cambyses, the Persian conqueror of Egypt, had failed in 525 BC – Cambyses' army having been allegedly buried by a sudden sandstorm? Was he motivated by deep religiosity? Did he wish to seek the advice of one of the most revered oracles and strengthen his authority? Historians' answers to these questions differ, since we have no reliable sources. These are not the only uncertainties surrounding Alexander's personality and actions. It is difficult to identify rational, ideological or emotional motives behind all of his decisions.

In Siwa, the high priest naturally greeted Alexander in the manner suitable to a pharaoh, as the son of the god Amun-Ra. This greeting could be translated in Greek as 'son of Zeus', since the Greeks identified Amun with their Zeus. The allusion to divine ancestry gave Alexander an aura that was to be developed further in the following years. He made dedications

2. Coin of Alexander with the horns of Ammon.

to 'Ammon, his father' (see p. 395) and the coins issued immediately after this visit depict him with the horns of Amun (see Fig. 2). His propaganda was quick to capitalise on the visit to Amun's sanctuary.

The third and most important event during Alexander's stay in Egypt is the foundation of Alexandria. To found a new city was hardly an original idea. Wherever the Greeks went, they founded cities; they had been doing so for centuries. Heracles, Alexander's mythical ancestor, allegedly did three things during his wanderings: he accomplished deeds that seemed impossible; he slept with virgins; and he founded cities. As regards at least two of these activities, Alexander continued the ancestral model. It was also not surprising that the new city was named after him. His father had already founded two eponymous cities: Philippi and Philippopolis. And as early as 340 BC, Alexander, then sixteen years old, had founded an Alexandropolis somewhere in Thrace after a successful military expedition. What made Alexandria significant, however, was its scale and the attention Alexander allegedly paid to the town planning. This city proved to be his most lasting achievement.

Alexander had arrived in Egypt as king of the Macedonians and general of the Hellenic Alliance. He left as a pharaoh, a *ktistes* (founder) and a living god. As pharaoh, he was the personal and absolute ruler of the most ancient kingdom known to his contemporaries. This kingship was very different from the Macedonian one; it reflected traditions that were three millennia old and corresponded to the specific administrative needs of the land of the Nile. As the founder of a city, he had elevated himself to the status of the legendary city-founders, larger than life figures that populated Greek myths and legends and were worshipped in the cities that they had founded. Through his visit to Siwa, he firmly associated himself with divine powers. The passage to Egypt brought closure: according to one of the rumours that circulated at the time, the oracle in Siwa confirmed that Alexander had punished his father's murderer. One more closure lay ahead: the punishment of the Persians for their sacrileges during the Persian Wars. This would be accomplished in the following year.

Passage to Persia: Alexander the Avenger (331–327 BC)

Darius had every reason to seek a conclusion to the war in a single battle. He had been defeated in person at Issos and his strategy to create a second front in the Aegean in order to distract Alexander's attention had failed. A prolonged war would only undermine his authority and embolden centrifugal powers in his empire. Allowing Alexander to invade the heart of Iran and to trap him there with a scorched-earth policy might have been an option from the perspective of military strategy but it was at odds with an ideology that endowed the monarch with invincibility.

In this phase of the war, the initiative belonged to Darius. After mobilising troops from the eastern and northern parts of his realm, especially cavalry, he chose the battlefield. Darius' army, much stronger than that of his opponent, expected the invader on a vast plain at Gaugamela, east of the Tigris, where the 30,000 riders and scythed chariots were at an advantage. Alexander took up the challenge with joy and good strategic sense. He allowed the Iranian horsemen to defeat the centre of his front, but the second line of defence was able to keep them engaged. This gave him the opportunity to penetrate with his cavalry the gaps that the Persian advance had created. He charged directly at the centre of the Persian troops, where the self-confident Great King had taken his position. Darius' troops could not stop the Macedonian cavalry and the King was forced to flee. This victory of daring strategy over sheer numbers marked the end of the Achaemenid Empire, and Alexander was declared king of Asia on the battlefield. In December 331 BC, he captured two major cities of the Persian Empire, Babylon and Susa, without resistance. The traditional capital of the empire, Persepolis, was seized and looted after some resistance in

January or February 330 BC. It was only months later, in May 330, that the royal palace was torched, probably as an act of revenge for the destruction of the Greek sanctuaries during the Persian invasion rather than because of a spontaneous decision of drunk officers encouraged by a prostitute, as was alleged. With this deed, Alexander could claim that he had fulfilled his obligations towards the Hellenic Alliance. It cannot be a coincidence that before he left Persepolis, Alexander discharged the troops from the Greek cities and federations. This marked the end of the campaign that he led as leader of the Greek alliance.

There is indirect evidence that he might also have been planning to send some of his closest officers back to Macedonia. If this is true, it means that at this point Alexander had not yet planned to continue the campaign beyond the Persian capitals. He was perhaps forced to carry on pursuing his defeated opponent with his Macedonian army and additional recruited troops because of unrest in the northern satrapies resulting from the power vacuum and the dangers emanating from the fact that Darius was still free. Having failed as a military commander, Darius had lost his legitimacy; he was arrested by his satraps and put to death in the summer of 330 BC. Alexander treated the dead monarch with the respect due not to an enemy but to a predecessor: he buried him in the royal cemetery at Persepolis and thus acquired additional legitimacy, especially in the eyes of Darius' former subjects. Then Alexander, once again, fulfilled the role of an avenger. He pursued and executed Darius' murderers and in a three-year campaign subdued the rebellious provinces in northern and eastern Iran (330–327 BC). At the end of this campaign, he did not return to any of his Persian capitals but instead continued campaigning eastward, reaching territories that Greek myths associated only with the eastern campaigns of the god Dionysus and the adventures of Heracles. No other Greek before him had ever reached the Indian subcontinent. In the winter of 327–326 BC, Alexander initiated a campaign against the tribes that refused to recognise his authority. This campaign brought him to the Punjab (see Map 2), to new frontiers and closer to the eastern Ocean, which, according to contemporary geography, was the end of the world. It also brought Alexander to his own limits.

Pothos: the desire to reach the limit (327–324 BC)

In 327–326 BC, after crossing eastern Iran, Afghanistan and Bactria, Alexander was testing the limits of his abilities by trying to take the fortress of Aornos, on Mount Pir-Sar in Pakistan, which was regarded as unconquerable. Even his ancestor Heracles had failed to conquer it, so the myth went. It was Heracles' easternmost challenge; Alexander, ancient authors assert, was driven to the limits of the world by *pothos* (longing). He was not the only *pothos*-driven Greek to meet previously unmet challenges and to investigate the unknown. While he was seeking to reach the eastern Ocean, a contemporary of his, Pytheas of Massalia (modern Marseille), was exploring the Ocean beyond the Pillars of Hercules, or Gibraltar (see p. 388). But it was Alexander's *pothos* that had the most immediate and profound impact on his contemporaries.

Having conquered the fortress at Aornos, Alexander pressed his campaign into India, desiring to reach the eastern Ocean. His endeavour was not driven by curiosity alone. As king of Asia, he had adopted the ideology of Oriental monarchy, and this meant that he could not tolerate rulers who did not recognise his authority. The campaign to India may have had an exploratory aspect, but it was primarily a military campaign to establish an authority whose limits could coincide only with the end of the inhabitable world.

Crossing the Indus, Alexander defeated Poros, king of the Punjab, in June 326 BC, appointed him to govern this territory and founded two new cities on opposite sides of the Hydaspes River. These are the only cities founded by Alexander that did not bear his name: Boukephala honoured his horse Boukephalas, which was killed in the battle with Poros, and Nikaia (City of the Victory, today's Mong) commemorated his success. Alexander could not know that this would be his last military victory.

When Alexander tried to continue his campaign in India, he was defeated by nature. Exhausted by hardship and continually plagued by storms caused by the monsoon winds, his soldiers refused to march beyond the Hyphasis (Beas) River. This mutiny forced Alexander to suspend his campaign and return to Persia. A sacrifice to Poseidon in the sea off the coast of the Indus Delta at Patala (see Map 2) marked the end of the campaign. Part of the army returned to Iran with a fleet under the command of Alexander's childhood friend Nearchos. Nearchos' orders were to sail from India to the Persian Gulf. His description of this journey, which provided a wealth of information about geography, flora, fauna and climate, has survived indirectly in Arrian's *Indike*, written in the second century AD. For unknown reasons – to face yet another challenge or to punish his troops for their mutiny – Alexander returned from India with an army of more than 30,000 men, following the most difficult course through the Gedrosian Desert. Two months into the march, during which at least 20,000 men died, Alexander arrived in Poura; four months later, in March 324 BC, he arrived in Sousa. He was thirty-one years old, undefeated and the absolute ruler of the greatest empire that mankind had ever known. The measures of comparison that he had chosen were not men, but gods and heroes of myth – Dionysus and Heracles – and he had surpassed them.

If we are to believe the sources, during his campaign Alexander kept his dagger and a copy of the *Iliad* under his cushion. We are not told whether he also had a copy of the *Odyssey*. This is unlikely. The subject of the *Odyssey* was *nostos*, the desire for homecoming, and Alexander showed no desire to ever return to Macedonia. The subject of the *Iliad* was closer to his taste. This epic treated the wrath (*menis*) of Achilles, a man whose honour had been wounded. The epic hero recognised that the only form of immortality granted to mortals is the one given by *kleos aphthiton* (undying glory). Achilles had been Alexander's model since childhood; he had even staged the beginning of his campaign in Asia as a tribute to the Homeric hero. If Alexander were to remain faithful to his emulation of Achilles, he would have to lose the person closest to him, as Achilles had lost Patroclus. He also had to die young. Life did not disappoint him in this.

Becoming immortal (324–323 BC)

In epic poetry there is no place for administrative challenges; in the real world conquerers do not usually retire to enjoy the pleasures of peace. Alexander had conquered; now he had to rule. The consequences of his extended absence in central Asia became visible when he returned to Persia: corruption, fear of revolts, threats to the cohesion of the empire. The worst blow had been delivered by his chief treasurer, Harpalos, who, afraid of punishment for the mismanagement of royal finances, had fled to Greece early in 324 BC with a large part of the treasury. Alexander's enemies might now use this money for the payment of mercenaries.

Affairs in Greece had been neglected for a long time, so Alexander made his presence felt in a radical manner: he issued a decree ordering the Greek cities to accept the return of their exiles – people who had left their cities in the course of civil wars or because of unpaid debts. If his aim was to win the exiles' support, he certainly achieved this. When the decree was announced at the Olympic Games of 324 BC it was greeted joyfully by thousands of exiles. If his aim was to assert his power, he achieved this as well, but his decision created turmoil in the cities. The return of exiles affected the composition of the citizen body; it was a radical intervention in the autonomy of a Greek city, which Alexander, as *hegemon* of the Hellenic Alliance, was obliged to respect. The Greek cities were confronted with a dilemma that would underlie the relationship between *poleis* and kings in the centuries to come: if they chose to defend their independence they risked war with an immeasurably stronger king.

In the past, Alexander's decisions had often been met with resistance, but nothing can be compared to the crisis he faced shortly after his arrival in Persia. He decided to release 10,000 Macedonian soldiers who had fought with him over the last ten years and to send them back to Greece. When the soldiers resisted, Alexander put an end to a mutiny at Opis by executing its leaders and replacing the troops with Iranians. Krateros, one of his generals, was to lead the veterans to Greece; the remaining Macedonian soldiers, totalling no more than 6,000, swore an oath of loyalty to Alexander alongside the Iranian troops. This change in the composition of the army, a foundation of his monarchical power, reflects the transformation of Alexander's rule from that of the king of the Macedonians to that of the king of Asia.

It was in this time of crisis that Alexander received from Greek cities the greatest honour imaginable: his person was to be ritually treated as if he were a god. Did Alexander demand this? It is doubtful, but the cities certainly knew that he would welcome the honour. Traditionally, the relation between humans and the gods was characterised by the principle of reciprocity. Mortals acknowledged the existence and power of the gods through rituals – sacrifices, dedications and prayers – as long as they could recognise manifestations of divine power. Reciprocity must have also motivated some Greek cities to approach Alexander ritually in the same manner as they did their gods, by sending sacred envoys with wreaths on their heads, making offerings and and stating requests. Without being or becoming a god, Alexander was assimilated with the gods, since his achievements excelled any human measure (see pp. 108–9).

Like humans, gods are powerless before fate, and Alexander was no exception. In autumn 324 BC, Hephaistion died. He was Alexander's childhood companion, closest friend and lover in a homoerotic relationship of the sort that characterised archaic Greek society. Alexander mourned Hephaistion no less than Achilles had mourned Patroclus. He ordered the construction of a monumental grave and in Macedonia Hephaistion was worshipped as a hero.

Hephaistion's death delayed the preparations for the restless king's next move: the exploration and conquest of the Arabian Peninsula. This plan was primarily dictated by Alexander's desire to complete the conquest of the world, but also by strategic reasons. He needed Arabia as a link between the two edges of his empire, Egypt and India. He ordered the construction of a fleet, the building of a bigger harbour in Babylon and the improvement of the canals in Mesopotamia. The new campaign was about to start when Alexander began showing symptoms of illness, which he initially did not take seriously. Weakened by wounds, excesses, fatigue and the loss of Hephaistion, Alexander died on 10 June 323 BC, before he had completed his thirty-third year. It is unlikely that the controversy over the cause of his death – malaria, another disease or poison – will ever be resolved. Alexander had finally achieved the only immortality of which mortals have a share: *kleos aphthiton*.

Alexander's legacy

From the time of Gustav Johann Droysen, who in 1837 wrote the first modern history of Alexander, it has become customary to see the legacy of the Macedonian conqueror in cultural terms. In Droysen's vision, Alexander consciously and systematically pursued the aim to overcome the separation between Orient and Occident:

Just as on the first day of Creation God separated light from darkness and from night and morning the first day was made, in the same manner the first day of history separated for the first time the people from the Orient and Occident, directing them to everlasting enmity and an everlasting longing for reconciliation ... The army of Alexander started to adopt the Asian way of life and to reconcile itself and merge with those whom the verdict of centuries had hated, despised and called barbarians; Orient and Occident started to permeate one another and to prepare a future in which both should disappear.

Generations of historians have modified this view, some in more radical ways than others. Although it is plausibly disputed that Alexander had a plan to assimilate East and West, his conquests are undoubtedly the first impetus behind the processes of assimilation that evolved in the centuries after his death. The empire that he had created lacked solid foundations and fell apart as an administrative entity; but the conquered remained joined in a network of political relations, economic exchange and cultural influence. Although Alexander did not leave a direct successor, his personality and his achievements inspired ambitious men in his immediate environment, the Successors who fought for control of the empire, and later Hellenistic kings and Roman generals and emperors. But the tangible impact of Alexander and his direct legacy are the measures and models on which the Greek East was based for the following three centuries.

If as a soldier Alexander was driven by passion and sometimes by irrational desires, as an administrator he was driven by pragmatism. From his Macedonian background, he was familiar with the complexity of exercising rule over a heterogeneous conglomerate of subjects and allies. In Macedonia, his father's subjects included the Macedonians, whose king he was; citizens of Greek cities, subjugated or founded by him and granted some form of autonomy; and citizens of the cities of the Thessalian League, which Philip commanded as chief magistrate. The members of the Hellenic Alliance were not under the king's rule, but they nevertheless accepted his military command. This construction had emerged gradually during the twenty years of Philip's rule. The conquests of Alexander had produced a far more complex situation. He had liberated the Greek cities of Asia Minor, which probably joined the Hellenic Alliance. He had founded several cities, although the number given by Plutarch (more than seventy) is rightly disputed. Their citizens were mostly Greek mercenaries raised in the traditions of free Greek cities, and yet the new cities were on land conquered by the king. Alexander had assumed the position of the pharaoh in Egypt and he had succeeded the Great King as the ruler of a multitude of ethnic groups and dependent regional dynasts. Governing this empire was a greater challenge than even the founders of the Achaemenid Empire, Cyrus I (c. 550–530 BC) and Darius I (522–486 BC), had faced.

Alexander must have realised that he lacked the experienced personnel needed to ensure a smooth transition from the rule of the Achaemenids to his own, the undisturbed collection of tribute and the upkeep of a functioning administration. He had to use local administrative traditions. The local populations were also interested in a quick and peaceful return to everyday life. The enthusiastic reception in 331 BC of the conqueror in Babylon as the new monarch was a clear expression of this desire, to which Alexander responded with prudence. He showed respect to the traditional gods and left the satraps in their positions, though he appointed Macedonian military commanders in the provinces to guarantee his rule. He sat on the throne of the Great King in Susa in December 331 and adopted external insignia of power that any Greek would immediately have identified as barbaric, such as elements of the Persian royal dress. He visited the grave of Cyrus in Pasargadai and buried Darius in the royal cemetery. He attempted to introduce a Persian ritual in the encounter between monarch and subjects called the *proskynesis* – obeissance or kneeling in front of the king, a gesture that the Greeks reserved for the worship of gods; the resistance of his court made him abandon this plan. His marriage with Roxane, the daughter of a local ruler in Sogdiana, established close connections with the indigenous aristocracy of Iran. He recognised Poros, one of the ablest military commanders that ever opposed him, as ruler of the easternmost territories. He incorporated 30,000 Iranians trained in the Macedonian manner into his army and accepted the best Iranian horsemen into the Macedonian cavalry units. Towards the end of his rule, Alexander surrounded himself with Persian bodyguards. He recognised the relationships of 10,000 soldiers with non-Greek, mostly Iranian, women as marriages and the children as legitimate. In a mass wedding in Susa, ninety of his closest companions wedded Iranian women in the Persian manner; during this wedding, Alexander and his close friends Hephaistion and Krateros took members of the Persian royal family as wives.

For some historians, these measures were the result of a great vision, while others saw them as an effort to face the challenges of administrating a huge empire, for which the limited number of Macedonian noblemen and a few men from Greek cities simply would not have sufficed. The latter assumption seems more plausible. With the incorporation of Iranians into his army and his administration, Alexander was following on a larger scale and in a more extreme form a measure that his father had already tested when he incorporated members of rival clans of Macedonian nobility and royalty into his court. Alexander seems to have been concerned more with enlarging the recruitment basis for his army and administration than with abolishing ethnic differences in a conquered world that had always been multicultural.

The consistency with which Alexander pursued this policy, against strong opposition, is remarkable. He eliminated some of the members of his closest circle because of their true or alleged involvement in conspiracies or because they openly criticised the king: Philotas, the commander of the cavalry, and his father, the old general Parmenion, were put to death in 330 BC; Kleitos, one of his highest officers, who castigated Alexander's new non-Macedonian habitus, was killed by the king in 328 BC; and his historian, Kallisthenes, who represented the spirit of free Greek citizens, was put to death in 327 BC, along with some royal pages whom he instructed. The struggle against such opposition leaves little doubt that Alexander had a plan and was not just acting on instinct or whim.

Alexander followed the only model that he knew: a personal monarchy in which everything depended on the king. Those close to him had the highest military and administrative functions. At the top of the hierarchy were the men who occupied the highest military ranks. Among them, the closest friends of the king were known by the honorary title of 'bodyguards' (*somatophylakes*). The highest-ranking officer was the *chiliarch*, 'commander of thousand men', a function that corresponded to that of the Achaemenid vizier and was probably adopted from the Iranian tradition. Some members of the Iranian aristocracy were also accepted into the inner circle of the 'relatives' (*syngeneis*), who were allowed to kiss the king. Elite soldiers served as *hetairoi*, or companions, in the *agema*, an elite troop within the cavalry, and as soldiers in the elite units of the infantry.

Alexander's monarchy had roots in three different monarchical traditions – those of Macedonia, the Achaemenid dynasty and pharaonic Egypt – as well as in Alexander's function as *hegemon* of the Hellenic Alliance. He never returned to Greece and none of the rumours about his last plans included a return to Macedonia. This does not mean, however, that he neglected affairs in Greece and Macedonia. With royal letters, regulations (*diagrammata*) and messages communicated through envoys he made his desires known to the cities, which were formally his allies and not part of his dominion. These media remained important instruments of power until the end of the Hellenistic period.

Alexander's decisions shaped the Hellenistic world in a very tangible way: Alexander determined the geographical limits of this world in the East, and he defined the character of monarchical rule, the relations between king and city, urbanisation and the integration of local populations and traditions. The thirteen years of his rule are one of those periods in history during which the clock seems to move faster than usual. Alexander's campaign began as a response to contemporary needs and trends and ended with the pursuit of personal desires. We cannot measure the extent to which Alexander changed the course of history. He certainly accelerated the collapse of the Persian Empire and the creation of a much larger network of regions than any of his contemporaries could have imagined. The resistance to Alexander and the fragmentation of his empire after his death show that he had given history's pace a beat that his contemporaries could neither understand nor follow.

It is doubtful that Alexander's own teacher and the greatest mind of his times, Aristotle, understood or approved of his disciple's policies. Apart from the distrust of absolute monarchy by a philosopher who was born in a Greek *polis* and chose to live, think and teach in Athens, the city that saw itself as a paragon of freedom and democracy, Aristotle had clear views concerning the natural superiority of the Greeks over the barbarians:

> There is another sort of monarchy, examples of which are kingships existing among some of the barbarians. The power possessed by all of these resembles that of tyrannies, but they govern according to law and are hereditary; for because the barbarians are more servile in their nature than the Greeks, and the Asiatics than the Europeans, they endure despotic rule without any resentment.

The incorporation of Iranian soldiers into the Macedonian army and the mixed marriages of Greeks and non-Greeks can hardly be reconciled with such teachings. I wonder how a city such as Alexandria, a Greek *polis* implanted in a land with theocratic traditions and the ubiquitous presence of royal power, would have fitted into the philosopher's taxonomy of constitutions. Aristotle died soon after Alexander, having captured a glimpse of the dawn of a new world. What this new world meant finds a magnificent expression in 'Anno 200' by the Alexandrian poet Cavafy:

And from this marvelous pan-Hellenic expedition,

triumphant, brilliant in every way,
celebrated on all sides, glorified
as no other has ever been glorified,
incomparable, we emerged:
the great new Hellenic world.
We the Alexandrians, the Antiochians,
the Selefkians, and the countless
other Greeks of Egypt and Syria,
and those in Media, and Persia, and all the rest:
with our far-flung supremacy,
our flexible policy of judicious integration,
and our Common Greek Language
which we carried as far as Bactria, as far as the Indians.

2

THE SUCCESSORS

Adventurers and Architects of Kingdoms
(323–275 BC)

The problem of the succession (323 BC)

Macedonian kings did not usually die in their beds; they fell in battle
or were murdered. In the traditional Macedonian monarchy a new king
acquired his legitimacy through acclamation by the army. He was first
and foremost a military commander. Just as in the *poleis* the assemblies
of citizens elected their military commanders and other officials, so did
the Macedonian assembly of warriors appoint the man who would lead
them to war. The dynastic principle of succession was respected, but the
new king was not always the eldest son of the deceased one – or even necessarily his son. When Philip himself died at the hands of a murderer in
336 BC, his succession by Alexander was not self-evident. Philip's nephew
Amyntas, the son of King Perdikkas III, still had a claim to the throne
and Alexander had two half-brothers: the older Arrhidaios, born in 359
BC, and Karanos, the infant son of Philip's last wife. Arrhidaios had some
kind of disability, but Karanos' claim to the throne might have been supported by his maternal relatives who were members of the Macedonian
nobility. Both Amyntas and Karanos were slain immediately after the

army declared Alexander king. The bloodshed of 336 BC had not been forgotten by the time Alexander died thirteen years later. And the older generals in Alexander's army had also witnessed royal murders and usurpations between 369 and 359 BC. Such experiences left little hope for a peaceful transfer of power.

If in 359 and 336 BC the question was who would be the king of the Macedonians, in 323 BC things were far more complex. Most of the Macedonian army, which was responsible for acclaiming the new king, was in Macedonia, except for roughly 6,000 soldiers left in Babylon. And Alexander was more than the Macedonian king and the chief magistrate of the Thessalian League. He was the commander of the Hellenic Alliance and, more importantly, the ruler of an empire that he had personally conquered. It did not make things any easier that Alexander himself had made no provisions for his succession.

Alexander died leaving his signet ring to one of his senior officers, Perdikkas, the *chiliarch* (vizier). This did not constitute bequest of the throne; it only authorised Perdikkas to supervise the transition of power. At the moment of Alexander's death, it was inconceivable that a man outside the Argead dynasty could be declared king. Only a close relative was an option: a brother, a son or a brother-in-law. The dead king had left two widows. Roxane, his wife since 327 BC, was pregnant when Alexander died. Stateira, the daughter of Darius III, married Alexander only a year before his death and bore him no children. Some sources suggest Alexander may have had an illegitimate son with his mistress Barsine, a boy called Herakles. Both of Alexander's older sisters, Kynnane and Cleopatra, were widows; a third sister, Thessalonike, now in her mid-twenties, was (surprisingly) still unmarried. For ambitious men of the Macedonian nobility, all three women were good matches, but none was in Babylon. They were in Macedonia with Alexander's mother, Olympias, still an influential figure in the court. Only Alexander's older half-brother Arrhidaios was in Babylon. Despite his disability he had accompanied Alexander in the campaign. Although the army declared Arrhidaios king, his rule must have been conceived as temporary, until Alexander's unborn child came of age, or until one of Alexander's generals succeeded in somehow legitimating his own rule over the kingdom of Macedonia or the entire empire. The new king, who took the royal name Philip III, was placed under the guardianship of Krateros, one of the senior officers, while the main army commanders were assigned duties in the administration of the empire.

When Roxane gave birth to a son a few months later, he too was acclaimed king, as Alexander IV, and placed under the same guardian.

What were the thoughts of the elderly men who had fought for Philip and then Alexander? And more importantly, what went through the minds of the younger men who had seen their childhood companion conquer the known world, become the ruler of a multi-ethnic empire, gradually distance himself from most of them, adopt some of the traits of an Oriental despot and even acquire the status of a god? All existing historical narratives view the events of these years with knowledge of their outcome – the splitting of the empire and the creation of three large and several smaller kingdoms. But in 323 BC no one could know what lay ahead, not even whether Roxane would give birth to a boy or a girl. It had taken Alexander less than seven years to subdue the Persian Empire; it took seventeen years for any of Alexander's officers to dare to have himself proclaimed king, and this demonstrates their hesitation to break with the tradition of the Argead dynasty. We do not know if in 323 BC a division of the empire was even considered as an option. The vision of a single ruler of the empire, or most of it, was not abandoned until 281 BC, more than forty years after Alexander's death.

Alexander continued to cast his shadow on his companions. It is said that when one of them, Kassandros, saw a statue of Alexander, he exhibited all the physical symptoms of fear: shuddering, trembling and dizziness. Alexander did not only arouse fear after his death; he inspired ambition and could bestow legitimacy. His corpse, the insignia of his power and his family members came to be important instruments of propaganda and legitimacy. For this reason Ptolemy, one of Alexander's generals, abducted Alexander's corpse in order to have it buried in his own province, Egypt. Although the ancient sources are explicit about the burial in Alexandria, they do not prevent imaginative archaeologists from looking for a grave elsewhere. The guardianship over the kings Philip III Arrhidaios and Alexander IV was also a highly contested privilege. Kassandros sought legitimacy by marrying Alexander's sister Thessalonike. An extreme example of the exploitation of whatever remained of Alexander is the behaviour of Eumenes, one of the senior officers, who displayed Alexander's throne in military councils during a war in Asia Minor, insinuating the dead king's presence.

It is said that when Alexander was asked on his deathbed to whom he would leave the kingship, he answered, 'To the best; I predict that my friends will organise a great funeral contest for me.' *Se non è vero, è ben trovato*. His death inaugurated a sequence of wars, which can be seen as a contest among ambitious and powerful men, and some of their women, for ultimate power. The outcome of these wars was not only an entirely new political geography but also a new conception of monarchical rule, one that was initially more strongly based on charisma than on dynastic legitimacy.

The Successors: a portrait gallery of ambition

The numerous protagonists of this period are called the Successors (*diadochoi*), and for this reason the period of uninterrupted wars between Alexander's death and the final division of the empire in 281 BC is known as 'the age of the Successors'. Some of these Successors were old men, belonging to Philip's generation, members of the Macedonian aristocracy. Antipatros, seventy-five years old and the regent in Macedonia since 334 BC, represented continuity and authority. The sixty-year-old Antigonos Monophthalmos (the One-Eyed), who had commanded the Greek allies during the campaign, was now governing Great Phrygia, one of the main provinces in Asia Minor (see Map 3).

Old these men may have been, but they were also fathers of ambitious sons. Antipatros' son, Kassandros, born in c. 350 BC, was in Babylon when Alexander died and must have hoped to succeed his father. The son of Antigonos Monophthalmos, Demetrios, was only fourteen years old, but he would soon become one of the most important Successors, eventually earning the epithet Poliorketes (the Besieger).

Among the numerous officers who were involved in the conflicts that ensued after Alexander's death, three men were to dominate the political scene for the following forty years. They were Alexander's friends since childhood and members of the close circle of 'bodyguards': Ptolemy, forty-four years old, was appointed satrap of the important province of Egypt; Lysimachos, about thirty-eight years old, became governor of Thrace, the province that connected Europe and Asia; and Seleukos, thirty-five years old, succeeded Perdikkas as *chiliarch*. Finally, Eumenes, the royal secretary of Alexander, held an important administrative position.

As much as the actual power vacuum invited these men to hope and dream, they had been accustomed to being equals in Alexander's court.

How could they now accept that one of them might rise to the position once held by the dead king? It was to be expected that if one of them attempted to gain too much power, the others would unite against him. This threat did not prevent the major players from trying to acquire more power, as they had seen Alexander do with great passion for more than a decade. Their conflicting ambitions made the political history of this period a confusing sequence of wars and *renversements des alliances*, usually accompanied by short-lived marriages arranged between one Successor and the sister or daughter of another.

Many details concerning the events of this period (see Chronology, pp. 428–9) are still uncertain, and newly discovered inscriptions occasionally provide more information. Only a few of the most important developments are summarised here, as they best characterise the nature of the conflicts and the plans and expectations of the protagonists.

The Lamian or Hellenic War (323–322 BC)

'If Alexander were really dead, the whole world would smell of his corpse,' the Athenian orator Demades allegedly said when news of Alexander's death reached Athens. When the news was confirmed, Demosthenes advised his countrymen to liberate themselves from the Macedonian hegemony. They had good reasons to follow his advice. The 'exile decree' (see p. 24) had caused a lot of discontentment and the Athenians were in a position to finance a war against Antipatros – ironically, with Alexander's money. In 324 BC, Harpalos, the king's renegade treasurer, had come to their city with an enormous sum of reportedly 5,000 talents and a small army of 6,000 mercenaries. This money was now available for use in hiring mercenaries. Thousands of them, unemployed after Alexander had disbanded the satraps' armies, were awaiting an employer in Cape Tainaron. Athens found allies among the Greek states that had reasons to oppose Macedonian leadership. The contemporary designation of this war as the 'Hellenic War' – that is, the war of an alliance of the Hellenes – indicates that the Greek cities and federations that joined forces with Athens propagated their struggle as that of the free Greek states against Macedonian rule. An inscription calls it 'the war that the people of the Athenians fought for the freedom of the Hellenes'.

After some initial successes by the Hellenes, Antipatros was forced to retreat to the Thessalian city of Lamia, where he was besieged from the winter of 323 to the spring of 322 BC – hence 'Lamian War'. But there the fortune of the Hellenes turned. After a Macedonian victory at Krannon in September 322 BC, the Hellenes capitulated unconditionally. Condemned by the Athenian assembly together with other anti-Macedonian leaders, Demosthenes came as a suppliant to the sanctuary of Poseidon in Kalaureia and committed suicide to avoid arrest. To scholars of the nineteenth and early twentieth centuries, Demosthenes' death signalled the end of the history of free Greek states.

The defeat of the Hellenes resulted in the establishment of oligarchic regimes and garrisons in the cities. Yet the dream of freedom endured. The promise of *eleutheria* (freedom), *autonomia* (autonomy) and liberation from the garrisons became an important propagandistic tool that was used by some Successors to gain the support of the Greek cities against their enemies. Although this promise was broken time and again, the Greeks did not stop dreaming until after the establishment of the Roman Empire.

From warlords to kings (322–306 BC)

The insurgency in Greece was not the only threat that the Successors faced immediately after Alexander's death. Large parts of Asia Minor were not really under the control of their satraps, and the unsuccessful wars of the Successors in the following decades led to the creation of small kingdoms (see Map 5). In Kappadokia, the rebel king Ariarathes I was crucified in 322 BC, but his nephew and adopted son Ariarathes II defeated the Macedonian satrap in 301 BC and founded a dynasty that lasted for more than two centuries. In Bithynia, the local ruler Zipoetes successfully defended his realm from Macedonian armies (326–301 BC) and assumed the title of king in 297 BC, founding one of the most important kingdoms on the periphery of the major empires that emerged from the wars of this period.

As soon as the wars in Greece and Asia Minor came to an end, the wars among the Successors broke out. In the first years, as long as Alexander's legitimate heirs were still alive, the main players directed their efforts towards the acquisition of military strength. This was achieved through alliances with Greek cities and through the control of provinces that paid tribute and served as a basis for the recruitment of mercenaries. The strategies varied, depending on the assets that each Successor possessed (see Map

3). Ptolemy had clear advantages in controlling Egypt, a homogeneous territory with immense resources and an age-old tradition of monarchical rule. Kassandros based his power on the possession of Macedonia and most of Thessaly, as well as on the control of a series of important cities, including Athens, where garrisons were placed and oligarchic regimes and tyrants were supported. Lysimachos' base was the strategically important province of Thrace. After 312 BC Seleukos controlled the heart of the empire, Babylonia and Mesopotamia, which gave him access to great wealth and the imperial army. Antigonos, who at a very early stage showed that he had the ambition to unite the entire empire under his rule, operated on different fronts, from Babylonia to Syria and from Greece to Asia Minor. His greatest assets were his fleet, the control of harbours and the support of the Greeks who trusted his promise to free their cities.

Whenever one of the Successors seemed to gain too much power, the others united against him. After his defeat, agreements were made, only to be broken as soon as an opportunity arose for one of the allies to increase his realm or even to take control of the entire empire. Then it was he who was abandoned by his allies and new alliances were formed, until the over-ambitious general was defeated. This was a time of ambition, hope and betrayal, of adventures and abrupt reversals of fortune. Unsurprisingly, the various histories of this period dwell on sudden turns of fortune (*peripeteiai*) and unexpected developments (*paradoxa*). One after the other, most of the protagonists of this period were murdered, betrayed by their officers or killed by their allies; in the best case, they fell in battle. By 309 BC, the Argead dynasty was eliminated, thereby opening the royal title to men of the Macedonian elite outside the old dynastic line.

The first major turning point in this period was the war waged by a coalition of most of the Successors against Perdikkas, who had invaded Egypt in 320 BC. This was where its satrap, Ptolemy, had taken Alexander's corpse and buried it in Alexandria in the autumn of 321 BC, thus acquiring one of the most important symbols of continuity with the Argead dynasty. While Perdikkas was murdered by his own officers, Krateros, the guardian of the kings, fell in battle in Asia Minor. The remaining Successors reached an agreement at Triparadeisos in north Syria in the summer of 320 BC, which confirmed Antipatros as regent in Europe and made him guardian of the two kings. Antigonos Monophthalmos succeeded Perdikkas in the command of the army. This position and the marriage of his son Demetrios to Antipatros' daughter Phila made him one of the most powerful men in the empire. He was also given the assignment of waging war against the remaining supporters of Perdikkas in Asia Minor. Although this was a burdensome task, it gave him the command of large armies. Of the other Successors, Ptolemy retained his province of Egypt and Lysimachos kept Thrace, while Seleukos, one of the officers who had betrayed Perdikkas, received Babylonia, an area with enormous resources. No one could foresee in 320 BC that this 'settlement of Triparadeisos' approximated the division of the empire forty years later.

Antipatros died a year later, having appointed Polyperchon, a Macedonian nobleman, as guardian of the kings, rather than his own son Kassandros. Disappointed by his father's arrangement, Kassandros allied himself with Antigonos and other Successors against Polyperchon, whose only support in Asia Minor was Eumenes, faithful to the legitimate rule of the Argeads. Four years of war, during which Olympias murdered King Philip III and Eumenes was killed in 315 BC, brought Kassandros closer to the throne in Macedonia. By arranging for the royal burial of the murdered king and his family in the royal cemetery at Aigai, he fulfilled the traditional duty of the heir to the throne. In addition, he was the guardian of the remaining king, Alexander IV, and he married Alexander's sister Thessalonike, giving her name to a newly founded city. The only obstacles that stood between him and the throne were a seven-year-old boy, the legitimate king, Alexander IV, and the ambitions of the remaining Successors. The eldest among them, Antigonos Monophthalmos, was now emerging as the most powerful man in the cracking empire. The youngest of the Successors was his son Demetrios, born in 337 BC, whose youth, beauty, strategic skills and ambition made him appear like a new Alexander. Antigonos united under his power a significant part of the Asian territory. Even Seleukos, the governor of Babylonia, felt the pressure and had to seek refuge in Egypt.

But then the most powerful Successor faced the opposition of all the others. Kassandros, Ptolemy, Seleukos and Lysimachos formed a new coalition in 314 BC and presented Antigonos with an ultimatum, proposing a new distribution of the provinces. Antigonos responded with a carefully staged scene: he gathered the army, which in the tradition of Macedonian kingdom was the source of legitimacy for important decisions, in Tyre and had it approve through acclamations a document that declared Kassandros an enemy of the empire and asked him to release Alexander IV, to remove the garrisons from the Greek cities and to let them be free. On the one hand, Antigonos was appealing to the loyalty of the army towards the legitimate Argead king, and on the other, to the wish of the Greek cities to remain free and autonomous. Polyperchon and his son Alexandros, who controlled parts of southern Greece, allied themselves with Antigonos, and a new war began. Antigonos and his allies had some success in Greece, but Seleukos managed to regain control of his province of Babylonia in 312 BC. A peace agreement in 311 BC restored the status quo of 314 BC, but it was clear that this peace would not last. Kassandros eliminated the final element of continuity by ordering the murder of Alexander IV in 310 BC. Herakles, a teenager believed to be Alexander's illegitimate son by a Persian noblewoman and, therefore, the next in the line of succession, was also put to death.

The biological end of the Argead dynasty meant that since the title of *basileus* (king) could no longer be borne by a member of Alexander's family; anyone could now lay claim to it. Surprisingly, no one did. One would have expected that at this moment Kassandros, the only Successor who, through his marriage to Alexander's sister, was connected with the Argead dynasty, would have staged his royal acclamation. But it was victory that made kings, not the murder of teenagers. That victory had yet to come, and it would belong to another Successor.

The vacancy of the throne was understood by most Successors as an invitation to cement the division of the empire and to try to acquire for their part as much territory as they could. For Antigonos it was a challenge to reunite the empire under his sole rule. Initially, his success was impressive. His son Demetrios liberated Athens in 307 BC from the garrison of Kassandros, an event of great symbolic significance for the freedom-loving Greeks. Soon after this, Demetrios defeated the fleet of Ptolemy in Salamis, Cyprus (see Fig. 3). The naval victory at Salamis was strategically not as important as its earlier namesake – the victory of the Greeks over the Persians at Salamis near Athens in 478 BC – but it did mark a decisive turn in the history of this period and the final emancipation of the Successors from Alexander's shadow. It is said that Demetrios dispatched an envoy, Aristodemos, to announce the victory to his father. Possibly following Demetrios' instructions – we know that Demetrios was a master in staging – the envoy at first left Antigonos and the gathered army uncertain about the outcome of the battle. Plutarch describes the dramatic scene, summarising the narrative of a contemporary historian:

3. Coin of Demetrios Poliorketes commemorating his victory at Salamis. Nike stands on the forecastle of a galley's prow holding a trumpet.

Aristodemos would not respond to anybody, but step by step and with a solemn face he approached in perfect silence. Very worried at this, Antigonos, no longer able to restrain himself, came to the door to meet Aristodemos; a large crowd was now following him, hurrying to the palace. When he had come near, he stretched out his hand and cried with a loud voice: 'Hail, King Antigonos, we have conquered Ptolemy in a sea battle, and now hold Cyprus, with twelve thousand eight hundred soldiers as prisoners of war.'

Aristodemos' announcement resembles a dramatic performance. In his movement, facial expression and body language he imitated the role of the envoy as people had many times seen acted on stage. Only after seizing the attention of his audience and creating suspense did Aristodemos announce the victory. Yet more important than the announcement was his greeting, 'Hail, King Antigonos.' The cheers of officers and soldiers in the 'court' of Antigonos resembled a royal acclamation by the Macedonian army and thereby lent Antigonos' kingship a sense of legitimacy. The new king founded the eponymous new city Antigoneia on the River Orontes, and there he assumed the diadem as a symbol of his newly acquired status. He also sent a diadem to his son.

After Antigonos and Demetrios assumed the title of king, the other Successors were quick to follow, and soon Ptolemy, Seleukos, Lysimachos and Kassandros had themselves acclaimed kings in 306 BC. But of what or whom were they kings? Were they kings as Alexander's successors?

Were they kings of territorial kingdoms? Neither the royal title of these kings nor that of any of their successors was accompanied by an ethnic or geographical specification, as, for instance, the title of the king of the Epirotans. This lack of an ethnic or geographical designation implies that the Successors were the kings of whichever land they could conquer and hold. But at least two of them, Antigonos and his son Demetrios, seem to have possessed the ambition to achieve 'universal' rule. The 'year of the kings', as the year 306 BC is known, did not settle the issue of Alexander's succession; it was only the beginning of a new phase of wars.

Dreams of empire (306–281 BC)

For almost five years Macedonia and the empire were kingless (310–306 BC). Now they suddenly had six kings and counting. In 297 BC, the ruler of Bithynia, Zipoetes, was the first non-Greek ruler in Asia Minor to assume the title of king. In Sicily, Agathokles was proclaimed king in 304 BC, following the example of the Successors (see p. 50). The intentional vagueness of the title 'king' invited its bearers to add to their realm as many regions as they could. This is what they attempted to do in a new phase of wars that cannot be narrated here in full.

The most memorable episode was Demetrios' siege of the island of Rhodes, an ally of Ptolemy, in 305–304 BC. Although Demetrios failed to take the city, his inventiveness during this siege earned him the nickname Poliorketes. His engineers constructed a mobile siege machine, the *hel-epolis*. It was a tower-like wooden structure, consisting of nine storeys and carried on wheels, equipped with devices against fire and with gangways; a long, projecting beam ended in a cone decorated with a ram's head. It was from the sale of the huge siege machines constructed by Demetrios' engineers that the victorious Rhodians funded the creation of a 100-foot-high statue of their patron god Helios, the Sun. The statue was set up in their harbour twelve years later as a war monument. An earthquake destroyed it in 226 BC, but its fame as one of the Seven Wonders of the Ancient World survives and its reconstruction stimulates the imagination of art historians. It is the Colossus of Rhodes (see Fig. 4).

Encouraged by military success, Antigonos and Demetrios indicated the extent of their ambition by reviving the Hellenic Alliance (see p. 14). As commander of this alliance, Alexander had led the Greeks in his Asian

4. A fanciful sixteenth-century reconstruction of the Colossus of Rhodes.

campaign. That Antigonos and Demetrios rekindled the alliance in 302 BC, uniting under their leadership many Greek cities, was a conscious effort to assume Alexander's position as the *hegemon* of the Hellenes. Their decision confirms the suspicion that, at this point, they aimed to succeed Alexander as the sole rulers of his empire. Of course, it also meant that they risked direct confrontation with the united forces of the other Successors, who reacted as expected: Seleukos, Lysimachos and Ptolemy joined forces against this 'clear and present danger'.

Whether the remaining Successors had ambitions similar to those of Antigonos is not certain, though this is more likely to have been the case for Seleukos than for the others. Having established his rule in Mesopotamia and east Iran, Seleukos too had recently imitated Alexander by launching a campaign in India. Although he did not succeed in establishing permanent rule east of the Indus, his campaign had direct military significance and indirect ideological and cultural consequences. It brought him into conflict with a kingdom that had come into existence in the aftermath of Alexander's campaigns. Chandragupta (Sandrokottos in Greek), an adventurer and military leader, had used military strength to establish political power, founding the Mauryan kingdom in the Ganges plain and gradually expanding his rule from the Ganges to the Indus. After failing to conquer him, Seleukos signed a treaty in 303 BC in which he conceded all territories between the Paropamisus and the Indus in exchange for recognition of his sovereignty and for 500 war elephants – a powerful weapon that gave Seleukos an unexpected military edge over his opponents. Ideologically, this campaign cast Seleukos as a second Alexander. His achievement was imitated a century later by his descendant, Antiochos III (see p. 164). The treaty had an unforeseen cultural consequence: Seleukos' envoy, Megasthenes, composed an account of his travels and of the organisation of the Mauryan court which is one of our most important sources for the early history of India. Strengthened by the war elephants and with his eastern borders secure, Seleukos now proceeded to Asia Minor to join forces with Lysimachos.

The decisive battle took place in Ipsos in Phrygia in 301 BC. Demetrios, positioned at the head of the cavalry, imitated Alexander's daring charges, defeating the front directly opposing him. Yet he committed a fatal mistake: he pursued the fleeing enemies without noticing the gap that he had created in his father's army. Seleukos exploited this opportunity. He penetrated the gap with his elephants and defeated Antigonos' troops. The eighty-one-year-old king fell in the battle, hoping until the end that his son would rescue him in time.

Demetrios remained a powerful player, controlling some coastal cities in Asia Minor, as well as the island of Cyprus and the important naval bases of Tyre and Sidon. It was also predictable that the victorious alliance would fall apart immediately after the victory. Indeed, Lysimachos made great territorial gains in Asia Minor, eliminating Seleukos' hopes of westward expansion. Ptolemy, who was not present at the battle, had taken the opportunity to conquer Koile Syria (Hollow Syria), which roughly corresponds to today's southern Syria, Lebanon and Palestine – an area whose control caused six so-called Syrian Wars between the descendants of Ptolemy and Seleukos over the next 100 years. When Ptolemy's daughter Arsinoe, an intelligent and ambitious woman, married Lysimachos, Seleukos realised that his ambitions were being checked by his rivals. A new *renversement des alliances* occurred. Only two years after the Battle of Ipsos, Demetrios arranged an alliance with Seleukos that was doomed to be as short-lived as all the previous ones. Yet, for the time being, Demetrios could at least count on Seleukos' tolerance of his effort to expand his power.

Demetrios had many advantages: he was still young, famous because of his innovations at the siege of Rhodes and admired as one of the most handsome men of his time; he was also cunning, ruthless and ambitious. His disadvantage was that he did not control a coherent geographical area as his rivals did. An opportunity was soon given to remedy this, by gaining Macedonia, the fatherland of all the Successors. Kassandros, who had established himself as king in Macedonia, died in 298/297 BC and his son, Philip IV, died only a year later, leaving his two younger brothers, Antipatros and Alexandros, fighting for the throne. As he waited for the right moment to strike, Demetrios built up his power in Greece and prepared his comeback.

In order to realise his plans, it was essential for Demetrios to control Athens, a traditional leader of the Greek *poleis*. Athens was the city where he and his father had achieved their first great success and where they had received honours that assimilated them with local heroes; it was the city that had betrayed him after Ipsos. In the spring of 295 BC, Demetrios captured Athens, but instead of punishing the Athenians he promised them more than a donation of grain. In the meantime, the dynastic conflict in Macedonia was reaching its climax. One of the contenders for the throne, Alexandros, made a fatal mistake: he invited Demetrios to assist him. Demetrios understood this as an invitation by Fortune herself and gladly accepted. He arranged for the murder of Alexandros and staged his acclamation as king by the army in the autumn of 294 BC. Now at the height of his power, he continued to stage his rule as a play, forgetting that every drama ends with the punishment of hubris.

In 291 BC, Demetrios married Lanassa, reportedly one of the most beautiful women of his time. Immediately after his marriage, he travelled to Athens, scheduling his arrival to coincide with the celebration of the Eleusinian mysteries. The Athenians celebrated his arrival as the advent of a god, burning incense on the altars, crowning statues and altars, offering libations, dancing in the streets and singing a hymn that assimilated his earthly power with that of the gods (see pp. 112–3).

> He is here full of joy, as befits the god, fair and laughing. His appearance is solemn, his friends all around him and he in their midst, as though they were stars and he the sun. Hail boy of the most powerful god Poseidon and Aphrodite! For other gods are either far away, or they do not have ears, or they do not exist, or do not take any notice of us, but you we can see present here, not made of wood or stone, but real.

Demetrios imitated Dionysus, exchanging the symbols of royal power for the Dionysiac costume, ivy wreath and fennel staff (*thyrsos*). At about this time, he ordered the weaving of a cloak, destined to remain unfinished, which represented the stars and the zodiac, an allusion to control of the annual cycle, control of the seasons and control of time itself. In his propaganda, he appeared among his friends as the sun surrounded by the stars. Following the example of Alexander and the other Successors, he founded a new city, Demetrias, in Thessaly, at a strategic location for his fleet and for receiving traffic from mainland Greece through the Aegean to Asia Minor and beyond. Demetrias was on the south side of the Gulf of Pagassai, facing Iolkos on the north side, the legendary embarkation point of the Argonauts. It is a sign of his military genius that he realised the importance of a fleet and safe harbours for the preservation of his rule, and most of his successors followed his example in pursuing a naval policy. It is not a coincidence that the Athenians referred to him as the son of Poseidon in their hymn. From Demetrios' actions it becomes clear that his aim was to expand his power beyond Macedonia, first in Greece, then beyond the Aegean.

Responding to the requests of the Athenians, who were suffering from attacks by Aetolian pirates, Demetrios waged a war against the federal state of Aetolia. The Aetolians were a rising power in western Greece and also controlled Delphi, one of Greece's most important sanctuaries. This war gave Demetrios the chance to prove genuine his intentions to protect the Greeks. But he failed to defeat the Aetolians and had to come to terms with them in 289 BC. His star was setting as fast as it had risen. His nemesis came in the person of another adventurer whose many turns of fortune resemble those of Demetrios: Pyrrhos of Epirus (see Fig. 5).

Pyrrhos was a member of the royal family that ruled the Molossians, a Greek tribe in Epirus in north-western Greece, and as such he was a distant relative of Alexander the Great, whose mother was a Molossian princess. He ascended the throne when he was twelve or thirteen years old in 306 BC but was soon exiled because of dynastic conflicts. In 302, he sought refuge in the court of Demetrios. In 298, he was sent to Ptolemy as a hostage. He returned to Epirus as king in 297 and, inspired by Alexander's success, he was looking for opportunities to augment his power. Almost thirty years after the death of Alexander he appeared to contemporaries like a new Alexander, as Plutarch asserts: 'Many of the Macedonians were moved to say that in him alone of all the kings could they see an image of

5. Portrait of Pyrrhos of Epirus.

the great Alexander's daring; whereas the others, and particularly Demetrios, did but assume Alexander's majesty and pomp, like actors on a stage.'

In 288 BC, when Demetrios was preparing a large campaign to reconquer Asia Minor, allegedly with an infantry of 98,000 men, 12,000 horsemen and 500 ships, Pyrrhos, Lysimachos, Ptolemy and Seleukos formed yet again an opportunistic alliance to stop him. Pyrrhos invaded Macedonia from the east and Lysimachos from the west, arousing fear and anger among Demetrios' troops and leading many soldiers to desert. Before a decisive battle against Pyrrhos could take place, some soldiers urged Demetrios to abandon the throne and Macedonia. So he did. Cavafy captures the mood in his 'King Dimitrios', inspired by Plutarch's account:

> He took off his golden robes,
> threw away his purple buskins,
> and quickly dressing himself
> in simple clothes, he slipped out –

just like an actor who,
the play over,
changes his costume and goes away ...

This was the beginning of the end for a king whose life still awaits a movie producer. Although he faced the attacks of Ptolemy in Greece, the Aegean and Phoenicia, and had lost a large part of his army and two of his most valuable possessions, the harbours of Sidon and Tyre, Demetrios still attempted to occupy Asia Minor, but the campaign was a failure. He was forced to retreat in Cilicia in southern Asia Minor and, passing Mount Taurus, to enter Seleukos' realm. There, he was trapped. Unable to reach the sea, he decided to surrender to Seleukos in 285 BC. Like his father, Demetrios had failed to create an empire comparable in breadth to that of Alexander. He died as Seleukos' prisoner two years later.

We do not need divinatory skills to foretell what comes next: the ad hoc alliance of Demetrios' allies split, and two Successors, Lysimachos and Seleukos, struggled to succeed where Demetrios had failed. Lysimachos drove his junior ally, Pyrrhos, out of Macedonia, thus becoming the sole king of the Macedonians; he now held in his possession not only Thrace but also most of Asia Minor. Seleukos, on the other hand, controlled most of Alexander's eastern possessions. A showdown between the two old kings, the only survivors of Alexander's generation after Ptolemy I died in 283/282 BC, was just a matter of time.

As was often the case in this period, ambitious women and dynastic conflicts triggered the war. Lysimachos' last wife was Arsinoe, daughter of Ptolemy I, who was forty-five years younger than her husband and the most influential woman in Hellenistic history before Cleopatra. Arsinoe turned against Agathokles, Lysimachos' eldest son and governor of Asia Minor. She probably realised that her own children could have a claim to the throne only if she got rid of Agathokles. Lysimachos was made to believe that his son intended to poison him, and he ordered his murder in 283 BC. When Agathokles' supporters fled to Seleukos, among them was Ptolemy Keraunos (the Thunder). Keraunos was the oldest son of Ptolemy I and therefore the half-brother of Arsinoe. He had fled to Lysimachos in 285 BC, when his father decided to appoint as his successor a son from another wife. Seleukos, now almost eighty, recognised a chance to expand his empire to the west, under the pretext of a campaign to avenge Agathokles' murder.

Lysimachos now found himself in a difficult position. First, there was the constant threat of invasion by barbaric tribes on the northern frontier of his kingdom. Second, he was confronted with an insurgence in Asia Minor, caused by the murder of Agathokles; in Pergamon, an important citadel in north-western Asia Minor, the commander Philetairos had revolted. And now Seleukos invaded his holdings in Asia Minor. For most of his life Seleukos had turned his attention to the east. Having campaigned twice to India and having appointed his son Antiochos I as regent in the eastern parts of his kingdom in 293 BC, he finally had a chance in the twilight of his life to return to his Macedonian fatherland, which he had not seen since he left it as a young officer to follow Alexander more than fifty years previously. The two old kings met in Kouropedion in Phrygia in 281 BC. Lysimachos was slain in the battle, opening to Seleukos the possibility of realising the dream that all of the Successors had once had: to unify as large an area as possible of Alexander's empire, from Macedonia to Iran. Yet he had not learned the lesson that the last forty years should have taught every actor in this drama: never to trust an ally after the common enemy had been defeated. Ptolemy Keraunos murdered Seleukos in the capital of Thrace, Lysimacheia, in September 281 BC and married Lysimachos' widow, his own half-sister Arsinoe, promising to spare the life of her children. In this way, he managed to declare himself king, ruling over Macedonia and Thrace. As soon as the mission was accomplished, he murdered two of Arsinoe's sons (the eldest managed to escape), forcing her to return to Egypt, where her brother King Ptolemy II was expecting her with open arms. He would become her third and final husband, and together they would consolidate the Ptolemaic kingdom of Egypt.

Sicilian adventures

The areas of Greek colonisation in the West (southern Italy and Sicily) and in the north (the western and northern coasts of the Black Sea) were only indirectly affected by the wars of the Successors. The political developments in Sicily are an instructive example of parallel developments in East and West (see Map 4). Although the Greeks in Italy and Sicily were organised into city-states, they had a long tradition of autocratic rule by tyrants. Ambitious men repeatedly took advantage of crises in order to establish their own regime. There was no lack of opportunities, due to three endemic problems: the efforts of the Carthaginians to enlarge their territory in Sicily at the expense of Greek colonies; the threat from the non-Greek peoples in Italy (Brutii, Lucani, Mamertines); and the political conflicts between the supporters of democracy and oligarchic groups.

Parallel to the wars of the Successors, a similar struggle for personal rule unfolded in Sicily. In 322 BC, the political crisis in the largest city of Sicily, Syracuse, had reached its dramatic climax. A civil war between the democrats and the oligarchs was threatening the very autonomy of the city, since the oligarchs sought the support of Syracuse's worst enemy, the Carthaginians. In 319/318 BC, the leader of the radical democrats, Agathokles, a cunning strategist and populist statesman, succeeded in winning the support of the majority of the citizens, promising to end the division and protect the political institutions. The assembly elected him general, a traditional office, adding to his title the designation 'protector of the peace'. One should never trust titles that recall the Orwellian ministries of Truth, Peace and Plenty. Agathokles gave an idiosyncratic interpretation of his role as 'protector of the peace': he had 4,000 opponents murdered; another 6,000 fled to Akragas. By claiming that he wished to return to the life of a private citizen, he only instigated his election to yet another extraordinary office in 317 BC: general with unlimited authority (*strategos autokrator*) entrusted with the 'care of the city' (*epimeleia tes poleos*). Through the application of populist methods – cancelling debts and giving land to the poor – he acquired the public support needed for his autocratic rule. In 314 BC, the cities of Akragas, Gela and Messana recognised the hegemony of Syracuse; however, other Sicilian cities formed an alliance against Syracusan supremacy. With the support of Carthage, which was successfully practising the policy of *divide et impera*, the enemies of Syracuse laid siege to the city. Agathokles responded to this threat by attacking Carthage and forcing the Carthaginians to withdraw their army from Syracuse in 310 BC.

In North Africa, Agathokles pursued the dream of a small-scale empire, a dream inspired by Alexander's conquests. Cyrene, the greatest Greek colony in Libya, was ruled by the Macedonian Ophellas, a close friend of Alexander. Soon after Agathokles had arrived in 308 BC, he had Ophellas killed and took over his army. The African expedition ultimately failed because the Carthaginian fleet was superior and Agathokles' two sons were killed by his own mercenaries. But Agathokles maintained his power in Sicily and in 306 BC he concluded a peace treaty with Carthage that made him sole ruler of the Greek parts of Sicily. Following the example of the Successors, he assumed the title of king in 304 BC, issued coins with his portrait and established relations with the other Hellenistic kings, marrying one of Ptolemy I's daughters. The restless ruler expanded his influence beyond Sicily by helping the Greek cities of southern Italy against their barbarian neighbours and occupying Korkyra. Agathokles was making preparations for a new invasion of Africa when he died in 289/288 BC.

His starting point had been a civil war in one Sicilian city, but in the course of three decades his adventures had brought him to North Africa and his policies and relations extended from Egypt to southern Italy and from Macedonia to Sicily. Like Alexander, he targeted a traditional barbarian enemy of the Greek cities, Carthage, and for the first time he brought the war to its territory. He used the same tactics as his contemporary kings – war, dynastic marriages, alliances, treason and murder – and he never set a geographical limit upon his ambitions. Although he failed to establish a dynasty, he accustomed the western Greeks to the idea that they needed a monarch as their champion against their barbarian enemies, Rome and Carthage. A new champion emerged in the person of Pyrrhos of Epirus.

The last adventurer: Pyrrhos

'Pyrrhic victory' is one of the numerous expressions bequeathed to posterity by the Hellenistic world. This expression has its origin in the adventures of Pyrrhos (c. 318–272 BC), king of Epirus from 306 to 302 and again from 297 to 272 BC (see Fig. 5). We have already encountered Pyrrhos as one of Alexander's most charismatic Successors and the victorious opponent of Demetrios Poliorketes (see p. 45). Following the example of other Successors, he exercised royal power in whichever area he could obtain. In 288 BC, he expelled Demetrios from Macedonia, but his rule there was short-lived, as he was driven out by Lysimachos in 284 BC. As a king of Epirus, he possessed the largest military power east of the Adriatic. It was only natural, then, that it was Pyrrhos to whom the Greeks of Italy and Sicily turned when they felt the pressure of Roman expansion.

From the mid-fourth century onwards, the Roman nobility who controlled the senate had pursued a policy of expansion. Aristocratic competition favoured this process, as the members of the ruling class were eager to receive military commands and promote their own prestige and that of their families through military victories. By the end of the century, Roman expansion had reached southern Italy, threatening the Greek colonies in the area. The citizens of Taras – today's Taranto – were sure of defeat if they were to face an attack from Rome without external support. Had the threat occurred one century earlier, their natural ally and protector would have been Sparta, Taras' mother-city. But the times had changed and in 281 BC they appealed to Pyrrhos for assistance. Pyrrhos' motivation in accepting the invitation to intervene is easy to understand: Lysimachos had put an end to his ambition to expand eastward; an opportunity to expand his power in the West was welcome at a time when royalty depended on successful warfare and acquisition of new territories. It is said that the philosopher Kineas, upon hearing of Pyrrhos' plans to sail to Italy, drew him into the following discussion:

'Pyrrhos, the Romans are said to be good soldiers and rulers of many warlike peoples; if, then, a god should permit us to defeat them, how should we use our victory?' Pyrrhos said: 'Your question, Kineas, really needs no answer; with the Romans defeated, there is neither barbarian nor Greek city there which would resist us, but we shall immediately possess all of Italy – and no man should know better than yourself how large, rich, and powerful she is.' Then, after a slight pause, Kineas said: 'And after taking Italy, O King, what are we to do?' Pyrrhos, not yet perceiving his intention, answered: 'Sicily is near, and stretches out her hands to us, an island abounding in wealth and men, and very easy to conquer, for there is nothing there, Kineas, but faction, anarchy in her cities, and excitable demagogues, now that Agathokles is gone.' 'What you say,' replied Kineas, 'is probably true; but will our expedition stop with the capture of Sicily?' 'May god grant us victory and success,' said Pyrrhos, 'and we will use this as preliminaries to great enterprises. For who could keep us away from Libya or Carthage, when they come within our reach, when Agathokles nearly captured them, secretly escaping from Syracuse and crossing over with a few ships? And when we have conquered these, none of our enemies, who are now treating us with scorn, will offer resistance; no one can dispute this.' 'None whatever,' said Kineas, 'for it is clear that with such a power behind us we shall be able to recover Macedonia and to rule Greece securely. But when we have got everything subject to us, what shall we do?' Then Pyrrhos laughed and said: 'We shall be much at ease, and we'll drink wine, my good man, every day, and we will entertain each other with conversations.' Now that Kineas had brought Pyrrhos to this point, he said: 'Well, then, what prevents us now from drinking wine and enjoying leisure among ourselves if we so wish? Surely this possibility is ours already and we can have it without taking any trouble; so why try to attain the same thing by bloodshed and great toils and perils, after inflicting on others and suffering ourselves great harm?'

World history might have been different if statesmen and kings had had a Kineas to talk to and had understood the point that he was making. It is unlikely that this discussion ever took place, but it is a good description of the imperialist drive in this period.

Pyrrhos crossed over to Italy in 280 BC. His strengths were his military genius, his strong cavalry and the use of war elephants. His misfortune was that his campaign began with victories (see Map 4). But these victories, at Herakleia in 280 and Asculum in 279, caused great casualties to his army without deciding the war. After Asculum, Pyrrhos reportedly said, 'Yet another victory over the Romans, and we are lost.' If he had received the good fortune of defeat right at the outset of his expedition, he may not have left to posterity the expression Pyrrhic victory; rather, he might have had the chance to end his life quietly drinking bumpers and entertaining himself with good conversation.

At first, the Roman weakness led indigenous peoples, the Lucanians and the Bruttians, and the Greek cities of Kroton and Lokroi to join him. Encouraged by his success, Pyrrhos did not return east to capitalise on the death of Lysimachos and the chaos in Macedonia resulting from the invasion of the Celts (see pp. 58–61). Instead of defending Macedonia from the barbarians and reclaiming its throne, he turned his attention to the barbarians in the West: the Carthaginians in Sicily. This was a mistake – it gave Antigonos Gonatas, the son of Demetrios Poliorketes, the chance to present himself as the champion of the Greeks.

Pyrrhos was initially victorious and proclaimed king of Sicily. But when he failed to capture the Carthaginian stronghold in Lilybaeum and concluded a peace treaty with Carthage, he lost the support of the Greeks. They regarded a monarch as a good king when he could defend them and as a tyrant when he failed to do so. The uprising of the Greeks against him forced him back to Italy, where he faced the Romans one last time at Maleventum in 275 BC. The battle was inconclusive, but with his army decimated and his financial resources exhausted, he called off his Italian adventures and returned to Macedonia.

Here he continued his military enterprises. He defeated Antigonos Gonatas and briefly regained the throne of Macedonia, leaving Antigonos only in control of the coastal cities. But his rule became unpopular, especially when his Gaulish mercenaries desecrated the royal graves at Aigai. In 272 BC, he agreed to help Kleonymos, the exiled king of Sparta, regain his throne, probably hoping to gain control of southern Greece. However, his attack on Sparta failed and his son was killed during the assault. He immediately moved north to intervene in a conflict in Argos, one of the most important cities of the Peloponnese. There, a roof tile hurled at his head by a woman during a street fight put an end to his life and his military adventures.

Pyrrhos failed to create a kingdom and to found a dynasty. All he had gained was his fame as a great military commander. It is said that when Hannibal and Scipio, the Roman general who had defeated him, were having a discussion about great generals, Hannibal ranked Alexander first, Pyrrhos second and himself third. Ironically, none of them created a lasting empire.

A new world in East and West: divided but connected

The division of Alexander's legacy and the death of Pyrrhos mark the beginning of an approximately 100-year period (until 188 BC) in which the political geography of the Hellenistic world remained largely unchanged (see Map 3). Until the first direct confrontation between a Hellenistic kingdom and Rome in 215 BC, the Hellenistic states were an almost closed zone, only temporarily disturbed by occasional barbaric incursions. Several kingdoms had emerged from the wars of the Successors. Each one of them had a relatively clearly defined geographical core. The additional external territories were often contested, sometimes lost and sometimes enlarged, but the core essentially remained the same.

Ptolemy I had organised his kingdom in Egypt, and although both he and his successors had significant possessions outside Egypt – Cyprus, Koile Syria, some of the Aegean islands and coastal sites in Greece and Asia Minor – the land of the Nile and Cyrenaica were the core of their kingdom. Ptolemy I died peacefully in 283/282 BC, bequeathing a stable kingdom to his children Ptolemy II and Arsinoe II. His dynasty of the Ptolemies or Lagids – Lagos was Ptolemy's father – was to rule Egypt until 30 BC.

With Seleukos' death in 281 BC, his successor, Antiochos I, was left to defend the Asiatic territories in Mesopotamia, Syria and large parts of Asia Minor, giving up the dream of also reigning as king of Macedonia. One of his descendants, Antiochos III, based territorial claims on Seleukos' victory at Kouropedion (see p. 170), but his dreams of expanding beyond Asia were shattered by the Romans. The dynasty of the Seleucids controlled a vast, culturally diverse and continually threatened territory. The populations of the former Achaemenid Empire were accustomed to monarchical rule, but the Greek cities in Asia Minor had to learn a new diplomatic 'script' for dealing with the Seleucid kings. The borders of this kingdom fluctuated more often than those of any other, until its final dissolution in 63 BC.

A new power was emerging in north-west Asia Minor, the realm of Philetairos and his successors in Pergamon; they were not yet kings, but were mighty rulers all the same. The dynasty of these Attalids – from Attalos I, the first ruler of Pergamon to declare himself king – had its greatest years of glory in the late third and early second centuries. Close to the Attalid territory, the minor kingdom of Bithynia was consolidated under the rule of Zipoetes (297–278 BC) and would last until 74 BC. In Kappadokia, bordering the possessions of the Seleucids in Asia Minor and Syria, Ariarathes II inherited the rule of his homonymous uncle and created yet another minor kingdom; his dynasty ruled until 95 BC. And finally, as a result of the Battle at Kouropedion and the events that followed, the kingdom of Pontos was created, which was ruled by another dynasty with Iranian ancestry but close to Greek culture, the Mithridatids, from 281 to 47 BC.

In Sicily, a Syracusan statesman succeeded where Agathokles and Pyrrhos had failed. Hieron of Syracuse was elected general with the support of the people in 275 BC, established a personal rule and was acclaimed king in 269. Under his rule, which lasted until 215 BC, the Greek part of Sicily developed along the same lines as the Hellenistic kingdoms. More kingdoms existed in the periphery. In the West, Epirus remained an independent kingdom after the death of Pyrrhos, but the tribe of the Athamanes, in its vicinity, was ruled by a separate king. In Dalmatia, kings ruled the Illyrian tribes. The Spartokids ruled the north-eastern part of the Black Sea.

Only one of the major Hellenistic dynasties was not in power after Kouropedion: the Antigonids in Macedonia, the descendants of Antigonos Monophthalmos and Demetrios Poliorketes. After Kouropedion, the kingdom of Macedonia, which also included Thessaly and Thrace, was in the hands of Ptolemy Keraunos. Yet his rule was not to last. Only a year after his treacherous deeds he faced the invasion of barbaric tribes from the far west, the Gauls. He was defeated, captured and beheaded – acts that many contemporaries must surely have seen as divine punishment. It was Demetrios' son, Antigonos Gonatas, who managed to consolidate this kingdom in 277 BC and found the dynasty of the Antigonids. The invasion of the Gauls, one of the most traumatic experiences in Greek history, occasioned his rise to power.

3

'OLD' GREECE IN THE SHORT THIRD CENTURY

Struggles for Survival, Freedom and Hegemony (279–217 BC)

The ubiquity of war

What do modern scholars regard as landmarks in the sixty years that separate the consolidation of the Hellenistic states around 275 BC from the first war between a Hellenistic kingdom and Rome? Certainly that a group of about seventy Hebrew scholars in Alexandria translated the Torah on the invitation of a king that legend identifies as Ptolemy II, that a mathematician jumped out of a bathtub in Syracuse shouting, *'Eureka!'* and that an astronomer claimed that the earth moved around the sun. These events that occurred in the 'short third century' changed world culture. The *Septuaginta*, the Greek translation of the Torah, enabled non-Jews to become acquainted with the Scripture. In Syracuse, Archimedes discovered a principle that bears his name and allows the measurement of the volume of irregular objects. Aristarchos of Samos laid the foundations for a heliocentric universe.

One might add other less known but equally fortunate moments of science and culture in these years: for instance, the startlingly accurate measurement of the circumference of the earth by Eratosthenes – his estimate was 25,000 geographical miles (only ninety-eight miles short of the correct distance); or the invention of the *hydraulis*, an early form of the pipe organ, by Ktesibios in c. 270 BC; or that the doctor Erasistratos, a native of the small island of Keos, discovered that the heart is not the centre of sensations but rather functions as a pump. Or the fact that Zenodotos of Ephesos, librarian of the library of Alexandria, prepared the first critical edition of Homer's epics and introduced the principle of organising a library according to subject matter and, within the subjects, alphabetically according to the name of the author; he also invented the tag that was attached to the end of each book scroll containing the basic identifying data (author, title and subject). It is not a coincidence that most of these developments occurred in Alexandria, the leading cultural centre of the world.

Only a very few contemporaries must have realised the momentous significance of these events. Even fewer must have paid any attention to the deeds of King Ashoka in India, who, after establishing an empire in most of the Indian subcontinent (269–232 BC), converted to Buddhism and dispatched missionaries to the West (see p. 377). Only the western Greeks must have noticed the war that was being waged between Rome and Carthage, later remembered as the First Punic War (264–241 BC). And understandably, no one knew of the wars in the Far East that led to the unification of China under the first imperial dynasty of the Qin in 221 BC. The Greeks of the third century were too busy contesting the frontiers of kingdoms, cities and federations to look beyond the borders of their world.

War dominated public and private memories in the short third century. It affected the lives of all; it was the most memorable experience a person could have – regardless of status, age or gender. The grave of a certain Apollonios of Tymnos, who did not fall in combat but died of old age in the mid-third century BC, was decorated with the symbol that had once adorned his shield: a snake. His epitaph mentions the events that he obviously liked to narrate: the battles he had fought for the fatherland and the innumerable spears which he had 'firmly stuck into the flesh of the enemies'. People remembered a father, a son, a brother and a friend who fell in battle; the daughter who had been abducted by pirates; the relative who had acquired distinction in war. Memories of war differed. They

ranged from the epitaph of a young soldier set up by his father and a dedication by a warrior after his safe return from a campaign to a long decree
in honour of an officer, the description of a battle by a historian and the *res
gestae* of a victorious king. It is not possible to narrate the full extent of the
wars of this period (see Chronology, pp. 429–31), but before we examine a
selection of the most important among them, it is necessary to summarise
the main causes of these wars.

The rise of the Hellenistic kingdoms was certainly the most important,
for three reasons. First, the expansion of the kingdoms limited the territory,
freedom and autonomy of Greek *poleis*; whenever an opportunity arose,
the cities rose in rebellion to regain their autonomy. Second, the kings
continually tried to enlarge their territory at the expense of other kingdoms. Third, although the type of the 'adventurer king', such as Pyrrhos,
Demetrios and Agathokles, became less dominant, it did not disappear,
and several adventurers, usually members of a dynasty, usurpers and renegade governors, attempted to create their own kingdoms. If monarchy
was a new factor in instigating war, the conflicts between and within cities
were as old as the Greek *polis*. Small and great wars often originated from
territorial disputes and from the efforts of large cities to exercise control
over smaller neighbours. Territorial expansion and hegemony were also
the principal policies of confederations; consequently, small-scale wars for
the acquisition of land or the subordination of a community abounded.
Large-scale invasions by barbarians, such as the invasion of the Celts in
280 BC and of the Parni in Parthia in 238 BC, were less common, but their
impact was dramatic.

The new barbarian: the Gauls enter the Greek world (279–277 BC)

According to a legend, the sacred Capitoline geese saved Rome from a
nocturnal attack of barbarians when their honking alerted the city's
defenders. These barbarians were the Gauls, a Celtic population group. It
is often forgotten that the geese did not save Rome, but only its last line of
defence, the Capitoline Hill. The city was sacked and plundered in 387 BC,
and although modern archaeological investigations do not confirm the
ancient reports of total destruction, the damage must have been considerable and the shock of the Romans tremendous. There were no sacred geese
in northern Greece to announce the Celtic invasion a hundred years later,

but if the rulers of Macedonia had not been so distracted by their wars against each other, they might have noticed the imminent threat.

The northern and north-western Greeks had always faced barbarian attacks. Macedonia was regularly invaded by various tribes who inhabited the lands south of the Danube, and Alexander the Great first had to fight against the northern barbarians before he could start his Asian campaign. King Lysimachos of Thrace and his son had been captured by the Getai and were forced to pay a large ransom for their freedom. Raids by Thracian and Scythian tribes were a constant threat for the Greek cities in Thrace and along the western coast of the Black Sea. In western Greece, cities and tribes in Epirus and Illyria often saw their territories plundered by raiders.

The Celtic tribe of the Gauls originally occupied territories in eastern France and Switzerland, whence they began to move towards the east and south in the fourth century. The sack of Rome is only an early episode of a migration that led to the establishment of Celts first in the northern Balkans and later in central Asia Minor. The early encounters of the Greeks with these barbarians were violent but not so dramatic as to leave lasting impressions. Sometimes the payment of tribute – declared a 'gift' in order to save face – prevented an attack. It is also reported that Alexander the Great received envoys from the chiefs of the Galatai (Galatians/ Gauls). Things turned out to be different in the *annus horribilis* of 280 BC. The numbers of the invaders were very large; they penetrated into areas of central Greece that had never seen them in the past. We can only speculate about the causes of this invasion. The usual suspects are famine, greed, population increase and pressure from other tribes further north and east – and these are the causes stated in the ancient sources. But it seems that the timing of the invasion was connected with developments in Macedonia and Thrace. The Celts were not so far away as to have been uninformed about the wars between the Successors and the conflicts in the court of Ptolemy Keraunos. There were regular contacts between Macedonia and Thrace and the northern barbarians, and in 281 BC, when Ptolemy Keraunos killed two sons of his wife and sister Arsinoe, the third one escaped to the Dardanians, one of the barbarian tribes. It is probable that the Celtic tribal leaders took advantage of these events when they launched the invasion of 280/279 BC. The available sources do not allow us to determine the exact number of people who moved – reportedly 85,000 men, servants and family members. Their aim was probably migration, not a raid.

The Celts moved in three army divisions: the eastern group under

Kerethrios attacked Thrace, the central group under Brennos and Akichorios invaded Paionia (to the north of Macedonia), while the western group moved against Macedonia and Illyria. Ptolemy Keraunos tried to defend his newly acquired kingdom but was defeated, captured and beheaded. His successor, his brother Meleagros, was forced by the army to resign after two months of rule; the next king, Antipatros, a nephew of King Kassandros, lasted for only forty-five days. The kingship was then offered to the general Sosthenes, governor of Asia Minor under Lysimachos. He probably declined the royal title, but he did not decline the mission. It was he who succeeded in repelling the invaders outside the kingdom's borders, and he ruled for about two years (279–277 BC).

In the second year of the invasion (279/278 BC), the main body of the Celtic army, under Brennos and Akichorios, invaded mainland Greece, in the first barbarian invasion of this part of Greece since the Persian Wars exactly two centuries earlier. And just as during the Persian invasion under Xerxes, a Greek alliance attempted to stop the invaders at the narrow pass of Thermopylai. The Greeks succeeded in defending the pass, but not in halting the invasion. The Celts circumvented the pass, and instead of moving southward, they proceeded to the west in order to plunder the sanctuary of Apollo at Delphi. The armies of two federations of central Greece, the Aetolians and the Phokians, arrived just in time and, exploiting the knowledge of the mountainous landscape and the bad weather conditions, they drove the barbarians away. The narrow escape was immediately attributed to divine intervention, a miracle of either Apollo or Zeus Soter (the Rescuer). Four centuries later, Pausanias gives an account of how Delphi was saved. His narrative, an expanded version of contemporary reports, gives us an impression of the way this event was announced by the defenders of Delphi to the other Greeks who were not there to fight against these tall, ghastly, fearless, godless and bloodthirsty warriors, whose number was reported to be many times that of the Greeks (40,000–60,000):

> The whole ground occupied by the Galatian army was shaken violently for most of the day with continuous thunder and lightning. The thunder both terrified the Galatians and prevented them from hearing their orders, while the bolts from heaven set on fire not only those whom they struck but also those who were standing next to them, themselves and their armor alike. Then there were seen by them ghosts

of the heroes Hyperochos, Laodokos, and Pyrrhos ... The night would bring upon them experiences far more painful. For there came on a severe frost, and snow with it; and great rocks slipping from Mt Parnassos, and crags breaking away, made the barbarians their target ... They camped where night overtook them in their retreat, and during the night a panic fell upon them ... At first only a few became mad, and these imagined that they heard the trampling of horses at a gallop and the attack of advancing enemies; but after a little time the delusion spread to all. So rushing to arms they divided into two parties, killing and being killed, neither understanding their mother tongue nor recognizing one another's forms or the shape of their shields ...

Earthquakes, storms and fog are very common in the region of Mount Parnassos. When such natural phenomena opportunely occur during a barbarian attack and, moreover, when they selectively slay the bad guys and save the good, then they must be the result of divine providence. This is what the Greeks believed when they decided, shortly after this event, to establish thanksgiving sacrifices and festivals for the salvation of Greece.

After the wounded Brennos committed suicide, Akichorios withdrew with the remaining army, suffering further losses. Greece was saved, but small groups of Celts had successfully established themselves in Illyria and Thrace. More importantly, Macedonia was again without a king. This was an opportunity that Antigonos Gonatas, the son of Demetrios Poliorketes, could never have dreamed of. He had inherited not only part of his father's army, fleet and strongholds but also his ambition and the claim to the throne of Macedonia. He rushed with his army to Macedonia and defeated the remaining Celtic troops at Lysimacheia, allegedly with the assistance of Pan, the god of terror. His victory gave his army the justification to proclaim him king in 277 BC. He was temporarily driven out of parts of Macedonia by Pyrrhos in 275 BC, but the death of Pyrrhos in 272 eliminated the last obstacle to the throne of Macedonia, which was to be ruled by the Antigonid dynasty until 167 BC.

What ultimately saved Macedonia and Greece from the Celtic menace, however, was not Antigonos' victory or Apollo's miracles but rather the imprudence of another king. Nikomedes I of Bithynia was in need of mercenaries in order to stabilise his rule in the kingdom that he had just inherited from his father, Zipoetes. So he invited two groups of Celts under Lonorios and Lutarios, who were plundering the area of Hellespont and Thrace, to fight for him. In 277 BC, the Celts crossed for the first time over to Asia Minor. Initially, they assisted Nikomedes in his wars, but soon they started to operate independently. The coastal cities and then the interior of Asia Minor became victims of their raids. The Celts had come to stay. Three tribes settled in central Asia Minor, in a region named Galatia, 'the land of the Galatai' – that is, the land of the Gauls (see Map 5). The Tolistoagii settled near Pessinous, the Trokmoi near Ankyra and the Tektosagoi near Tavium. Here they organised chiefdoms founded on Celtic traditions and maintained Celtic culture, place and personal names, types of settlements and burial customs. The Galatian federation survived until 25 BC, when this area was incorporated into the Roman Empire.

The Celtic invasion changed the ethnic composition of large areas from the Danube to the Aegean, especially in the northern Balkans and to a lesser extent in Thrace, Illyria and Asia Minor. It also triggered important political developments. In Greece, the greatest beneficiaries were the Aetolians. Hitherto unimportant on the great international scene and mostly regarded as a factor of instability due to their raids in southern Greece, the Aetolians had played an important part in the defence of Delphi and presented themselves as champions of Greek freedom. Once the Celtic threat was removed, the Aetolians united in their federal state a large number of cities in central Greece and beyond, promising to offer protection from a more permanent threat to their independence: Macedonia. Those who did not join the Aetolians became victims of their raids. The conflicts originating from the confrontation between Aetolia and its enemies, especially Macedonia and the federal state of the Achaeans in the Peloponnese, dominated the political history of the late third century. In Asia Minor, the Celtic invasion contributed to the rise of the Attalid kingdom of Pergamon. It was only after a great victory over the Galatians in c. 238 BC that the dynast of Pergamon, Attalos I, assumed the title of king.

In Greek collective memory and ethnic consciousness, the Celts somehow replaced the Persians as the barbarians who threatened Greek freedom and committed sacrileges but were finally defeated. The invasion of 279 BC was a shock comparable to that of 9/11, and both the horrors and the victory were remembered for decades thanks to narratives, commemorative anniversaries, festivals, monuments (see Fig. 6) and, above all, the efforts of those who had fought against the Gauls to exploit their victory in the political arena. A commemorative festival, the Soteria (the festival for the saviour Zeus), was established in Delphi shortly after the victory. The

6. Statue group of a Gaul killing his wife and himself.

Aetolians reorganised it a few years before 246 BC, inviting participants from the entire Greek world to compete in athletic and musical contests.

On the Athenian Acropolis, near the Temple of Athena Nike, whose sculptural decoration showed the Athenians defending their fatherland from barbarian invaders – the Amazons and the Persians – the commander of the Macedonian garrison of King Antigonos Gonatas dedicated to Athena Nike a monument 'containing memorials of the king's deeds against the barbarians for the salvation of the Greeks'. This monument, probably consisting of painted panels, commemorated Antigonos' victory over the Gauls in 277 BC. Standing in the shadow of the temples of Athena Parthenos and Athena Nike, and borrowing themes from their sculptural decoration, it was erected in an ideal setting to convey its message: it was Antigonos Gonatas – and not the Aetolians – who had saved the Greeks from the barbarians. This claim, however, did not go unchallenged. Fifty years later, the enemy of the Antigonids, the king of Pergamon, Attalos I, chose the same location for the dedication of a sculptural group representing dying Gauls. The Athenian Acropolis became a battlefield of works of art presenting contrasting versions of recent history.

Divine epiphanies were an important feature of the commemoration of the Celtic Wars. In no other period of Hellenistic history do we find a concentration of narratives about miracles comparable to those from the years of the Galatian invasion. Stories of the gods defeating the sacrilegious barbarians were told not only in Delphi and in the Macedonian court but also in the cities of Asia Minor. In Kyzikos, Heracles was represented in a relief standing over a Galatian; in Themisonion, Heracles, Apollo and Hermes are said to have appeared in the dreams of magistrates and advised them to save the entire population by hiding them in a cave; at Kelainai, the barbarians were repelled by the mythical musician Marsyas and his music. Most likely, the narrative about the miracle at Delphi inspired the other accounts as well. By bringing the gods to earth, the Greeks who experienced the horrible invasion of the Galatians assimilated their battles with the Homeric narratives in which gods and men fought side by side, as well as with miracles narrated in connection with the Persian Wars. In this way, the defeat of the Gauls with divine assistance acquired epic dimensions and was elevated to the status of a Hellenic victory over the archetypical barbarian. The next barbarians to invade Greece, the Romans, came upon Greek invitation. They found the Greeks divided as ever. But this time the Olympians did not come to help.

The Chremonidean War (267–261 BC)

For the inhabitants of mainland Greece and the Aegean, freedom and autonomy had precise meanings: freedom in the foreign policy of their cities; freedom from royal or other garrisons; freedom from the payment of tribute; and freedom in the management of their internal affairs. The dominant position of the Macedonian kings curtailed many of these freedoms. Those who lost them were eager to believe anyone who promised to restore them. Antigonos Monophthalmos first exploited this desire in 311 BC (see pp. 38–9), but other Hellenistic kings also tried to profit from this love of freedom in their dealings with Greek communities instigating a rebellion that would weaken one of their opponents. Strongholds in central and southern Greece were vital for the kings of Macedonia, who had more limited resources and access to manpower than the Ptolemies and Seleucids. The Antigonids effectively controlled traffic in Greece by holding Demetrias in Thessaly, the two most important cities of Euboia, Chalkis and Eretria, the forts on the Mouseion Hill in Athens and the hill of Mounychia in Piraeus, and the citadel of Acrocorinth at the entrance to the Peloponnese. For this reason, Demetrias, Chalkis and Acrocorinth later became known as the 'fetters of Greece'. Whenever *poleis* saw their autonomy threatened or lost because of the expansion of a king, they sought alliances with another king or with other *poleis* and federations and took up arms for their freedom. This is the background of the War of Chremonides.

In 268 BC, the Athenian statesman Chremonides proposed in the Athenian assembly a treaty of alliance between Athens, Sparta, their respective allies and Ptolemy II. The target of this alliance was Antigonos Gonatas. The aim of the Greeks was clear: liberation from the Macedonian garrisons. The aim of Ptolemy II was to weaken Gonatas. The Ptolemies traditionally had strong interests in the Aegean, as they controlled several islands through the the Nesiotic League (*Koinon ton Nesioton*), a confederacy of the islands of the Cyclades. Its chief magistrate (*nesiarch*) was in the service of the king. His immediate superior was the Ptolemaic admiral Philokles, who was also king of the Phoenician city of Sidon. Antigonos' presence in the Aegean and his control of harbours were obstacles for Ptolemaic maritime supremacy. But perhaps wide-ranging ambitions were behind Ptolemy's involvement in this war.

His policy of naval domination and leadership in Greece had been to a large extent determined by his wife, Arsinoe (see Fig. 7). Before she married her brother in 279 BC, Arsinoe had been the wife of two kings of Macedonia, Lysimachos and Ptolemy Keraunos. The kingdom that was now ruled by Gonatas had been her kingdom. Her only surviving son from her marriage to Lysimachos, Ptolemy Epigonos (the After-Born), was a sworn enemy of Gonatas and had already attempted to gain the throne of Macedonia. It is doubtful that the royal couple of Egypt had concrete plans to reign in Macedonia or to establish direct control in Greece. But they may have aimed at establishing a hegemony over the Greeks, similar to that of Philip II and Alexander.

People close to Ptolemy II adopted the idea that the Greeks should

7. Arsinoe II Philadelphos.

be united under a single leader to oppose those who threatened their freedom. In Plataiai, where the Greeks ultimately defeated the Persian army on Greek soil in 477 BC, Glaukon, an Athenian in the king's service, promoted the idea of Greek freedom and concord by sponsoring a sacrifice in honour of Zeus Eleutherios (the Bringer of Freedom) and Homonoia (Concord). In Athens, Glaukon's brother Chremonides promoted the same Panhellenic spirit. Reminding the Persian Wars and praising Ptolemy as the champion of Greek freedom, Chremonides justified an alliance of Athens, Sparta and Ptolemy II with these words:

> In the past, the Athenians, the Lakedaimonians, and their respective allies established a common friendship and alliance with each other and jointly fought many glorious battles against those who sought to enslave the cities, winning fame and bringing freedom to the other Greeks. And now that similar circumstances have affected the whole of Greece because of those who seek to subvert the laws and ancestral constitutions of each city, King Ptolemy following the policy of his ancestor and of his sister conspicuously shows his zeal for the common

freedom of the Greeks. The people of Athens have made an alliance with him and the other Greeks and now they pass a decree to invite all to follow the same policy.

From Ptolemy's perspective, a war 'for the common freedom of the Greeks' was one that would weaken his main opponent in Greece and the Aegean.

Military operations took place in Attica, the Peloponnese and many Aegean islands. The anti-Macedonian alliance was victorious at first, but Ptolemy failed to provide strong support, despite his fleet's operations in the Aegean. The Athenian countryside was plundered, the population faced food shortages and the alliance suffered two great blows: the defeat and death of the Spartan king, Areus, near Corinth in 265 BC and the loss of the Athenian fleet in a sea battle near Kos in 261 BC. Athens, weakened by siege, blockade and raids on its countryside, short of grain and deprived of its fleet, was forced to surrender in 261 BC. The city was to remain under Macedonian control for more than thirty years. The Athenians failed in the struggle for freedom. The idea of a Panhellenic alliance was forgotten for forty years and Sparta withdrew once again from the Panhellenic stage. But where Athens and Sparta had failed, a statesman from Sikyon would later succeed.

Aratos and the rise of the Achaeans (251–229 BC)

Alexander was twenty years old when he was given the throne of Macedonia and the responsibility to lead the Greeks in a campaign against Persia. Demetrios Poliorketes was the same age when he liberated Athens and received divine honours from the Athenians in 307 BC. When he returned to Epirus to reclaim his throne in 298/297 BC, Pyrrhos was twenty-one years old. And at the age of twenty, Antiochos III put an end to the rebellion in the eastern provinces of the Seleucid kingdom that he had inherited when he was seventeen in 220 BC. In monarchies, the death of kings presented young men with challenges and opportunities. In the world of the poleis, when the institutions functioned properly, young men had to wait for a position of leadership; they spent their youth learning tasks and acquiring a reputation through personal achievement, social connections and inherited money. It was only in times of deep crisis that men who had barely reached the age of citizenship took initiatives. Aratos was one such man, who took advantage of the political and social crisis in the northern Peloponnese to leave his imprint on the history of all of Greece.

The Peloponnese of the third century was still a world of *poleis*; but their political order had been disturbed by decades of social unrest and interventions of monarchs. As in Syracuse and Asia Minor, ambitious men had established personal rule. They were known in contemporary sources as 'tyrants', although they usually concealed their autocratic rule under the mantle of a traditional office. Argos was ruled by a line of tyrants belonging to an elite family that had acquired and retained power with the support of Antigonos Gonatas. Tyrants also ruled Megalopolis and Sikyon. Corinth was under the direct control of Antigonos Gonatas, who had placed his half-brother Krateros as commander of the garrison and effectively governor of the city. By removing these tyrants Aratos changed the fate of the Peloponnese for a century.

Aratos, born in c. 271 BC, had experienced political violence in his childhood. His father, Kleinias, was a member of one of the leading families of Sikyon and an opponent of tyrants. When Aratos was seven years old, a new tyrant seized power (see p. 144); his father was killed, but Aratos managed to escape to Argos. Although in exile, he received the education to which people of his rank were accustomed, was admired as an athlete and became a leader of the exiled Sikyonians. He was twenty years old when he led a small group of exiles back to Sikyon in 251 BC. They climbed the steep city wall at night, captured the guards and spread news of the revolt. The citizens rose against the tyrant Nikokles and set his palace on fire, and at the end of the day, with only one casualty, the tyranny of Sikyon was overthrown. In order to avoid civil war as the returning exiles reclaimed their property, Aratos took two measures. He made Sikyon a member of an old but hitherto unimportant confederation, the Achaean League, and he received financial assistance from the one king who would profit from the weakening of Macedonian power in Greece: the king of Egypt. Aratos' decision to have Sikyon join the Achaean League had far-reaching consequences for the entire Peloponnese and for Greek history.

Until the mid-third century BC, the Peloponnese had been divided into groups of communities that spoke different dialects, traced their history back to different mythical founders and had heterogeneous political institutions. Some of the groups were organised in loose federations known as *koina* (Achaeans, Eleians, Arkadians). In the Classical period, the most important federation was that of the Arkadians in the central

Peloponnese. The *koinon* of the Achaeans had never played any important role. It originally consisted of twelve communities in the north-western Peloponnese. Two of the cities, Helike and Olenos, were destroyed by an earthquake and the resulting tsunami in 373 BC, and the remaining ones fell into a state of disunity due to the interventions of the Macedonian kings. Around 280 BC, the league was revived at the initiative of the cities of Dyme, Patrai, Pharai and Tritaia. In 275/274 BC, the other cities followed, expelling tyrants and garrisons, and the federation was reorganised under the leadership of a federal secretary and two generals (later reduced to one), who were elected on an annual basis (see p. 131). The possibilities that such a collaboration offered for freedom from the rule of tyrants and independence from Macedonia attracted Aratos to the Achaean League. When Sikyon, a city at the opposite side of the Peloponnese, joined the League, this changed its character as a regional federation. The Achaean League ventured onto a path that would make it first a Peloponnesian and then a Greek power.

In 245 BC, Aratos was elected to the highest office, the office of the general (*strategos*). In order to transform this federal state into an influential power in Greece, he had to oppose the Macedonian domination of southern Greece. The most important target was Corinth, a city with the utmost strategic importance. Here a Macedonian garrison guarded the citadel of Acrocorinth, which controlled traffic from central Greece to the Peloponnese. Aratos led a small detachment of 400 men into the citadel through a secret passage, defeated the garrison and freed Corinth, which immediately joined the League. Encouraged by this success, Megara, Troizen and Epidaurus followed suit, expelling the Macedonian garrisons and joining the League. While serving continuously as a general from 241 to 235 BC, Aratos ejected tyrants from several cities, although he failed to incorporate Argos, the city where he had spent his childhood, into the League. A landmark in the League's rise to power was the decision of Lydiadas, tyrant of Megalopolis, to bring his city into the League. In the following years, he alternated with Aratos in the office of the *strategos* (234–230 BC). A temporary alliance with the Aetolian League enabled further expansion, and in 229 BC Aratos was standing with his troops at the gates of Athens. Once a leader of the Greeks, Athens had remained under the control of a Macedonian garrison since 261 BC. Aratos convinced the garrison commander to withdraw his troops by offering him an honorarium of 150 talents; twenty talents were contributed by Aratos himself, while the remaining sum was in part procured by the Athenian statesman Medeios and in part donated by the king of Egypt, eager to damage the interests of Macedonia. The island of Aigina, Hermione, the majority of the Arkadian cities and Argos joined the League, which had now reached the apex of its territorial expansion and power, overshadowing Sparta as the greatest power on the Peloponnese and rivalling the Aetolian League in influence. Polybius, a citizen of the League and early in his life a commander of its cavalry, offers a very flattering appraisal:

> In general, there is no difference between the entire Peloponnese and a single city, except that its inhabitants are not included within the same city wall. In other respects, within the League and in each individual city they all have similar institutions ... Nowhere will you find a constitution and an ideal of equality, freedom of speech, and, in a word, of genuine democracy more perfect than among the Achaeans ... None of the original members is allowed to enjoy any special privilege, and equal rights are given to all newcomers.

Polybius' favourable view is not surprising; Aratos' memoirs, now lost, were his main source of information about the events of this period. It is natural that the rise of an unimportant peripheral power to become one of the main players of international politics was presented as a success story by its main protagonist. Yet a closer study of the evidence reveals tensions and fractures that ultimately prevented the Achaean League from uniting the Greeks. Aratos and the other leaders of the League were representatives of a wealthy elite of landowners who for decades had monopolised power, sometimes as elected magistrates, sometimes as tyrants. Although the League developed procedures for the peaceful resolution of territorial disputes among its members, traditional enmities persisted. The biggest problem, however, was that the League utterly failed in resolving the social problems that had built up over the previous centuries in the Peloponnese (see p. 306). The League could not become a credible champion of the freedom of the Greeks under the leadership of statesmen who were not willing to ease the tensions caused by economic and social inequality. This problem became apparent less than two decades after the liberation of Corinth and precipitated a war that threatened the League's very existence (see p. 72).

Restorers of power: Doson and Kleomenes (239–221 BC)

Things did not look good for Antigonos Gonatas in Greece at the end of his life. For two decades after the Chremonidean War he had dominated Greece; following a victory over the Ptolemaic fleet around 256 BC, he controlled the majority of the Aegean islands. But Aratos' policies had deprived him of his most important fort in southern Greece, the Acrocorinth, in 245 BC. Although he managed to retain Athens and Euboia under his control, the regimes that he supported in the Peloponnese collapsed one after the other. His successor, Demetrios II, had to spend most of his short reign (239–229 BC) fighting against the combined forces of Aetolians and Achaeans in order to successfully defend his influence in central Greece; his greatest success was to prevent the federal state of Boiotia from joining the Aetolian League in 236 BC. When he died of his wounds during a war against northern tribes, his son Philip was only nine years old. His half-cousin Antigonos, a grandson of Demetrios Poliorketes, assumed the regency until Philip came of age. In addition to the royal title, he was also given the nickname Doson (the One Who Shall Give [the Kingship]).

The circumstances in 229 BC could not have been more difficult for a Macedonian king. The northern border was threatened; in the neighbouring kingdom of Epirus, a revolution had overthrown kingship and established a republic around 233 BC, encouraging the ambitions of the Aetolians for expansion in this area. Roman troops were for the first time east of the Adriatic Sea, fighting against the Illyrian queen Teuta (see p. 151). The Aetolians and the Achaeans, although traditionally opponents, had united forces against Macedonia, and the most important Antigonid stronghold in the south, Athens, was lost for ever when the commander of the Macedonian garrison accepted a huge sum of money and withdrew his troops.

In this disastrous situation Doson proved as energetic as his grandfather Demetrios Poliorketes, and not only secured the northern borders of his kingdom by defeating the barbarian tribes, but also revived a traditional policy of the Antigonids: he attempted to secure the control of the Aegean Sea, which in the last decades had been dominated by the Ptolemies. His military operations in Caria in 228 BC, about which little is known, were not an unplanned adventure but an effort to establish firm naval bases on both sides of the Aegean. Doson's decision to operate in an area with vital Ptolemaic interests must have been a strategic move that aimed to open a new phase in the competition between the two kingdoms for naval supremacy. Although Doson failed to establish permanent Macedonian control in south Asia Minor, he did win a reputation as a significant political and military leader.

Doson had more potential adversaries than he could handle: the Ptolemies, the Achaean and Aetolian Leagues and Rome. This entanglement became more complex when a young Spartan king, Kleomenes III, king since 235 BC, initiated social reforms that aimed at restoring Sparta's military power by enlarging the body of the citizens who possessed land and had the financial basis for military training and army service in 228 BC (see p. 306). This Spartan project stirred up the hopes of the dispossessed and indebted elsewhere in Greece, and voices called for redistribution of land and abolishment of debts, a recurring theme in social conflicts (see pp. 305–7). When Kleomenes attempted to export his reforms and regain for Sparta a leading role in the Peloponnese (227–222 BC), the Achaean League was forced to react. Unable to successfully face Kleomenes' military operations in the Peloponnese and recognising a great leader in Doson, Aratos took a momentous decision. Putting an end to the enmity between the Achaean League and the Macedonian kingdom, he approached the former enemy and asked him to take the leadership in a war against Kleomenes. Following the example of his great-grandfather Antigonos Monophthalmos, Doson revived the Hellenic Alliance in Corinth in 224 BC and became leader of a coalition of all the major federal states in Greece. In addition to the Achaean League and the Thessalians, who were under Macedonian rule, the major federal states of central Greece, Phokians, Boiotians, Akarnanians and Epirotans also joined the alliance. Sparta's few allies were the states of the Peloponnese that refused to join the Achaean League. The revival of the Hellenic Alliance under the leadership of the Macedonian king put an end to Ptolemaic influence in Greece. Two years later, Doson's victory at Sellasia in 222 BC put an end to Kleomenes' ambitions, and the defeated Spartan king had to seek refuge in Egypt, where he was later murdered.

The 'Social War': the last great war the
Greeks fought alone (220–217 BC)

At the height of his power, Doson was forced to return to Macedonia to face an attack by Illyrians in the north; victorious but weakened, possibly by a wound, he suddenly died in 221 BC. His nephew, now eighteen years old, ascended the throne as Philip V. He also succeeded Doson as leader of the Hellenic Alliance. The upbringing of Philip, exactly as that of his contemporary the Seleucid Antiochos III, their family traditions and the expectations inherent in their royal position led both kings to military enterprises that shook the world for thirty years, from 219 to 189 BC. None of their ambitions was fulfilled. On the contrary, at the end of their lives they left their kingdoms much weaker than at the beginning of their rule.

Philip V was soon called to continue Doson's work; he led the Hellenic Alliance in a war against the Aetolian League, Sparta and Elis from 220 to 217 BC. The war had been provoked by the raids of the Aetolians in central and southern Greece. The rising power of Aetolia was threatening Macedonia's allies (Epirus and Akarnania) and even the kingdom's borders; and in the Peloponnese, cities of the Achaean League had been victims of Aetolian attacks. This so-called 'Social War' ('social' from the Latin *socius*, ally) brought devastation all over Greece, but showed Philip's military skills; the fact that Aratos, an experienced leader, was his adviser, contributed to the young king's success. Despite significant victories, Philip agreed in August 217 BC to negotiate a peace treaty with the Aetolians. The treaty restored the status quo before the beginning of the war. Although it cancelled all of Philip's gains it increased his reputation as a leader. It is not a coincidence that a Cretan alliance, the Cretan Koinon, elected him *prostates* (leader of the alliance).

To understand why Philip ended the war and why 217 BC proved to be one of the most important turning points in Hellenistic history we have to look at events that occurred far away from Greece: the conflicts between the Ptolemies and the Seleucids over south Syria (see pp. 77–84) and the bitter competition between Rome and Carthage for domination in the western Mediterranean.

4

THE PTOLEMAIC
GOLDEN AGE

(283–217 BC)

Ptolemaic hegemony in the short third century

Shortly after his father's death, Ptolemy II founded a festival in Alexandria, the Ptolemaia. He declared this festival to be of the same status as the Pythian festival of Apollo. Cities from the entire Greek world were invited to participate by sending sacred envoys (*theoroi*) as they did on the occasion of the traditional great festivals. During the first celebration of the festival – the date is disputed (c. 274 BC?) – in the presence of these foreign envoys and visitors, the king staged the greatest procession that the Greek world would ever know. It was so impressive that, half a millennium later, the author Athenaios was able to quote a long description preserved in the work of Kallixeinos of Rhodes. The various sections of the procession highlighted the relationship of the Ptolemies with their divine patrons, Zeus and Dionysus, and with Alexander the Great, their contribution to the freedom of the Greeks and the extent of their power. Actors, dressed in colourful and luxurious costumes, impersonated the companions of Dionysus and abstract ideas such as the Year and the Four Seasons. A veritable army of satyrs marched in silver, gold and bronze panoplies; Silenoi, boys and girls represented Dionysus' triumphal return from India.

> There were statues of Alexander and Ptolemy, crowned with ivy wreaths made of gold. The statue of (military) Virtue, which stood beside Ptolemy, held a gold olive wreath ... The city of Corinth standing beside Ptolemy was crowned with a gold band ... This cart was followed by women wearing luxurious garments and ornaments; through announcements they were identified as the cities in Ionia and the other Greek cities settled in Asia and the islands, which had been ruled by the Persians ... After all these, the cavalry and the infantry, all armed in a manner that caused amazement, marched. The infantry numbered about 57,600 men, the cavalry 23,200 ...

The celebration was a complex propagandistic enterprise that was orchestrated to convey the Ptolemies' legitimacy of rule, divine protection, affluence and power. This unforgettable spectacle had military overtones and alluded to the claim of the Ptolemies to a hegemonic position in the Greek world.

Among all the Hellenistic dynasties, it was only in Ptolemaic Egypt that the transition of power had taken place without incident from the generation of the Successors to the next in 283/282 BC. Exploiting the rich resources of his kingdom, safe from direct threats to his territory and applying a cunning policy of alliances, the 'sibling-loving' kings Ptolemy II and Arsinoe II (see Fig. 7) made the Ptolemaic kingdom into the leading political power in the eastern Mediterranean. Theocritus described Egypt and its ruler with the following verses around 270 BC:

> Countless countries and countless nations,
> helped by the rain of Zeus, cause their crops to grow,
> but none is as productive as the lowlands of Egypt
> when the Nile floods and breaks up the soil,
> nor does any have as many towns of skilled workmen.
> Three hundred cities are built there,
> then three thousand in addition to thirty thousand,
> and twice three and three times nine besides.
> Over all these mighty Ptolemy rules as king.
> In addition, he cuts off for himself a part of Phoenicia, Arabia,

Syria, Libya, and of the dark-skinned Ethiopians.
He gives orders to all Pamphylians, to the Cilician spearmen,
to the Lycians and to the warlike Carians,
and to the islands of the Cyclades, since his are the finest ships
that sail the seas. All the sea and land
and the roaring rivers are ruled by Ptolemy,
and a host of horsemen and a host of shielded warriors,
equipped with glittering bronze gather about him.
In wealth he could outweigh all the kings,
so great are the riches that come daily to his opulent home,
from everywhere. His people go about their occupations in security ...
So great is the man who reigns over the broad plains,
fair-haired Ptolemy, a skilled spearman,
who cares deeply for the preservation of his fatherly inheritance
as a good king, and adds to it himself ...

If court poets were to be trusted, future historians might have a rather misleading impression of the North Korean dynasty of the Kims. Ptolemy II was not really master of Libya. Magas, his stepbrother and governor of Cyrene, had declared himself an independent king in 276 BC, and Cyrene remained an independent kingdom until his death in 250 BC. Only when Magas' daughter Berenike married Ptolemy's son in 246 BC did Cyrene return to the realm of the Ptolemies.

But despite his exaggerations, Theocritus' portrayal of wealth, military might, domination of the seas, external influence and internal security is as accurate as the genre of encomiastic poetry allows. Ptolemy knew well how to promote this image of superiority, although he did not deceive attentive observers. It is said that Aratos used to admire the wealth of Egypt, 'hearing tales of its elephants, and fleets, and palaces'; but when he went behind the scenes, 'he saw that everything in Egypt is play-acting and painted scenery'.

Ptolemaic diplomacy reached as far as Ukraine. In the harbour of Nymphaion, a graffito on a wall of a shrine of Aphrodite represents, in great detail, a ship by the name of *Isis*, possibly that which carried ambassadors of Ptolemy II to the cities of the north shore of the Black Sea. It is to this king that Greek cities turned in times of need and conflict. Ptolemy II was involved in the Chremonidean War and assisted Aratos in the liberation of Peloponnesian cities from tyrannies and garrisons (see pp. 65–7 and 70).

Ptolemy's foreign policy had two main aims: to secure domination of the Aegean through control of the islands and coastal cities in Asia Minor, and to control a region that has never ceased to be contested among empires, nations and religions. In antiquity it was known as Koile Syria (Hollow Syria) and it corresponds to today's southern Syria, Lebanon and Palestine (see Map 3). Six Syrian Wars were waged between the Ptolemies and the Seleucids for the possession of this land.

Nothing quiet on the eastern front: the Syrian Wars (274–253 BC)

During the First Syrian War around 274–271 BC, Ptolemy II successfully defended the occupation of Koile Syria and his strongholds in Asia Minor. His ambitions and those of his adopted son and co-regent Ptolemy Epigonos must have been significantly broader in the Second Syrian War (260–253), which broke out under unclear circumstances shortly after the Chremonidean War. This younger Ptolemy was the only surviving son of the king's beloved sister and wife Arsinoe, from her marriage to Lysimachos (see p. 65). To be distinguished from Ptolemy's eldest son, the later Ptolemy III, he was given the epithet Epigonos (the After-Born). After unsuccessful efforts to reclaim his father's throne and to rule over Macedonia and Thrace (279–277 BC), Ptolemy Epigonos came to Egypt. No later than 267 BC, around the time of the outbreak of the Chremonidean War against Antigonos Gonatas, Ptolemy II appointed him – and not his eldest son – as co-regent. As a son of Lysimachos, Epigonos would be the natural opponent of Antigonos Gonatas, who was occupying the throne that his biological father once had.

Around the time Ptolemy II launched a new Syrian War against Antiochos II, around 260 BC, Epigonos was in Miletos, probably to represent the interests of his adopted father. However, possibly disappointed by the lack of support for his dream to reign in Macedonia, Epigonos joined forces with Timarchos, a tyrant in Miletos, and revolted against Ptolemy II in 259–258 BC. Initially, he was supported by Antiochos II, but the revolt ended with the capture of Miletos by Antiochos II, the death of Timarchos and possibly the reconciliation of Epigonos with the king of Egypt. The strong Ptolemaic presence in Asia Minor alarmed both Rhodes, a sea power in the southern Aegean, and Antigonos Gonatas, who decided to take Antiochos' side. At a great naval battle near Kos (256 BC?), the

Ptolemaic fleet was defeated. Antigonos Gonatas was now in control of the Aegean, apart from Thera, where Ptolemy retained a garrison. Antiochos II recaptured most of the territory that the Seleucids had lost in the First Syrian War.

These Syrian Wars, and the ones that followed, were more than the efforts of kings to control an area of strategic importance for military communications and trade. They were part of efforts to legitimise their authority through military success (see pp. 105–8). Koile Syria remained contested between the two kingdoms for another century. The first Syrian Wars are also paradigmatic for the way regional conflicts could easily expand through the involvement of additional powers, both kingdoms and cities.

The peace treaty was sealed with a dynastic marriage in 253 BC. Antiochos II divorced his wife Laodike, accepting a marriage to Ptolemy's daughter Berenike. This marriage had important consequences, although not the ones intended by the two kings, who underestimated the repudiated queen's grudge.

Cherchez la femme: the war of Laodike (246–241 BC) and the lock of Berenike

With the death of Ptolemy II in January 246 BC, an era marked by his influence in 'international politics' came to an end. Antiochos II may have recognised here an opportunity to attempt expansion at the expense of the Ptolemaic territories outside Egypt. But Ptolemy III also had reasons to start a war. The peace of 253 BC had dealt a significant blow to Ptolemaic influence in Asia Minor and the Aegean, and this would justify an effort to regain the lost ground and legitimate his rule through military achievement. In 246 BC, Antiochos II was in Asia Minor, presumably having reconciled himself with Laodike, who was living in Ephesos. Since his rejection of his marriage with a Ptolemaic princess affected the peace agreement, he must have been planning for war. But Ptolemy III was not unprepared either; his army was already operating in the northern Aegean at an early phase of the conflict.

Antiochos II died suddenly in August 246 BC, possibly murdered by Laodike, who immediately assumed leadership of the kingdom. She had her eldest son, Seleukos II, proclaimed king and orchestrated the murder of Berenike's son and later of the queen herself in the Seleucid capital of Antioch. For Ptolemy III, the war was a matter not just of defending or conquering territory but also of protecting his sister and his nephew, and then avenging their deaths. His success was impressive. He led a campaign into the heart of the Seleucid kingdom, conquering the capitals, Seleukeia and Antioch, then crossed the Euphrates and continued the march into Mesopotamia. That Ptolemy III reached southern Mesopotamia was both a daring enterprise and a splendid success. This is the place whence, almost eighty years previously, his grandfather, the companion of Alexander, had started his journey to Alexandria. When the governor of Ephesos defected to Ptolemy, the most important city of Asia Minor passed under Ptolemaic control.

Up to this point the war had been a conflict between the Ptolemies and the Seleucids; but, as it often happened in this period, the war had a domino effect. When Ainos in Thrace, a city of strategic value for sea traffic in the northern Aegean, came under Ptolemaic control, this alarmed Antigonos Gonatas, the Ptolemies' traditional competitor in the Aegean. With his entry into the fighting, the 'Laodikean War' turned into one of the Hellenistic Great Wars. The Macedonian king, who had recently lost his principal strongholds in southern Greece, recognised a chance to regain control in the Cyclades. In a great naval battle at Andros, the Ptolemaic fleet was defeated in 246 or 245 BC.

Ptolemy III had to suspend the campaign around 243 BC, possibly because of troubles in Egypt caused by his long absence. Seleukos II did manage to regain ground in Asia Minor and Syria, but not without paying a hefty price: he had to accept as co-regent his younger brother Antiochos Hierax (the Hawk), who later declared himself king in Asia Minor around 240 BC. As for Antigonos Gonatas, the impact of his success in Andros was soon almost completely cancelled out. Aratos liberated Corinth and Acrocorinth from the Macedonian garrison in 245 BC (see p. 69). Under his leadership, the Achaean League allied itself with Ptolemy III, who was declared its *hegemon* on land and sea in 243 BC.

This position was of little practical significance – Ptolemy III never commanded any Achaean troops or ships. It did, however, send a political message. It was not the first time that a confederation of states had elected a king as its military leader: this is the position that Philip II held in the Hellenic Alliance and the Antigonids Antigonos Doson and Philip V would have in its revival in 224 BC. But for the first time, a king whose realm was outside Greece was in that position, which reveals far-reaching political claims on the part of both the nominator, Aratos, and his nominee, Ptolemy III. We may assume that for Aratos this meant that the Achaean League was stepping into the role that the Hellenic Alliance had once had. It would be surprising if such a statesman with foresight and consciousness of his historical role – Aratos was one of the first authors of a memoir – had not realised this. And it would be equally surprising if Ptolemy were ignorant of earlier alliances with Panhellenic aspirations and of the significance of his position as *hegemon* of an alliance in Greece. Ptolemy III was also conscious of his historical role: he left us short accounts of his deeds via an inscription in which he proudly recounts his unprecedented achievements (see p. 81). This is not to say that Ptolemy III was resurrecting dreams of a succession to Alexander in Europe and Asia. Still, one cannot deny continuities in the instruments of political operation applied by kings and leading statesmen. We recognise a recurring pattern: a group of Greek cities, united to face an enemy of their independence, accepted as their leader a monarch whose policy seemed at that moment to favour their plan; and a monarch accepted the leadership, not out of love of freedom, but rather to gain prominence on the Panhellenic stage.

The War of Laodike continued until 241 BC, when Seleukos II and Ptolemy III finally concluded a peace treaty. Ptolemy III's greatest success was that he not only retained Koile Syria but also expanded his realm, seizing the most important harbour in Syria, Seleukeia in Pieria. With control of Cyprus, several Aegean islands, coastal cities in Thrace and cities in Asia Minor, Egypt under Ptolemy III confirmed its position as the most important power in the eastern Mediterranean. Ptolemy III's predominance was also favoured by the political problems confronting his main opponents. The biggest loser in the war was Seleukos II. After a civil war, his brother Hierax ruled large parts of northern and western Asia Minor as an independent king. And in Pergamon the local dynast Attalos I acquired the royal title after a great victory over the Celtic tribes in north-western Asia Minor in 238 BC. Around 228 BC, he expelled Hierax from Asia Minor. Hierax continued his adventures first in Mesopotamia and then in Thrace, where he was killed in 226 BC. In the East, Andragoras, the governor of Parthia, had taken advantage of Seleukos II's involvement in the War of Laodike and ruled his province as an independent king (c. 245–238 BC). When the nomadic tribe of the Parni – later known as the Parthians – invaded the eastern provinces of the Seleucids and occupied all of Parthia (238–209 BC), Seleukos II was unable to offer the protection that the satrapies expected from the king (see p. 198). Consequently, Diodotos, the satrap of Bactria, declared his independence and founded the Graeco-Bactrian kingdom. When Seleukos II fell from his horse and died in 226 BC, his kingdom was almost half the size of his father's.

Ptolemy had cause to celebrate. Shortly after the war, he ordered a huge throne erected at Adulis, the southernmost part of his kingdom, on the Erythraian Sea, the modern Red Sea. An inscription written in Greek and Egyptian proudly declares his achievements. A monk, Kosmas Indikopleustes (the one who sailed to India), saw this text in AD 525 and left us a drawing of the throne and the text:

> King Ptolemy the Great ... having taken over from his father the kingship over Egypt, Libya, Syria, Phoinike, Cyprus, Lycia, Caria and the islands of the Cyclades, marched out into Asia with infantry, cavalry, a fleet, and elephants from the land of the Troglodytes and from Ethiopia, which his father and he himself were the first to hunt from these lands and after bringing them to Egypt they equipped them for military use. Having gained possession of all the land on this side of the Euphrates, of Cilicia, Pamphylia, Ionia, the Hellespont, Thrace, and of all the forces in these countries and of the Indian elephants, and having made all the rulers of these areas into his subjects, he crossed the river Euphrates, and having subdued Mesopotamia, Babylonia, Sousiane, Persis, Media and the rest of the land as far as Bactria, and having sought out all the sacred objects that had been carried out of Egypt by the Persians, and having brought them back to Egypt together with the rest of the treasure from these areas, he sent his forces across the rivers [canals] that were dug out ...

Ptolemy III Euergetes (the Benefactor) presents himself as a guarantor of dynastic legitimacy, as a ruler of more lands than any other king after Alexander, as a warrior who followed the great conqueror's footsteps as far as Bactria, as a military innovator and as an avenger of the injustice that was perpetrated by the Persian king Cambyses against the Egyptian temples in 525 BC. Despite his exaggerations, he was, in fact, the most powerful man in the eastern Mediterranean. It is rather surprising that Ptolemy III decided not to exploit his clear advantage over Gonatas and Seleukos II to pursue a more aggressive policy. Was he the only Hellenistic king who had learned from the failures of the Successors and realised that acquiring too much power would unite his enemies against him? Or did he desire a less adventurous life in Egypt? If his actions give a clue to his intentions, Ptolemy III was interested in preserving a balance of power, supporting those who weakened his opponents – more often with funds than with armies. A less aggressive policy also meant fewer risks, and unlike his opponents, who were continually embroiled in wars until their deaths, Ptolemy III spent the last twenty years of his reign in Egypt, turning his attention to his patrimony. He is the first Ptolemaic king for whom the Egyptian priests set up inscriptions with long honorary decrees in Greek, Egyptian hieroglyphic and Demotic; and he reformed the administration of the provinces. From Alexandria, he could comfortably monitor the struggles in Greece, Asia Minor, Mesopotamia and the Far East.

The memory of Laodike and her war faded away. However, a small incident has forever left its imprint on the night sky. When Ptolemy III was fighting in Mesopotamia in 243 BC, his young wife Berenike vowed to Aphrodite that she would offer her long blonde hair to the goddess if she would protect the king and bring him back. Ptolemy returned safely and Berenike placed her hair in Aphrodite's temple in fulfilment of her vow. When on the next day it was nowhere to be seen, the court astronomer offered an explanation. He identified the hair with a constellation, claiming that the goddess of love had taken such great pleasure in the offering that she had placed the hair in the firmament, where the Coma Berenices can still be seen by the naked eye. The court poet Callimachus composed a poem inspired by this incident. Most of it is now lost, except for fragments of verses in a papyrus. Yet a Latin translation survives in Catullus' *Carmen 66*, a beautiful praise of love. Was Berenike's love stronger than the drive for conquest? Is this what kept Ptolemy in Egypt and made him resist the temptation to pursue new conquests? This thought can never be proved or disproved; it remains a nice albeit implausible thought, a serene intermezzo between one chain of wars and the next.

The last Ptolemaic victory: the Battle of Raphia

In 221 BC, important positions of leadership in the Mediterranean came into the hands of a new generation of young men. The king of Macedonia Antigonos Doson died and was succeeded by Philip V, then eighteen years old (p. 73). In Egypt, Ptolemy III died, leaving on the throne the seventeen-year-old Ptolemy IV. In the East, Antiochos III, who was twenty-two years old and had succeeded his brother Seleukos II four years earlier, had just defeated the usurper Molon and re-established his authority in Asia Minor. Exploiting this victory, he started a campaign against Egypt, with the aim of regaining the lost territory of Koile Syria.

This Fourth Syrian War (219–217 BC) ended with one of the greatest battles of the Hellenistic period, the Battle of Raphia near Gaza on 22 June 217 BC. If the numbers given by Polybius are to be trusted, the two armies totalled 150,000 men and were supported by 175 war elephants. For the first time a substantial part of the Ptolemaic forces consisted of native Egyptians trained in the Macedonian way – reportedly 20,000 men. At the beginning of the battle, Ptolemy's African elephants, who could not stand the smell and sound of Antiochos' Indian elephants, panicked and caused disorder within Ptolemy's army. While Antiochos defeated the cavalry on the left wing and was pursuing the fleeing enemy, under the impression that he had won the day, Ptolemy led a successful attack in the centre. By the time Antiochos realised that his phalanx had been driven back, it was already too late. Defeated, he retreated to Gaza and asked for a truce to bury his dead, reportedly one-sixth of his army. Koile Syria was to remain Ptolemaic for another twenty years.

But despite the victory, the war had negative consequences for Egypt. The high cost weakened the royal treasury and, more importantly, the contribution of the native Egyptians to the victory increased their self-confidence. Only ten years after the battle, the natives revolted against Ptolemy under the leadership of Hugronaphor, who established himself as a pharaoh in Upper (south) Egypt. The Ptolemies were to lose control of a large part of their kingdom for twenty years, from around 205 to 185 BC. Polybius describes this conflict as 'a war that apart from the savagery and lawlessness each side displayed to the other involved no regular battle, sea-fight, or siege, nor anything else worth mentioning'. Its consequences for the Ptolemaic economy and the acceptance of the authority of the kings were severe.

Although the Fourth Syrian War was treated here as a regional war, it should be mentioned that it was loosely connected with two wars fought in distant regions between 222 and 217 BC: a war on Crete and the 'Social War' of Philip V of Macedonia and the Achaeans against the Aetolians (see p. 73). This common feature of Hellenistic wars, which makes any narrative of Hellenistic history confusing, can be observed in an exemplary way in these years. To understand it we have to turn to the Greek mercenaries who fought in the Battle of Raphia, 6,500 Greek in Antiochos' army and another 11,000 in Ptolemy's. Of the mercenaries serving on both sides, 5,500 came from Crete alone. The Cretans who served Antiochos were commanded by a man from Gortyn, while those in the Ptolemaic army were under the command of a man from Knossos, Gortyn's greatest opponent. The presence of Cretan mercenaries in the armies of both the Seleucids and the Ptolemies is connected with the political division on Crete. In 222 BC, Gortyn and Knossos had joined forces against the only city that defied their hegemony: Lyttos. But they met with opposition, probably connected with social conflicts. The war against Lyttos caused civil wars in several cities, ultimately splitting the alliance of Knossos and Gortyn. And this Cretan conflict took place in parallel and in connection with the war of Philip V and the Achaeans against the Aetolians. The Gortynians and their allies supported Philip V, while the Knossians were allied with the Aetolians.

The contemporary historian, Polybius, designated this phenomenon of interconnected wars in Greece, Asia and Africa as *symploke* (entanglement). From 217 BC onwards, a major player was added to the entanglements in the eastern Mediterranean: Rome. We shall examine this development after an overview of the political organisation of the Hellenistic world.

5

KINGS AND KINGDOMS

Basileia: the heterogeneous origins of Hellenistic kingship

An anonymous Hellenistic author defines kingship as follows: 'Monarchical power [*basileiai*] is given to men neither by nature nor by law; it is given to those who are able to command troops and deal prudently with political matters.' By placing military success above legitimacy, this definition breaks with earlier Greek traditions of kingship. Until Alexander, the Greeks had only known of men who had the title *basileus* (king) in accordance with institutional traditions: because they belonged to a certain family – for example, in Macedonia the Argeads – or because they had been elected to the annual office of a *basileus* that existed in some cities. But the contemporaries of Alexander and his Successors experienced how military victories made kings. It was victory that had made Alexander first a pharaoh in Egypt and then the king of Asia. All Successors were acclaimed kings on the basis of military success, not of dynastic legitimacy. Antigonos Gonatas was not acclaimed king immediately after his father's death in 283 BC, although he commanded an army and controlled territories, but only after his victory over the Gauls in 277 BC. Similarly, the first dynasts of Pergamon hesitated to be acclaimed kings. Only Attalos I's victory over the Gauls around 238 BC allowed him to assume this title. The western Greeks of Sicily had long experienced the monarchical power of tyrants, but the first man to assume the title *basileus* was Agathokles (see p. 50), exploiting his success in wars. Following the example of the

Successors, he did not add a geographical or ethnic specification of his kingship. He was not 'King of Sicily' or 'King of the Syracusans'. Agathokles was simply 'King Agathokles': that is, king of whichever territory he could control. Only Kassandros used a title with an ethnic specification: 'King of the Macedonians'. The intentional vagueness of the title of Hellenistic kings opened the possibility of a continuous expansion of power; it was an invitation to conquest.

After the establishment of the Hellenistic dynasties a king's legitimacy depended on the dynastic principle of succession that usually passed power from father to son; a king's power depended on his army. The proclamation of the king by the army assembly was an old ritual with great symbolic power. We assume that in pre-Hellenistic Macedonia when a king died the influential members of the court presented to the army the man upon whom they had agreed, voluntarily or under pressure, as the next monarch. Through acclamations the army recognised him as king and commander. This practice continued after the end of the house of the Argeads. After the period of the Successors, royal proclamations are only mentioned in the context of usurpations or problems in the succession, but this does not mean that they did not also occur under normal conditions. In the Ptolemaic kingdom, it is likely that the royal proclamation took place in front of not only the army but also the population of Alexandria, the capital.

But the Macedonian traditions were only part of what constituted Hellenistic kingship. Foreign influences were equally significant. When Alexander took control of Egypt, he was probably enthroned as a pharaoh; when he sat on the throne in the old Achaemenid capitals, he did so as the successor of the Great Kings, adopting elements of their royal attire. We do not know how the Macedonian circle of friends reacted to the Egyptian rituals. But we know that their reaction to Alexander's adaptation of Persian traditions in royal dress and ceremony was criticism, ridicule and outright rejection. One of the ceremonial traditions, the *proskynesis*, or obeisance, was so vehemently opposed as barbaric that Alexander had to abandon it. Things were different with the diadem, an ornamental headband that the Greeks could easily associate with the headband given to victorious athletes. From the 'year of the kings' onwards, the diadem was the most important *insignium* of royalty. When Antiochos IV was placed on the Seleucid throne by King Eumenes II of Pergamon and his brothers in 175 BC, the coronation ceremony is described with these words: 'They adorned him with the diadem and the other insignia as was proper, offered the sacrifice of an ox and exchanged promises of trust with all goodwill and affection.'

To fully understand the adoption of non-Greek traditions by Hellenistic kings, we need to change the perspective for a moment. Instead of viewing it from the Greeks' standpoint, we should consider it from that of the local elites, the personnel of the courts – scribes, astrologers, eunuchs and servants – and the local populations, especially in cities such as Babylon or Susa. At the beginning, the local elites – officers, administrators and priests, without whom the running first of the Alexander's empire and then of the Seleucid and Ptolemaic kingdoms would have been impossible – succumbed to military power; after the initial shock of the end of the Achaemenid dynasty had subsided, they required gestures that would allow them to integrate into a new system or rule. They needed measures that would guarantee continuity in complex administrative duties, such as surveying the land for taxation, maintaining infrastructure and communication, administering justice and policing the vast territories of the kingdoms. The Hellenistic kings, who had to negotiate their power with multiple partners (see pp. 115–7), were willing to make these gestures of goodwill. The acceptance of non-Greek symbols of royalty was one of their negotiation strategies. In Egypt, the Nile rose every year in August, whether the power was in the hands of an Egyptian pharaoh, a Persian satrap, the descendant of a Macedonian general or a Roman monarch; the cultic, administrative and technical duties connected with the flooding of the Nile remained the same. The change of ruler was a challenge; discontinuity spelled disaster. A similar *horror saltus*, or fear of leaps and sudden breaks, characterised the administration of the territories in Asia. From the perspective of the keepers of tradition, only the names of rulers changed, not the duties and the structures. The traditional documents – the astronomical diaries, the lists of kings and the chronicles found in Babylonia – record the passage of time under Alexander and the Seleucids in the same manner as they had for hundreds of years. They employ the same language and script, reveal the same mentality and correspond to a similar concept of monarchy as the one that had existed under the Achaemenids. In Egypt, the priestly decrees in honour of Ptolemaic kings address them with the same laudatory phrases that gave pleasure to pharaohs for centuries: for example, 'the King of Upper and Lower Egypt Ptolemaios, the Everliving, Beloved of Ptah, son of Ptolemy and Arsinoe, the Sibling-Gods'. The Hellenistic world was full of illusions, both intentional and unintentional. One of them was the illusion of continuity, when in reality so much had changed. What never changed, however, was the significance of the principle of dynastic succession: the preservation of rule within the circle of a single, admittedly often quite extended, family.

Kingship as a family affair

Consider this story: a woman marries her brother and then, after his death, her second brother; but then her new husband leaves her to marry her daughter from her previous marriage and kills their only son. These things do happen, you might say. And, indeed, they do, in bad soap operas and in Hellenistic courts; this is the story of Cleopatra II (see p. 205). Hellenistic royal families faced all the challenges that confront powerful families: the preservation, division and transmission of family power; struggles for affection and attention; jealousy and envy; ambition and disappointment. To study Hellenistic kingship only as an institution without examining interpersonal relations and emotional tensions is as wrong as banning emotions from the study of the British royal family. But naturally, when we deal with families that lived more than two millennia ago, what we study is filtered information.

The Hellenistic monarchies assimilated themselves with a household and were run as such. In theory, all the power was in the hands of the head of the household but, depending on his age, experience and personality, the influence of his wives, mother, children and court members, or 'friends', could be significant. The perception of Hellenistic monarchy as a family is not modern. It is precisely the way that monarchies presented themselves to their subjects and the outside world. Although Laodike, the wife of Antiochos III, was not the king's sister, she was officially designated as such. The royal epithets by which Ptolemaic monarchs were known highlighted their familial relations. Ptolemy II was 'sister-loving' (Philadelphos); Ptolemy IV, Ptolemy VII, Berenike III, Ptolemy XIII and Cleopatra VII (the famous Cleopatra) were 'father-loving' (Philopatores); Ptolemy VI was 'mother-loving' (Philometor), as were his two wives, his sister Cleopatra II and her daughter Cleopatra III. These epithets sometimes reflected reality – Ptolemy II really loved his sister Arsinoe II – and sometimes they did not – the relationship between Cleopatra II and Cleopatra III was dysfunctional at best. Be they expressions of genuine feelings or not, these epithets always served the same aim: to present to subjects the image of dynastic continuity and harmony.

The story of a son who falls in love with his father's second wife is familiar to us from Verdi's (and Schiller's) *Don Carlos*; but it is also a Hellenistic love drama with a happy ending, featuring the love of Antiochos I for his stepmother Stratonike. It would inspire paintings by David and Ingres, as well as one of the most popular comic operas of the late eighteenth century, Étienne Méhul's *Stratonice* (1792). This love story provides a good example of how royalty presented itself as a loving family. In 294 BC, Antiochos fell in love with Stratonike, his father Seleukos' young wife. In his despair, he decided to starve himself to death, abstaining from food under the pretence of having some disease. He could not, however, deceive his physician, Erasistratos, who was determined to identify the young man's object of desire, male or female. Spending day after day in his patient's chamber, Erasistratos noticed that whenever Stratonike came to see him Antiochos responded with the typical symptoms of lovesickness: 'stammering speech, fiery flushes, darkened vision, sudden sweats, irregular palpitations of the heart, and finally, as his soul was taken by storm, helplessness, stupor, and pallor'. Eventually, relying on Seleukos' affection towards his son, the doctor took the risk of telling the king that Antiochos' trouble was a love that could be neither satisfied nor cured: love for Erasistratos' wife. When Seleukos begged Erasistratos to give him his wife, since he was Antiochos' friend, Erasistratos asked the king whether he would do the same if Antiochos were in love with Stratonike. With tears in his eyes, Seleukos claimed that he would gladly give up his whole kingdom, if only he could save Antiochos. Having provoked this statement, Erasistratos revealed the truth.

Consequently Seleukos called an assembly of the entire people and declared it to be his wish and decision to make Antiochos king of all the upper satrapies and Stratonike his queen, the two being husband and wife. In his opinion, his son, accustomed as he was to be compliant and obedient in all things, would not oppose his father in this marriage; and if his wife were reluctant to take this extraordinary step, he called upon his friends to teach and to persuade her to regard as good and just whatever the king thought beneficial.

We cannot be sure about what transpired in the royal chambers of the

Seleucids; that we know the story of the lovesick son is probably because such information was revealed with the court's approval. After all, the feelings that the three protagonists expressed were not reproachable. This is a story of an affectionate father willing to make a sacrifice, of a respectful and obedient son, and of a dutiful and prudent wife – a loving family supported in its decision by their friends. There is probably also an element of theatricality in this story: the royal family appeared to their subjects as people with emotions. 'The king and his son are one of us,' people might have thought. This is a PR strategy that we know from modern politics. That Seleukos called an assembly to announce his decision is significant: the assembly probably consisted of the population of the capital and the army and was used for the presentation of the co-regent and future king, in accordance with the old Macedonian tradition of royal proclamations by the army (see p. 86).

Almost a decade later, around 285 BC, Ptolemy I made his son Ptolemy II his co-regent. Such declarations later became a common practice in Hellenistic kingdoms as a means of safeguarding the dynastic succession. However, the transmission of power did not always take place in such a peaceful manner. As royal marriages were usually a medium for the creation of new alliances, it was quite common for a king to repudiate his wife for a female relative of another king when the need arose. The children from the king's multiple marriages regularly spawned conflict, and often the repudiated wives as well. Let us take the case of Ptolemy I of Egypt. Before he became king, he had married Eurydike, the daughter of the powerful regent Antipatros. Eurydike bore him three sons and two daughters. In 317 BC, Berenike, a niece of Antipatros and the widow of a Macedonian nobleman, came to Alexandria with her son Magas and her daughters Antigone and Theoxena. While attending the queen, she caught the eye of Ptolemy, who repudiated his first wife to marry her; she bore him two daughters, Arsinoe and Philotera, and a son, the later Ptolemy II. From just these two marriages (and there were more) Ptolemy had eight children and three stepchildren. When he chose Ptolemy II as his successor, his eldest son, Ptolemy Keraunos, fled to the court of Lysimachos, where his half-sister Arsinoe was queen and his sister Lysandra was married to the king's son Agathokles. When Arsinoe's intrigues led to the execution of Agathokles, Keraunos and Lysandra fled to the court of Seleukos. Keraunos helped Seleukos defeat Lysimachos at the Battle of Kouropedion, but his ambition was stronger than his gratitude. He murdered Seleukos after the victory and had himself proclaimed king in Macedonia. When he raised a claim to the throne of Egypt as well, Ptolemy II tried to come to terms with his older half-brother and arranged for him to marry their sister Arsinoe. But Arsinoe conspired against her new husband and Keraunos had two of her sons murdered. Arsinoe finally returned to Egypt, where she married her brother Ptolemy, becoming one of the most influential women in Hellenistic history and, after her death, a popular goddess (see Fig. 7).

With such entanglements it is not surprising that dynastic struggles were commonplace. Lysimachos had his son Agathokles executed (284 BC); Magas, ruler of Cyrene, turned against his stepbrother Ptolemy II (274 BC); Antiochos I had his rebellious eldest son, Seleukos, put to death (267 BC); Antiochos Hierax fought his brother Seleukos II for the throne and ruled for a short period in parts of Asia Minor (c. 246–235 BC); and Philip V ordered the execution of his son Demetrios (180 BC), whom he suspected of plotting with the Romans. For forty years the Ptolemaic kingdom suffered under the struggles for power between Ptolemy VI and his brother Ptolemy VIII, and later between Ptolemy VIII and his sister Cleopatra II (c. 163–118 BC). Dynastic struggles between different branches of the Seleucids were endemic in that kingdom from 161 BC until its demise in 63 BC (see pp. 200–3).

In all of these dynastic struggles, women played a prominent role. Following a tradition that had deep roots in the tribal kingdoms of Macedonia and Epirus, the kings' wives were influential; they were well-travelled women with political experience and sometimes even military skills. Olympias, Alexander's mother, was a protagonist in the Wars of the Successors, as was Eurydike, the wife of King Philip III Arrhidaios. The so-called War of Laodike (246–245 BC) is an example of the political influence of Hellenistic queens (see pp. 78–80). However, none of these queens was a match for the last Hellenistic queen, Cleopatra VII, who was interested in science and had a personality that fascinated two of the greatest generals of Rome (see pp. 223–30).

Dynastic struggles sometimes also involved the illegitimate children sired by kings with their courtesans. A certain Herakles, allegedly a bastard of Alexander from his relationship with Barsine, a Persian noblewoman, was a minor figure in the Wars of the Successors (see p. 39). Another bastard of a royal house, Aristonikos, the illegitimate son of Attalos II, declared himself king when his half-brother Attalos III bequeathed his kingdom to Rome in 133 BC (see p. 187), and illegitimate children of

Seleucid kings also play an important part in the dynastic struggles of the second century BC.

The usurpation of power by relatives of kings is a related phenomenon. This was done on a small scale by Alexander, nephew of King Antigonos Gonatas. The king appointed him commander of Corinth, the most important Macedonian garrison in Greece. Taking advantage of weakening Macedonian power in southern Greece, Alexander revolted and for a short period established a personal rule in Corinth and Euboia. Molon, who governed the upper Seleucid satrapies, revolted against Antiochos III on account of his hatred of his chief minister (223–220 BC). The same Antiochos also faced the rebellion of Achaios, a distant relative, who managed to have himself proclaimed king in parts of Asia Minor (220–214 BC). The usurpers probably intended to rule just those lands on which they could lay their hands and not the entire Seleucid Empire.

Despite these challenges, Hellenistic dynasties were longer-lived than any Roman dynasty. The Antigonids ruled, with interruptions, from 307 to 167 BC, the Attalids from 281 to 133 BC and the Ptolemies from 323 to 30 BC. Even the protracted death of the Seleucids (150–63 BC) was preceded by a vigorous period of imperial politics (312–163 BC). By contrast, the Antonines, a dynasty of adopted Roman emperors, did not manage to last for even a century (AD 96–192). What explains the longevity of Hellenistic dynasties? The first factor was that the principle of hereditary succession was generally respected in all aspects of law and society. More importantly, only members of the ruling dynasties, their close relatives and their chief advisers had access to the political experience, the resources – money and armies – and the network of relations with military commanders, governors, civic elites and later Roman senators that was necessary for the establishment of personal power. Consequently, shifts of power from one ruling family to another could only occur in limited circumstances: when the governors in loosely controlled and inadequately defended areas on the periphery of a kingdom renounced their loyalty and created independent kingdoms, such as the Graeco-Bactrian kingdom in Iran and Afghanistan (see pp. 198–200); or when the shift of power was the result of foreign involvement, usually Roman intervention. Additionally, Hellenistic courts were very successful in applying a range of media in order to make their rule seem acceptable to the various partners involved in complex negotiations: to the army, the dependent cities, the native population, the population of the royal capitals and, for a certain period, Rome.

New administrative challenges: ruling empires

What should you do, when you are in your mid-twenties and have been trained to govern a kingdom whose breadth you can walk in less than ten days, if suddenly you are faced with the rule of an empire that stretches from the Balkans to Iran in the east and Egypt in the south? Assuming success has not blinded your common sense, then you adopt the administration system that you have found in place and make only as many changes as are absolutely necessary. But what do you do if you bring to the newly subdued areas a population that is not familiar with the local institutions and traditions? Do you introduce their institutions into the conquered territories or do you accustom the newcomers to the existing structures of their new environment? These were the two challenges that Alexander the Great faced as soon as he set foot in Egypt. The challenges intensified after he had defeated Darius III in Gaugamela and was sitting on the throne of the Achaemenid kings in Susa. Alexander also confronted them throughout his campaign in the Far East while settling veterans in the conquered areas; he encountered them again in the short period between his return from the campaign and his early death.

In addressing the first challenge, Alexander followed common sense by taking advantage of the existing infrastructure. For two centuries the Achaemenid kings had ruled their empire by exploiting a system of satrapies and combining the centralised, autocratic rule of the king and his court with the decentralisation of certain tasks – the local recruitment of troops, the preservation of law and order, and the collection of tribute – at the level of the province. Another traditional authority that Alexander could not ignore was the clergy, especially in Egypt. But the settlement of veterans who had been raised in the political, social and cultural traditions of the Greek *poleis* was a new phenomenon in Egypt and the rest of Alexander's vast empire. For the organisation and administration of the new *poleis* Alexander turned to the model of the Greek colonies. As regards the settlement of and assignment of land to soldiers in conquered areas, Alexander and his successors may have followed an already existing Macedonian system. Therefore, the organisation of the Hellenistic kingdoms and their administration had their roots in many different backgrounds, including Greek and Macedonian institutions as well as local traditions; but there was always room for innovation.

Alexander died before he could face the day-to-day administrative business of running an empire. But for his successors there was no escape from this challenge; they had to deal with administrative tasks immediately. The main characteristics of the administration must have already been in place by 300 BC. Despite many significant differences, the Hellenistic kingdoms shared common features with regard to the position of the king, the ideology of monarchy and the administration. The main tasks consisted of military organisation and the defence of territory, fiscal matters and the collection of tribute, the administration of justice and maintenance of sanctuaries.

The king was surrounded by top officials, who formed his court. Unless the king was a minor, he personally recruited these officials on the basis of merit, ability and loyalty. Very often, especially in the early period, the officials were not born in the kingdom where they served but hailed from Greek cities and achieved their rise to the court through a variety of factors. Descent from a family with influence and connections contributed to a position in the court, but competent men, especially army officers, could climb up the hierarchy due to their merit and loyalty. Their loyalty was personal and to the king, not to the kingdom or the 'state'. The administrative incompetence of a king or his defeat in war could, therefore, disturb the relationship of trust between king and officer, causing the officer to seek another employer.

The members of the court and high officials were directly bound to the person of the king. They were his 'friends' (*philoi*). Their titles indicated their proximity to the king and their hierarchical position. In the Ptolemaic kingdom, where these titles were formalised in the early second century BC, the high officials and members of the court were called 'bodyguards' (*somatophylakes*), 'followers' (*diadochoi*), 'friends' (*philoi*), 'chief bodyguards' (*archisomatophylakes*), 'first friends' (*protoi philoi*), 'relatives' (*syngeneis*) and, later, 'equal in honour with the relatives' (*homotimos tois syngenesin*) and 'equal in honour with the first friends' (*isotimos tois protois philois*). Similar designations existed in the Seleucid kingdom: 'friends', 'honoured friends' (*timomenoi philoi*), 'first friends' and 'first and distinguished friends' (*protoi kai protimomenoi philoi*). The 'friends' were one of the most significant administrative and military organs of a Hellenistic kingdom. They were commanders of the important army units, governors of districts and provinces, envoys and advisers. They accompanied the king when he went hunting and attended his banquets; they were teachers of the princes and sometimes they were truly friends. Over time, the position as a 'friend' of the king passed from one generation to the next and a hereditary aristocracy developed, which, however, always left opportunities for competent or cunning newcomers to become part of the court.

The court was where the king was, and the king, when not on a military campaign, was in his capital, or in one of his capitals if more than one existed. For the Ptolemies this capital was Alexandria, a city that in the course of the Hellenistic period grew into a major urban centre with approximately 1 million inhabitants, truly a megacity of antiquity. The royal palace, close to the royal graves, was the undisputed centre of power. It was connected with a centre of learning and a library, the Mouseion (see pp. 2 and 295). The Seleucid kingdom had three capitals: Antioch and Apameia on the Orontes, and Seleukeia on the Tigris. Pergamon, the capital of the Attalids, developed into a major urban centre during the course of the third century BC. In Macedonia, neither the traditional capitals in Aigai and Pella nor the secondary capital in Demetrias acquired the scale of the capitals in the new kingdoms.

The complex administrative tasks made life in Hellenistic courts more sophisticated than in the rudimentary court of the old Macedonian monarchy. The fundamental feature of court life remained the banquet, or *symposion*, which brought together the king, his family and the highest military and administrative officers in convivial drinking. The banquet offered an occasion for deliberations on matters of foreign policy and military strategy, exchanges with foreign guests and envoys, and general discussion. In Hellenistic courts, especially in Alexandria, the cultural activities of a banquet – recital of old and new literary works, lectures on history, discussion about works of art and musical performances – often reached a high level of sophistication. This depended on the intellectual capacities and interests of the king and his courtiers. At one extreme we have men such as Ptolemy I, an accomplished historian himself, who gathered in Alexandria leading scholars of his time to create the Mouseion and its library as centres of learning, or Pyrrhos and Antigonos Gonatas, who were surrounded by philosophers; at the other we find kings who liked to exhibit their own performative skills, Antiochos IV as a mimic dancer and Ptolemy XII as a flute player, but were criticised by their contemporaries for damaging the dignity of kingship. Needless to say, the competition among courtiers for influence, ambition, enmity and conspiracy flourished in Hellenistic courts as they did in any other court in history, as did love affairs between the kings and female relatives of courtiers.

The larger kingdoms adopted a system of provincial administration that essentially followed earlier traditions. In Egypt, an elaborate system of administration had existed since pharaonic times, in order to best exploit the annual flooding of the Nile for agriculture. The Ptolemies adopted it. Important tasks, especially the construction and maintenance of canals and dams, and the preparation of the fields for the rising of the Nile, had to be coordinated by a central authority, to which local administrators had to report. The heart of the administration was the court in Alexandria, where the 'chief administrator' (*dioiketes*) headed the fiscal administration. The land was divided into about forty provinces or districts, called *nomoi*. Each *nomos* was governed by a 'general' (*strategos*) with police and judiciary duties. The 'chief of the *nomos*' (*nomarches*) was responsible for the agricultural production, while a 'steward' (*oikonomos*) oversaw fiscal matters and the payment of tribute to the royal treasury in Alexandria. He was assisted by the 'royal scribe' (*basilikos grammateus*), who was responsible for accounting. These duties were very important, because in the Ptolemaic economic system almost all economic activities were under the strict control of the royal administration. The central administration determined what would be produced, as well as where, by whom and in what quantities, and in addition the prices of goods and the amount of tribute to be paid. Many products, in particular various vegetable oils, were state monopolies, and government limitations restricted trade with the outside world. To run this system, the administration used the services of tax farmers, who prepaid the estimated tribute for a certain product, receiving the right to exact the tribute from the population. In the second century BC, 'territorial generals' (*strategoi* or *epistrategoi tes choras*) were responsible for units larger than the provinces, namely Middle and Upper Egypt, Thebais and Cyprus.

Each *nomos* was divided into *topoi* (districts), which were made up of *komai* (villages). Each *topos* and each *kome* was governed by local officials, the *toparches* and *komarches* respectively, who were assisted by scribes. For the administration of justice there were local courts, which were separate for the Greeks, the native population and possibly also for different ethnic groups, such as the Jews. In addition, the Ptolemies respected to a certain extent the authority of the native priests as mediators between the mortals and the gods. The administrative and fiscal system of Egypt also applied, with minor modifications, to the administration of Egypt's external possessions in south Syria and Palestine, Asia Minor and the Aegean.

These external possessions were governed by generals as well, while *oikonomoi* oversaw fiscal and economic matters and were the link between tax farmers and the royal treasury. Each administrator reported to the higher authority in a strictly hierarchical chain of command that started on the level of the village and moved through the district and the province to the central administration in Alexandria. For matters of safety and justice, the provincial 'generals' reported directly to the king, while the fiscal administration was headed by the 'chief administrator'.

An important task for the royal administration was the maintenance of the armed forces. Warfare had reached high levels of tactical sophistication in battle and in long sieges, as well as a high degree of specialisation, because of the existence of different kinds of troops with specific weapons, such as the heavy phalanx with its long lances, the light-armed forces with small round shields, the archers and slingers, the operators of siege engines and artillery devices, the cavalry and the fleet; these troops required special training. The armies mobilised by the kings were sometimes huge – for example, 140,000 men fought in the Battle of Raphia (see p. 83) – and heterogeneous, consisting of a professionalised standing army, additional mercenaries, troops from allied cities and federations and, in some cases, soldiers recruited from the non-Greek population.

The conditions in the Seleucid kingdom were quite different. There was no geographical unifying element such as the Nile; the distance from the capitals to the satrapies on the periphery favoured centrifugal tendencies that led to usurpations and secessions. But the principles of the administration did not differ from those in Ptolemaic Egypt. Here too the empire's founders based their rule on a combination of local traditions, especially in the administration of the eastern provinces, and Greek civic traditions which were applied to the administration of the cities. The 'overseer of the affairs' (*epi ton pragmaton*), a sort of vizier, was the most important administrator under the king; his position had been adopted from the old Oriental kingdoms. The tribute and revenues were collected by the royal treasury (*to basilikon*), which was under the charge of the 'supervisor of the revenues' (*epi ton prosodon*); local financial officials in the provinces reported to him. In the late third and early second centuries BC, the provinces in Asia Minor were governed by a sort of vice-king, the 'overseer of the affairs beyond the Taurus'. Another important official was the 'chamberlain' (*epi tou koitonos*). The kingdom was divided into provinces that roughly corresponded to the satrapies of the Persian Empire. Their governor, the general (*strategos*), combined military and civil functions. The internal subdivisions of the satrapies into districts and subdistricts, or *topoi*, varied, depending on each satrapy's size and location. The chain of command is revealed by inscriptions that contain the king's orders as well as cover letters instructing subordinate authorities to act accordingly and to inscribe them. For instance, a dossier of documents dating to 209 BC found at Philomelion in Phrygia contains the king's order (*prostagma*) appointing Nikanor as high priest of all the sanctuaries in the provinces of Asia Minor. This order was first sent to Zeuxis, the vice-king, who forwarded it to Philomelos, the satrap of Phrygia; in his turn, the satrap sent it to a district governor, Aineias, who gave it to Demetrios, presumably the commander of a subdistrict. Finally, Demetrios handed a copy to another addressee, possibly a local official or priest. The whole procedure of transmission took less than a month. In their realm the Seleucids found an already existing infrastructure, especially a network of roads that facilitated communications and trade. They improved it, primarily through the development of cities and harbours in suitable locations that could serve as centres of transit trade from east to west.

The kingdom of the Attalids was relatively small until 188 BC, when the Roman senate rewarded King Eumenes II with huge territories in Asia Minor that had previously been part of the Seleucid kingdom (see p. 173). In these areas, the Attalids adopted the pre-existing administrative structures. The Antigonid kingdom of Macedonia and Thessaly was much smaller than the other Hellenistic kingdoms throughout its existence, and its most important challenge was the control of subordinate cities in southern Greece and the Aegean islands. This required complex negotiations between the kings, who wanted to impose their authority, and the cities, which never ceased in their fight for autonomy (see pp. 100–5).

Hellenistic kingdoms were multi-ethnic and multilingual, and this presented another administrative challenge. Even in the culturally more homogeneous Antigonid kingdom of Macedonia, part of the population of the countryside was not of Greek origin; but these people – mostly but not exclusively Thracians – used Greek for epitaphs and dedications and were deeply Hellenised. Things were more complex in Asia and Egypt. In the kingdoms of Asia Minor, the old and new Greek cities, with their almost exclusively Greek population, coexisted with settlements in the countryside whose inhabitants belonged to various indigenous Anatolian populations: Mysians, Carians, Phrygians, Lydians, Paphlagonians,

Thracians and others. Mercenary service brought additional immigrants: Iranians, Gauls and Jews. In the kingdom of the Ptolemies, in addition to the native population of Egypt and the Greek settlers, we also find a large number of Jews and mercenaries of different origins. The Seleucid kingdom was the most diverse with regard to ethnic groups and languages, especially in the period of its greatest expansion in the third century BC. As regards these diverse populations, the royal administration had to deal primarily with two tasks: taxation and justice.

The indigenous populations who lived in royal lands while keeping some form of self-administration for their local affairs are known under the name *laoi* (the peoples). They cultivated the land of the king and collectively paid tribute either to the king or to the individual to whom a king may have donated the land – a courtier, a former officer, a divorced queen. The tribute of a village – not an individual farmer – usually consisted of a tenth of the land's produce and a percentage (between 2 and 12 per cent) of the value of timber, livestock, wine and other commodities. But also a capital tax is occasionally attested. The modern term 'serfs' does not accurately represent the position of the *laoi*. The *laoi* were free individuals, in the sense that they were not the property of another person or institution. When the land that they cultivated changed hands, through conquest or donation, the recipient of their tribute changed, but this does not mean that they became the property of the new owner of the land or that they were bound to the soil. When the king attached their land to the territory of a city, they became *paroikoi* (those who live near the city). Generalisations about the condition of the *laoi* are likely to be wrong. Given the frequency of wars and the need of kings to fill their treasuries with money in order to pay for their armies, suppression and exploitation must have been common. In Egypt, where we have more information about the life of the indigenous population, in the second century BC, especially under the chaotic conditions of the civil wars, part of the population became the victim of exploitation and lawlessness, abandoned the fields and turned to brigandage. The Ptolemaic amnesty decree of 118 BC, after a long period of dynastic wars, makes an explicit reference to this problem. The royal proclamation decreed that 'those who have fled because they were charged with brigandage and other offences shall return to their homes, resume their former occupations and recover those of their belongings which were seized for these reasons but which have not yet been sold'. In Asia Minor, Aristonikos gained support in his rebellion against Rome in the late second century BC (see pp. 187–9), in part because of the dissatisfaction of this population in the Attalid kingdom.

In the urban settlements, foreigners, mostly mercenaries, were organised in self-governed communities called *politeumata* (communities of citizens). We know of such *politeumata* in the Ptolemaic kingdom. The people from Kaunos and Termessos who were resident in Sidon were organised each in its own *politeuma*; similar groups of Boiotians, Cretans, Cilicians, Jews and Idumaeans (from a region south of the Dead Sea) are known in Egypt. The *politeumata* of Phrygians and Lycians, attested only in the Imperial period, must have already existed earlier. The *politeumata* had separate sanctuaries and priests. To judge from the Jewish *politeumata*, which are attested in several cities (Alexandria, Herakleopolis, Leontopolis, Berenike) and better documented, the members of a *politeuma* lived in separate quarters; there, the magistrates of the *politeuma* had administrative and judiciary duties granted to them by the Ptolemaic administration. The chief magistrate of the *politeuma* was the *politarches* or *ethnarches*.

The high degree of flexibility and the adaptation of different traditions allowed the royal courts to deal with the complex administration of vast and heterogeneous territories with rather limited personnel. However, problems inherent in Hellenistic kingship – dynastic conflicts and the military character of kingship that obliged the king to continually legitimise his rule through wars – undermined the stability of rule, as we shall see in the next chapters.

Cities and kings: struggles for autonomy and illusions of freedom

In 318 BC the Athenian general Phokion was put on trial for opposing King Philip Arrhidaios. According to some sources he was universally condemned. But an anonymous Hellenistic historian of Athens, whose narrative survived indirectly in Plutarch's *Life of Phokion*, gives a different version:

> Their transportation [of Phokion and his followers] presented a sad spectacle, as they were brought from Kerameikos to the theatre. After they had been brought there Kleitos [a supporter of the king] put them under arrest, until the magistrates called the assembly, allowing everyone access to the podium and the theatre, not preventing anyone

from attending, neither slaves nor citizens who had lost their citizenship. Then the letter of the king was read out, in which he said that as for his part, he regarded these men as traitors, but since the Athenians are free and autonomous, they have the right to pass their own judgment. After that, Kleitos presented the men. Then some covered their heads and others looked down shedding tears. Someone found the courage to stand up and say that since the king had entrusted such an important decision to the people, it was proper that the slaves and the foreigners leave.

The anonymous historian intended to show that the popular assembly, the most important expression of democracy and the people's sovereignty, had become a theatrical performance. By mentioning details that at first sight seem insignificant, he evokes the image of a spectacle. The assembly took place in the theatre, the locus of shows. It did not consist of the citizens alone, who were the usual decision-making body, but the usual audience of the theatre: men and women, citizens and foreigners, free and slaves. During this spectacle someone read out the letter of the king, in which he recognised the right of the Athenians to pass their free judgement, but only after he had informed them of his own judgement. In the theatre – the venue of illusion and deception – the king staged a theatrical presentation of 'freedom'. This parody of an assembly functioned like a theatrical mask that attempted to conceal the bitter reality: the loss of sovereignty.

The victory of Philip II at Chaironeia in 338 BC was not the end of the Greek *poleis*, but it was certainly a turning point in their history: from that time on many citizen communities in Greece and Asia Minor found themselves under the direct or indirect control of kings; and those that were not were sooner or later incorporated into federal states and had to accept the parallel existence of federal sovereignty (see pp. 129–33).

The advantages that kings gained from the control of *poleis* were manifold. Cities supported their 'international' policy. Their armies served as allies. Their manpower was important for the recruitment of mercenaries. Their forts and harbours allowed the kings to control strategic sites as well as land and the seaborne traffic. For example, the Macedonian garrisons in Chalkis and Acrocorinth controlled important travel routes. The control of the harbours – Athens by the Antigonids, and Ephesos and Itanos in Crete by the Ptolemies – as well as the possession of islands such as Thasos, Thera and Samos were sought-after assets for royal fleets. In some cases kings could also impose regular tribute or extraordinary contributions on cities.

A variety of media enabled kings to exercise control over cities. The most direct and effective, but also the most hated, was the establishment of a garrison, which the kings presented as protection but the citizens resented as an amputation of their freedom. From the early fourth century onwards the term *aphrouretos* (free of garrison) became almost synonymous with *autonomos*. In the words of one of the Hellenistic sources quoted in Plutarch's *Life of Aratos*, the Achaeans were 'bridled like a horse' when they accepted a Macedonian garrison and delivered hostages to King Antigonos Doson. Garrisons exercised pressure on the political institutions of a civic community; to some extent they exploited its economic resources; they occupied its military facilities – forts, citadels and harbours. In addition to the garrison commander, an influential representative of a king's interests, in some cases royal control was institutionalised through the appointment of an official who represented the king. An 'overseer of the city' (*epistates epi tes poleos* or simply *epi tes poleos*) was usually appointed by kings for cities within the borders of their kingdom. Such 'city governors', sometimes identical to the garrison commanders, are attested for the Ptolemaic external possessions in Cyprus, Asia Minor and the Aegean, for the Attalid kingdom of Pergamon, for the Bosporan kingdom in the Black Sea and for the kingdoms of Bithynia and Kappadokia. In the Macedonian kingdom, the king exercised his control of cities by sending instructions to 'overseers' (*epistatai*); it is not certain whether these *epistatai* were elected civic magistrates or 'city governors' appointed by the king. The kings made their wishes known through regulations of general value (*diagrammata*) and letters that dealt with particular questions. Kings could also exercise influence on the cities through local statesmen who were loyal to them. However, it was up to the city to implement the royal instructions by having a decree or a law approved by the popular assembly.

By appointing 'overseers' or supporting tyrants, establishing garrisons, offering support to political friends and communicating their wishes through letters, Hellenistic kings exercised a close control of the cities in the areas under their influence and limited people's sovereignty. Nevertheless, an effort was made to save face, to retain the illusion of democracy and sovereignty, and to give the cities the impression that they were more than nominally free. This was achieved through the deliberate choice of words in the correspondence between kings and cities and through theatrical behaviour. The correspondence between the Antigonid Philip V and the nominally sovereign city of Larisa in Thessaly is very instructive. In 217 BC, the Lariseans sent an embassy to Philip V to explain that their city had suffered population loss due to the wars. In response to the embassy of a free city, Philip gave his instructions, which, however, required formal approval by the assembly of the recipients:

> Until I think of others who are deserving of your citizenship, for the present it is my judgment that you must pass a decree to grant citizenship to the Thessalians or the other Greeks who are resident in your city. For when this is done and all keep together because of the favors received, I am sure that many other benefits will result for me and the city, and the land will be more fully cultivated.

The granting of citizenship, which constituted the acceptance of new members into the *polis* community with full rights, was a decision that only the sovereign community could make, through a vote in the people's assembly. No matter how great the king's real power, he could never award to anyone the citizenship of any *polis* in his realm. Yet what he could do was to ask the community to make this decision in accordance with its own constitutional procedures. Of course, the king could make his will clear. Philip did this by using the strong verb *krino* (to rule, to pass a judgement); but he combined his judgement with arguments, in order to allow the Lariseans to save face by passing the decree as the result not of his ruling but of persuasion. The phrase 'my judgement is that you must pass a decree' shows the discrepancy between the nominal sovereignty of Larisa ('you must pass a decree') and the true power of the king ('my judgement is'). Philip's recommendation was too strong to be ignored, but the story did not end there. While the king was distracted by a war, the Lariseans cancelled the decree that had been forced upon them. Philip had to send a second letter in 214 BC:

> I hear that those who were granted citizenship in accordance with the letter that I sent to you and your decree, and whose names were inscribed on the stele, have been erased. If this has happened, those who have advised you have ignored the interests of your city and my ruling ... And yet, I even now exhort you to approach the matter with

impartiality, and to restore to those chosen by the citizens their rights of citizenship.

This time Philip explained in more detail the advantages of this measure, and made clear what the city should do. Again, he could not pass a decree, but he could dictate its content. He then asks the Lariseans to put off any decision on persons who were regarded as not deserving citizenship and concluded: 'But warn in advance those who intend to lodge accusations against them, that they may not be seen to be acting in this way for partisan reasons.' This second time the city complied. Philip was a master of theatrical behaviour; he knew how to wear the mask of the affable ruler, the friend of the people. When he visited Argos a few years later (209 BC), 'he laid aside his diadem and purple robe, wishing to produce the impression that he was on a level with others, a lenient individual, and a man of the people'. Besides altering his dress to produce a deceiving image, he also used words to disguise a command as advice. The correspondence between Philip V and Larisa is a good example of how royal letters could serve as an important medium for the indirect exercise of power.

The relations between kings and nominally sovereign *poleis* were characterised by reciprocity. Kings needed the cities but the cities also needed the support of the kings, especially for their defence against the attacks of pirates in the Aegean and of neighbours and barbarians in Asia Minor, the northern Aegean and Thrace. For this reason, kings sometimes justified the establishment of a permanent garrison as an act of benefaction aimed at protecting a city, while at the same time it offered strategic advantages to the king.

Citizen communities appealed to kings to arbitrate in disputes. They hoped for financial support and donations which decorated the cities with representative buildings and works of art, supplied the citizens with cheap corn, provided the athletes with olive oil for their anointment in the palaestras and rendered the worship of the gods more luxurious. The most important material contribution of the kings was towards the defence of cities: they donated horses for the cavalry, weapons and warships, timber for the construction of ships and funds for the construction or repairs of city walls. But nothing was appreciated more than a king's willingness to recognise a city's freedom and autonomy, to grant exemption from taxes and to make a city garrison-free.

Cities showed their loyalty to those kings who had served their interests by offering them godlike honours (see pp. 108–15). The relationship between kings and cities was based on a complex negotiation of power and reciprocity, similar to the one that existed between the people and the elite (see p. 139). It is said that when an old woman insisted that Demetrios Poliorketes give her a hearing and the king replied that he had no time, she shouted to him: 'Then stop being a king!' Acceptance of a king's rule required services from the king in return.

The military character of Hellenistic kingship

When Hellenistic documents refer to a Hellenistic kingdom, they use the phrase 'the king, the friends and the troops' (*ho basileus kai hoi philoi kai hai dynameis*). A Hellenistic kingdom therefore consisted of the king, the high commanders of the army and officers of the administration (the friends), and the army. A Hellenistic king was first and foremost a military leader (see Figs. 8 and 9). In this regard he did not differ from most pre-Hellenistic *basileis*. We may recognise the military character of Hellenistic kingship in the duties of the kings, the training of the princes, the organisation of their courts, the symbols of their power, their self-representation and their relation to the army.

In his praise of Ptolemy II, the court poet Theocritus asserted: 'As a good king he cares deeply for the preservation of his fatherly inheritance and adds something thereto himself.' The main duties of a Hellenistic king included the defence of the patrimony, the reclamation of lost land and the conquest of new territories. He was expected to fight, to offer effective military protection, to be victorious and to die fighting when necessary. The Seleucid Antiochos III corresponded to this model of an ideal Hellenistic king. He ascended the throne at the age of only twenty and in a series of wars he subdued a revolt by Molon, the governor of the upper satrapies, who had proclaimed himself king in Media (220 BC), almost succeeded in restoring Koile Syria to his kingdom (219–217 BC) and re-established control of the largest part of Asia Minor by defeating the usurper Achaios (216–213 BC). Then, in imitation of Alexander the Great, he launched a large-scale campaign that brought his army to the territories beyond the Hindu Kush (212–205 BC), where he forced the local kings to recognise his supremacy. By the time of his return (204 BC) he was known as Megas (the Great).

*8. Coin of the ruler of Bactria Eukratides I (c. 297–281 BC);
he holds a spear and wears a helmet with horns.*

To fulfil such expectations, a prince had to be educated from an early age. Military training, horsemanship and hunting were top priorities in the education of a king's male offspring. By accompanying his father or other commanders on campaigns, a young prince acquired experience and legitimated his claim to succession. Some kings developed a strong interest in military theory and the use of 'applied science' in war. Demetrios Poliorketes owes his nickname, the Besieger, to the new mechanical devices that he employed during his siege of Rhodes in 305–304 BC. He had Epimachos of Athens construct for him a mobile, nine-storey siege machine (*helepolis*) with a long projecting beam that terminated in a cone decorated with a ram's head. It is reported that Pyrrhos and his son Alexandros were the authors of works on military tactics. The Ptolemies were keen on ballistic research, and Hieron II of Syracuse used the skills of Archimedes to solve problems of siege warfare (see p. 159). Kings were expected to launch attacks at the front of the ranks, although it was regarded as a mistake to expose themselves to dangers without good reason. Most kings of the third and early second century, with the exception of the Ptolemies, spent the greater part of their reigns on campaigns, and many of them were often wounded and sometimes killed in action.

Some of the nicknames under which kings were known had their origin in acclamations, spontaneous or staged cheers, that highlighted military success and prowess: Soter (the rescuer), Nikator (the victorious), Nikephoros (the one who brings victory), Kallinikos (the one with the fair

9. Bronze statue of a Hellenistic king.

victories) and Epiphanes (the one with the manifest power). The military nature of Hellenistic kingship is also visible in symbols of power. The helmet was a standard attribute in a king's portrait (see Fig. 8). A famous statue of Hellenistic royalty (see Fig. 9) shows a king naked and in a relaxed posture; a virtual diagonal line leads the gaze of the spectator to the top of his spear, thereby making clear that a violent manifestation of his might is possible, whenever necessary. Military qualities and power played an important part in celebrations organised by kings. Military elements were prominent in the greatest festival known to have taken place in this period, the procession organised by Ptolemy II in honour of his father in Alexandria (c. 274 BC; see pp. 74–5). The spectators were given visible proof of the king's military strength, as they saw 57,600 infantry soldiers and 23,200 horsemen, accompanied by military equipment, march through the avenues of Alexandria towards the stadium. When Antiochos IV failed to take control of Egypt and was humiliated by a Roman officer (see p. 195), he compensated for his failure and indicated future plans by organising an impressive military parade of more than 50,000 men, partly equipped with exotic weapons.

When a king failed to fulfil the expectation to offer military protection, those who could were encouraged to step into his position, either by usurping the throne or by creating their own kingdoms. Continually confronted with attacks by nomadic tribes, the Seleucid upper satrapies, in northern Iran and Afghanistan, broke away when the attention of the Seleucids was diverted to other affairs. Timarchos, the satrap of Media, exploited his wars against the invading Parthians to become king of that part of the empire (163–160 BC). Almost all the small kingdoms on the periphery of the Hellenistic world had their origins in the ambitions of renegade governors and dynasts who capitalised on the weakness of the king.

The military character of monarchy led to the perception of the good monarch as a continually victorious man, responsive to the requests of his subjects and the indefinitely weaker dependent cities. Not all kings lived up to these standards. When they did, their power could not be measured by human standards; it could only be compared with that of the gods. They therefore deserved the honours usually reserved for gods.

The mortal divinity of Hellenistic kings

The first mortal to receive godlike honours during his own lifetime in Greece was the Spartan general Lysandros, after the defeat of Athens in the Peloponnesian War in 404 BC: the Samian oligarchs, returning from exile, gratefully erected an altar, offered him sacrifices, sang cultic songs and changed the name of the festival of Hera to Lysandreia, the festival of Lysandros. Although these honours were ephemeral, they foreshadow later developments, for which Philip II of Macedonia and Alexander the Great provided some impetus. Philip's cult existed in Philippi, the city that he founded, and probably also in several other Greek cities. On the day that he was murdered, he had his image carried in a procession together with the images of the twelve Olympians; with such a display, Philip was not directly declaring himself as a god, but rather indirectly assimilating his power with that of the gods (see p. 16).

Alexander's cult is a more complex phenomenon. Until the end of his life, Alexander behaved as a pious mortal, never neglecting to sacrifice to the gods. When he was wounded, he made a joke, assuring his companions that what they saw was blood, not 'ichor, that which runs in the veins of the blessed divinities'. Alexander counted among his ancestors Heracles and Achilles, worshipped as heroes and gods. His consanguinity with heroes and gods was not an innovation. Other Greeks before him had been regarded as sons of gods and heroes due to their extraordinary achievements: for example, the famous Thasian athlete Theagenes was believed to be the son of Heracles. This tradition was later continued by the Ptolemies, who claimed descent from both Heracles and Dionysus, and by the Seleucids, who considered Apollo to be their ancestor – or even the father of Seleukos I. When Alexander assumed the status of pharaoh in Egypt, he was ex officio son of the sun god Ra and a divine being himself. During his stay in Egypt or shortly thereafter, rumours circulated that his father was not Philip but Zeus. But in addition to this, what enhanced the perception of Alexander as a man whose power was comparable to that of the gods and who ought to receive commensurate honours was his unprecedented military achievements and his efforts to surpass the heroes and gods. He competed with Heracles when he attacked Aornos (see p. 22) and his conquest of India was compared with the god Dionysus' Indian campaign.

During Alexander's campaign, his cult was established in several cities in Asia Minor: altars were erected for sacrifices in his honour, contests took place and tribes (civic subdivisions) were named after him. His friend Hephaistion was worshipped as a hero after his death. A true innovation came in 323 BC when the cities of the Greek mainland, possibly urged by Alexander or encouraged by his court, sent sacred envoys to Babylon to honour him as a god (see p. 24). Alexander died soon after and, with a few exceptions, his cult was discontinued. In Asia Minor, Erythrai still offered sacrifices to Alexander in the early second century BC, and priests of King Alexander are still attested in Ephesos in the second century AD and in Erythrai as late as the third century AD.

By the late fourth century BC, the offering to kings of the honours usually reserved for gods was an established practice. One of the earliest examples is the cult for Antigonos Monophthalmos and Demetrios Poliorketes in Athens. When Demetrios liberated Athens from the garrison of Kassandros (307 BC), the Athenians declared Antigonos and Demetrios 'saviours' (*soteres*) of the city; an altar was erected and the newly introduced 'priest of the saviours' offered sacrifices; two new tribes were named after the saviours, Antigonis and Demetrias; and an annual festival, with a procession, sacrifice and contest, was founded. In most cities, the worship of kings and a few queens consisted of the same elements. A precinct (*temenos*) was dedicated to and named after the ruler. In the precinct, an altar for sacrifices to the king was erected. His statue was set up in an already existing temple, near the statue of a traditional god, with whom the king now 'shared the temple' (*synnaos*). A priest was appointed annually to supervise the performance of the sacrifice, which took place during a festival. Greek festivals were usually held on the birthday of a god and included a procession, a sacrifice and athletic contests. These features served as models for the civic ruler cult. The festival was named after the king (e.g. Antiocheia for Antiochos).

An instructive example is the establishment of divine honours for Seleukos I and Antiochos I in Aigai in Asia Minor immediately after their victory at Kouropedion in 281 BC. In addition to honouring the two kings with the epithet Soteres for awarding freedom to the city, Aigai took a series of measures: building a temple next to the precinct of Apollo, erecting two cult statues, setting up two altars for the kings and an altar and a statue of Soteira, 'the rescuing goddess' (probably Athena), and sacrificing bulls to Seleukos and Antiochos during Apollo's festival. Further sacrifices were offered every month to commemorate the city's liberation, as well as in the month Seleukeon (named after Seleukos). For this worship, a priest was to be elected annually. Donning a laurel wreath, a headband and splendid dress, he was to offer the preliminary sacrifice on the kings' altar before every meeting of the assembly. The sacred herald included the kings in all prayers, and incense would be offered and prayers recited in all libations made before the magistrates. Also, two new tribes were named after Seleukos and Antiochos; the seat of the councillors was named after Seleukos, that of the generals after Antiochos. We can observe similar features but additional honours as well in Teos in Asia Minor in 204 BC, when the city showed its gratitude to Antiochos III for freeing Teos from taxes and recognised the city as inviolable. The grateful citizens bestowed upon Antiochos and the queen, his 'sister' Laodike, honours that assimilated them with the gods. Statues of Antiochos and Laodike were erected beside the statue of Dionysus, the city's patron,

> in order that those who made the city and its territory sacred and inviolable, freed us from the tribute, and gave this favor to the people and the association of the Dionysiac artists, receive from us all honors, as best as possible; by sharing with Dionysus the temple and the other worship, they shall jointly be rescuers of our city and will jointly give us good things.

A new festival was established, named after the royal couple (Antiocheia kai Laodikeia). Every civic subdivision was required to erect an altar for the king and the queen and to offer sacrifices in the same manner as sacrifices were offered to Poseidon. Additionally, the inhabitants who did not have citizenship were asked to join in the celebration, offering sacrifices in their houses. On the day of the festival, everyone had to wear a wreath to mark the festive character of the day; the lawcourts were closed and all work was suspended. The place where Antiochos the Great announced his benefactions, the town hall, was consecrated and a statue was erected in it. All the magistrates had to offer a sacrifice on the first day of the year. As the king's statue stood in the seat in the council, all deliberation of the councillors took place under the king's gaze, as it were. Besides Antiochos, a sacrifice was also offered to two personifications that symbolically stressed the nature of the honour: the Charites, the personification of gratitude and favour, and Mneme, remembrance. The sacrifice expressed the idea that the Teians would forever remember the favours and continually feel gratitude. On New Year's Day, all annual magistrates were to 'offer a sacrifice for their inauguration in their office, in order that they enter their office with a good start'; in this manner, the New Year's festival became a festival of the king. On that day, the young men who had finished their training as ephebes (see pp. 330–3) and entered the citizen body offered a sacrifice to the royal couple, 'in order that they will not start any public activities without first giving thanks to the benefactors, in order that we accustom our offspring to regard everything else as secondary to the expression of gratitude'. Upon entering the city, the winners of athletic contests crowned the statue of the king and offered a sacrifice. To thank the king for securing the cultivation of the land and making it fruitful, first fruits were placed in front of the king's statue and the priest crowned the statue with a seasonal wreath. A fountain was dedicated to Queen Laodike:

> Since the queen is pious towards the gods and benevolent towards the people, it is proper that all who honor the gods and perform purifications draw from this fountain the water for the preparation of the sacrifice ... All priests and priestesses, who offer a sacrifice on behalf of the city, shall use this water in all sacrifices that require water.

These rituals associated central aspects of life with the royal couple: decision-making in the council, the executive power of the magistrates, the education of the young, citizenship, victories in athletic contests, agriculture, family and the cult of Dionysus. The king and the queen were symbolically present in political activities and civic rituals; they were associated with abstract ideas of memory, salvation, protection, freedom and gratitude. The rituals assimilated the impact of the king's power with that of the gods. Like a god, Antiochos had given prosperity.

By honouring him like a god, the Teians displayed gratitude but also expressed the hope that the king's grace would be beneficial to them in the future. As a display of gratitude the ruler cult was a strategy of persuasion: it obliged the king to perpetuate his benevolence. In order to elicit royal benefactions, the cities chose to present themselves as weak, suffering and dependent, thereby constructing the image of the powerful king. By assimilating the power of a king with that of a god, the cities indirectly obliged the ruler to act as such. A term that is sometimes used in connection with the ruler cult is *isotheoi timai* (godlike honours). The attribute *isotheos* stresses the fact that the Hellenistic kings were *not* gods; they were honoured only *like* gods. This concept allowed the Hellenistic Greeks to raise the kings to a higher status than that of ordinary mortals without deifying them.

The worship of kings and queens had an official character; even when the sacrifices were offered at home, they were officially prescribed. People did not individually pray to kings for their personal concerns. Only Queen Arsinoe II received a private cult after her death around 268 BC. As a patron of sailors she was a popular goddess in the eastern Mediterranean and was identified with traditional patrons of sailors, such as Aphrodite and Isis.

The mentality behind the ruler cult can be observed in the hymn that the Athenians sang in 291 BC as they received Demetrios Poliorketes. When he staged his arrival in Athens to coincide with the celebration of the Eleusinian mysteries of Demeter, processional choruses and *ithyphalloi* (costumed men with erect phalluses) came to meet him with dancing and singing in the streets:

How the greatest and dearest of the gods are present in our city! For the circumstances have brought together Demeter and Demetrios; she comes to celebrate the solemn mysteries of the Kore [Persephone], while he is here full of joy, as befits the god, fair and laughing. His appearance is solemn, his friends all around him and he in their midst, as though they were stars and he the sun. Hail boy of the most power-ful god Poseidon and Aphrodite! For other gods are either far away, or they do not have ears, or they do not exist, or do not take any notice of us, but you we can see present here, not made of wood or stone, but real. So we pray to you: first make peace, dearest; for you have the power. And then, the Sphinx that rules not only over Thebes but over the whole of Greece, the Aetolian sphinx sitting on a rock like the ancient one, who seizes and carries away all our people, and I cannot fight against her – for it is an Aetolian custom to seize the property of neighbors and now even what is afar; most of all punish her yourself; if not, find an Oedipus who will either hurl down that sphinx from the rocks or reduce her to ashes.

The song celebrates the *epiphany* of the gods – that is, the manifestation of their presence; it praises their visible and effective power with epithets in the superlative; it refers to the willingness of gods worthy of this designa-tion to listen to prayers. These are significant features of Hellenistic divine worship (see pp. 369–72). According to the religious concept that under-lies this hymn, a true god is willing to communicate with mortals and to listen to their prayers, as opposed to mute images. Demetrios is 'true' because of his visible and effectual presence, in the same way that only gods who are present and manifest their power are true gods. By declaring that only the gods who listen to prayers matter, the poet implicitly warned Demetrios that his divinity, too, depended on this. As a true god, he had to demonstrate his ability to listen to the prayers of the Athenians and to save them from their enemies. Mortal divinity was based on efficacy. In the words of the early-third-century-AD historian Dio Cassius: '*arete* [extraordinary, effective power] makes many men godlike [*isotheos*], no one has become a god through a vote'.

While the ruler cult established by the cities responded to benefac-tions, past or hoped for, and thus fostered communication between city and king, the dynastic ruler cult introduced by the court had a different origin and aim: it provided a unifying element throughout the vast ter-ritories and connected the king with his subjects. Initially, the dynastic cult consisted of the deification of a deceased king; later, it also com-prised living kings. When Ptolemy I died in 283 BC, his son and successor, Ptolemy II, declared him a god; the same honour was bestowed upon Ptolemy's widow, Berenike, in 279 BC. The deceased royal couple were worshipped as 'the saviour gods' (*theoi soteres*). When Arsinoe, Ptolemy II's wife and sister, died (268 BC?) – or possibly even before her death – her cult was introduced in the temples of all the native gods in Egypt. In a subtle manner, Ptolemy II also propagated and legitimated his rule by associating himself and his sister with the cult of Alexander the Great. Alexander's priest became the priest of 'the sibling-loving gods' (*theoi philadelphoi*) as well. All his successors did the same, adding their epithets to the priest's title. In this way, the cult of Alexander in Alexandria was transformed into a dynastic cult. Public documents were dated with the reference to this 'eponymous' priest, underlining both dynastic continuity and the monarchy's divine nature.

In addition to this cult, the Ptolemies were also worshipped as 'temple-sharing deities' (*synnaoi theoi*) in the Egyptian temples, receiving daily libations and incense offerings. The primary addressee of this cult was the native population. The dates of dynastic festivals often followed Egyptian traditions: the cult of Arsinoe II was funded with money that used to be paid to the native Egyptian temples; and the decrees of the Egyptian priests, inscribed on stone in the native script, referred to the members of the royal family with the traditional Egyptian religious vocabulary. Such practices allowed the native population to recognise in the Ptolemaic king their pharaoh. Outside Egypt, in the Ptolemaic possessions in Asia Minor, Cyprus and the Aegean Islands, the dynastic cult was practised by the soldiers who served in the Ptolemaic garrisons, establishing a connection with the centre of power in the distant capital. The Ptolemaic dynastic cult was of critical importance for the maintenance of a network of contacts and for the display of grandeur. The greatest monarch of this kingdom, Ptolemy II, consciously exploited it to such ends by establishing the Ptolemaia (see p. 74), to which cities from the entire Greek world sent their sacred envoys (*theoroi*).

The Seleucids ruled a less homogeneous realm than that of Ptolemaic Egypt. Although they could not found their dynastic cult on pre-existing practices such as the pharaonic traditions, they could still make use of the unifying power of religious worship. The deification of the deceased monarch was a standard procedure from the time of Antiochos I, but an innovation was introduced when Antiochos III established his own cult during his lifetime. He introduced the office of the high priest for himself and his ancestors (209 BC?) and sometime later a high priest for his wife Laodike.

Within their kingdoms, the dynastic cult gave monarchs ideological support for their power and allowed the native population to participate in a form of worship in which it recognised familiar elements. On the other hand, the cities used the royal cult as an instrument with which they established a close relationship with a monarch and directly expressed their gratitude for past benefactions and their expectation of future ones. Similarly, the kings and queens responded to these honours by promising to consider the interests of the cities. In the delicate negotiations between *polis* and king, the cities encouraged royal liberality and constructed an image of a monarch with supremacy and unlimited, godlike power.

Negotiating power

Hellenistic kings ruled over all the territories that they could gain and maintain through their military might: the territories that they inherited and were in a position to defend; the territories that they could conquer; and the territories of cities to which they offered their protection. Consequently, their realms were heterogeneous as regards the origins of their inhabitants, their legal positions – citizens, military settlers and dependent populations – and their institutions. Each kingdom had a geographic nucleus. These were Macedonia and Thessaly for the Antigonids, Egypt for the Ptolemies, north Syria, Babylonia and parts of Asia Minor for the Seleucids, and north-western Asia Minor for the Attalids; the small peripheral kingdoms of Bithynia, Kappadokia, Pontos and Armenia had the respective regions as their nucleus. Because of numerous external possessions, the territories of the larger kingdoms were rarely enclosed within a continuous border. To rule such kingdoms was a challenge. The acceptance of the king's rule depended on the successful conduct of delicate negotiations with other kings (and their daughters), his 'friends', his army, the population of his cities and especially the capital(s), the Greek cities, the indigenous elites and the local populations, the gods and, from the early second century BC onwards, also with Rome. The strength of a Hellenistic king depended on this complex field of interactions with 'others', in a game of promises and expectations, requests and offers, achievements and threats, power and tolerance.

Hellenistic kingship was highly personalised. What we would today call 'state affairs' were called in Hellenistic Greek 'the affairs of the king' (*pragmata tou basileos*); the vizier of the kingdom was the 'man in charge of the affairs' (*epi ton pragmaton*); the kingdom was assimilated with a household (*oikos*); the court consisted of the king's 'friends' (*philoi*). Their increasingly formalised titles indicated how close they were to the person of the king and how much they were trusted. The term 'friend' implies a relationship of trust and affection, which was based on the acceptance of the hierarchically higher position of the king and the expectation of rewards for loyalty.

The kings were conscious of the impact that their generosity would have on the loyalty of their friends, their officers and their army. For this reason, they made sure that their policy of generously rewarding those who served them well was explicitly referred to in relevant documents that were publicly inscribed. A similar reciprocal arrangement determined the relationship between the king and his army. It was expected that loyalty and successful service would be rewarded with promotion, patronage, honours and material gain, such as land, money, prizes and a share in the booty after a successful campaign. The recipients of royal favours mentioned this in their dedications to gods or their dedications for the well-being of kings. By communicating the idea of reciprocity to others, they strengthened loyalty and propagated the principles on which kingship was predicated. For the soldiers, the most important reward was the grant of land. As in the case of the friends, the loyalty of the army could be easily lost when the fear of defeat became apparent, the promise of booty was not fulfilled and a king's rule was too weak or too authoritarian. Not even Alexander the Great was spared the experience of a mutiny of angry soldiers; mutinies of armies and especially of mercenaries, as well as cases of desertion, are well attested.

From the late third century BC onwards, the Hellenistic kings more often than not were forced to negotiate their position with an external power: Rome. They concluded treaties of alliance with the Romans; they negotiated the terms of a peace treaty after their defeat in a war; they appealed to the Romans as arbitrators or supporters in their dynastic conflicts; they looked upon them as potential supporters in their foreign policy; and when they found themselves short of options, they bequeathed them their kingdoms. The creation of satellite, allied kingdoms is the result of the increasing influence of the Romans, as well as their initial hesitation to annex territories and to undertake their administration; they preferred to leave this task to 'client kings'.

These negotiations were particularly frustrating because of the different 'diplomatic languages' used by Greeks and Romans, the fluidity of Roman policies, as well as the sometimes puzzling balance of power between the senate and ambitious military commanders. In 168 BC, Antiochos IV experienced Roman diplomacy in a manner that was to be long remembered. After a victorious invasion of Egypt, and close to annexing the Ptolemaic kingdom, he was confronted by the Romans' demand that he withdraw his troops. Antiochos did not have much room, as it were, to manoeuvre. The Roman envoy drew a circle around him with his staff and told him not to step outside it before he gave an answer. The Seleucid had to comply (see p. 195). At the same time, Prusias II, King of Bithynia, demonstrated how a weak king might approach the Romans, who had just defeated his brother-in-law Perseus, in order to achieve his aims:

> When Roman envoys first came to him, he met them with shorn head and wearing a cap, toga, and shoes, and in fact exactly in the costume worn by those recently manumitted at Rome, whom they call *liberti*: and greeting the envoys, he said. 'Behold your freedman, who is willing to please you in all things and to imitate your customs!' ... And now, again, when he reached the entrance of the Senate house he stopped at the door facing the senators, and, dropping both his hands, he performed obeisance to the threshold and the seated Fathers, exclaiming, 'Hail, rescuing gods!' surpassing all others who came after him in lack of manliness, in effeminate behavior, and in flattery.

By adopting the habitus of a freedman, Prusias obliged the senate to assume the responsibility that a *patronus* had for his freedman. By elevating the senate to the status of saviour gods, the king challenged the senate to behave as such, just as contemporary cities sought the support of kings by establishing ruler cults. This is theatrical behaviour and it is a significant feature of Hellenistic kingship.

The staging of monarchy

Demetrios Poliorketes was certainly the most tragic but also the most theatrical of kings. In his persistent efforts to succeed Alexander as ruler of the empire, he experienced more reversals of fortune than any other

Hellenistic king; he repeatedly lost and regained kingdoms. Plutarch, following Hellenistic sources, perceived Demetrios' life as a drama. When Demetrios and the other Successors altered their behaviour as soon as they received the diadem, Plutarch compares them with tragic actors who 'adapt to their costumes their gait, voice, posture at table and manner of addressing others'. He describes Demetrios' change of fortune as a movement from the comic to the tragic stage. The king's wardrobe is described as 'great drama' and thus likened to an actor's costume. With passages from Sophocles' *Menelaos* and Euripides' *Bacchae*, Plutarch comments on Demetrios' situation after his defeat. His funeral is described as a dramatic performance. While the most celebrated flautist played a solemn melody, 'to this melody the oars kept perfect time, and their splashing, like funeral beatings of the breast, answered to the cadences of the flute-tones'. The oars of the ships assumed the role of a tragic chorus. Finally, Plutarch closes the king's life with the words 'and now that the Macedonian drama has been performed, let us introduce the Roman'.

Demetrios was not a pawn in Fortune's play but a skilful performer in his role as a king. *His* life was compared with a play because he lived it as a good performer. Demetrios knew how to apply theatrical behaviour in the construction of his image. A characteristic example is his carefully staged appearance in Athens in 295 BC, after he had captured the city that had betrayed him a few years earlier. Choosing as the date for his appearance the day on which the Athenians usually celebrated the dramatic contests the Dionysia, the king ordered the Athenians to assemble in the theatre – spectators of their own drama, as it were. He fenced the stage building round with armed men and encompassed the stage itself with his bodyguards. After these arrangements had puzzled and terrified the Athenians, Demetrios finally made his appearance through one of the upper side entrances like a tragic actor. In full control of the emotions of the frightened Athenians, Demetrios staged in the theatre a reversal of fortune, a true *peripeteia*. With the right tone of voice and the selection of the proper words, he forgave the Athenians and won them over – the result that he desired by his performance.

What explains the use of theatrical behaviour by Hellenistic rulers? An answer is provided by a treatise on kingship attributed to a certain Diotogenes. The text was probably composed in the second century AD, but its ideas concerning monarchical rule apply to Hellenistic kingship as well. The author advises the monarch to dissociate himself from human failings and to astonish onlookers with his staged appearances and studied pose:

> The monarch should set himself apart from the human failings and approach gods, not through arrogance, but through magnanimity and through the greatness of his virtue, surrounding himself with so much trust and authority with his appearance, his thought, his reason, the morality of his soul, deeds, movement, and the posture of the body, so that those who watch him shall be overwhelmed and shall be adorned with shame and wisdom and the feeling of trust.

The author concludes: 'And above all, one should remember that kingship is the imitation of the gods.' Indirectly, he regards the king as an actor who performs on earth the part played by the gods in heaven: a man who imitates the gods, without being a god. To achieve this, the king requires more than moral and intellectual abilities; his staged behaviour requires careful use of body language. In another passage, the author stresses again the importance of appearance:

> As regards public addresses, the good king needs to pay attention to suitable posture and appearance, forming a political and serious image of himself, so that he appears to the multitude neither harsh nor contemptible, but sweet and considerate. He shall achieve this if he is, first, majestic to watch and to listen to and seems worthy of his rule; secondly, if he is kind in conversation and in appearance and in benefactions; thirdly, if he is fearsome in his honesty and in punishing and in swiftness and, generally, in the experience and practice of kingship. Majesty, being an imitation of the gods, will make it possible that he will be marveled at and honored by the people; kindness will make the people be favorably disposed towards him and love him; and finally, severity will terrify his enemies and make him invincible, but to his friends it will make him magnanimous and confident.

A crucial issue in the public appearance and image of a Hellenistic king was not to disturb the balance between affability, which was necessary for his popularity, and remoteness, which was necessary for the respect of his leadership. Remoteness and affability are essential both for the acceptance of military leadership and for relations with autonomous cities.

Commanding an army requires a clear hierarchical distance between king and soldier. But a successful commander must be visible in training and on the battlefield, responsive to the needs of the soldiers and willing to reward them for their loyalty and services. A king's relationship with a free city was based on a similar balance between authority and friendliness, distance and proximity, inequality and affability, between his claim to loyalty and a city's claim to autonomy. Kings had to use a theatrical display of equality in order to achieve their purpose.

Enough occasions were provided for kings to stage appearances: the assembly of the army, celebrations in the court, processions and ceremonial receptions in cities. Philip V is said to have manipulated his dress in order to create the illusion of equality and affability:

> After he celebrated the contest of the Nemea, he returned to Argos, taking off the diadem and the purple garment, wishing to create the impression of equality with the many, of a mild person, of a friend of the people. But the more popular the dress he wore, the more monarchical the power he possessed.

Dress was for Philip what the mask was for an actor: a medium for the creation of an image. Polybius describes similar behaviour in the case of the Seleucid Antiochos IV, who was keen to construct the desirable public image:

> Many times he used to take off the royal garment and to wear a toga, going around in the agora, participating in the elections and asking the people for their vote, embracing some and begging others, in order to be elected as *agoranomos* [supervisor of the market] or *demarchos* [head of the town].

In order to create the illusion of the popular king, he is said to have joined common people in their celebrations, playing musical instruments. At the end of the great festival he had organised in Daphne in 166 BC (see p. 195) he was carried to the palace by mimic dancers as though he were one of the performers. There he danced naked and acted with the clowns. This staged gregariousness did not appeal to all, and Polybius ironically turned his royal title Epiphanes (the one with manifest power) to Epimanes (the lunatic); when the balance between distance and sociability was disturbed, such behaviour was taken for madness. But careful staging had a tremendous impact. When, around 185/184 BC, two of the sons of Attalos I visited Kyzikos, the native city of their mother, Apollonis, they staged their visit as a reminiscence of the most famous 'virtuous sons' of Greek history. According to legend, when there were no oxen to pull the cart of the priestess of Hera from Argos to Hera's sanctuary, her sons, Kleobis and Biton, did the job. Attalos' sons placed their mother between them and walked all around the sanctuaries of the city holding her hands. 'The spectators approved of the young men and held them worthy; remembering the deeds of Kleobis and Biton, they compared their conduct to this.' This story nicely summarises some of the aspects of a royal family that have been previously discussed: the representation of the ruling dynasty as a loving family, the right balance between affability and remoteness, the elevation of the royal family above normal mortals and their comparison with legendary figures, and the effort to achieve approval. Even in the years leading to her demise, Cleopatra, the last Ptolemy, excelled in one thing: enchanting spectators through the glamorous enthronement of her children (see p. 230). But, according to Cavafy:

The Alexandrians knew of course
that this was all mere words, all theatre.

6

THE CITY-STATE IN A
WORLD OF FEDERATIONS
AND EMPIRES

The *polis*: physical decline and ideological longevity

What impression did the greatest city of the Classical period, Athens, leave on a visitor two centuries after the death of Pericles? Herakleides, a traveller, wrote down his impressions of this and other cities in the mid- or late third century BC:

> The city itself is all dry and does not have a good water supply; the streets are narrow and winding, as they were built long ago. Most of the houses are cheaply built, and only few reach a higher standard; a stranger would find it hard to believe at first sight that this was the famous city of Athens, though he might soon come to believe it. There you will see the most beautiful sights on earth: a large and impressive theatre, a magnificent temple of Athena, something out of this world and worth seeing, the so-called Parthenon, which lies above the theatre ... They have festivals of all sorts, and philosophers from everywhere pull the wool over your eyes and provide recreation; there are many opportunities for leisure and spectacles without interruption. The produce of the land is all priceless and delicious to taste, though

in rather short supply. But the presence of foreigners, which they are all accustomed to and which fits in with their inclination, causes them to forget about their stomach by diverting their attention to pleasant things. Because of the spectacles and entertainments in the city, the common people have no experience of hunger, as they are made to forget about food, but for those who have money there is no city comparable in the pleasures it offers.

A city full of contrasts: between past and present, rich and poor, illusions and realities. In his description of Athens and other cities, Herakleides presents vivid images of a heterogeneous world. Impressive buildings, spectacles, festivals, lectures, safe roads and good infrastructure count among the positive aspects. In neighbouring Boiotia, Tanagra is praised for the hospitality of its people and their love of justice; and for the fact that the woods in its vicinity are free of bandits. If the author highlights such features, it is only because they were not to be expected everywhere. In many places, he observes signs of decline. With regard to Plataiai, he quotes the contemptuous verses of the comic poet Poseidippos:

> It has two temples, a portico, and its name ...
> Most of the time it is a desert,
> and only at the festival of the Eleutheria
> does it become a city.

With no recent achievements to be proud of, Plataiai could point only to the commemorative festival to celebrate the last battle against the Persians in 478 BC. A famous history was the one thing old Greek cities had in abundance. Athens lacked water, Anthedon grain. A traveller to Athens might find numerous buildings to admire – the theatre, the Parthenon, the still-unfinished Temple of Zeus Olympios, the philosophical schools in the Academy and the Lyceum, and the gymnasium at Kynosarges – but none of these buildings was built in the Hellenistic period. If Thebes had a more modern outlook, it was only because it had been razed to the ground by Alexander in 335 BC and rebuilt twenty years later.

The principal cause for decline was war. The number of wars increased after Alexander due to royal ambitions, territorial conflicts, barbarian invasions, piracy and Roman expansion. Their results were disastrous: loss of manpower, devastation of the territory and its resources, heavy debts for the community and individual citizens, strong dependence on powers that offered protection. And yet what impresses, despite all problems, complaints and signs of decline, is the vitality of the *polis* as a political point of reference. When in the early second century BC Polybius wanted to praise the achievements of the Achaean League, he compared it with a city-state: 'In general, there is no difference between the entire Peloponnese and a single city, except that its inhabitants are not included within the same city wall.' Three centuries later, in AD 155, when the orator Aelius Aristides composed his *Roman Oration* in praise of the Roman Empire, he described it as a network of urban centres and a commonwealth of city-states:

> When were there so many cities both inland and on the coast, or when have they been so beautifully equipped with everything? Did ever a man of those who lived then travel across country as we do, counting the cities by days and sometimes riding on the same day through two or three cities as if passing through sections of merely one? ... Cities gleam with radiance and charm, and the whole earth has been made beautiful like a garden.

For Polybius as for Aristides, the point of reference against which any political entity should be measured was the *polis*, or city-state. Since the eighth century BC at the latest, the *polis* was the predominant form of political organisation in ancient Greece. A *polis* typically consisted of an urban centre (*asty*), usually with a fortified citadel (*acropolis*). The main settlement was surrounded by a territory (*chora*), where a large part of the population lived and worked. On the *akropolis* or in suitable places near it were altars, sanctuaries and temples, the place of the assembly, the market (*agora*), the seats of the magistrates and other public buildings. Depending on its location, a *polis* could have one or more harbours, territorial subdivisions, usually called *demoi*, and dependent settlements. Some farmers who possessed citizenship were country dwellers and exercised their rights as citizens in rural communities scattered in the territory of the *polis*. But whether the citizens of rural areas attended the assembly in the city depended on how far away they were and how feasible it was for them to travel to the urban centre and spend some time there.

The city-state remained the only political reality of which large parts of the population in the Hellenistic world and the Roman Empire had direct experience. For the intellectuals it offered the main framework of thought. For poets and novelists it competed with idealised pastoral landscapes as a setting for their literary creations. Although Aristides' praise is as exaggerated and one-sided as any encomiastic oration, on one point he is right: the unparalleled number of cities, big and small, that existed in the Roman Empire. In the western provinces and in North Africa, this was the result of colonisation and urbanisation at the initiative of the Romans. In the Greek-speaking East – Greece and its islands, Asia Minor, and the Near and Middle East – urbanisation had much older roots than in the West, and some differentiations are necessary. It is true that numerous *poleis* disappeared from mainland Greece, some islands and Asia Minor in the course of the Hellenistic period, either through complete destruction or by losing their status as autonomous communities. But when vast territories from the Aegean coast to modern Afghanistan were incorporated into Greek culture, so many new *poleis* were founded or pre-existing settlements upgraded to *poleis* that if we were to apply purely quantitative criteria the period from Alexander to Hadrian would be the period of the greatest rise of the Greek *polis* and the greatest diffusion of its institutions and architectural features: assemblies, councils, magistrates, gymnasia, theatres, marketplaces and town halls. But purely quantitative criteria would be deceiving. The period in which we observe an unprecedented increase in the number of *poleis* was at the same time a period in which power was shifting from the *poleis* to federations and kingdoms, and then to the Roman Empire.

That cities were in one form or another politically dependent on hegemonic powers was not new. For most of the fifth and fourth centuries BC numerous Greek *poleis* were dominated first by Athens, then by Sparta, Thebes and Macedonia; from 387 BC to Alexander's campaign the free *poleis* of Asia Minor were under the rule of the Persian king. The establishment of the Hellenistic monarchies brought a new qualitative change: many cities, including a traditional hegemonic power such as Athens, fell under direct or indirect royal control for long periods. The rise of federal states shifted the centre of power from the statesmen of city-states to the statesmen of federations. And finally, the gradual establishment of Roman provincial administration brought another shift.

Although the city-states, as communities of citizens, remained the stage of vibrant political life, their impact on the grand political stage was limited – apart from the wars that they often provoked. City-states produced first-rate statesmen, such as Aratos of Sikyon, but whenever these statesmen had an impact on history it was because they were active outside the narrow confines of their own cities, as leaders of federations or as royal advisers. City-states competed for distinction and honour in the present, but their claims on privileges were based on achievements in the past. These contrasts are explained by deep changes in society and institutions, as the borders of the world in which the cities had existed until the fourth century BC expanded.

A world full of *poleis*

In no other period of Greek history since the time of the great colonisation of the eighth and seventh centuries BC did so many new *poleis* come into existence as in the 450 years from Alexander to Hadrian; but also in no other period did so many *poleis* disappear from the map or lose their status as autonomous states, usually due to wars. Within this period we can distinguish separate phases.

The first phase, from around 330 to around 220 BC, began with the conquests of Alexander and the struggle of the Successors to establish their own kingdoms. Many new *poleis* were founded in the territories conquered by Alexander and ruled by his successors. Alexander alone is said to have founded more than seventy cities, but this certainly is an exaggeration. The exact number of his Alexandrias, the most famous of which are Alexandria in Egypt and Alexandria Arachosia, modern Kandahar, cannot be determined. They served as models for the Successors. A wave of new foundations that served as administrative centres and were named after kings and members of the royal families started already in the first years after his death. Small settlements were renamed and reorganised as *poleis*, settlements that already had military and religious functions acquired the status of a *polis*, destroyed cities were rebuilt and new cities were founded near the site of villages and sanctuaries. For instance, Therme became Thessalonike, named after Alexander's sister, wife of King Kassandros; Kassandros also founded Kassandreia in 316 BC at the site of Poteidaia, a city that had been destroyed in 356 BC. Thebes too owes its refoundation in 316/315 BC to Kassandros. The small settlement of Pharmake on the Orontes became the royal treasury of Seleukos I under the name of Apameia, after his wife Apama; Seleukos I founded two more capitals for his empire, naming them after himself and his son Antiochos: Seleukeia on the Tigris and Antiocheia on the Orontes. Demetrios Poliorketes founded Demetrias in Thessaly. Ptolemy I established Ptolemais Hermiou as the capital of Upper Egypt, while his son founded two harbours on the Red Sea, one named after his wife Arsinoe and the other after his mother, Berenike. The important cities in the royal realms fulfilled central administrative functions, as royal residences and the seats of provincial governors. Their populations were organised as civic communities, but the presence of a king, his court, his treasury and his army distinguished them from 'normal' *poleis*. Governors of kings also founded cities: Antigonos Dokimos, a governor under Antigonos Monophthalmos, founded Dokimion in Phrygia in the late fourth century BC; Themison, a courtier of Antiochos II, founded Themisonion, also in Phrygia; and Nikanor, a Seleucid official, founded Antiocheia Arabis.

Another significant phenomenon in this period is the incorporation of small communities into larger neighbouring cities, either on the basis of an interstate agreement (*sympoliteia*) or as the result of war and conquest. To give but a few examples: in Asia Minor Miletos incorporated Myous and Thebai, Ephesos did the same with Pygela and Teos with Kyrbissos. Because of the rise of Pergamon to a royal capital, old cities in its vicinity were incorporated into its territory, gradually lost importance and were abandoned. When a *polis* and its territory were absorbed by another, its population usually acquired citizenship and constituted a civic subdivision, but sometimes it was demoted to the status of a dependent population. The settlement sometimes survived as a fortress or urban settlement, but sometimes the population abandoned it and moved to the larger city.

In this first phase the foundation of new cities in Asia attracted large numbers of settlers; this impact is comparable to that of the foundation of cities in the New World from the late seventeenth century to the nineteenth. For 'Old Greece', this meant the loss of population. In the first decades of this process, and in isolated cases later, this was indeed a desired effect. People who did not own land, as well as the members of factions defeated in political conflicts, were offered a new beginning. This movement from west to east also contributed to a shift in the economic and cultural centres from mainland Greece to the capitals of the new kingdoms and to cities that had close connections with the new centres of power, such as Rhodes and Ephesos. The position of a city was now determined by new parameters: its relation to a king, as a royal foundation, a capital or host of a royal garrison; its administrative position in a kingdom; its location on one of the roads that connected the new territories with the Mediterranean; its membership of a federation.

The second phase, from around 220 to around 64 BC, was dominated by wars between Greek cities and wars to do with the Roman expansion. Many *poleis* in mainland Greece and the islands were destroyed, lost their independence or were absorbed into greater political communities. The razing of Corinth to the ground by the Romans in 146 BC was lamented as a tragedy and remembered as an act of unsurpassed barbarity. Dozens of small cities suffered the same fate, more often at the hands of victorious Greek neighbours than at those of Roman soldiers; some recovered from physical destruction, others were obliterated. When ancient sources mention the destruction of seventy sites in Molossis (Epirus) in 167 BC, this number certainly includes small *poleis*. On Crete, a particularly bellicose place, the second century BC saw the destruction of at least eight *poleis*. When Crete became part of the Roman Empire, only fifteen or sixteen settlements retained the *polis* status, a small portion of the more than fifty city-states known to have existed there at the beginning of the Hellenistic period.

Due to dynastic crises in the Ptolemaic and Seleucid kingdoms, in this phase we also observe a significant change in the political influence of royal capitals such as Antioch and Alexandria. The populations of these cities gradually became an important political factor, exercising pressure on the court, making demands, organising uprisings and even overthrowing kings.

Beginning in the early second century BC, the impact of Rome is noticeable with regard to the legal status of *poleis*. The Roman senate and Roman magistrates took decisions concerning the status – and sometimes the very existence – of a *polis*, the payment of tribute, the assignment of a city to the realm of a king and the allocation of territories to allied cities. For instance, in 167 BC Delos, until then an independent city-state, passed to the ownership of Athens, while Rhodes lost the territories of Lycia and Caria and the control of cities in these regions, which it had been given twenty years earlier.

But while this period saw a decrease in the number of *poleis* in 'Old Greece', new *poleis* were still being created in Egypt and Asia. For instance, Boethos, a governor of the Thebaid in Egypt, founded three cities of military character around 140–130 BC: Euegetis, Philometoris and Cleopatra. But the emergence of new *poleis* was now less often the result of new foundations at the initiative of kings and royal governors; it more often occurred through the promotion of existing garrison sites to *poleis* at the initiative of local officers. Taking advantage of the waning Seleucid power in Asia Minor, some settlements claimed for themselves the status of a *polis*. Tyriaion, on the border of Phrygia and Pisidia, is a case in point. Its population consisted of soldiers and natives. After the defeat of Antiochos III and the Peace of Apameia of 188 BC (see p. 172), Tyriaion sent an embassy to Eumenes II, to whom these territories had been given by the Romans, requesting that the settlement be given its own laws, a council and a gymnasium – in other words, the status of a self-governed *polis*. Another settlement that must have acquired *polis* status in the same way is the later flourishing city of Aphrodisias in Caria.

The third phase for the *polis* begins with Pompey's new order in the East in 64 BC, but the most important part of this phase comes after the end of the Roman civil wars. In this phase, the status of Greek *poleis* depended on the Roman senate and Roman generals, and later on the emperor. The colony of Roman citizens was a new type of civic community with significant impact on Greek society and culture (see pp. 248–50).

Hellenistic federalism: great expectations and great failures

The rise of the Aetolian and Achaean Leagues introduced a new type of power into Greek history besides kingdoms and *poleis*: the federal state. Of course, federations existed already before Alexander's conquests. The populations in central Greece and in parts of the Peloponnese were organised in federations of various forms; their members were both cities and loosely organised tribal communities. The usual designation of such federations is *koinon* or *ethnos*. Thessaly was divided into several *koina*, and further *koina* existed in Aetolia, Akarnania and Boiotia in central Greece, in Achaia, Arkadia and Messenia in the Peloponnese, and in Asia Minor.

The federal states experienced their greatest growth and importance in the third and early second centuries BC. They were the protagonists in major political developments and military events, from the defeat of the Gauls in 278 BC by the Aetolian Koinon to the final resistance of the Achaean Koinon against Roman expansion in 146 BC. Two factors triggered the rise of federal states as influential political organisations: the need for Greek communities to develop forms of military cooperation in order to better defend themselves against external threats; and the pressure exercised by Hellenistic kings, who threatened the autonomy of the free *poleis*. Since federal states had larger territories, they could mobilise larger armies than individual cities. Statesmen with foresight and ambition, such as Aratos in Achaia, recognised the advantages of unity, although they never succeeded in eradicating the antagonisms and traditional enmities that often provoked foreign interventions and ultimately led to the conquest of Greece.

Despite significant local differences, the Hellenistic federal states shared certain features. With very few exceptions, such as Crete, they had a double citizenship, so that individual citizens were citizens of both the federal state and the member state: for example, the official name of the historian Polybius was Polybios, son of Lykortas, Achaean, citizen of Megalopolis. Each member state understood itself to be an independent and sovereign community of citizens, which for certain purposes yielded some aspects of its sovereignty to federal magistrates. So, for instance, in wartime the supreme military command was in the hands of a federal general. Other areas in which the member states cooperated included the joint celebration of festivals and contests, common procedures in certain legal issues, the resolution of territorial and other disputes – through arbitration, adjudication by a foreign city and adjudication by invited foreign judges – and the use of the same standards of weight. Usually, although not always, the members of a federation had similar constitutional forms. The individual members administered their local affairs and also had their separate territory, local magistrates and often separate coinage. Some federations expanded well beyond the geographical borders of the original tribal territory. The Aetolian Koinon had members as far as Crete and Asia Minor, the Boiotian Koinon expanded beyond the borders of Boiotia and the Achaean Koinon united large parts of the Peloponnese.

The federal states had a common foreign policy: in other words, they fought wars, made alliances with other states, concluded peace agreements jointly and mobilised troops under joint command. In this regard, they resemble alliances of equal partners, with a coherent internal structure and permanence. For all affairs of federal interest the *koina* summoned a federal assembly to regular and extraordinary meetings, while the day-to-day business was conducted by a council in which the members were represented and by federal magistrates – military commanders, a secretary and treasurers. The Achaean Koinon was governed by a board of ten executive officials (*damiourgoi*), a general (*strategos*), a commander of the cavalry (*hipparchos*), a secretary (*grammateus*), a commander of the fleet (*nauarchos*), deputy generals (*hypostrategoi*) and a treasurer (*tamias*). These officials were elected without any effort to achieve equal representation of the member states. Trusted statesmen could be re-elected – Aratos sixteen and Philopoimen eight times. In the Aetolian Koinon, the magistrates were elected by the assembly, where every citizen had a vote. In addition to the general and the commander of the cavalry, there were commanders for each of the seven sections of the army (*epikletarcheontes*), a secretary and seven treasurers who administered the contributions paid by the member states according to their population.

The federal assembly, which was open to all citizens, met regularly on the occasion of great festivals and irregularly whenever an important decision had to be taken. The assembly usually met in a federal sanctuary or a major city. The Achaean assembly met four times during the 'war season', in early May, early June, late July and late September. It originally met at the sanctuary of Zeus Homarios near Aigion, but after 189 BC the city members rotated as hosts of the meetings. Each city had one vote; during the meeting, the citizens of the different member states who were over the age of thirty and could attend voted separately, in order to determine the vote of their community. The Aetolian Koinon met twice every year as well as whenever need arose; the meeting for the election of magistrates took place in autumn at the federal sanctuary at Thermon, while the other meetings rotated in different cities. The decrees of the Aetolian assembly were valid in the entire territory of the federal state; from time to time, the assembly elected a board of 'law writers' (*nomographoi*), who registered the new laws and made sure that there were no contradictions between new and old laws.

The federal council (*synhedrion* or *boule*) was an important organ of a federal state. It met more often than the assembly, prepared proposals for the assembly, received foreign envoys and cooperated with the magistrates on important political matters. In the council of the Aetolian Koinon, the member states were represented according to their population. By 167 BC, the council had more than 550 members, so a smaller committee of thirty councillors (*apokletoi*) dealt with the day-to-day matters.

Some federal states developed elaborate structures in order to facilitate efficient mobilisation of troops, better representation of the city members in the federal organs and harmonious relations among the members. The Boiotian Koinon was divided into seven districts, or *tele*, with roughly equal numbers of citizens. Each *telos* was also a military unit and was represented in the council, the board of the seven 'magistrates of the Boiotians' (Boiotarchai) and other magistracies. The four biggest cities – Thebes, Orchomenos, Tanagra and Thespiai – formed one district each, whereas smaller cities were grouped together into three districts. An eighth district was added when Opous was annexed by the Koinon in the late third century BC. In Achaia, the federal territory was also divided into districts (*synteleiai*), each of which was obliged to make an equal contribution to the armed forces.

There were divergences from this general scheme. A loose artificial federation of Cycladic islands, the Nesiotic League, was created by Antigonos Monophthalmos in the late fourth century BC in order to unite his allies in the Aegean Sea; in the first half of the third century BC this organisation was controlled by the Ptolemies and later by Rhodes (c. 188–167 BC). The Nesiotic League did not have double citizenship and 'the chief of the islands' (*nesiarchos*) was not an annually elected magistrate but a Ptolemaic official, who was appointed by the king and, together with the admiral (*nauarchos*), represented Ptolemaic interests in the Aegean. In the mountainous areas of south-west Crete, a 'League of the Highlanders' (*Koinon ton Oreion*) was created in the late fourth century BC. It consisted of only four or five cities, which possessed joint citizenship and common territory, concluded alliances together, issued federal coins and developed a sense of regional identity. A second federation on Crete, the 'League of the Kretaians', emerged in the early third century BC. The league's artificial name, the 'Kretaians' (*Kretaieis*), made a distinction between the Cretans (*Kretes*), which referred to the inhabitants of the island of Crete and men of Cretan origin living abroad, and the Kretaians, the citizens of those cities that participated in the *koinon*. This league was essentially an alliance between two hegemonic powers, Gortyn and Knossos, and often fell apart because of their conflicts, only to be resurrected under the influence of foreign kings. It lacked federal citizenship, magistrates and an army; the members were represented in a council, and a general assembly discussed matters concerning foreign policy. This league's main achievement was the establishment of rules for conflict resolution among the member cities, citizens of different *poleis* and Cretan citizens and foreigners.

Outside Greece, the concept of a federation of independent communities is best attested in Lycia. There is no secure evidence for the existence of a Lycian League in the period of Ptolemaic control in the third century BC, but it is likely that the Ptolemies favoured the creation of a federation to assist their rule. A League certainly existed during the period of the Rhodian occupation in Lycia (188–167 BC), opposing Rhodian control. After the liberation, the League had all the features of a federal state. It consisted of twenty-three cities governed by a council, with the bigger cities sending three representatives each and the smaller cities two or one. The contributions of the communities to the federal finances corresponded to their size. The council, whose meetings were hosted by different cities in rotation, elected the chief magistrate – 'the leader of the Lycians' (*lykiarches*) – as well as other magistrates and the judges of a federal court. The League had a common foreign policy: for instance, it signed a treaty of alliance with Rome under Julius Caesar in 46 BC.

The development of procedures for conflict resolution by the federal states and the refinement of a system of proportional representation are major achievements of Hellenistic political culture. Federations broke the political, geographical and ethnic frontiers of communities with different traditions; in the federal council, statesmen from different communities exchanged arguments with shared interests in mind. But precisely because the federal states favoured regional identities and often followed an aggressive policy of annexation of neighbouring communities, they failed to suspend the political fragmentation of the Greek world. Obsessed with conflicts against cities that resisted their expansion and against other *koina*, they sought allies among those who presented the greatest threat to their autonomy: the kings and Rome. In the late third and the second centuries BC, they both provoked and contributed to the wars that brought Roman rule to Greece.

Political institutions

At first sight, until Roman institutional influences and interventions became apparent in the first century BC, little seems to have changed in the political structure and institutions of the Greek *polis*. These institutions were similar all over the Greek world, from the colonies of Magna Graecia and the cities of Greece and Asia Minor to the military colonies founded by Alexander and the Hellenistic kings in the Near and Middle East. The *polis* communities had an assembly, usually designated as *ekklesia*, which met regularly to discuss and approve of proposals submitted by the council. The council, usually called *boule*, was responsible for the day-to-day business, but its most important function was to carry out the preliminary discussion of proposals initiated by magistrates (*probouleusis*), sometimes also by ordinary citizens. The council usually had an executive committee, which remained in office for a limited period, usually a month or six months. Finally, annual executive officers, known under the generic designation *archai* or *archontes* (those who rule), were responsible for diverse military, financial, religious and administrative tasks, far too many to be listed here. The number, designation, duties and mode of appointment of these magistrates differed depending on the size of the city, its traditions and the nature of its constitution. Important magistracies that are found in most Hellenistic cities include the military offices of the *strategoi* (generals), who usually formed a board, and the *hipparchoi* (commanders of the cavalry); financial officers called *tamiai* (treasurers) and *epi tes dioikeseos* (in charge of the public finances); magistrates who were 'in charge of the town' (*astynomoi*) and 'in charge of the market' (*agoranomoi*), supervising public facilities – streets, public buildings and the market; the supervisor of the gymnasium (*gymnasiarchos*); and priesthoods. One of the officials was 'eponymous': that is, the year in which he was in office was named after him. In Asia Minor, this eponymous magistracy was often held by the *stephanephoros* (the wreath-bearer); many cities had eponymous priests.

In democratic constitutions, the assembly met more often than in oligarchies – there were forty regular meetings per annum in Athens – and more space was given to discussions. In some cities – for example, in Iasos in Asia Minor – the citizens received an honorarium for participation in the meetings of the assembly (*ekklesiastikon*). In democracies, at least some magistrates were appointed by lot and not elected, thus providing some opportunities for political activities to all citizens, regardless of property and other qualifications. Citizenship depended on birth in a citizen family and not on property or occupation. By contrast, oligarchies had property requirements both for citizenship and for service in offices and the council. Certain offices, especially those including financial duties, required wealth in both democracies and oligarchies. In Teos in Asia Minor, only men with an estimated property value amounting to at least four talents – the equivalent of the lifetime income of a mercenary soldier – had the right to be appointed to the office of the commander of the garrison in the fort of Kyrbissos. Some priesthoods were the hereditary privilege of elite families, even in democracies. Facing the problem of funding religious worship in a polytheistic religious system, some cities sold the priesthoods of certain gods to men and women who were willing to accept the obligation to perform the tasks connected with a cult in exchange for priestly privileges and exemption from certain fiscal and other obligations.

Caution is required when attempting a characterisation of political life in Hellenistic cities: the heterogeneity of their institutions was so vast and short-term changes – introduced under the influence of kings, as a result of civil wars or due to the establishment of an autocratic government – so common that the following general remarks do not apply to all cities. However, one can distinguish a general line of development that still allows for local variations. Important factors that determined the nature of the constitution include the existence of property requirements for political activity: that is, for participation in the assembly and for holding public positions, and in some cases even for citizenship; the appointment of councillors and magistrates through election, by lot among the entire citizen body or by lot among preselected citizens; the confirmation of all political decisions by the assembly; the accountability of magistrates; and the exercise of external control, through, for example, the presence of a garrison, a tyrant supported by a foreign king or a royal 'supervisor' of the city.

Athens and other cities that provide sufficient source material, especially Samos, Rhodes, Kos, Miletos, Pergamon, Magnesia on the Maeander and Priene, allow us to see how these factors could differ. In Athens, for instance, a census was imposed by the Macedonians in 322 BC, excluding from political participation 12,000 citizens whose property was worth less than 2,000 drachmas and reducing the citizens who qualified for the council and offices, possibly also for the assembly, to just 9,000 men. In 317 BC, the requirement was reduced to 1,000 drachmas, and in 307 BC, it was probably abolished. Similar regulations must have existed in cities that our sources describe as oligarchic. For most of its history, from 322 to 229 BC, Athens was under the direct control of Macedonian kings. Although the democratic institutions continued to exist, the Macedonian garrison, the representatives of the Macedonian kings and loyal local statesmen made sure that the decisions of the assembly were in conformity with the wishes of the kings.

The radical democracy that had existed in Athens in the fifth century BC and had been imposed by the Athenians on their allies went through significant modifications in the course of the fourth century BC both in Athens and in the rest of the Greek world. One of the fundamental modifications was that more executive power and influence were given to magistrates, who were now almost always elected and not chosen by lot. Also, the meaning of the word *demokratia* had changed. In the mid-second century BC, Polybius characterised the constitution of the Achaean League as a democracy: 'Nowhere will you find a better constitution and more genuine ideal of equality, freedom of speech, and in a word a true democracy than among the Achaeans.' And yet in the Achaean League a small minority of wealthy landowners monopolised political power; and Polybius' praise of 'true democracy' presupposes the existence of 'false democracies'. While a very vague concept of *demokratia* was idealised, at the same time the concrete institutional meaning of the word varied from city to city and from time to time. 'To respect democracy' became a catch-phrase that admitted multiple interpretations. The meaning of *demokratia* gradually shifted from 'rule of the *demos*' – rule of the citizens regardless of wealth and ancestry – to 'sovereignty of the *demos*' – sovereignty of the citizen body primarily in opposition to external interventions. This semantic shift allowed even cities in which many of the citizens were excluded from political offices, participation and initiatives to be designated as *demokratiai*.

This does not mean that the old conflicts between 'democrats' and supporters of oligarchy or aristocracy had been eclipsed. Laws that prevented the establishment of oligarchic regimes continued to be issued; cities continued to celebrate the restoration of democracy when foreign garrisons departed or authoritarian regimes collapsed; and civil wars between supporters and opponents of democracy were not uncommon.

What will a future historian make of the tickets for the New Jersey Transit? These inform the passengers that they are entitled to a seat regardless of race, colour, gender, national origin or religious faith. A future historian will notice that by condemning discrimination this text only acknowledges its existence. Race, colour, gender, national origin and religious faith may be irrelevant for seating in the New Jersey Transit trains, but fifty years after the Civil Rights Act of 1964 they do matter in many and far more important aspects of American society. An ancient historian is faced with similar problems when trying to detect contradictions between appearances and reality. And this holds true for the study of 'democracy' in the Hellenistic cities, because the greatest limitations of democracy were not institutional but factual: a few wealthy families monopolised power and assured the transfer of important political positions from one generation to the next. Although the Greek cities continued to cherish the ideal of the sovereignty of the people, for the cities in which sources permit an insight into the reality of political life democracy seems to have been only an illusion.

Illusions of democracy and realities of plutocracy

Elite families, with wealth, connections and prestige based on tradition, had always been a prominent feature of Greek political life, even in the radical democracy of Classical Athens. They continued to be influential throughout the fourth and third centuries BC, but from the late third century BC and far more clearly from the mid-second century BC onwards, there was a trend towards monopolisation of power by members of a few families and the transfer of important political positions from one generation to the next. The roots of this process are to be found in the dependence of public finances on private sponsors: that is, in the role of benefactors. By providing the funds for public tasks, as donations, loans or contributions to public subscriptions, they promoted their own public image and achieved approval for the political leadership of their families (see pp. 318–22).

A set of questions can help us assess the level of democracy in various Hellenistic cities, as well as the extent of the power monopoly of wealthy families. Which men were elected to office and how often? How many offices did they accumulate? Is political activity attested for their ancestors, family members or descendants? Was participation of the less wealthy citizens in the meetings of the assembly encouraged through the payment of an honorarium? Were proposals from men other than magistrates submitted to the assembly? Honorific inscriptions that provide some biographical information and also data about a prominent man's ancestors offer relevant evidence. For instance, in Kos a certain Diokles, who flourished around 200 BC, was born into a distinguished family. His grandfather Praxagoras was a prominent physician; his father, Leodamas, occupied the highest civic office, that of a *monarchos*, in the *deme* of

Halasarna. As a young man Diokles acquired fame as a winner in the greatest local athletic contest in 217 BC. In 206 BC, he occupied the priesthood of Dionysus. When his city faced attacks by Cretan raiders in 201 BC, he proposed in the assembly a subscription that provided the funds for the defence of Kos. With a contribution of 7,000 drachmas – an amount for which a mercenary soldier would have to work for more than twenty years – Diokles was also its greatest donor. The honorific decrees that praise his achievements during the war do not fail to mention the tradition of his family in public service. 'Acting in accordance with the virtue which has been handed down to him by his ancestors', Diokles showed leadership and tactical thinking; he secured the fort of his *deme*, recruited, organised and guided its defenders; he brought weapons, supervised the construction of fortifications, procured the necessary funds and lent money whenever necessary.

Another example of the influence exercised by an elite family comes from Athens, a city whose political life in the late third century BC was dominated by two brothers: Eurykleides and Mikion. Eurykleides served as a general of the infantry and treasurer of the military treasury, using a good deal of his own money while in office. As an organiser of contests he spent the enormous sum of seven talents; when the land was lying fallow and unsown because of the wars, he procured the necessary money for cultivation. In 229 BC, 'he restored freedom to the city together with his brother Mikion' by procuring the money needed to pay off the Macedonian garrison and 'persuade' it to withdraw from Athens. 'He fortified the harbors and repaired the walls of the city and of Piraeus, together with his brother Mikion'; he made alliances with other Greek cities, made sure that loans were repaid to Athens, proposed new laws, organised spectacles to honour the gods, introduced an athletic competition of armed men to commemorate the restoration of freedom and excelled in building activities. Eurykleides not only worked closely with his brother but also introduced his son to political life. After serving for a year as treasurer of military funds, a magistracy for which wealth was required, he continued performing these duties for a second year 'through his son', also named Mikion, who was thus introduced into political activities. One of the most expensive and prestigious *liturgies* was the *agonothesia*, the financial responsibility for the organisation of a contest. Eurykleides 'provided again his son for this charge'. Mikion, who learned his duties under the guidance of his father, is known to have later been an *agonothetes*, a member of a commission for the purchase of grain, and a donor of money. This is not an isolated case. Helikon, commander of the guard in Priene, was assisted by his son during his term of office in the late third century BC. Sometimes the honours bestowed upon a prominent citizen were inherited by his descendants. The Athenians decreed, for example, that Philippides, comic poet, statesman and benefactor in the early third century BC, was to receive for all time free meals with the executive committee of the council and a seat of honour at all the contests organised by the city. Not only was Philippides elevated above the ordinary citizens and associated with the most prominent men, but these honours were also given to the eldest of his descendants, thus perpetuating the prominent position of the benefactor's family.

These trends can also be observed on the periphery of the Hellenistic world. Protogenes was one of the wealthiest men in Olbia, on the north shore of the Black Sea, in the late third century BC. He was elected to the office of 'the Nine' (probably treasurers), served as ambassador to the Scythian king and was put in charge of the public finances, serving in this office for three years. The decree in his honour begins with a reference to his father, who had 'rendered many and great services to the city with regard both to money and to the public affairs', thus stressing the importance of family traditions and inherited duties. There was only a small step from inherited status, inherited wealth, inherited leadership and inherited gratitude to the institutionalisation of a class of privileged citizens. This step was taken when the Greek cities were integrated into the Roman Empire (see pp. 282–6).

Although democratic institutions continued to exist in the Hellenistic cities, political life increasingly accrued oligarchic and aristocratic features: offices and political activity gradually became the exclusive privilege of a small number of wealthy families, as in oligarchic regimes; and this privilege was inherited within these families, as in hereditary aristocracies. We often find the accumulation of offices and political functions, the iteration of office, the occupation of offices by members of the same families and the monopolisation of political initiative by a small elite. The *demos* accepted the elite's leadership in exchange for the services that the elite provided through benefactions. This relation of reciprocity was observed by the geographer Strabo in first-century-BC Rhodes:

The Rhodians care for the *demos*, although they do not live under a democracy. They wish nonetheless to keep the mass of the poor in good condition. And so the common people are provided with food, and the wealthy support those in need according to an old tradition. They have *liturgies* [mandatory services to the community imposed on the propertied classes] for the provision of food, with the result both that the poor receive sustenance and the city has no lack of available manpower, particularly as regards the fleet.

This is not to say that the political leadership and influence of the elite were unchallenged or were the same in every place and throughout the period under examination. Also, the nature of the leading political position of benefactors gradually changed from the third to the second century BC. In the early phases of this development, members of the elite families aimed at holding the first rank among their fellow citizens; however, from the mid-second century BC onwards, when a city's public expenses were primarily funded by benefactors, the members of this elite were no longer seen as the first among peers, respected for their patriotism, but constituted a closed group that was clearly placed above the rest of the citizen body. This internal development coincided with the expansion of direct Roman rule, first in Greece and then in Asia Minor. The Roman political leaders, raised in an aristocratic system of government, found their natural allies in the Greek cities among the supporters of oligarchy, who favoured reforms that opened political offices and membership in the council only to those who met property criteria. After their conquest of Greece in 146 BC, the Romans imposed oligarchic constitutions according to which political participation and election to office were dependent on property requirements (*apo timematon*). Thus the de facto leadership of an elite was also increasingly connected with legal requirements and census qualifications. This process was completed in the Imperial period.

The citizens who did not belong to the circle of elite families had limited possibilities, if any, to exercise executive powers or to prepare and submit proposals to the council and thus initiate the legislative procedure. But they found ways to influence political life. First, groups of citizens could make their wishes known through acclamations, through rhythmical loud shouting in formal gatherings in the assembly or in informal gatherings, usually in the theatre, whenever an important event occurred. Secondly, when important issues, such as alliances, the declaration of war or the conclusion of a peace treaty, institutional changes, public finances and private debts, deeply divided a community, crowds of citizens actively engaged in violent incidents that sometimes grew into civil wars. Thirdly, and most importantly, the elite was never an entirely homogeneous group. Individuals and families competed for power and followed different agenda. In this competition, they vied for the support of citizens for election to magistracies and for successful proposals in the assembly. This support could shift from one statesman to another, depending on the wishes of the citizens. The rise and fall of statesmen, designated in our sources as demagogues or tyrants (see p. 144), is nothing but the result of such shifting support.

The competing statesmen had to bring to their sides large groups of citizens. This required persuasion strategies that went beyond simple rhetorical skills. They had to maintain the illusion of the people's rule and at the same time either exercise personal political power as autocratic rulers or maintain privileged positions as members of an almost hereditary oligarchy. Such a discrepancy between the principle of equality and the factual rule of elites is not unknown as a structural problem in contemporary mass democracies. As the modern Greek philosopher Panajotis Kondylis has observed, the asymmetry between reality and expectation can be observed in the manner in which the elite presents itself to the 'ordinary person':

Populism needs to continually satisfy psychological needs as well, creating substitutes for equality where practically no equality exists. Such a substitute is provided for instance by the advanced abolishment of the borders between the private and the public, so that the 'ordinary people', but also the 'mature citizen', can be persuaded on the basis of what is told him by the mass media that this or that member of this or that elite generally behaves in a 'human' manner and is, generally, 'one of us'. The inherent populism of mass democracy makes it a principal duty of the members of the elite to display on every occasion how close they are to the ordinary people.

Hellenistic statesmen faced the challenge created by the asymmetry between expectation and reality by adopting staged and theatrical behaviour in their interaction with citizens: carefully composed texts, particular costumes, body language, facial expressions and control of the voice. Statues of statesmen show men with orderly draped cloaks, avoiding the display of luxury; the unmoved arms evoke self-control and reservation; when they

10. Statue of a Hellenistic statesman.   *11. Portrait of a Hellenistic statesman.*

are freed from the cloak's drapery and are projected forward, they indicate energy and strain (see Fig. 10). Contemporary portraits encapsulate in their facial expressions the vigour and the strenuousness with which the good citizen carried out toilsome civic duties (see Fig. 11). These images bring to mind the advice given by Quintilian to orators: they should demonstrate their exhaustion by letting their dress fall in careless disorder and their toga slip loose, by streaming with sweat and showing signs of fatigue, thus signalling that they had spared no strength for the interest of their clients. The similarity with an account from the congressional campaign of George Bush Senior in Houston in 1964 is striking: 'Over and over again, on every television screen in Houston George Bush was seen with his coat slung over his shoulders; his sleeves rolled up; walking the streets of his district; grinning, gripping, letting the voter know he cared. About what was never made clear.' By Hellenistic times political oratory had developed into a carefully staged dramatic performance through which the statesman controlled the emotions of the assembly. Taking lessons from actors, political orators learned the proper use of body language. When the author of *Rhetorica ad Herennium*, which is partly based on Hellenistic models, observes that 'good delivery ensures that what the orator is saying *seems* to come from his heart', the emphasis is on appearances (*videatur*), on the creation of an illusion.

One of the most effective ways of strengthening the power of the elite and making it acceptable was to keep visible their services and benefactions. With voluntary contributions, they displayed their willingness to spend part of their private property on the community. But this willingness was combined with the expectation that the community would accept their political leadership. The elite continually employed theatrical behaviour to control the emotions and thoughts of the people, to create the illusion that they were not distant from ordinary citizens. Already in the late fourth century BC Demetrios of Phaleron took great care with his make-up in order to appear merry and affable; centuries later the representations of virtuous citizens show them with facial expressions indicating exhaustion after their demanding efforts for public welfare. One is reminded of Fred Ebb's lyrics for *Chicago*:

> Give 'em the old razzle dazzle
> Razzle dazzle 'em
> Give 'em an act with lots of flash in it
> And the reaction will be passionate.
> [...]
> Razzle dazzle 'em,
> And they'll make you a star.

The Hellenistic star system: demagogues, tyrants, dynasts and heroes

Hellenistic political life, at least the political life that was exciting enough to leave its traces in the written sources, was dominated by stars. The conquests of Alexander had made clear that even the apparently impossible could be achieved through the passionate pursuit of a task (*pothos*), the zealous emulation of glorious men of the past (*zelos*) and, of course, fortune (*tyche*). Inherited family power was not negligible as an asset but one could do without it.

Personal rule did not need to be as extensive as that of one of the

Successors; it could be limited to a city or a region. Let us consider a few examples of men who rose to power exploiting military skills. In the late fourth century BC Agathokles (see pp. 49–50) rose to an ephemeral kingship in Sicily with a civic office as his starting point. In 319 BC, the Macedonian officer Alketas sought refuge in Termessos in Pisidia and, thanks to his military skills, achieved an extraordinary position of power. He recruited young men, organised raids and became popular because of his generous distribution of booty. Only the treacherous behaviour of the 'old men', who tried to seize Alketas and hand him over to Antigonos Monophthalmos, made Alketas commit suicide. Had he lived, he would have become one of those powerful men who controlled cities and are sometimes referred to in our sources as 'tyrants'. A certain Timarchos, tyrant of Miletos around 260 BC, was probably a commander of mercenaries or a high-ranking soldier who rose to autocratic power by exploiting his martial experience. Another way to achieve a small-scale autocratic rule was through royal support. For instance, from 317 to 307 BC the orator and philosopher Demetrios of Phaleron ruled Athens as a tyrant with the support of Kassandros. Telmessos in Lycia was ruled from around 250 BC and for about a century by dynasts related to Ptolemy I of Egypt.

From the Archaic period onwards, tyranny thrived in cities under two conditions: external rule and civil strife. Sikyon was for decades dominated by both civil strife and tyrants:

> The city of Sikyon ... became victim of civil strife and the ambition of demagogues, falling in a permanent state of illness and turmoil, changing one tyrant for another, until, after the murder of Kleon, Timokleides and Kleinias were elected magistrates, men of the highest repute and influence among the citizens. But no sooner did the government appear to be somewhat settled than Timokleides died, and Abantidas, son of Paseas, slew Kleinias attempting to make himself tyrant. Of Kleinias' friends and kinsmen he sent some to exile and killed others.

The killings and the succession of tyrants continued, until Kleinias' son Aratos put an end to that, returning from exile. Five hundred citizens also returned from exile, reclaiming property which the previous regime had confiscated and distributed among its followers. The tyrannies in the Peloponnese at the time of Aratos were established and overthrown after conflicts between members of the elite. The vague reference to demagogues indicates that tyrants sought and had the support of citizens, in addition to the support of mercenaries. It seems likely that they won the support of some citizens by promising them land that would be confiscated from their opponents.

Some statesmen owed their political leadership to the advice they gave, their military skills and their courage. They fought against tyrants and foreign enemies, protected their communities from taking the wrong side in military confrontations and served as envoys. When they met a heroic death in battle, their example inspired future generations. Eugnotos, commander of the Boiotian cavalry, illustrates such a case. Realising that the battle against Demetrios Poliorketes at Onchestos in 294 BC was lost, he committed suicide on the battlefield. His statue, next to the altar of Zeus in the marketplace, commemorated his heroic death and urged the young men: 'Thus in glory become fighters, thus become brave men, defending the city of your fathers!' Eugnotos' statue and the inscription became an exemplum for the youth. For generations after his death, the base of his statue was used to inscribe the names of conscripts who probably took their oath precisely in front of the altar of Zeus and Eugnotos' statue.

Usually men were placed above their fellow citizens during their lifetime through their undisputed leadership as commanders and advisers. During Alexander's reign, Lykourgos of Athens was such a leader. The scion of one of Athens' most prestigious families, a man of wealth and a prominent orator, he repeatedly occupied the office of the supervisor of financial administration and excelled as a proposer of decrees. He put the city's finances in order, launched an extensive building programme and reformed Athenian institutions. Due to his leadership, a whole period of Athenian history is called 'Lykourgan Athens'. Aratos and Philopoimen were the political and military leaders of the Achaean League for decades. Eurykleides and Mikion did the same in Athens in the late third century BC (see p. 138), and in the early first century BC Diodoros Pasparos was the leading man in Pergamon in the years following the end of the Attalid monarchy.

As a result of marriage and migration, the influence of a wealthy family could expand in more than one city and span several generations. A certain Chairemon in Nysa was one of the wealthy Greeks who took the Roman side during the War of Mithridates in 88 BC. His son Pythodoros moved to Tralleis and, with his enormous fortune, became one of the leading citizens. His daughter Pythodoris married into another wealthy family in Laodikeia and became queen of Pontos in 14 BC (see p. 298), and around 25 BC another member of the family, Chairemon, travelled to the senate in Rome and to the emperor in order to request help for the reconstruction of Tralleis after a devastating earthquake. Members of this family belonged to the elite of Tralleis and Nysa until the second century AD. After their death such men were often raised above all ordinary men: annual sacrifices were offered to them; gymnasia were named after them; their memory was kept alive.

The troubled years of the first century BC see the rise of a new type of political leader: the ambitious, often educated and rhetorically skilled man, who rose to power by allying himself with a Roman commander (see pp. 300–1). One such man was Nikias in Kos, a man of apparently humble origins. Allegedly, one of his sheep gave birth to a lion, thus predicting his future rule. The support of Mark Antony allowed him to establish an almost monarchical rule in Kos. His portrait decorated the coins of his city and dozens of altars were erected in private houses responding to an appeal – or ordinance – to pray for his well-being. The inscribed dedications are addressed 'to the ancestral gods for the salvation of Nikias, the son of the people, lover of the fatherland, a hero, a benefactor of the city'. The designation 'hero' shows that he had already been elevated above the rank of mortals. But after Antony's defeat his grave was desecrated and his corpse mutilated.

In many cases, rhetorical skills and demagogy proved to be important assets of 'tyrants'. Athenion in Athens had acquired his wealth as a teacher of oratory; as a demagogue and an advocate of King Mithridates VI in Athens, he established a rule described as 'tyranny', although it was concealed by the mantle of a public office (see p. 211). Another man of letters who supported Mithridates and held political power in his city, Adramyttion, is the philosopher Diodoros , who, serving in the office of general, ordered the massacre of the entire council.

The importance of persuasion strategies explains why we find a significant number of philosophers and teachers of oratory – such as Euthydemos and Hybreas in Mylasa (see p. 297) – among the powerful men of Hellenistic cities. At an undetermined date in Tarsos, the Epicurean philosopher Lysias, who had been elected priest of Heracles and served as the eponymous 'wreath-bearer', refused to lay down his wreath at the end of his annual term and 'became a king through his garment, putting on a purple tunic with white stripes, a splendid shawl, white shoes from Lakonia and a golden wreath'. Clothes make the man; a golden crown makes the king. But what made Lysias an autocratic ruler? We have no other information, but the dynast's philosophical background and, associated with this, his rhetorical skills suggest that we are dealing with a demagogue who must have exploited social tensions in order to establish his own rule. As a priest of Heracles, the patron god of the gymnasium, he may have been connected with the education of the ephebes, and his attire closely resembles that of the supervisor of the gymnasium. It is possible that he was supported by young men, often an important factor in civil wars.

Long biographical inscriptions narrate the deeds of heroic generals, wise advisers, generous benefactors and courageous envoys to Rome. The honorific statues of such protagonists decorated in unprecedented numbers the civic public space. But with the firm establishment of Imperial power under Augustus, one single protagonist was tolerated in the empire: the emperor.

7

ENTANGLEMENT

The Coming of Rome
(221–188 BC)

Symploke: the birth of global history

In 221 BC, the year in which new kings came to power in both the Antigonid and the Ptolemaic kingdoms, an event at a very distant place was certainly not noticed by any statesman in the Greek world. In Spain, an Iberian slave murdered the Carthaginian commander Hasdrubal and a twenty-six-year-old relative succeeded him as commander-in-chief in Spain: Hannibal, the son of Hamilcar Barca. Hannibal's father had commanded the Carthaginian army in the First Punic War, which ended with Roman victory in 241 BC. From his childhood Hannibal was a sworn enemy of Rome; as a youth he had seen his father's efforts to revive Carthaginian power in Spain (237–229 BC). Now he was given the opportunity to continue this work. His military operations in Spain from 221 to 219 BC were the overture that led to the invasion of Italy, the Second Punic War and an alliance with Macedonia in 215 BC.

'Does the flap of a butterfly's wings in Brazil set off a tornado in Texas?' was the title suggested to Edward Lorenz, the mathematician and pioneer of chaos theory, for his talk at the 139th meeting of the American

Association for the Advancement of Science in 1972. 'Did a slave in Spain ultimately cause the conquest of Greece by the Romans?' It is futile to look for butterfly effects in history. But the extent of the interdependence of events in different geographical areas is intrinsically connected with fundamental features of a historical period. It is not a coincidence that such an interdependence was observed for the first time by a historian in connection with events in and around 220 BC. The historian was Polybius, his observation concerns the interdependence of historical events in the entire Mediterranean from 220 BC onwards and the word he coined for this phenomenon is *symploke*: entanglement.

In the first book of his *Histories*, Polybius explains why he decided to start his narrative with events in 220 BC:

> Previously the events of the inhabited world had been, so to say, dispersed, since the individual actions were not held together by a unity of initiatives, results or location. But from this time on, history has been an organic whole, and the affairs of Italy and Libya have been entangled with those of Greece and Asia, all leading to one end.

In Greece, Asia Minor, the Near East and Egypt, regional entanglements had been a permanent phenomenon since the wars of the Successors. Major wars, such as the Chremonidean War (see pp. 65–7) and the War of Laodike (see pp. 78–80), had involved all great and most small powers. But Polybius was right in recognising the beginning of a period of an unprecedented entanglement of political and military events starting around 220 BC.

'Woman, fire and the sea': the war that brought the Romans to the Balkans (229 BC)

Ancient historians who narrated the beginnings of Roman expansion in the East had no difficulties identifying the guilty party: *cherchez la femme*. If we were to believe them, Rome's eastward expansion is a series of just wars that began and ended with campaigns provoked by the evil queens Teuta of Illyria and Cleopatra of Egypt. Male prejudice is to blame if women are more often mentioned by name by ancient authors for their notoriety than for their prudence. The moral of their stories is that female agency causes disaster. This stereotype has been immortalised in a verse by the Hellenistic comic poet Menander, 'woman, fire and the sea', the only ancient verse that has made its way to *Playboy*, as the title of a short story. But male prejudice and stereotypes are not the best tools of historical interpretation, and nor do we have to believe historians simply because they wrote in Greek or Latin.

Teuta comes into the picture when her husband Agron, the king of the Illyrian tribe of the Ardiaioi, died suddenly as a result of excesses while celebrating a victory in 231 BC. He left behind an infant son, Pinnes, from his first wife, Triteuta. Teuta ascended the throne on his behalf, ruling a people accustomed to making their living through raids, as did many other peoples in the Adriatic and the Aegean Sea.

> With a woman's natural shortness of view, she could see nothing but the recent success and had no eyes for what was going on elsewhere. So, in the first place she authorized privateers to pillage any ships they met, and next she collected a fleet and a force of troops as large as the former one and dispatched it, ordering the commanders to treat the entire seaboard as belonging to their enemies.

With a Greek man's perspective, this is how Polybius saw things seventy years later. The raiders reached the Ionian Sea and even conquered the important island of Korkyra (Corfu), which Teuta placed under the command of Demetrios, the ruler of the island of Pharos (Hvar). When the raids claimed victims among Roman and Italian merchant ships and threatened the safety of routes in the Adriatic Sea, the Roman senate decided to take action. Two Roman envoys met Teuta to demand reparations and termination of the raids. Allegedly, during that exchange Teuta claimed that sea raids were a legitimate means of acquiring property – a view that many maritime communities would have shared – and that she would not deprive her subjects of the profits from this activity. One of the Roman envoys responded that Rome would ensure that better customs were brought to Illyria. During its journey home, the Roman ship was attacked and one of the envoys was killed. Rome declared war in 229 BC.

It is unlikely that increased Illyrian piracy alone motivated the senate's decision to deploy more than 20,000 men and 200 ships to take possession of Korkyra and to cross over to Illyria. Raids by Illyrian ships were not new. The new factors in 229 BC that made all the difference were that now the interests of Rome extended to the Adriatic coast of Italy and that part of Sicily had become a Roman province in 241 BC. What ignited the conflict in 229 BC – and could not have kindled it before the mid-third century – was not a woman but the obligation of the Romans to protect an increased number of allies and dependent communities.

The First Illyrian War did not last long (229–228 BC). When the Roman fleet and army, under the command of both consuls, reached Korkyra, Demetrios of Pharos changed sides, gave his island to the Romans and served as their guide. Teuta retreated to the northern part of her kingdom, capitulated and then disappeared from the historical record. The Roman senate had done what was necessary: it had kept the allies' trust. It was satisfied with a peace treaty that obliged Teuta to pay tribute and retreat from most of Illyria; no more than two ships, unarmed, were permitted to sail beyond Lissos, the border of Illyria. Rome was not interested in the establishment of a protectorate in Illyria, the occupation of strategically important places or the conquest and annexation of territories. It was primarily interested in affirming its leadership by protecting the interests of its allies. By requiring Teuta to abandon her leadership of all Illyrian tribes, Rome sought to prevent the rise of a united Illyrian state. When this task was achieved, the Romans withdrew, leaving Demetrios of Pharos in control of a large part of Illyria. Yet the war had far-reaching consequences, since at that point Rome also concluded treaties of friendship with Teuta's earlier victims, Epidamnos, Korkyra and Apollonia. These agreements, harmless at first sight, could potentially oblige the Romans to take political and military action.

From trust and loyalty to expansion: Rome's first steps towards imperial rule

Generations of modern scholars have attempted to explain Roman expansion, continually modifying their interpretations. It is unlikely that this process of reinterpretation will ever be completed, since what determines a modern historian's perspective is more often his or her experience of imperialism – British, German, Soviet, American or whatever the future may bring – and, consequently, new theoretical models rather than new evidence.

For those who in antiquity believed in teleology, in a purposeful historical progression, Rome's expansion was a natural development. Humankind naturally strives towards ecumenical unity, under the guidance and rule of the best man or the best nation. An extreme expression of this teleology is voiced in the mid-first century AD by Pliny, who interpreted the Roman Empire as a commonwealth of nations. For him, Italy was chosen by the gods 'to join the scattered powers, mollify the customs, bring together the discordant and wild idioms of so many peoples by the shared use of one language for communication, to give humanity to mankind, and in short, to make all the peoples in the whole world have one single fatherland'. Some ancient authors formulated the question differently: why was Rome successful in the conquest of the world? The Greek historian Polybius attributed this success to the superiority of the Roman constitution, whereas the Roman historian Sallust ascribed it to the manly virtue (*virtus*) of the Romans. Such ideas appealed to historians in Nazi Germany, who, following Hitler's view that the proper understanding of Roman history is a good political teacher, ascribed Roman success to biological supremacy and a natural instinct to rule.

Historians with less rigorous ideological agendas than Pliny or Hitler realised that unsatisfactory answers are usually responses to the wrong questions. The question for them was neither one of teleology ('What purpose did the Roman expansion serve?') nor one of simple causality ('Why did the Romans decide to conquer the world?') but rather one of recognising dynamic processes and trying to understand the primary objectives of Roman policy in different phases of Roman expansion. Thus some historians favoured the idea of a 'defensive imperialism', according to which Rome's eastern policies from the Second Punic War to the abolishment of the Macedonian kingdom (216–167 BC) were determined by the wish of the Roman senate to avert real or imaginary dangers; others denied the existence of a plan and saw in the eastern expansion one of the greatest accidents of world history or the result of a chain of coincidences; still others denied Roman expansion the character of a homogeneous and continuous development, recognising instead a gradual shift from defensive policies to a strong interest in annexation and economic exploitation of regions east of the Adriatic. But no approach can really explain Roman expansion in the East if it views it as a phenomenon of Roman history and the result of Roman agency alone. Until the annexation of territories in Greece in 146 BC, for most Hellenistic states the Romans were primarily instruments in the pursuit of their own agendas. Roman expansion is an important episode of Hellenistic history as much as it is part of Roman history.

From the abolition of kingship in the late sixth century BC to the First Punic War (264–241 BC), the policy of the noble families that dominated the senate aimed at first establishing a leading position among the cities of Latium and then at expanding this hegemony to the rest of Italy. Roman expansion is a continuous process, from the first alliance of Rome with the neighbouring cities in Latium in 493 BC to the expansion to northern Italy from around 232 to 218 BC. If the measures that Rome took after a victorious war give a clue as to the policies of the nobility, Rome was not primarily interested in the conquest and annexation of territories, although this did happen when the enemy's territory was nearby. Rome's main concern was the recognition of its leadership in Italy and the creation of a network of allies that would support it in the event of war. Rome's relations to the defeated communities were determined by local peculiarities, specific challenges and potential advantages – political, military and economic; hence, they differed from case to case. In many cases, Rome allowed the defeated communities to exist as autonomous allies with different rights and obligations. Various types of allied, semi-autonomous and subordinate communities made up the Roman system of rule. Etruscan, Italian and Greek cities and tribes in central and southern Italy that had been recognised as allies of Rome, either peacefully on the basis of a treaty or after military defeat, retained their autonomy but were obliged to assist the Romans in their wars with troops under their own commanders. Other subordinate communities with a certain amount of autonomy contributed troops to Roman wars. Colonies – that is, settlements of Roman citizens in Italy and later in the provinces – were very important for the military control of Italy, and at the same time provided Rome a place to settle some of the poorest population of the city. This flexible system of rule guaranteed the unlimited military and political leadership of Rome in Italy, without imposing on Roman nobility the burdensome task of taking care of the internal affairs of allies and subordinate communities; it provided a large reservoir for the recruitment of reliable soldiers; and it gave the Romans possibilities for economic activities beyond their territory. The weaknesses of the system became evident later, from the mid-second century BC onwards: an army consisting of small landowners was forced to be away from home for long periods, as senatorial policies brought the Roman legions to ever more distant regions; and the traditional Roman institutions were no longer sufficient for the control of a large network of subordinate communities.

Roman leadership in this complex system of alliances and dependent communities was based on a value underlying Roman aristocratic society: *fides*, or trust. *Fides* obliged a hierarchically higher individual (*patronus*) to offer protection to a dependent individual (*cliens*), receiving in exchange the client's support in the competition among the noblemen for political power and social prestige. Transferred onto Roman foreign policy, the value of *fides* obligated Rome to intervene in favour of those who had accepted its leading position as allies or its rule as subordinate communities. Roman expansion had brought communities on the east coast of Italy and in Sicily into the Roman system of *fides*. This is why, in the late third century BC, Rome could not ignore Illyrian piracy as it had done in the past, when the victims of the Illyrian raiders were not yet part of its network.

Therefore, in a nutshell, the First Illyrian War presents several important features of Roman expansion: Rome had established a claim on leadership, with all the political, military and economic advantages that a hegemonic position brings; a local war compelled Rome to intervene in order to affirm this leadership; this intervention resulted in the further expansion of Rome's contacts and the introduction of new members into the Roman hegemonic network. New contacts meant further obligations and so new interventions were already to be expected. A serious problem confronting a new friend would oblige Rome to display leadership and to give protection; this intervention would in turn take Rome further east, to new contacts, new obligations and new interventions. This process seems familiar, because we have seen it unfold in the case of other hegemonies, most recently in the case of the USA.

Demetrios of Pharos and the Second Illyrian War (219–218 BC)

If the Romans did not already know that a traitor could not be trusted, they would learn that lesson soon enough. Demetrios of Pharos, whose treason had helped them win the war, established his own rule, strengthened his position by making alliances with Macedonia in 222 BC and the Illyrian tribe the Histri in 221 BC, and attempted to revive precisely the policy that had brought about Teuta's downfall. A new Illyrian fleet sailed beyond the city of Lissos in 220 BC in violation of the treaty with Rome, plundered the south of the Peloponnese and terrorised the islands of the Aegean.

In the 'Social War' in Greece (see p. 73), Demetrios chose to side with Macedonia. Presumably, his objective was to revive the power of Illyria. He must have determined that this was the opportune moment, since Rome's attention was diverted towards problems first with Celtic tribes in northern Italy (225–222 BC) and then with Carthage (219 BC), and that Macedonia was the right ally. Therefore, he expanded his power at the expense of Roman allies and rendered traffic in the Adriatic insecure. He did not expect Rome to deliver an immediate and vigorous response. But just before the beginning of the war with Hannibal, the Roman senate decided to secure the harbours in Illyria, and the Second Illyrian War broke out in 219 BC. What started as a raid had a domino effect due to the entanglements between different parties. The cunning strategy of the Roman consul Aemilius Paullus, who attacked Demetrios in the centre of his power, the island of Pharos, decided the war in favour of Rome in 218 BC. Demetrios fled to the Macedonian court and small independent tribal states emerged in Illyria.

While Aemilius Paullus was celebrating a triumph in Rome, Hannibal's army was heading to Italy. Having conquered Spain in 220–219 BC, Hannibal passed the Pyrenees and then the Alps in September 218, invading the valley of the River Po in October 218 with an infantry of 20,000 men and a cavalry of 6,000. Only two years later, Aemilius Paullus would perish on the battlefield at Cannae, Rome's power would be tottering, and Greek and Roman history would become entangled in ways that no one could have predicted at the end of the Second Illyrian War.

Clouds in the West (217–205 BC)

At about the same time as the Battle of Raphia triggered important developments in Egypt (see p. 83), another major military event occurred in a distant place with momentous long-term consequences. In late June 217 BC, a Roman army had taken position near Lake Trasimene to stop Hannibal's invasion of northern Italy. In a battle on the shore of the lake, the Romans suffered one of the most humiliating defeats in their history. The defeat and the tremendous casualties (allegedly 15,000 men) created panic in Rome, causing the senate to request the nomination of a *dictator* – a military commander with authority over all magistrates for a period of up to six months – an exceptional measure allowed only in times of despair.

As Hannibal was continuing his campaign in central and southern Italy, bringing some of Rome's allies onto his side, and the Romans were beginning to fear for the very existence of their city, Philip V took an unexpected decision: he invited the Greeks to a peace conference in Naupaktos in August 217 BC. His major opponent, Aetolia, was represented by its leading statesman, Agelaos. The historian Polybius presents him delivering a speech, in which the Aetolian leader urged Philip V to consider the wide-ranging consequences that the war between Hannibal and Rome would have:

> Whether the Carthaginians conquer the Romans, or the Romans the Carthaginians, it is in every way improbable that the victors will remain content with the empire of Sicily and Italy. They will move forward and will extend their forces and their designs farther than we could wish ... If you are eager for action, turn your eyes to the west, and let your thoughts dwell upon the wars in Italy. Await with coolness the turn of events there, and seize the opportunity to strike for universal dominion. Nor is the present crisis unfavorable for such a hope. But I entreat you to postpone your controversies and wars with the Greeks to a time of greater tranquility; and make it your supreme aim to retain the power of making peace or war with them at your own will. For if once you allow the clouds now gathering in the west to settle upon Greece, I fear exceedingly that the power of making peace or war, and in a word all these games which we are now playing against each other, will be so completely knocked out of the hands of us all, that we shall be praying heaven to grant us only this power of making war or peace with each other at our own will and pleasure, and of settling our own disputes.

Polybius wrote these lines half a century later, after the clouds that were then seen gathering in the west had already settled over Greece. Although Agelaos never said the exact words that Polybius puts in his mouth, his speech conveys thoughts that were current at that time. That the Greeks should unite in order to face external threats is an idea with a long tradition in Greek ideology: the Greeks – most of them – faced the Persian invasion under Xerxes in 480 BC; and Philip II and Alexander the Great led a Panhellenic alliance against the Achaemenid Empire. The leading Greek statesmen were aware of developments in Italy. Agelaos' counsel to Philip, to postpone his wars against the Greeks, corresponds to the opportunist policies of that period and to Philip's notorious cunning. The hope of expanding one's power was inherent in Hellenistic kingship; and Agelaos' reference to the imperialistic drive, which compels the victor in a conflict to attempt further expansion, is a notion that can be traced in Greek literature back to Herodotus.

The speech may be fictitious but the views that it expresses are not necessarily anachronistic. What is entirely anachronistic, however, is the prediction that the Greeks might be deprived of their freedom to make peace and war. No one could predict that in 217 BC. Likewise, no one could foresee the consequences of Philip's decision to agree to a peace in Greece and then, two years later, to ally himself with Hannibal.

Did Philip terminate the 'Social War' in Greece in order to attack the weakened Romans and achieve world domination? Although the timing of his decision, only a few weeks after Rome's devastating defeat, speaks in favour of such an interpretation, other factors may have forced the king's hand. It is likely that Philip had to defend his kingdom from one of the common attacks of barbarian tribes and to re-establish his influence in Illyria. But regardless of his original motives in negotiating a peace in Greece, it is significant that Philip chose a confrontation with Rome. This decision alienated him from his major adviser, Aratos. The king ordered the construction of 100 *lemboi*, small fast ships suitable for the transport of troops and sudden attacks but not for sea battles. These *lemboi* were certainly not the means to acquire world dominion but were ideal for the establishment of control on the east coast of the Adriatic Sea and its islands. When a Roman fleet of ten ships arrived in the Ionian Sea to offer support to the Roman friends (Apollonia, Epidamnos and Korkyra), Philip immediately abandoned his operations. He was neither prepared for nor expecting a major war. In the initial phase of their confrontation, both Rome and Philip were cautious. The Romans could not abandon their allies in the Adriatic Sea but nor could they become engaged on a second major front; Philip's priority was to secure his realm.

The great entanglement: the First Macedonian War (215–204 BC)

Things changed dramatically a year later. In August 216 BC, the Romans suffered yet another devastating defeat, this time at Cannae. According to Polybius, almost the entire Roman army that had marched against Hannibal (90,000 men) was annihilated, with 70,000 killed and 10,000 captured. The numbers are exaggerated, but they do indicate the enormity of the loss and its impact. Similarly exaggerated was the news that reached Rome: two consular armies with their commanders were entirely lost. The impact on the population was tremendous. According to modern estimates, in the first years of the war Rome had lost one-fifth of male citizens over seventeen years of age. And yet, surprisingly, only a few of Rome's allies decided to defect, among them Syracuse, the greatest Greek colony in the West.

It was at this critical moment that Philip V signed a treaty of alliance with Hannibal in 215 BC, unintentionally making future Greek history a chapter of Rome's expansion. A Greek translation of the treaty has been preserved in Polybius' *Histories*. The two parties swore alliance and mutual protection against their enemies, but the scope of the treaty in case of a victory over Rome was very limited. The relevant passage, in which Hannibal formulates the obligations and expected gains of his ally, is revealing:

> As soon as the gods have given us the victory in the war against the Romans and their allies, if the Romans ask us to come to terms of peace, we will make such a peace as will comprise you too, and on the following conditions: that the Romans may never make war upon you; that the Romans shall no longer be masters of Korkyra, Apollonia, Epidamnos, Pharos, Dimale, Parthini, or Antitania; and that they shall return to Demetrios of Pharos all his friends who are in the dominions of Rome.

Philip wanted the Romans expelled from any place on the east side of the Adriatic Sea. His focus was on Greece, where he continually intervened in the political affairs of Greek cities. Philip had no ambitions to expand his power in Italy, nor had Hannibal any plans to annihilate Rome. Hannibal never requested troops in his war in Italy; he was content to know that the Romans would have a second front in Illyria. But although limited in scope, this treaty had tremendous consequences. Aratos, the senior statesman of the Achaean League, repeatedly opposed Philip's actions but died after a long illness in 214 BC, allegedly slowly poisoned by the king, who also had a love affair with Aratos' daughter-in-law.

On his way back to Macedonia, the Athenian envoy was captured by the Romans. When the Romans became aware of the agreement, they decided to face the new front in the East by sending a fleet under the pro-praetor Marcus Valerius Laevinus. Illyria was the main battlefield in this First Macedonian War, which lasted from 214 to 205 BC. Philip's greatest success was the capture of the important harbour of Lissos in 212 BC, which gave him access to the Adriatic and control of the adjacent territories. In Italy, things were not developing well for Hannibal. His hopes that Rome's allies would take his side were shattered. Most of the allies remained loyal to Rome, and those who did not were captured by the Romans.

The siege of Syracuse in 214 BC was one of the most dramatic episodes of the Second Punic War, confronting a great strategist, Marcus Claudius Marcellus, with a great mathematician, Archimedes. When Marcellus started the siege by erecting a huge siege engine on a platform, created by fastening eight galleys together, Archimedes invented technological devices that made the life of the besieger difficult. All sorts of missiles and stones were thrown with incredible speed upon the Romans; their ships were destroyed by beams suddenly projected from the walls; iron claws seized their ships at the prow, lifted them up into the air and then let them fall. If Marcellus ultimately managed to capture the city, it was because during some negotiations he noticed a tower which was not well guarded, estimated its height, had scaling ladders prepared and attacked while the Syracusans were celebrating a festival. Archimedes was killed during the tumult. He was approached by a Roman soldier while he was absorbed by a geometry problem, having drawn shapes on the sand. 'Don't disturb my circles' were his famous last words. But more than geometrical designs were at stake during this war.

The Romans needed allies in Greece. Naturally, their potential allies were their enemy's enemies, the Aetolians, who were observing with anxiety Philip's growing power. In the autumn of 212 BC, Rome and the Aetolians made an alliance, whose text is preserved in Livy's histories and in part in an inscription. As in the treaty between Hannibal and Philip, the clause concerning the time after the war is revealing. All areas con-quered north of Aetolia were to be incorporated into the Aetolian state, while the captives and the movables would be Roman booty; cities that capitulated would become members of the Aetolian League, keeping their autonomy. Rome was not declaring any interest in territorial expansion. But two clauses that were at first sight less significant had unforeseen repercussions. First, the treaty forbade the allies to conclude a separate peace treaty. The Aetolians did precisely this in 206 BC; by violating the treaty, they freed the Romans from any obligation towards them. And second, the treaty allowed further states to join the alliance, thus facilitating Rome's contacts in Greece and beyond.

That the kingdom of Pergamon joined the alliance had long-term consequences. Pergamon had established itself as a regional power in north-west Asia Minor under the dynasts Philetairos (281–263 BC) and Eumenes I (263–241 BC). In 238 BC, the new ruler, Attalos I (241–197 BC), won an important victory against the Galatians, who had been plundering Asia Minor for three decades. His victory also brought territorial gains in Asia Minor at the expense of the Seleucid kingdom. Attalos' greatest enemy was his neighbour Prusias I, king of Bithynia (c. 228–182 BC), Philip's ally. This left Attalos with no other choice but to ally himself with Philip's enemies. By joining the alliance of Rome and Aetolia, Attalos for the first time made the Pergamene kingdom a political factor in Europe and established a connection between Rome and Asia Minor. His decision resulted in a major war, in which almost all states in Greece and two kingdoms in Asia Minor were involved.

The diplomatic relations between Rome and Greek states reveal an important feature of the political history in this period: the fragmentation of the Greek world into many competing states that concluded alliances with only one criterion – their own security – and broke them whenever a better opportunity emerged. In the interstate relations of a world in which a state had only enemies, the foes of a foe were friends, as long as they served a state's offensive or defensive objectives. In the First Macedonian War, the Achaean League supported Philip V against Rome, since their opponents in the Peloponnese (Sparta, Messene and Elis) were Philip's enemies. The Aetolians supported the Romans, because they were the enemies of their competitor for power in mainland Greece. Attalos I took the side of the Aetolians, because his adversary in Asia Minor, the kingdom of Bithynia, was an ally of Philip. Any small change in this fragile system of alliances had wide-ranging consequences.

Although Philip had to face a large coalition on different fronts in central Greece and the Peloponnese, he stood his ground, and in 207 BC he forced Attalos I of Pergamon to abandon the campaign and return to Pergamon. Having lost an ally and receiving no significant help from Rome, the Aetolians were compelled in 206 BC to conclude a separate peace treaty with Philip, thus violating their own treaty with Rome. If only they had waited! The Romans also signed a peace treaty with Philip a year later – the Peace of Phoinike of 205 BC – so as not to be distracted in the final stages of their war against Hannibal, which ended with the Battle of Zama and Carthage's defeat in 202 BC. The Peace of Phoinike acknowledged the status quo before the start of the war, thus confirming Rome's position as a protector of small independent cities in the Ionian Sea, Epirus and Illyria. Philip V had failed to remove the Romans from the Balkans.

Deprived of Aratos' leadership in 214 BC and distracted by the perennial Peloponnesian problems, the Achaean League did not play any important part in this war. It is worth briefly looking at the war that took place parallel to the First Macedonian War in the Peloponnese; it is just one of many regional conflicts of this scale in Greece and Asia Minor in these years. Three major causes of conflict defined regional history in the Peloponnese: territorial disputes, especially that between Megalopolis, a member of the Achaean League, and Messene; the efforts of Sparta to regain the influence and territories that it had lost after Kleomenes' defeat at Sellasia (see p. 72); and the Achaean League's conflicts with the cities and federations that defied its hegemonic position, especially Sparta, Elis and Messene. In the person of Philopoimen, a great military commander who was for the first time elected general of the Achaeans in 209 BC, the League again found a strong leader. After reorganising the federal army, Philipoimen turned to the problems caused by revived Spartan ambitions. Sparta was traditionally ruled by two kings, descended from two royal houses. Around 209 BC one of the two kings was a child by the name of Pelops. This name probably alluded to hegemonic ambitions. Pelops is the name of the mythical hero after whom the Peloponnese (the island of Pelops) was named. No individual is known to have had this name before, so this seems to express ambitions for regional power. But whatever ambitions were associated with the child, they were not to be fulfilled. Under unclear circumstances, a certain Machanidas, a man of obscure origins and possibly a mercenary, became regent and usurped the rule. As an Aetolian ally, he raided the Peloponnese as far as Olympia, until Philopoimen killed him with his own hands in a battle in Mantineia in 207 BC. Machanidas was succeeded as regent by another adventurer of obscure origin, Nabis, who continued this expansionist policy, defying the Achaean League, until he was defeated by Philopoimen in a battle at Tegea in 201 BC and was forced to look for a new opportunity. 'The best thing of all is that the Greeks should not go to war with each other at all': Agelaos' advice was not followed.

Now that Philip V had for the first time brought a Greek kingdom into a war with Rome, the entanglement of the fortunes of the western and eastern Mediterranean was complete. Only the Greeks of the north shore of the Black Sea, distracted by far more imminent threats from the neighbouring barbarian tribes, may have failed to notice 'the clouds gathering in the west' and settling over Greece. From now onwards, every contact between a Greek community and Rome had an impact not only on that community, but on all cities, federations and kingdoms with which that community might have relations. The Mediterranean world looked like something from the second act of Rossini's *La Cenerentola*.

Questo è un nodo avviluppato,
Questo è un gruppo rintrecciato.
Chi sviluppa più inviluppa,
*Chi più sgruppa, più raggruppa.**

The Egyptian crisis and an opportunistic alliance (204–201 BC)

The Peace of Phoinike coincided with unexpected developments in the Ptolemaic kingdom that presented Philip V and Antiochos III with an opportunity for expansion that they could only have dreamed of. When Ptolemy IV died in 205 BC, he left on the throne of Egypt a child, his four-year-old son Ptolemy V. The courtier Agathokles, whose sister was the late king's mistress, seized this opportunity, murdered Queen Arsinoe III and became the child's guardian. The southern part of the kingdom, where a native revolt had started around 206 BC, was from 205 BC on under the control of a local pharaoh, Haronnophris. And as Agathokles' abuse

---

* 'This is an enmeshed knot, this is a tangled web. When one attempts to unravel it, he tangles it all the more; if one tries to unpick it, he pulls it tighter still', Jacopo Ferretti, libretto of G. Rossini's *La Cenerentola*, Act 2, Scene 8.

of power became noticeable, the indignation of the Alexandrian population against the king's guardian grew. The crisis in the Ptolemaic kingdom could not be concealed from the traditional competitors of the Ptolemies, the Antigonids and the Seleucids.

The Peace of Phoinike allowed Philip to turn his attention, once again, to the East. It is conceivable that he ended his war with Rome precisely in order to pursue plans of expansion beyond the Aegean Sea. The Antigonids had always been interested in dominating in the Aegean; neither Philip nor his predecessor had forgotten that the founders of their dynasty had once ruled parts of Asia Minor. Only two decades earlier, in 228 BC, Antigonos Doson had attempted to occupy parts of Caria. It was now Philip's turn to pursue similar plans. His natural opponent in the southern Aegean was the island of Rhodes, a naval power with strong commercial and military interests. In order to stop its rising influence, Philip V used his authority in Crete – since 217/216 BC he had been the leader of an alliance of Cretan cities. Upon his instigation, Cretan ships raided Rhodes, other islands of the southern Aegean and coastal cities in Asia Minor. This so-called First Cretan War (c. 206–201 BC) had no lasting results for Philip. On the contrary, it alienated many Greek communities from the king and increased the prestige of the Rhodians as defenders of the safety of the seas. By 201 BC the Rhodians had undermined the Cretan alliance by winning allies on Crete, and even established a garrison in the east of the island.

While Philip failed to win control in the southern Aegean, he was successful in his enterprises in an area of strategic importance: Thrace, at the entrance of the Hellespont, a region that controls the passage both from the Mediterranean to the Black Sea and from Europe to Asia (see Map 5). Parts of European Thrace were still under Ptolemaic control; on the Asian side of the straits, the kingdoms of Pergamon under Attalos I and Bithynia under Philip's brother-in-law Prusias I were involved in an endemic territorial conflict; and a series of Greek cities with strategic positions for communications between the continents, such as Byzantion, Abydos and Kios, were allied with the Aetolian League. It is here that Philip had his greatest success. He captured Kios and Myrleia and gave them to Prusias, asking the Bithynian king in return to expand at the expense of Pergamon. The next victims were two further Aetolian allies, Lysimacheia and Chalkedon, as well as the island of Thasos.

For Antiochos III the developments in Egypt were an invitation to act and to avenge the defeat at Raphia. In the years after that battle, he had spent all his energy on recovering the lost parts of his empire. First, he subdued a revolt of his cousin Achaios, who had declared himself king in Asia Minor (216–214 BC). In the following campaigns, which lasted until 209 BC, Antiochos regained the northern and eastern provinces that had seceded under governors and local rulers. Xerxes, the ruler of Armenia, recognised Antiochos as overlord, Parthia was reconquered and Euthydemos, the Greek king of Bactria, was defeated but recognised as a king. Then Antiochos proceeded to his greatest enterprise, a campaign into India, modelled on Alexander's campaign. Crossing the Hindu Kush in 207 BC, he reached the Indian kingdom of Sophagasenos (Subhash-sena). This campaign did not bring him permanent territorial gains in Afghanistan and India, but it did bring him treasures, 150 war elephants and prestige. When he returned to Syria in 205/204 BC, having restored the empire that was once ruled by Seleukos I, he was known as Antiochos Megas (the Great).

It might have been expected that Philip V and Antiochos III, two powerful and ambitious kings, would fight against one another for the occupation and control of Ptolemaic territories, now that the Ptolemaic kingdom faced a crisis. Instead, they decided to cooperate, in order to take as much of the Ptolemaic realm as they could. In the winter of 203/202 BC, they reached an agreement to divide the Ptolemaic Empire between them. Antiochos was to receive Cyprus, the Ptolemaic possessions in south Asia Minor (Lycia and Cilicia) and Koile Syria; Philip would gain the northern possessions of the Ptolemies in Thrace, the Thracian Chersonesos (at the entrance of the Hellespont) and the islands of the Cyclades. No one expected that this (secret) treaty, concerning operations in areas where the Roman had no interests whatsoever, would soon lead to new wars with Rome.

A turning point of Roman imperialism? The Second Macedonian War (200–197 BC)

Philip and Antiochos started their operations in 202 BC, but Philip's advancement had a domino effect with unforeseen consequences. Philip's operations in Thrace and in parts of Asia Minor, where he devastated the territory of Pergamon in 201 BC and took over territories in Ionia and

Caria, did not threaten Rome. But they directly threatened Pergamon, encroached upon Rhodes and alarmed the free Greek cities. The Rhodians and King Attalos I, supported by Athens, decided to appeal to Rome. Their envoys appeared in front of the senate in the summer of 201 BC, informed the Romans about the agreement between Antiochos and Philip, and requested Roman help against Philip's expansion. Rome had only recently come out of her long war with Carthage; it was a victorious war, but it had caused the loss of many men, the neglect of agricultural activities and high war expenses. The senators had, of course, not forgotten that Philip had allied himself with their enemy precisely when they were facing the most severe threat. But their response was not and could not be a declaration of war – not yet. Instead, they dispatched an embassy consisting of three senators, who presented Philip with an ultimatum. Rome forbade Philip to launch war against Greek communities and recommended international arbitration for the resolution of conflicts, especially that between Macedonia and Pergamon. At that moment, Philip was besieging the city of Abydos in north-west Asia Minor. He initially ignored and then rejected the ultimatum.

In Rome, the consul P. Sulpicius Galba, to whom Macedonia had been assigned as his area of political responsibility, summoned the popular assembly and, supported by the senatorial elite, presented a motion according to which war should be declared against King Philip and the Macedonians because of acts of injustice and attacks against allies of the Roman people. This motion was rejected, reportedly because the Romans were tired of the dangers and pains of war. It was only during a second meeting that the consul succeeded in convincing the assembly to declare war.

This decision, which led to the Second Macedonian War (200–197 BC), is regarded as a turning point in the political history of the entire Mediterranean. Unlike their earlier military conflicts in Greece, this time the casus belli for the Romans was not a direct threat to them. Philip's operations in Thrace and Asia Minor had no impact on their interests and the interests of their allies in Italy. In addition, the treaty between Philip and Antiochos concerned the fate of regions far away from Rome and Italy and its adjacent zones of interest. These factors distinguished this decision from the earlier interventions of Rome on the east coast of the Adriatic Sea. Neither Rhodes nor Athens was an ally of Rome. Only Attalos I, who had been an ally of the Romans during the First Macedonian War and probably remained an ally after the Peace of Phoinike, might have had a plausible justification to request military support, although at the moment of the declaration of war he was no longer under attack by Philip.

So, is the year 200 BC the beginning of a new, offensive, imperialistic Roman policy in the East? For Theodor Mommsen, the 1902 Nobel Laureate in Literature for his Roman history, the Romans needed to fight this war for their own safety. Mommsen wrote at a time when statesmen were as sure as George W. Bush was a century later that there was such a thing as an unreservedly just war. Today, in order to understand a decision, we are inclined to take into consideration the impact of the emotions, mentality and values of the people who made them. The Romans and their leaders certainly observed with suspicion and fear the rise of a great power in the East only a few years after Carthage had been subdued in the West; they were indignant at Philip's arrogant rejection of the ultimatum; they wished to take revenge against the man who had allied himself with Hannibal and whom the Peace of Phoinike had left unpunished. Also, the social values with which the Romans had been raised had an impact on that decision, especially the value of *fides*, which the Romans applied in their international relations (see p. 154). Denying support to allies would violate the relationship of *fides* and directly undermine Rome's claim to a position of leadership.

But it is unlikely that the Roman statesmen who proposed the declaration of war realised the mid- or long-term consequences of an involvement in Macedonia and Asia Minor – although Rome's involvement in Spain might have served as an instructive parallel. Both the initially negative response of the assembly and the persistence of the consul, who would not take no for an answer, clearly show that in 200 BC Roman positions concerning leadership and expansion were still unsettled. The decision of the Roman assembly to ultimately choose war over inertia determined the route of history in the eastern Mediterranean and the choices of the Romans in their future foreign relations. In the words of Cicero, writing in the final phase of the Roman expansion, the Romans made wars *aut pro sociis aut de imperio* (either for the sake of their allies or for hegemony). As the number of allies and the position of hegemony continually grew, the choices of the Romans to ignore invitations to act diminished.

In the Second Macedonian War, Rome could count on the support of all the Greek states that were alarmed by Philip's expansion in various fronts in Greece and Asia Minor. The Aetolians, traditional opponents of

Macedonia, joined Pergamon, Rhodes and Athens. In the first years of the confrontation (200–198 BC), Philip successfully faced this large coalition in a war that was fought with little enthusiasm. The Achaean League did not participate at the beginning, as it was engaged in a war against Sparta's monarch, Nabis (see p. 162); the Spartan ruler offered Philip his support in exchange for the important city of Argos, which Nabis occupied in 199 BC. Things changed in 198 BC, when Titus Quinctius Flamininus, a young general born around 229 BC, with a strong admiration of Greek culture and a deep understanding of the values of the Greek communities, was appointed commander of the Roman troops. Under Flamininus' command, the war's objective was no longer to prevent Philip from attacking the Greeks but to force him to withdraw his garrisons from the Greek cities. Flamininus adopted the slogan of freedom that had already often been used in the past by Hellenistic kings against their opponents. The Greeks were eager to follow Flamininus' call for a war for freedom. At his side in his campaign to win over the Greeks he had the king of Pergamon, Attalos I. But while Attalos was holding an oration in favour of Rome in Boiotia, he suffered a stroke and had to be brought back to Pergamon.

Flamininus forced Philip to retreat to Thessaly, and his campaign received fresh impetus when many members of the Achaean League abandoned their pro-Macedonian or neutral stance and joined the Romans. Then Nabis betrayed Philip, hoping to be able to keep Argos in the event of a Roman victory. While Philip was willing to negotiate a peace, abandoning his conquests in Thrace and Asia Minor, Flamininus was not interested in a peace treaty, wishing his command to be prolonged. He demanded that Philip withdraw from Greece and limit himself to Macedonia and Thessaly: that is, to the borders that the Macedonian kingdom had before the Battle of Chaironeia in 338 BC. This was clearly unacceptable for the Antigonid king. While the negotiations were slowly proceeding, Flamininus received the desired prolongation of his command and resumed war. Abandoned by his allies, except for Akarnania, Philip was finally defeated in Thessaly. The decisive battle took place in the hills of Kynos Kephalai in June 197 BC, and was a triumph of Roman military tactics over the heavy Macedonian phalanx, which was unable to be fully deployed on the hilly ground and was surrounded by the flexible Roman maniples. Suffering great losses and fleeing from the battlefield, Philip was forced to accept the Roman terms for peace.

Philip agreed to evacuate all of Greece, in addition to his conquests in

Asia Minor, Thrace and the northern Aegean (Lemnos and Thasos). Thessaly, which since the time of Philip II had been part of the Macedonian kingdom, was lost, including one of the Macedonian capitals, the city of Demetrias, where Demetrios Poliorketes, Philip's great-grandfather, was buried. Without his traditional strongholds, Chalkis and Corinth, Philip lost all influence in Greece. In addition, parts of Macedonia in the west (Orestis) and the north became autonomous. Philip was forced to surrender his navy, except for five ships, pay a war indemnity of 1,000 talents and send his younger son, Demetrios, to Rome as a hostage. The conditions of peace were humiliating. Although the kingdom of Macedonia was preserved as a state, it was brought to its knees as a hegemonic power. Attalos I died in Pergamon at about this time, probably never learning of his foes' defeat.

Freedom: an announcement with consequences (196 BC)

Flamininus knew how to stage the announcement of the victory to a Greek audience. Every second year all the Greeks celebrated a great festival with athletic and musical games at Isthmia, near Corinth. The place had a manifold symbolical and ideological significance. It was in Isthmia that the first Hellenic alliance was established during the Persian Wars and it was here that later Hellenic alliances were renewed. Poseidon, in whose honour the festival was held, was the patron of Demetrios Poliorketes, and the nearby citadel of Acrocorinth had been the most important Antigonid garrison in Greece. Flamininus chose the celebration of this festival to announce to the gathered Panhellenes their liberation. In the ensuing tumult, many in the audience were not sure about what had been announced. The herald was called again into the stadium to repeat it. It is said that the shouts of approval were so loud that birds were seen falling from the sky. The Thessalians established a festival of freedom (Eleutheria) to celebrate their liberation and the re-establishment of their federal state.

With the proclamation of freedom, a Roman general did what Hellenistic kings had done in the past: he appeared as saviour and liberator. Flamininus received divine honours in Chalkis, like Hellenistic kings before him. Rome had become a power whose presence was strongly felt from the east coast of the Adriatic Sea to Asia Minor, assuming a role that was previously held by Hellenistic kings. It is therefore not surprising that Rome was honoured by the Greek communities in exactly the same manner as Hellenistic kings had been honoured in the past: as a goddess. Her name was Thea Rhome (the goddess Rome), and since the word *rhome* means 'might', the Greeks were worshipping at the same time a personification of might and a personification of the greatest military power of their times. The award of divine honours to Rome started immediately after the declaration of freedom. The federation of Euboian cities established in 196 BC the festival Rhomaia – that is, the festival of the goddess Rome – and evidence for Rome's worship appears in Asia Minor from 189 BC onwards. The worship of the entire Roman people and the Roman senate followed soon after.

Freedom was declared. But what did this mean? Flamininus meant something very precise: freedom from Macedonian garrisons. But some Greeks would give this word a more comprehensive meaning: freedom from any power that might limit their autonomy, freedom to fight wars and make peace as they pleased. With such an interpretation of freedom, new conflicts were inevitable.

Rome had now stepped into a field of conflicting interests that its senatorial leadership could not ignore. The traditional role played by Hellenistic kings, as arbitrators in territorial conflicts and supporters in time of need, was now a role that the Greek states expected Rome to play. Rome was viewed as responsible for the safety of Greece from barbaric invasions in the north – for this reason, the preservation of the Macedonian kingdom was important to the Romans – but also as responsible for the resolution of all small and large conflicts in Greece.

To play this role, the Romans had to become Greeks. They were admitted to compete in various Panhellenic festivals and legends that documented their kinship with the Greeks were remembered or invented. Rome seemed to have entered the Hellenistic world not like an external conqueror but as a great Hellenistic power, with which many Greek states concluded treaties of alliance, thus creating more responsibilities for the Romans and drawing them deeper into the political complexities of the Hellenistic East.

A fatal confrontation: Antiochos III and Rome (196–189 BC)

The dynamics of this development became apparent immediately after the declaration of freedom. With one ambitious king subdued, Rome was now confronted with another: Antiochos III. Conveniently forgetting his secret agreement with Philip and undisturbed by Pergamon, Rhodes and Rome, who were engaged in the Second Macedonian War, he expanded at the cost of the Ptolemaic kingdom. In Alexandria, the courtier Agathokles, who ruled as the guardian of the infant king Ptolemy V, was killed during an uprising of the population in 202 BC. The paralysis of the central authority and a revolt in south Egypt allowed Antiochos to complete the reconquest of Koile Syria in 198 BC. He could then continue his expansion in Asia Minor, threatening Pergamon. When, in the spring of 196 BC, Flamininus was announcing the peace treaty with Philip in Isthmia, Antiochos III and his troops were already on European soil, in Thrace. His envoys, who were present at the festival, were summoned by Flamininus, who presented demands that derived from the declaration of freedom. Antiochos should respect the freedom of the free cities of Asia Minor and evacuate the cities that he had taken from Philip and the Ptolemies. He was not to cross the Hellespont with his army. These demands did not immediately lead to war; the Romans needed a break. In a conference at Lysimacheia, in Thrace in early 195 BC, when the Romans repeated their demands and interpreted Antiochos' presence in Europe as part of a plan to attack Rome, the king publicly presented his standpoint:

> The king said that he could not understand on what grounds the Romans were arguing with him over the cities in Asia; the Romans had less right to do this than anyone else. He next asked them not to meddle at all in the affairs of Asia; he himself had not interfered in any way in Italian affairs. He said that he had crossed into Europe with his army to recover possession of the Chersonese and the cities of Thrace. Sovereignty over those parts belonged to him more than to any other. At first Lysimachos held power over this area, but when Seleukos waged war on him and was victorious [281 BC], the whole kingdom of Lysimachos fell to Seleukos as the spoils of war … As for the autonomous cities of Asia they must obtain their freedom not from an injunction of Rome but through an act of favor on his part.

From his early youth, Antiochos had pursued one plan: to restore the empire of his dynasty's founder. He had done this in the eastern satrapies, Syria, Palestine and Asia Minor. Since Seleukos I had defeated Lysimachos, the Seleucids in Antiochos' view had a legitimate claim to Thrace. The Romans and Antiochos agreed on only one point: Asia was not part of the Roman zone of interests. But as regards Europe, the claim of the Romans that Antiochos' presence was a threat is not as absurd as it appears. Only twenty-three years earlier, Hannibal had started his campaign against Rome from a far more distance place than Thrace. And Hannibal, Rome's defeated enemy, was himself in Antiochos' court, advising the king to bring the war to Italy. Besides, Greece now was part of the Roman zone of interest and Rome could not ignore Antiochos' expansion. In this conference, two worlds collided: the old world of a king who was called 'the Great' and whose claims were rooted in the Wars of the Successors and the new world in which Rome's obligations towards her allies had made her an important factor of Greek politics. We cannot blame Antiochos for his failure to understand how much had changed with Rome's victory.

In the following years, Antiochos III proceeded with dynastic marriages that strengthened his position. He had already appointed his eldest son, Antiochos, as co-ruler in 196 BC, marrying him to his sister Laodike – such sibling marriages were common in Egypt, but this was the first instance of the practice in the Seleucid kingdom. When this younger Antiochos died in 193 BC, Laodike married the next in line of succession, Seleukos, who was now appointed co-regent. Antiochos' daughter Antiochis married the king of Kappadokia, Ariarathes IV, in 194 BC, thus assuring an alliance in eastern Anatolia; and in 193 BC, Antiochos settled his conflict with Egypt by marrying his daughter, Cleopatra I Syra, to Ptolemy V – she was the first of the Egyptian queens with this name.

Two other powers turned the cold war between Antiochos and Rome into a real war: the Aetolians, who were disappointed because they had gained nothing from Macedonia's defeat in the Second Macedonian War, although they had assisted the Romans; and the new king of Pergamon, Eumenes II, who saw most of the possessions that his father, Attalos I, had acquired being lost to Antiochos. For different reasons, both the Aetolians and Eumenes were keen on a war between Rome and Antiochos. The Aetolians made the decisive move in 192 BC, when they invited the Seleucid king to come to Greece in order to arbitrate between Aetolia and Rome. Antiochos arrived in October 192 in Demetrias with a very small army of 10,000 infantry, 500 cavalrymen and six war elephants. His hope that all of Greece would stand behind him was immediately dashed. Even Philip V took the Roman side, thus punishing his old foe, the Aetolians, and his disloyal partner Antiochos. The Romans could not remain inactive when Antiochos arrived in Greece and the war started. Unable to hold his position in Greece, Antiochos returned to Asia Minor in the spring of 190 BC. The newly elected consul Lucius Cornelius Scipio, accompanied by his brother Scipio Africanus, the man who had defeated Hannibal, won an important victory in a battle near Magnesia ad Sipylum in 190 BC. Even if Livy gives exaggerated numbers for the losses of the two armies – 400 Romans and 50,000 Seleucid soldiers – the outcome of the battle was a disaster for Antiochos and a turning point in the history of the Seleucid Empire. Soon after, in 189 BC, the Aetolians were also forced to seek a peace agreement.

The Peace of Apameia: a turning point in the history of the Greek East (188 BC)

The arrangements imposed by the Romans after the end of the war against Antiochos are important milestones in the development of Roman expansion and international law. The Aetolians were forced to accept the Roman hegemony (*imperium maiestatemque populi Romani*) and to have the same friends and enemies as the Romans – in other words, to make their foreign policy subject to Rome's wishes. This arrangement differed from the earlier Roman practice of concluding treaties of friendship (*amicitia*) or alliances for specific wars. The peace arrangement with Antiochos was concluded in 188 BC in Apameia.

Antiochos lost all his possessions in Asia Minor (see Map 5) north of Mount Taurus and the River Kalykadnos, amounting to nearly one-third of his territory. His garrisons withdrew from the cities and his war elephants were given to Rome, along with hostages. Antiochos agreed to pay an enormous war indemnity of 15,000 talents – this amount roughly corresponds to the annual salary of 300,000 mercenaries. His ships were not allowed to sail north of Kalykadnos. On the western borders of his kingdom, the Romans permitted him to fight only defensive wars. In Asia Minor some cities were declared free and a few garrison sites took advantage of the power vacuum to elevate themselves to the status of *poleis*. The Romans rewarded their allies with huge territorial grants. Rhodes, which already had possessions on the coast of Asia Minor, received Lycia and Caria, thus becoming for a short period the Greek *polis* with the largest territory, holding areas that neither Athens at its apogee nor Sparta had ever dreamed of. Eumenes of Pergamon saw the borders of his kingdom in Asia Minor expand, as he was given formerly Seleucid lands. The Romans were forced to wait for a few years to deal with Hannibal, who as an old man – he was born in 247 BC – had continued fighting, first against the Romans as a commander of Antiochos' army and fleet (until 189 BC) and then against Eumenes as a commander of Prusias I of Bithynia. Under pressure from Rome, Prusias considered delivering the Carthaginian general to the Romans, but Hannibal preferred to take poison, in 182 or 181 BC, to finally free his ancestral enemies from their fears. 'Let us free the Romans from their continual worry, since they do not have the patience to wait for an old man to die,' he wrote in the letter he left behind.

When Greece ceased to bear good men

The victory over Antiochos was an important turning point in the relations between Rome and the Greek states. Just as with the declaration of freedom in 196 BC, the decisions about the fate of the Greek cities of Asia Minor were one-sided resolutions of the Romans, by a committee of ten senators under Cnaeus Manlius Vulso. Although the Romans did not make any territorial gains themselves and still declined to take any administrative responsibility in the Greek East, they appeared as a sovereign power that could make decisions about territorial questions and the payment of tribute to other states as well as about the legal status of Greek cities. The Roman senate had achieved its principal aims, which were to break for ever the power of its opponents and to strengthen its allies. The Roman troops retreated and left it to the Greek states to learn how to deal with this new balance of powers.

Already in the years immediately before the Peace of Apameia the Roman senate and Roman magistrates had stepped into the power vacuum left by the decline of the Antigonid kingdom. In the two decades that followed the peace, this role intensified: the senate and Roman commanders arbitrated in boundary disputes and conflicts between Greek communities; the embassies that used to be sent to the royal courts now crossed the Adriatic Sea and approached the leaders of Rome; and Roman envoys were a common sight in Greece and in royal courts. But Rome neither possessed nor directly administered any place in the Balkans or in Asia Minor.

This left enough space for the traditional monarchs to pursue their own policies and live under the illusion that little had changed.

There were still statesmen who thought that Rome should not exercise any influence in Greek affairs. Philopoimen (see p. 161) was called 'the last of the Greeks' by an anonymous Roman precisely for this reason, for his firm belief that the Achaean League should remain truly independent. He died while pursuing this policy. Unwilling to tolerate Messene's revolt against the League in 183 BC, he campaigned against the city, where he fell from his horse behind enemy lines and was captured. His enemies forced him to drink poison. His death united the League against the rebellious Messenians and Philipoimen received divine honours in his fatherland, Megalopolis, for centuries. The future historian Polybius was chosen to carry the general's urn in one of the most impressive funerals ever staged in Greece. Four centuries later, the traveller Pausanias would comment that Greece ceased to bear good men after his death. This is debatable. What is certain is that neither the efforts of states to leave the Achaean League nor Roman interventions ceased after his death, until Greece became a Roman province.

8

THE GREEK STATES BECOME ROMAN PROVINCES

(188–129 BC)

Rule as a habit

In an illuminating study on theories proposed to explain Roman imperialism, Zvi Yavetz adduces a Polish joke in which a Catholic priest attempts to explain to a peasant what miracles are. 'If I fell from the church tower and landed unhurt, what would you call this?' 'An accident,' the peasant responds. 'And if I fell again and was unhurt?' the priest insists. 'Another accident.' 'And if I did it a third time?' The peasant's clear-headed answer is: 'A habit.' If until the defeat of Antiochos Rome's military engagements in the East might be seen as accidents, soon after that event they surely became a habit.

Within forty years, the Hellenistic world had experienced a real revolution: the decline and fall of the three traditional monarchies – the Antigonids, the Seleucids and the Ptolemies – and the rise of a new power and its allies – Rome, Rhodes and Pergamon. What the Roman leaders had achieved, and probably intended, was territorial expansion in the West, with the creation of two provinces in Spain and consolidation in

Italy with a stronger linking of the Italian communities with Rome. The construction of the Via Flaminia in 220 BC, a highway that connected Rome with the important harbour of Ariminum (Rimini) on the Adriatic Sea, contributed to this consolidation, along with other measures such as the foundation of colonies of Roman citizens in Italy and the grant of Roman citizenship. In a period in which the senatorial leaders had not yet achieved the merging of Italy into a union, they could not have been interested in the subjugation of territories in the East. Things gradually changed, as Rome's hegemonic position in the Mediterranean transformed its economic structures with the import of a large number of slaves, the decline of small holdings and the rise of large units of agricultural production, the dependence of part of the population on the war spoils and the development of economic interests outside Italy. After Rome's continual victories in wars on all four sides of the Mediterranean its foreign policy was certainly no longer primarily a policy of response; it was a policy of action. Although we shall follow the development of this policy separately in different venues, first in Macedonia and Greece, then in Asia and Egypt, in the new 'entangled' world they were interconnected.

The end of the Macedonian kingdom (179–167 BC)

In Macedon, Philip V spent the last years of his reign (until 179 BC) defending the now reduced borders of his kingdom and strengthening its army. His son and successor, Perseus, continued this policy, avoiding provocations and respecting the freedom of Greek cities. But he still behaved as a self-confident ruler. He was king of a kingdom reduced in size but also a member of a dynasty that for centuries had played an active part in Greek politics. He lacked the garrisons that had once supported his father's control of parts of Greece, but he did not lack diplomatic and propagandistic tools to regain an influential position. In 178 BC, he married the daughter of the Seleucid king, Seleukos IV; his own sister was married to Prusias II, king of Bithynia. In mainland Greece, the sanctuary of Delphi, respected by all the Greeks, had once been under the patronage of his ancestor, Demetrios Poliorketes. The Macedonians were represented in the council of the sacred federation (*amphiktyony*) that governed it. It is here that Perseus appeared in 174 BC, during the celebration of the Pythian festival, with a military escort indicating an ambition to play a leading part among the Greeks. It is around this time that he erected a monument in Delphi, inscribing on it old documents that evidenced the protection that his ancestors had offered to the sanctuary. In 173 BC, he concluded a treaty with the federal state of Boiotia.

Perseus' actions were carefully observed by Eumenes II of Pergamon. When he survived an attempt on his life in Delphi, he accused Perseus of masterminding the assassination. Following the example of his father, Attalos, who had instigated the Second Macedonian War by alarming the Roman senate about Philip V's operations, Eumenes appeared in front of the senate in 172 BC and, with an engaging oration, argued that every action of Perseus was a direct threat to Rome. His speech was successful, not because of the plausibility of his arguments, but because the Roman elite was receptive to prospects of a war in Greece.

For several years Rome had not been engaged in military conflicts and this frustrated the younger senators, who looked with envy upon the victories, triumphs and glory of the older generation. Aristocratic competition was fed by wars. Influential Roman knights, the members of the equestrian order that held the second rank in Roman society, were actively engaged in trade and manufacture. They therefore had a keen interest in new booty and the enslavement of war captives, and such a prospect also seemed attractive to part of the population. Economic interests are a more likely suspect for Rome's new war than the defence of allies or obligations deriving from *fides*.

Unsurprisingly, the newly elected consuls requested that they be assigned Macedonia as their area of responsibility for the next year. Embassies were sent to Greece to confirm the support of the Greeks in a potential war against Perseus. At the same time the Macedonian king took measures to increase his prestige in Greece, but without wishing a military confrontation. In the Greek cities, many of those who had reasons not to be satisfied with their situation, especially indebted people, looked upon him with hope, probably not because Perseus had any concrete plans for social reforms or the cancellation of debts, but because they resented the oligarchic political leaders who supported the Romans.

While the Roman ambassadors were touring Greece to recruit allies, Perseus' efforts to arrange meetings with them and avert the war failed. The Roman senate had no intention of negotiating in order to prevent a military conflict that had already been decided. At no point did the Romans present any demands or give an ultimatum. One has the impression that from the very beginning of this confrontation the intention of the Roman political leaders was to prosecute a war for booty. The war declaration came early in 171 BC. Shortly before the beginning of this Third Macedonian War, the Romans sent a letter to Delphi in which they summarised their grievances against Perseus. This text, inscribed in large letters in the sanctuary, is an excellent source for the presentation of a casus belli. Perseus was accused of coming with his army to Delphi during the sacred truce of the Pythian festival; for allying himself with the barbarians who lived across the Danube, the same barbarians who had once tried to enslave Greece and sack the sanctuary of Apollo in Delphi; for attacking friends and allies of the Romans; for killing ambassadors who were sent to conclude treaties with Rome; for attempting to poison the senate and assassinate King Eumenes; for instigating confusion and strife in the Greek cities, corrupting the leading statesmen and trying to win the favour of the masses through promises of cancellation of debts; for planning a war against Rome in order to deprive the Greeks of their protector and enslave them. More accusations followed, no longer preserved on the stone, probably as false or exaggerated as the ones that are still there. Presenting grievances before an attack is a universally applied strategy of persuasion. One of the fables of Babrius (second century AD) is an ironic comment on this practice:

> Once a wolf saw a lamb that had gone astray from the flock, but instead of rushing upon him to seize him by force, he tried to find a plausible complaint by which to justify his hostility. 'Last year, small though you were, you slandered me.' 'How could I last year? It's not yet a year since I was born.' 'Well, then, aren't you cropping this field, which is mine?' 'No, for I've not yet eaten any grass nor have I begun to graze.' 'And haven't you drunk from the fountain which is mine to drink from?' 'No, even yet my mother's breast provides my nourishment.' Thereupon the wolf seized the lamb and while eating him remarked: 'You're not going to rob the wolf of his dinner even though you do find it easy to refute all my charges.'

No one was going to rob the she-wolf from her dinner. In this war, Perseus was almost entirely isolated, in spite of the sympathies of many Greeks and resentment at the Roman intervention. In the early phase of the war (171–170 BC), he had some success, but this did not bring him any allies, except for the Illyrian King Gentios, and the Romans had no intention of negotiating. The efforts of Rhodes to arbitrate in this conflict were rejected by Rome and met with suspicion. In 168 BC, Gentios was defeated and captured. The new consul of 168 BC, Lucius Aemilius Paullus, met Perseus in the decisive battle near Pydna in 168 BC. At the beginning, the Roman army was unable to resist the advance of the terrifying Macedonian phalanx with its long pikes. But as the Roman legions retreated to the uneven ground of the hills, the phalanx lost its cohesion and Paullus' maniples proceeded into the gaps, attacking the Macedonian soldiers on their exposed flanks. The short swords of the Macedonians were of little use against the legionaries' longer swords and heavy shields. At the critical moment in which the battle turned, the Macedonian cavalry did not engage, either because the king had been wounded at the beginning of the battle or because, according to hostile reports, he fled in a cowardly fashion. The Macedonian army was annihilated; allegedly 30,000 Macedonians fell. Perseus escaped to the island of Samothrace, but, realising his desperate position, he finally surrendered to Paullus, to be taken to Rome and displayed in a triumph. He died in prison in Alba Fucens soon after, in 165 or 162 BC.

The Roman arrangements after this victory have a different quality than their earlier responses to victories, revealing a significant change in Roman policy. The Antigonid kingdom of Macedonia was dissolved. This time the senate's decision affected not only the territorial integrity of a Hellenistic state but its very existence. The territories of the kingdom were divided among four independent republics called *merides* (districts), which may have corresponded to already existing administrative and military units (see Map 1). The easternmost *meris*, with Amphipolis as its capital, extended between the rivers Nestos and Strymon; Thessalonike was the capital of the second *meris* in central Macedonia, between the rivers Strymon and Axios. The heart of the old Macedonian kingdom, in the west, became the third *meris*, with the traditional royal residence, Pella, as its capital. The fourth *meris* consisted of the mountainous regions of upper Macedonia (Pelagonia), with Herakleia Lynkestis as its capital. The four states were not allowed to have any relations among themselves and even intermarriages were not allowed. Forbidden also was the exploitation of Macedonia's natural resources, timber and mines, until 158 BC. Half of the tribute that was previously paid to the royal treasury was now to be paid to Rome; for the first time, the Romans were imposing a regular payment of tribute, a clear sign of subordination, east of the Adriatic Sea. The king, the members of the court and the royal treasures were taken to Rome. These arrangements were presented to the Macedonian representatives in Amphipolis as a declaration of freedom, since the population was freed from the monarchy. In Illyria, monarchy was abolished and the territory was divided into three *merides* that were nominally independent.

The new quality of the Roman presence in Greece is also revealed by measures concerning the rest of the Greeks, even communities that were not engaged in this war. Men in neutral or allied states who had a favourable attitude towards Perseus were denounced by their political opponents, arrested and deported to Italy, along with hostages who would guarantee future loyalty towards Rome. The Achaean League alone had to deliver 1,000 hostages, among them the commander of the cavalry, Polybius, the son of a prominent statesman who had favoured Achaea's neutrality and a member of the ruling oligarchy of the Achaeans. His misfortune is the modern historian's luck. Polybius became the tutor of Aemilius Paullus' sons, was introduced to the circle of leading senators and had access to documents and first-hand information about recent and contemporary history; this information is the basis of his historical work that covers Roman expansion from 264 to 146 BC. Caught between a nostalgic view of the world of independent Greek states and admiration for Roman institutions and values, he gives us impressive reflections not only on political history but also on the role of the historian as a teacher of pragmatic politics.

In Epirus, the only significant ally of Perseus, seventy settlements were destroyed and plundered; their population, allegedly 250,000 people, was sold into slavery. The Rhodians, traditional friends of the Romans, were severely punished just for wishing to arbitrate between Rome and Perseus. Rhodes lost its territories in Asia Minor – Caria and Lycia – which were declared free. But its greatest punishment was that the island of Delos, independent from Athens for most of the Hellenistic period (314–167 BC), was returned to the Athenians and was declared a free harbour: that is, a harbour in which no customs were levied on exports and imports. Rhodes suddenly had a strong competitor in trade, and Delos became the most important centre of transit trade in the eastern Mediterranean, attracting many traders from Italy (*Italici*). Even Eumenes II, who after all had provoked the war and had fought on the side of the Romans, was viewed with suspicion by the senate because of rumours that during the last phase of the war he may have intended to avert Perseus' total defeat. With these measures Rome now emerged not as an ally or protector but as a sovereign ruler.

The events of these years show a change of Roman policies in the East. War was declared without good cause; the defeated state lost its integrity; new states were created, with institutions dictated by the Romans; tribute was paid to Rome; territories changed hands on the senate's one-sided decisions; kings were humiliated (see p. 195). In 167 BC, King Prusias of Bithynia visited Rome with shorn head and the garments of a manumitted slave in order to ask for the senate's pity (see p. 117). The psychological impact in the Greek world was enormous, and fortunately we can see it in contemporary documents. In 167 BC, ambassadors of Teos in Ionia went to Rome to intervene in favour of their colony Abdera in Thrace in her conflict with the Thracian king Kotys. A decree in their honour shows the emotional tension that emerged when the traditional pride of a free community was confronted with the need to supplicate the Romans: 'When they went to Rome as ambassadors, they patiently endured psychical and bodily hardship, appealing to the Roman magistrates and, with their perseverance, offering themselves as hostages ... They even laboriously dedicated themselves to the daily visits of the atria.' No other Greek inscription ever mentions hardships of the soul. By having to appeal to Roman magistrates and to perform the daily rituals of the *clientes*, the envoys received the impression that they were no longer free men, but hostages, like the innumerable hostages that had been dragged to Rome at that time. The prediction allegedly made by Agelaos in Naupaktos was fulfilled: the clouds from the west had settled over Greece.

Graecia capta: the provincialisation of Greece (167–146 BC)

With the dissolution of the Antigonid kingdom and the other one-sided arrangements of 167 BC, the Romans demonstrated their claim to hegemonic rule in Greece and Asia Minor. And yet it took another twenty years for them to proceed to the final step: direct rule through the annexation of territory and the introduction of direct administration through the creation of provinces. The opportunity was offered to them by an uprising in Macedonia and the perennial conflicts in the Peloponnese.

In 153 BC, a certain Andriskos, ruler of Adramytteion in north-west

Asia Minor, claimed to be Perseus' son and the legitimate king of Macedonia. His 'uncle', the Seleucid king Demetrios I, did not support his claim to the throne and instead delivered him to the senate. He thus acknowledged the senate as a higher authority that had if not the right, then certainly the power to recognise kings. In Rome, no one took Andriskos seriously (his name means manikin). But in 149 BC, he managed to escape from Rome and, with the help of the Thracian king Teres, who was married to Perseus' sister, invaded Macedonia, restored the monarchy and started raiding the territory of Thessaly. Allegedly, the lower classes supported him, pinning on him their hopes for the cancellation of debts and redistribution of land. The Romans originally underestimated this danger and considered the possibility of letting the Achaean League deal with him. But in 148 BC, the third and final Punic War started, and Andriskos made the fatal mistake of allying himself with Carthage. A Roman legion sent against him failed to defeat him and Andriskos even conquered Thessaly. But when two legions under the praetor Quintus Caecilius Metellus arrived in 148 BC, Andriskos had no chance of victory. Lacking support from the Macedonian elite and without allies in Greece, he was soon defeated, captured, displayed in a triumph in Rome and executed.

Around the same time, in the Peloponnese the endemic conflict between the Achaean League and Sparta had taken a new turn. After the assassination of King Nabis in 192 BC, Sparta had been forced to join the League, but this was perceived by the Spartans as a loss of independence. The tensions culminated when the League was asked by the senate to arbitrate in a territorial conflict between Megalopolis and Sparta in 165 BC and took a decision that favoured Megalopolis. Sparta's wish to leave the League was favourably received by the senate. The senators, either ignorant of or indifferent towards local sensitivities, went as far as to recommend, in 147 BC, the exit of several important cities from the League, including Corinth and Argos. The situation became explosive when the conflict also acquired a social dimension. The Achaean statesman Kritolaos linked the integration of Sparta into the League with the promise of social reforms in favour of the indebted and the dispossessed. Whether this was the result of a genuine interest in social reforms or simply a populist measure to win the support of the masses is difficult to determine. Kritolaos did not propose cancellation of debt but only the freezing of payments and the liberation of those who had lost their freedom because of failure to pay their debts. His social programme, originally directed against Sparta, united all those who profited from it and turned their hostility not only against Sparta but also against Rome. The conflict was exported to central Greece, as a series of federal states (Boiotia, Euboia, Phokis, Lokris) supported Kritolaos' policies.

Metellus, who after his victory had remained in Macedonia, sent three envoys to the assembly of the Achaean League, but the assembly sent them away, declaring war against Sparta and thus provoking Rome's reaction. The legions of Metellus marched from Macedonia without delay and defeated the Achaeans in Skarpheia. Kritolaos fell in this battle and his successor, Diaios, hastily organised the defence in Corinth. In their desperation, the Achaean leaders promised freedom and citizenship to all the slaves who were willing to fight. In Leukopetra, near Corinth, the last battle of the Greeks was fought and lost. The new Roman consul Lucius Mummius took the city of Corinth and, probably in accordance with a senatorial decision, razed it to the ground in 146 BC, the year in which Carthage suffered the same fate. Diaios committed suicide; the population of Corinth was either killed or sold into slavery. If, with the destruction of Corinth, the senate wanted to set an example for the Greeks – the most likely interpretation of this act of brutality – then it succeeded. For two generations, mainland Greece caused no headaches for the Roman senators.

Rome's measures after these victories were unprecedented not only in their brutality but also in their institutional dimension. The four Macedonian states were abolished and their territories became the first Roman province in Greece. The new province was under the responsibility of a proconsul, a consul whose command was prolonged after his annual term in office and who was assigned a region directly ruled by Rome. The proconsul's jurisdiction extended to Illyria, which after the removal of its last king, Gentios, in 167 BC was nominally independent. The first governor after Metellus' departure, Cnaeus Egnatius, arrived in 146 BC. With the Via Flaminia as his model (see p. 176), he immediately initiated the construction of a highway known as the Via Egnatia, connecting the important harbour of Epidamnos (Dyrrhachion, Durazzo) on the Adriatic Sea to Thessalonike, contributing to the consolidation of the province and improving traffic and communications with Italy. Repaired many times, this route is still used today (see Fig. 17).

A senatorial committee of ten men regulated the affairs in central and southern Greece; the historian Polybius was assigned the duty of the political reorganisation of southern Greece. Most measures can only be inferred indirectly from later sources. The allies of Rome (Sparta, Athens, Aetolia, Akaranania, the federal states in Thessaly) remained nominally free. All other states (the Achaean League, Megara, Lokris, Boiotia, Phokis, Euboia) were assigned to the jurisdiction of the provincial governor of Macedonia. The federal states were dissolved for a short period, and when they were re-established their membership was reduced: for example, the Achaean Koinon was reduced to the borders of the homonymous region of Achaia, in the north-western corner of the Peloponnese. The cities remained free and autonomous. Since there is no evidence for tax farmers (*publicani*) in Greece, it is unlikely that they had to pay tribute to Rome initially. Part of the territory of Corinth and the land owned by those who had led the opposition against Rome became Roman public land. The new freedom of the Greek communities was radically different from the freedom once declared by Flamininus. Now there was a Roman governor in Macedonia, and no Greek community thought of taking any measures in its foreign policy without first consulting the governor and the senate. As for their internal affairs, they were in the hands of the leaders of the oligarchic regimes that were established everywhere and supported Rome. After 146 BC Greece was subject to the authority of the Roman senate.

Comparative research on imperialisms has recognised certain shared features that characterise the behaviour of an imperialistic power towards its dependent states. Rome's measures after 146 BC – as well as some instituted before that date – correspond to most of these features: Rome limited the freedom of Greek states with regard to their foreign relations, established provincial administration, annexed territories, intervened in local affairs, obliged some of the dependent communities to pay tribute and expected unconditional military support; it exploited economic resources, allowed its own citizens to acquire land in the dependent areas and obliged the dependent states to conclude treaties with Rome as unequal partners.

After the sack of Corinth, innumerable works of art were transported from Corinth to Rome, giving an impetus to artistic production in Rome and Italy. One hundred years later, Horace would recognise the impact of this event in a famous verse: '*Graecia capta ferum victorem cepit et artes intulit agresti Latio*' ('Conquered Greece conquered the savage victor, bringing arts to rustic Latium'). But contemporaries of the event could not recognise any positive cultural impact in the destruction of one of the oldest cities of Greece. The Greeks were shocked beyond measure.

With a long chain of rhythmically arrayed questions, the contemporary poet Antipatros of Sidon laments the sack of this city, bitterly stressing the ephemeral nature of power and the destructive force of war:

> Dorian Corinth, where is your admired beauty, where are the crowns of your towers, where is your old wealth? Where are the temples of the Blessed? Where are the palaces? Where are the wives, and the myriads of men, the descendants of Sisyphos? Not a single trace has been left of you, most miserable. For war has seized and devoured everything.

From allied kingdom to province: the last Attalids (159–129 BC)

Although the kingdom of Pergamon had been Rome's most loyal ally in its wars, the attempt of Eumenes II to arrange for a peace between Perseus and Rome in 168 BC earned him the senate's suspicion. The Pergamene king had provoked a war thinking he could use the Romans against his Macedonian enemies; but he had only provided them with an excuse to fight a war for their own interests. In the next decades, the Pergamene kings faced two threats: they had territorial disputes with the neighbouring kingdom of Bithynia and, further east, the Galatian rulers repeatedly raided the territory of Pergamon, Greek cities in the area and the temple-state of Pessinous in Phrygia. In 166 BC, although Eumenes successfully faced an uprising of Galatian tribes, Rome recognised the autonomy of the Galatian state, punishing Eumenes for the lack of enthusiasm in the last phase of the war against Perseus.

Eumenes was succeeded by his brother Attalos II (159–139/138 BC). The new king was already an old man, conscious of the dependence on Rome. In a letter that he sent to the priest of Pessinous, he tries to explain why he had hesitated to wage war against the Gauls of Asia Minor and, therefore, failed to offer the protection expected of him:

> To launch an undertaking without their participation began to seem fraught with great danger; if we were successful, the attempt promised to bring us envy and detraction and baneful suspicion – which they also felt toward my brother – while if we failed, we should meet certain destruction. For they would not, it seemed to us, regard our disaster with sympathy but rather would be delighted to see it, because we had

12. The Altar of Perganon (detail of the battle between the Olympian gods and giants).

undertaken such projects without them. As things are now, however, if – which may God forbid – we were worsted in any matters, having acted entirely with their approval we would receive help and might recover our losses, if the gods favored.

Attalos' decisions were subject to Rome's approval, not on the basis of legal arrangements and treaties but on the basis of the new political reality.

Bithynia's expansion under Prusias II caused a long war, from 159 to 154 BC. Supported by the kings of Kappadokia and Pontos, Attalos II defeated Prusias II, who was obliged by Rome to pay war indemnities to Pergamon. A few years later, in 149 BC, Prusias II was assassinated by his own son Nikomedes. In Kappadokia, Attalos helped King Ariarathes V in his war against his brother Orophernes (158–156 BC), thus acquiring significant influence there as well. In his last years, Attalos II and his nephew Attalos III jointly ruled a kingdom that accumulated treasures through the payment of tribute by subject cities and populations and contributed to stability in western Asia Minor. The Pergamon altar (see Fig. 12), built sometime between 184 and 166 BC, is the most famous testimony of the Attalid power; the representations of a battle between the Olympians and giants alluded to the Attalid victories over the Gauls, while other images commemorated the mythical founders of Pergamon.

Attalos II was succeeded by Attalos III, who died after a short rule (139/138–133 BC). Although a long inscription celebrates a military victory with which Attalos III earned divine honours, the erection of a huge statue, an extravagant festival and the establishment of a commemorative anniversary, it seems that the king's real interest was in medical and botanical studies. Neither his victory nor his medical treatises had any lasting impact. His testament did. Dying childless, he left his kingdom to the Roman people, but at the same time made the city of Pergamon and its territory free; it seems that he left it to the Romans to decide whether the other Greek cities in his kingdom, hitherto subject to tribute, would also be freed. Modern historians assume that Attalos III feared social unrest or that he opposed his succession by his half-brother Aristonikos. That at the moment of his death direct Roman rule in Greece had been a reality for more than a decade and no significant political decision was taken anywhere in the eastern Mediterranean without previous consultation with the Roman senate might have influenced his decision.

The conditions at the moment of Attalos III's death were such that his will triggered unforeseen developments. First, Rome was in a deep social crisis, mainly because of the impoverishment of small landholders. It was the time at which Tiberius Gracchus was proposing the agrarian reforms that his brother Caius Gracchus would implement a decade later. The Pergamene bequest was for Rome an unexpected source of funding for solutions to urgent social problems and Tiberius immediately proposed to auction Attalos' treasures and distribute the money among the recipients of land. Second, Attalos had a half-brother, Aristonikos, an illegitimate son of Eumenes II, who was not prepared to leave his patrimony uncontested. Third, the Greek cities that were part of the Attalid kingdom and subject to the payment of tribute saw an opportunity to regain their full autonomy. And finally, every serious political development was doomed to arouse hopes of broader changes in those who were unsatisfied with their financial and social conditions. The convergence of these factors made the situation explosive. Aristonikos took the royal name Eumenes and asserted his claim to the throne. There must have been some opposition to the will and possibly some support for Aristonikos. The people who were deprived of citizenship because they left Pergamon after Attalos' death may have been Aristonikos' supporters. But in view of the new prospect of freedom, neither Pergamon nor other Greek cities were willing to accept a new king. An inscription from Metropolis in Ionia honouring the local statesman Apollonios, who was killed in the first year of the war in 132 BC, formulates these feelings:

> After King Philometor [Attalos III] died and the Romans, the common benefactors and saviors, returned to all who used to be subject to the royal rule of Attalos their freedom, in accordance with their decree, and Aristonikos came and wanted to deprive us of the freedom that had been returned to us by the senate, Apollonios submitted himself to the obligation to oppose with words and deeds that man, who had conferred upon himself royal rule in spite of the decision of the Romans, the common benefactors, genuinely taking upon himself the protection of the freedom in accordance with the will of the people.

It seems that the Roman senate had immediately promised to free the cities from the tribute that they had to pay to the kings. This is confirmed in a speech given by Mark Antony to the assembly of the Greeks in Asia in 41 BC: 'We released you from the taxes that you used to pay to Attalos.' The cities understood this as a return to the original, lawful status.

Lacking the support of the cities, Aristonikos won the support of the rural population by promising freedom to the slaves and property to the dependent farmers. In control of a few cities (Thyatteira, Apollonia and Stratonikeia on the Kaikos), he also founded a city in Mysia that was given the name Heliopolis, 'the city of the Sun'. Traditionally interpreted by Marxist historians as a social revolution, Aristonikos' policies were probably no more than a pragmatic response to the needs of his struggle for power. Military commanders and cities regularly attempted to expand the recruitment basis of their armies by promising the liberation of slaves, the cancellation of debts and the granting of citizenship. Serious socioeconomic reforms were primarily instruments for the revitalisation of a state's military power. This is not to say that there were no demands for social and economic reforms in that period. On the contrary, at the same time as Aristonikos was starting his uprising, Rome was for the first time facing a slave rebellion in Sicily, under the leadership of a certain Eunous, a slave from Syria (135–132 BC), and the Stoic philosopher Caius Blossius in Rome was advising Tiberius Gracchus to proceed with agrarian reforms and to distribute land to the dispossessed. After Tiberius' assassination in

133 BC, Blossius left Rome and joined Aristonikos. It is possible that his philosophical ideas, about which almost nothing is known, influenced the creation of 'the city of the Sun'. However, Aristonikos probably did not start his revolt in order to bring about social reforms but simply exploited social dissatisfaction for his own purpose; those who were unhappy with their situation gladly joined someone who could become their champion, even though their primary concern was not who would rule Pergamon but who would give them land and freedom.

For different reasons, most cities and all of the neighbouring kingdoms (Pontos, Bithynia, Kappadokia and Paphlagonia) joined a coalition under the leadership of Rome against Aristonikos. The cities feared social unrest, hoped for independence and wished to demonstrate loyalty to Rome; the neighbouring kingdoms objected to the rise of a strong state in their vicinity. Aristonikos had some success at the beginning, and the Roman consul Publius Licinius Crassus was killed during one of the early battles in 131 BC. Things changed with the arrival of reinforcements under Marcus Perperna, who besieged Aristonikos in Stratonikeia, captured him and brought him to Rome in 129 BC, where he was executed by strangulation during the celebration of Perpena's triumph.

Immediately after the end of the war, a commission of ten senators under the consul Manius Aquillius was sent to Pergamon in order to implement the arrangements of an earlier decision of the senate concerning acceptance of the will. The eastern territories of the kingdom (parts of Phrygia and Lykaonia) were probably given to the kingdoms that had allied themselves with Rome (see Map 5). There remained enough territories in Asia Minor to form a new province called Asia. It consisted of the Hellenised and urbanised areas of north-western and central Asia Minor (Mysia, Troas, Ionia, Lydia, south-western Phrygia and parts of Caria). The European possessions of the Attalids – the Thracian Chersonesos and the island of Aigina – were added to the province of Macedonia. Pergamon and other important cities became free, except for the cities that had supported Aristonikos. After a war against pirates in south-east Asia Minor in 102 BC the territory of Cilicia Pedias became the second Roman province in Asia.

Expansion as exploitation: Roman tax farmers in Asia

During the process of its expansion, Rome exacted tribute from its provinces, including Macedonia. Public finances depended heavily on this taxation, especially as an extensive programme of social reforms had to be funded. Although the new province of Asia probably did not pay tribute in the first years after its creation, it was to be expected that the Romans would follow the model of other provinces, such as Sicily and Macedonia, and demand tribute. The organisation of the payment of tribute was the work of Caius Gracchus and was an essential part of his efforts to find the financial means to make the implementation of his social reforms possible. Expanding the reforms proposed by his brother, Caius proposed a series of laws that provided for the granting of land to Roman citizens, the creation of settlements in the provinces, the purchase of grain and its distribution to the citizens at a low price, the construction of roads and the equipping of soldiers at public expense (123–122 BC). Who would pay for such a programme? A more efficient collection of tribute from the provinces was Caius' answer, and the newly created province of Asia, believed to be the source of unimaginable wealth, provided an opportunity to test the new system.

A widespread method for collecting taxes was to auction the right to collect the taxes to the entrepreneur or group of entrepreneurs who made the highest offer. The bidders based their offer on a rough estimate of the various taxes expected from a region – taxes on transactions and on land, customs duty at harbours and so on. In this way the treasury received the taxes in advance, did not require an administrative apparatus for the collection of taxes and transferred the risk for shortfalls – for instance, because of bad harvest – to the tax farmers. Naturally, the individual or the 'company' that had acquired this right did everything to exact all possible taxes and surpass the amount already advanced to the treasury; the surplus was their gain. The tax farmers in Rome, who were organised in companies called *societates publicanorum*, are securely attested by 184 BC but must have existed earlier. The *publicani* mostly belonged to the equestrian order, the class of wealthy Romans who were engaged in trade, mining, manufacture and financial enterprises, and for this reason, since 218 BC, were not allowed to become members of the senate or be elected to high public office. The *publicani* became notorious for the relentless exaction of taxes and the ruthless methods that they applied in order to demand higher rates.

Caius Grachus' *lex Sempronia de provincia Asia* arranged for the collection of taxes in the new province of Asia. The contracts for the tax collection for a period of five years were no longer made in the province, under the responsibility of the governor, but were to be auctioned in Rome under the responsibility of the *censor*, a respected magistrate responsible for the publication of a register of Roman citizens and their property. Thus Caius hoped to reduce the danger of bribery and corruption. The tax on agricultural production was fixed at 10 per cent of the produce; a 2.5 per cent customs duty was imposed on imports and exports. It is very likely that a law concerning the customs to be paid for imports and exports to and from Asia by land and sea – in the economically important region from the Bosporus to Pamphylia – was first drafted in the same period. This law (*lex de portorii Asiae*) was modified several times and, thanks to an inscription, we have the form it had taken under Emperor Nero (AD 62). This very detailed law reveals the effort to strictly regulate fiscal issues in the provinces and thus prevent arbitrary decisions and corruption, but also loss of revenues. Even the free cities were not exempted from customs duty fixed at 2.5 per cent of the value of the goods. Only a tax-free zone in Lycia was exempted; exemption was also granted to Roman officials, soldiers and tax collectors.

Although Caius Gracchus introduced a law allowing for the provinces to appeal against illegal seizure of property by Roman authorities (*lex Sempronia repetundarum*), abuses were not prevented. In the decades that followed, the actions of the *publicani* in Asia repeatedly became the subject of complaints and appeals to Rome. For instance, in 101 BC the *publicani* tried to exact taxes even from territory belonging to the free city of Pergamon.

Caius Gracchus once wrote an account of how his brother, travelling through Etruria, saw the countryside abandoned by its free farmers and the fields cultivated by foreign slaves; this, he claimed, had prompted Tiberius' reforms. His own reforms were the work of a Roman citizen sensitive only towards the prosperity of Roman citizens. In a surviving fragment of an oration, he explains his motivation: 'I recommend the increase of taxes in order that you may more easily achieve your own advantage and administer the Republic.' His mentality was that of a representative of an imperialistic state that would not hesitate to exploit subject populations for the benefit of its citizens. For Cicero, writing in 66 BC, the *publicani* were the most honourable and accomplished men; the tributes that they provided were 'the sinews of the Republic' (*nervos rei publicae*). The view of the populations in the Roman provinces in the East was quite different, as summarised one century after Caius' reforms by the historian Diodoros: 'He threw the provinces to the recklessness and greed of the tax-farmers; what he gained was the justified hatred of the subject peoples against Roman rule.'

When the author of the Gospel of Luke looked for a character who needed repentance most urgently, the choice fell easily upon the tax collector, in the parable of the Pharisee and the tax collector. The attitude of the Greek provinces towards Rome in the following decades was to a great extent determined by the experiences they had with this most visible representative of Roman rule.

9

DECLINE AND FALL OF THE HELLENISTIC KINGDOMS IN ASIA AND EGYPT

(188–80 BC)

Götterdämmerung in the East

The long twilight of the Seleucids, during which their kingdom, continually reduced in size and torn by internal conflicts, became irrelevant as an international power, started immediately after the Peace of Apameia. It lasted for more than a century and cannot be narrated in detail. The efforts of Seleucid kings to retain or regain parts of their realm were futile. Weakened by dynastic conflicts and uprisings, the Seleucids gradually lost not only the eastern satrapies but also most of their kingdom. In 83 BC, the Seleucid throne was captured by the Armenian king Tigranes II; twenty years later the last 'shadow king' of a once great dynasty was killed.

To compensate for his losses in the West, Antiochos III launched a new campaign in the East, in Luristan (western Iran), immediately after the humiliating Peace of Apameia. He died plundering a temple in 187 BC; his death while committing sacrilege must have appeared to many contemporaries as divine punishment. He was succeeded by his son Seleukos IV, who inherited the huge war indemnity imposed by the Romans on his father. Instead of continuing his father's expansionist policy, Seleukos tried to face his kingdom's financial problems by improving the exaction of tribute from the provinces. One of the measures he took was centralising the appointment of priests to oversee temples in the provinces and their revenues. An episode narrated in the Old Testament and immortalised in Raphael's painting in La Stanza del Eliodoro in the Vatican is directly connected with the king's policy. His chief minister, Heliodoros, was sent to Jerusalem to seize the Temple's treasures, probably consisting of money deposited in the Temple, but this was averted through God's intervention. It is left to the reader's faith to assess the historicity of the biblical narrative, but for Seleukos' measures we now have hard evidence. Epigraphic finds in Israel contain copies of a royal letter addressed to this very Heliodoros in 178 BC and informing him about the appointment of a priest overseeing the temples in Koile Syria and Phoenicia.

A short period of peaceful relations between the Seleucids and the Ptolemies ended abruptly when, in 176 BC, the queen of Egypt, Cleopatra the 'Syrian', died, leaving her son Ptolemy VI, still a minor, on the throne. Her brother Seleukos IV was assassinated a year later by Heliodoros, who had hoped to see Seleukos' son Demetrios, who was still an infant, on the throne. But instead, the murdered king's brother, Antiochos IV, seized power, also taking the king's widow as his wife – for Laodike this was her third and last marriage with one of her bothers. The fact that she had children with both Seleukos and Antiochos was the root of dynastic conflicts that lasted for a century (see pp. 201–3).

When the guardians of Ptolemy VI demanded the return of Koile Syria, Antiochos IV launched an attack against Egypt (the Sixth Syrian War), invading its territory, reaching Alexandria and capturing the king (170–169 BC). The population of Alexandria revolted, bringing to the throne Ptolemy's brother, known as Ptolemy VIII. The two children – sixteen and twelve years old respectively – agreed to a joint rule, but Antiochos used Rome's apparent distraction because of the Third Macedonian War to launch a second attack to capture both Egypt and Cyprus in 168 BC. He was close to Alexandria when a Roman envoy, Caius Popillius Laenas, responding to a call from the Egyptian kings for help, met him in Eleusis, a suburb of Alexandria. Laenas demanded that Antiochos withdraw his armies from Egypt. When the king responded that he wished to discuss the matter with his council, Laenas drew with his staff a circle in the sand around the perplexed king and said: 'Give me an answer for the Roman senate, before you cross this circle.' Confronted with the prospect of a war with Rome, Antiochos agreed to withdraw. Those who witnessed this scene, known as 'the day of Eleusis', must have realised that the world had changed.

'The day of Eleusis' fell upon Antiochos IV unexpectedly, at a time when the conquest of part or all of Egypt seemed within his grasp. According to a common pattern, a ruler must compensate for a military failure with a demonstration of power. Antiochos IV was a master of illusion (see p. 120); it required some staging for him to present his humiliation in Eleusis as a triumph. He did this by organising an impressive military parade of more than 50,000 men at Daphne, near the capital city of Antioch, upon his return from his campaigns, in 166 BC. This demonstration of military power, wealth and exotic weapons was doomed to be the Seleucids' swansong.

More than a century separates the humiliation of a Seleucid on 'the day of Eleusis' from the dethronement and death of the last Seleucid 'shadow king' in 63 BC. It is a period of unceasing decline caused by a convergence of factors: an ethnic revolt in Judaea, the loss of the eastern provinces and, above all, a chain of dynastic conflicts and usurpations. Although the events on all three fronts developed parallel to each other and were in part interconnected, we must examine them separately.

A clash of cultures in Judaea: from high priests to kings

Antiochos IV was still campaigning in Egypt in 168 BC when a local conflict in Jerusalem triggered a series of events that ultimately led to the creation of the first Jewish state since the times of the Babylonian captivity in 587 BC. Jerusalem and Judaea, which were controlled by the Ptolemies in the third century BC, had fallen into Seleucid hands in 198 BC as part of the province of Koile Syria and Phoinike. Jewish elite families that had served the Ptolemies presented a threat to the new rulers, but a garrison in Jerusalem controlled the city. To win local support, Antiochos III and his successors allowed the Jews to observe their religious traditions and laws, and to enjoy a certain amount of autonomy under the authority of a high priest. The Seleucid kings were interested in taxes, not in Jewish rituals.

Already during the Ptolemaic rule representatives of the Jerusalem Jewish elite had adopted Greek names and Greek customs. These 'Hellenisers' faced the contempt of the *hasidim*, the devoted Jews who were under the influence of the conservative exegetes of the Torah, the so-called 'scribes'. Since the devout Jews were mostly, but not exclusively, found among the lower strata of the population, this opposition between the two Jewish groups was also a social conflict. But the confrontation defied simplistic designations; it had social, economic, religious and cultural aspects. The Hellenisers were anything but a united front with a clear agenda. Personal ambitions and enmities, as well as competition for the office of the high priest, turned this complex confrontation into a bloody conflict.

A Helleniser known under his Greek name, Jason, the Greek rendering of Jesus, succeeded in becoming high priest in 175 BC by promising to increase the tribute paid to Antiochos IV. It is doubtful that his reforms followed a coherent political programme, but there were clear steps towards the acceptance of Greek institutions, such as the establishment of a gymnasium as a place of athletic and military training and the introduction of the *ephebeia* – the civic and military training of future citizens. Jason dedicated a place of worship on the Temple Mount, where the Second Temple stood, to the cult of Zeus Olympios. He did not desecrate the traditional Jewish place of worship of Yahweh, whose altar remained intact, but he intended to allow the mixed community of military settlers of Greek and Oriental origin who lived in Jerusalem to worship their own gods of the skies – the Greek Zeus Olympios and the Syrian Baal-Shamen. But in 172 BC, Menelas, a more fervent Helleniser, promised the king an even higher tribute and ousted Jason from his office; as a result, Jerusalem became the stage of a violent conflict between the two ambitious men, with Menelas occupying the citadel and Jason taking possession of the city. Despite the rumours that he had been killed in Egypt, Antiochos IV arrived in Jerusalem in 168 BC, determined to put an end to these troubles by supporting Menelas and taking harsh measures against the troublemakers. But he went too far. The rights granted to the Jews by his father and respected until then were revoked: traditional rites, such as circumcision, were abolished; the Jews were not allowed to observe the Law; and a fortress (Akra, the citadel) was constructed for the Seleucid garrison. These measures, intended by Antiochos as a solution to a local problem and neither as an ambitious programme of Hellenisation nor as an anti-Jewish campaign, led to a Jewish revolt known as the War of the Maccabees. Those who opposed the new measures left Jerusalem and organised resistance in the countryside and desert under the leadership of Mattathias (until 165 BC) and then his sons Judah Maqqabi or Makkabaios (165–160 BC) and Jonathan (160–143 BC). Antiochos was unable to deal with the revolt because he was engaged in a war in Iran, where he died in 164 BC. Judah occupied Jerusalem, except for the citadel, and reconsecrated the Temple in 164 BC. The restoration of the Temple to Jewish worship is still commemorated today with the festival of Hanukkah. Antiochos' vizier Lysias, anxious to become the regent for the new king, Antiochos V, hastily agreed to a peace treaty that restored the rights of the Jews. But this was not the end of the revolt.

In the following years, the internal Jewish conflicts continued. When an army under the Seleucid commander Nikanor was defeated by Judah in 161/160 BC, the new Seleucid king, Demetrios I (see p. 201), began a new campaign. Although Judah met with defeat and death in 160 BC, the rebels had already established relations with Rome, and Judah's brother Jonathan continued the struggle for a few years against the Seleucid general Bakchides. A peace treaty with the Seleucids allowed him to increase his power, with Machmas (or Michmash) as his stronghold. The turning point in the rebellion came in 150 BC, when Jonathan took the opportunities offered by dynastic conflicts in the Seleucid kingdom. He offered his services to the usurper Alexander Balas (see p. 201), receiving in exchange not only the office of the high priest but also the political position of the *meridarches* (the head of the *meris*, or governorship of the region of Judaea). This was the first step towards the creation of a Jewish state. When the next usurper appeared, Diodotos Tryphon, Jonathan again offered his services, but he fell victim to treachery. Tryphon invited him to a conference, arrested him and executed him in 143 BC. To avenge his death, Jonathan's brother Simon sided with the legitimate king, Demetrios II, and achieved freedom from taxation, as well as recognition as the first ruler of a semi-independent Judaea in 142 BC. The next year an assembly of the priests, the elders and the people elected him high priest for life. This was the beginning of the Hasmonean dynasty, which ruled Judaea until 63 BC. After Simon's assassination in 135 BC, his son John Hyrkanos (135–104 BC) continued his work, conquering Transjordan, Samaria, Galilee and Idumaea, but remaining a vassal of the Seleucids until 110 BC, when his state became fully independent. Judaea survived as a state until the Roman occupation of Jerusalem in 63 BC, albeit torn apart by dynastic conflicts and civil war, and engaged in frequent wars with Seleucid kings and usurpers.

The rise and fall of Greek kingdoms in central Asia

Parallel to the developments in Judaea, the Seleucids were struggling to maintain possession of most of their territories in the eastern part of their empire. Although they ultimately lost the so-called upper satrapies, in today's Iran and Afghanistan, Hellenic culture and institutions continued to thrive there until the late second century BC, having significant impact on art and culture in central Asia.

The loyalty of the upper satrapies depended on the ability of a monarch to offer protection against the raids of nomadic tribes and foreign invasions. With his great campaign between 210 and 204 BC, Antiochos III had restored his authority there, forcing renegade satraps and local dynasts to accept him as overlord. But his defeat by the Romans and the following troubles created a power vacuum. The kingdom that profited the most from the resulting Seleucid decline was that of the Parthians.

The Parthian kingdom was created when the satrapy of Parthia in north-east Iran seceded from the Seleucid kingdom in 247 BC and the satrap Andragoras declared himself king. His realm was conquered in 238 BC by the Iranian people of the Parni, henceforth known as the Parthians. Unable to re-establish his rule there, Antiochos III was left with no other option but to tolerate Arsakes II as king and to demand, in 209 BC, that the Parthian king recognise him as overlord. When Mithridates I (171–138 BC) ascended the throne, an opportunity for expansion presented itself. Antiochos IV had turned his attention to his Egyptian campaigns and then to the problems in Judaea. In the first years of his reign, Mithridates conquered Herat as well as parts of Bactria (see Map 6). Antiochos IV's death in 164 BC, during his campaign against the Parthians and the dynastic conflicts that followed, gave Mithridates the opportunity to gradually conquer the Seleucid territories east of the Tigris (Media and Persia) and parts of Mesopotamia and Babylonia. In 141 BC, Seleukeia on the Tigris, the first Seleucid capital, named after the dynasty's founder, fell into the hands of Mithridates and became the western capital of the Parthian Empire. The territories that were not conquered by the Parthians came under the rule of local dynasts, who are known from their coins. Although later Seleucid kings resumed the struggle against the Parthians, they never succeeded in reconquering the lost territories. When the Seleucids were deprived of all their possessions in Iran, the easternmost Greeks in Bactria and India were cut off from the rest of the Hellenistic world.

The Graeco-Bactrian kingdom emerged out of the need of the easternmost satrapies to defend themselves against the rising Parthian state. King Euthydemos had been forced into subordination by Antiochos III, but Euthydemos' son Demetrios I made the Graeco-Bactrian kingdom autonomous again and, taking advantage of the collapse of the Mauryan Empire in India in 185 BC, he reconquered Arachosia (south Afghanistan/northern Pakistan; see Map 6). An inscription found somewhere in eastern Bactria praises Euthydemos as 'the greatest of all the kings' and his son Demetrios as 'the one who has won fair victories'. Demetrios' campaigns, which probably brought him as far as northern India, had already started during his father's reign. After Demetrios' death, in around 180 BC, his kingdom was divided due to usurpations by generals. A separate Indo-Greek kingdom emerged around 175 BC, with Gandhara (in modern Pakistan) as its nucleus; in periods of expansion it possessed additional territory in Arachosia, Paropamisades and Punjab. The Graeco-Bactrian kingdom proper was divided into two parts, ruled by different dynasties. The most important ruler was Eukratides (c. 170–145 BC; see Fig. 8). He ruled over a vast area but failed to take possession of the eastern territories controlled by King Menandros (c. 165/155–c. 130 BC), the greatest of the Indo-Greek kings.

The later history of these easternmost Hellenistic kingdoms is also an episode in the history of central Asia. The movement of populations in the steppes of central Asia initiated the movement of tribes to the west and south. The invasions of nomadic tribes, first the Scythians from the north and then the Yuezhi (Tocharians?) from the western border of China, destroyed central authority and brought about the dissolution of the Graeco-Bactrian kingdoms around 130 BC. Although the Indo-Greek kingdom also lost its unity around that time, Greek rulers continued to control most of Menandros' realm. We know their names from their coins, which carry bilingual Greek-Indian legends, and from scattered pieces of information in Greek, Indian and Chinese sources. Isolated and protected from invasions by the Hindu Kush range, they could hold power longer than the Graeco-Bactrians, but the invasions of the Scythians, the Parthians and the Yuezhi gradually reduced their territories. An inscription from Mathura (in modern Uttar Pradesh in northern India) refers to the construction of a well in 'the 116th year of the reign of the Yavanas' (the Ionians, i.e. the Greeks); if this local era started with Demetrios (c. 186/185 BC), the implication is that Greek rulers controlled this area until the early first century BC. The last Indo-Greek dynasty still ruled the eastern Punjab in the first century BC, when the territories of Straton, its last king, were conquered by Indo-Scythians around AD 10.

The Graeco-Bactrian and Indo-Greek kings preserved Greek language and culture and promoted a syncretism of Greek religion and Buddhist beliefs (see p. 395). The amalgamation of Greek art and Buddhist religion is evident in the Buddhist reliefs from the area of Gandhara. From here Greek artistic influence spread into the Indian subcontinent and is recognizable as late as the second century AD. An inscription with a long and elaborate poem from Alexandria Arachosia (Kandahar) in the late first century BC (see pp. 390–1) is evidence of the preservation of a sophisticated Greek culture beyond the collapse of the Graeco-Bactrian kingdoms.

The Seleucid dynastic conflicts and the slow death of the Seleucid dynasty

The loss of territories in the eastern and western parts of the Seleucid Empire coincided with and was caused in part by dynastic conflicts that started after the death of Antiochos IV in 164 BC and lasted for a hundred years. Apart from the problems inherent in every system in which a position of leadership is occupied on the basis not of merit but of heritage, the Seleucid crisis became worse because of the confluence of additional factors. Unlike most early kings, who ascended the throne after they had been associated with their fathers in the government of the kingdoms and had acquired sufficient training and experience to govern, beginning in the late third century BC the royal infant or child, placed under the guardianship of an ambitious courtier or a widowed queen, becomes a very common phenomenon. The main concern of the guardians was not the education of the young kings but the preservation of their own power and survival. Other new factors – new, at any rate, in this density – were interventions by foreign kingdoms and Rome in questions of succession. The weaknesses of the rulers offered the female members of the dynasties possibilities for political interventions. In the early Hellenistic period, princesses had mostly been diplomatic tools, given by fathers and brothers in marriage to foreign kings. However, many royal women in the second and first centuries BC were conscious of their political power and the role they could play in offering legitimacy to the rule of a brother or a son. Conscious also were the populations of the capital cities that raised demands in order to accept a king's legitimacy. That the populations of the capital cities became active participants in dynastic changes was not a cause of the crisis but it certainly was one of its symptoms.

The very confusing history of the Seleucid civil wars cannot be narrated here, but we should at least examine what triggered the unprecedented chain of dynastic conflicts. Their early history is instructive. At the time of Seleukos IV's assassination in 175 BC, his six-year-old son Demetrios was being held as a hostage in Rome. In Demetrios' absence, Seleukos' brother Antiochos IV usurped the throne and married his brother's widow, who was also his sister. When Antiochos IV died in 164 BC, his son Antiochos V was a child of nine years old. Demetrios recognised his chance to reclaim the throne. He turned to the Roman senate for support, assigning to them the authority to recognise the legitimacy of a Hellenistic king. The senate preferred a child on the throne rather than an ambitious young man and rejected his claim, but this did not discourage the twenty-two-year-old prince. Demetrios escaped from Rome and returned to Syria in 161 BC, where he killed Antiochos V and the vizier Lysias, and started a reign that is thus summarised by Cavafy in the first verse of his poem 'Of Demetrios Soter': 'His every expectation turned out wrong!'

At the beginning, it looked as if Demetrios might have a chance to reunite the empire. In Judaea he defeated Judah Maccabee, and in Media he defeated the satrap Timarchos, who had defended the satrapy from the Parthians and had declared himself king (162–160 BC). Both foes were killed but both had brothers, who contributed to Demetrios' downfall. In Judaea, Jonathan Maccabee continued the revolt, and Timarchos' brother Herakleides discovered a young man in 152 BC who would raise a claim to the Seleucid throne: Balas. He was of obscure origins but was presented as a son of Antiochos IV and was given a name associated with royalty and glory: Alexander.

By this point in his short reign, Demetrios I had already accumulated so many enemies by interfering in dynastic conflicts in the neighbouring kingdom of Kappadokia and in Egypt that his struggle against the usurper Alexander Balas was doomed to fail. The Roman senate upheld Balas' claim, Jonathan Maccabee supported the usurper in exchange for the high priesthood and Ptolemy VI gave Balas his daughter Cleopatra Thea as his wife. Demetrios I, known as Soter (Rescuer), was unable to save himself. He was defeated and killed in 150 BC.

This was not the end but the beginning of the dynastic wars. Demetrios' son, Demetrios II, successfully challenged Balas' rule in 147 BC, but his own rule was short, unpopular and unhappy. He owed his throne to foreign patronage and to the military support of mercenaries. The plundering of Antioch by these mercenaries led to a popular uprising. The revolt was drowned in blood, but Demetrios' days in Antioch were numbered, and with them also the days of a unified Seleucid kingdom. Torn apart by the claims to the throne of a continuously increasing number of sons of dead kings, the efforts of the rulers of semi-autonomous regions to gain their autonomy and the ambitions of royal widows and generals, the Seleucid kingdom was divided and the provinces east of the Tigris were either lost to the Parthians or became autonomous kingdoms. It is probably around the time of Demetrios II that the Seleucid satrap in the area of the Persian Gulf, Hyspaosines, declared his independence, founding the kingdom of Charakene, which controlled the area south of the confluence of the Tigris and the Euphrates, and the Persian Gulf at least as far as Bahrain. An inscription from Bahrain, a dedication made by the general of the district of 'Tylos and the Islands' to the Dioskouroi on behalf of King Hyspaosines and Queen Thalasia, shows the preservation of Seleucid administrative institutions, Greek language and Greek culture in the new kingdom.

In the first decades of the first century BC, after years of wars and atrocities, the divided Seleucid kingdom was hardly more than the territory around Antioch. Surrounded by enemies, the kingdom had lost its significance and the kings the power to legitimise their authority by offering security and prosperity to the population, privileges to the cities, spoils of war to the army and favours to the courtiers. In 83 BC, the population of Antioch invited the most powerful king in the area to take the throne: Tigranes II, king of Armenia. In the previous years, Tigranes had expanded the borders of his kingdom at the expense of the Parthians, conquering territories in northern Iran and Iraq. Tigranes accepted the offer, thus annoying the Roman senate, which preferred to recognise a Seleucid prince as a 'shadow king'. This did not prevent Tigranes from adding to his realm not only Syria but also Cilicia, bringing his borders to those of

Asia Minor. For the first time since the Battle of Gaugamela in 331 BC, when Alexander defeated the Great King and was declared king of Asia, a king of Iranian origin with the title King of Kings ruled an empire that extended from the Caspian Sea to the Mediterranean. If 83 BC is not the year that marks the end of Hellenic culture in this area, it is only because of Pompey's victory over Tigranes in 63 BC. Syria was re-established as part of the Greek world, albeit as a Roman province.

Game of thrones: the civil wars of the Ptolemies

A screenwriter straining to create plotlines for a soap opera full of family rivalry, intrigue, incestuous relations, murder and the most incredible turns of fortune should look no further than the last 150 years of the Ptolemaic dynasty for inspiration. The glory of this house had reached its apogee with two siblings who married, ruled together and were known as the Philadelphoi, 'the sibling-loving' king and queen: Ptolemy II and Arsinoe II. Royal epithets such as Philopator (father-loving, for Ptolemy IV, VII and XIII, as well as for Cleopatra VII) and Philometor (mother-loving, for Ptolemy VI) transmitted the image of a loving family. The reality was different.

Ptolemy V was a child of eleven when Antiochos III conquered Koile Syria and Phoinike in 198 BC. During most of his reign south Egypt was also lost to Egyptian rebels ruled by the native pharaoh Ankmachis. The famous Rosetta Stone, an inscription in Greek, hieroglyphic and demotic that made the decipherment of the hieroglyphic script possible, dates to the time when Ptolemy took personal control of part of the kingdom in 196 BC. It contains a decree of Egyptian priests in Memphis honouring the thirteen-year-old king with divine honours in acknowledgement of the tax exemption that he had granted to the temples. This text is evidence of the king's dependence on the traditional priests, rather than his power. It took Ptolemy another eleven years to have the usurper in south Egypt arrested and it was only in 183 BC that the rebels were finally defeated. His marriage with Cleopatra I 'the Syrian' in 193 BC brought peace with the Seleucids, at least temporarily. When Ptolemy V died in 180 BC, Cleopatra became the first queen to rule Egypt on her own, while her eldest son, Ptolemy VI, was only six years old. The death of Cleopatra I in 176 BC marked the beginning of a long period of bloody dynastic conflicts, civil wars and turmoil that only ended when the last Cleopatra (VII) successively rid herself of her brother-husbands Ptolemy XIII in 47 and Ptolemy XIV in 44 BC and remained the sole, and last, ruler of Egypt.

Upon the death of Cleopatra I, the ten-year-old Ptolemy VI Philometor remained sole ruler. According to the Ptolemaic practice, he married his sister Cleopatra II, with whom he had four children. With no consideration of the problems this might create for future historians, he named both sons Ptolemy and both daughters Cleopatra. The boys, Ptolemy Eupator (the one with the good father) and Ptolemy VII Neos Philopator (the new lover of his father), are of little historical significance, apart from brief periods in which they co-ruled with their father, before dying at a young age. We cannot say the same for the two Cleopatras. Cleopatra Thea became queen in Syria (see p. 202), married in succession to Alexandros Balas, Demetrios II, Antiochos Sidetes and again to Demetrios II. Her sister Cleopatra III surpassed every other Hellenistic queen in her struggle for power.

The factors that contributed to dynastic crises in Ptolemaic Egypt do not differ from those already mentioned in connection with the dynastic crisis in the Seleucid kingdom. Inexperienced minors were placed on the throne; siblings were forced to jointly rule the kingdom but ended up struggling for sole power; queens – royal mothers and sister-wives – were now strongly involved in the struggle for power, as were courtiers. Foreign interventions, especially by Rome and the Seleucids, unknown in the third century BC, were now common and contributed to the crisis of leadership. Kings deposed by their brothers or sisters acquired the habit of going to Rome to beg for support. The weaker the royal authority, the stronger the role played by the population of the capital, whose uprisings contributed to the fall of a king and his replacement by a relative. Unlike the Seleucids, Egypt did not face foreign raids – except for the invasion by Antiochos IV during the Sixth Syrian War of 170–168 BC – but its kings instead encountered local problems: the control of two remote provinces, Cyrenaica and Cyprus, which in times of civil war were often ruled by separate kings; and the dissatisfaction of the indigenous population with the royal administration which resulted in small-scale uprisings of farmers and, more often, in their desertion from the fields.

Between 170 and 118 BC, Egypt was the stage of repeated civil wars between sibling kings and queens who invariably had the names Ptolemy and Cleopatra. A few episodes of these troubled decades exemplify the magnitude of the crisis. Afraid of real or imaginary attempts on his life, one of the kings of this period, Ptolemy VIII Physkon (the Pot-Belly), who ruled Cyrenaica, took an unprecedented measure in order to make sure that even if his brother Ptolemy VI succeeded in assassinating him, he would have nothing to gain. In the spring of 155 BC, he published a will, according to which in case of his death his kingdom would become the property of the Roman people. Although the terms of this will were never fulfilled (Physkon survived his brother), it became the model for three similar bequests, through which Rome took control of the territories of the kingdoms of Pergamon in 133 and Cyrenaica and Bithynia in 74 BC.

The second episode concerns Physkon again. When his brother Ptolemy VI died in 145 BC, he was succeeded by his son Ptolemy VII and his widow Cleopatra II. Encouraged by the population of Alexandria, which was demanding his return, Physkon captured Cyprus and advanced towards the capital. Cleopatra II, supported only by the Jewish population of the capital and the scholars of the Mouseion, recognised that resistance would be futile and agreed to marry Physkon. This sealed her son's fate: Ptolemy VII was murdered on her wedding night. Physkon showed himself relentless in his revenge. He prosecuted all those who had opposed him in the past, including many intellectuals, who were sent into exile. Other centres of learning were to profit from this exodus of scholars, among them Pergamon.

A new dramatic turn in this game of thrones occurred in 142 BC. Physkon fell in love with his wife's daughter (and his own niece), Cleopatra III, and took her as a second wife. The incestuous *ménage à trois* did not work well and the struggle between the two Cleopatras led to a division of the kingdom in 131 BC. With the support of the population of Alexandria, who set the palace on fire, Cleopatra II succeeded in occupying the throne alone, while Physkon escaped to Cyprus together with Cleopatra III and the only son he had fathered with Cleopatra II: Ptolemy Memphites. From Cyprus, Physkon sent his sister-wife a gruesome present: the head, hands and feet of their son. He regained control of Egypt in 127 BC, and Cleopatra II went into exile until 124 BC, when reconciliation with her brother and daughter became possible.

Amnesty was declared in 118 BC; the document survives, and it reveals how deep the division of the country had been, with various groups – the Greek population, the Egyptian priests, the indigenous farmers and the soldiers – participating in or becoming victims of the civil war. When

Roman envoys under Scipio Aemilianus had visited Egypt in 140/139 BC, they had admired the fertility and prosperity of the land, the large number of cities and settlements, the large population, the infrastructure and the security. Twenty years later, the carefully chosen formulations of the amnesty decree could not conceal the impression of a kingdom where law and authority had been disregarded for years. The countryside had been abandoned by farmers who had become brigands; the royal treasury had suffered from delays in the payment of taxes and the temples from disruption in the payment of contributions; land had been illegally occupied, houses destroyed and suppliants removed from places of asylum; officials had abused their power; and the infrastructure had been left without the proper care.

The dynastic conflicts continued, and by the end of the second century BC, the Ptolemaic kingdom was de facto divided into three parts: Egypt, Cyrene and Cyprus. Cyrenaica was lost for ever in 96 BC, when its last ruler, Ptolemy Apion, left the cities free and bequeathed his kingdom to the Roman people. The Romans created a new province in Cyrenaica in 74 BC. Ptolemy IX Lathyros temporarily reunited what was left of the kingdom in 88 BC, but his death in 81 BC opened the last phase of the Ptolemaic game of thrones.

10

A BATTLEFIELD OF
FOREIGN AMBITIONS

(88–30 BC)

Longing for the freedom to fight wars

For if once you allow the clouds now gathering in the west to settle upon Greece, I fear exceedingly that the power of making peace or war, and in a word all these games which we are now playing against each other, will be so completely knocked out of the hands of us all, that we shall be praying heaven to grant us only this power of making war or peace with each other at our own will and pleasure, and of settling our own disputes.

When Polybius wrote these lines, around the mid-second century BC (see p. 156), he knew that what had worried an Aetolian statesman in 217 BC had become a reality: the increasing power of Rome had deprived the Greeks of their freedom to make their own wars. War had been omnipresent in the two centuries that followed Alexander's death. With the exception of occasional barbaric invasions on the borders of the Hellenistic world, these wars had been between Greek states, federations and kingdoms. But from the late third century BC onwards, the Macedonian Wars brought about a qualitative change in Greek war: they made the Romans part of 'all these games which the Greeks were playing against each other'. And by the mid-second century BC the establishment of direct Roman rule in most of Greece and a large part of Asia Minor made wars among the Greeks impossible. Yet another qualitative change, one that Polybius could never have predicted, occurred in the first century when Greece and Asia Minor became the battlefield of wars motivated by the personal ambitions not of Greek kings but of foreigners: first the wars between Rome and Mithridates, king of Pontos, then the civil wars between ambitious Roman statesmen.

The Roman expansion brought to Greece and Asia Minor a large number of Italian tradesmen and manufacturers (*negotiatores*) known as the Italici. They exploited the possibilities offered by the subdued Greek regions for trade with slaves, luxury items and agricultural products, especially those that could be easily stored in jars and transported by ship: wine and olive oil. They were also increasingly involved in banking, manufacture and, wherever they could acquire land, also in agricultural production. Although we cannot determine the number of Italian settlers in the East, various sources, such as documents of private associations, epitaphs and honorific inscriptions, leave no doubt that their presence was visible.

The newcomers were not only entrepreneurs but also tax collectors (*publicani*). For the Greeks of Asia Minor, the payment of tribute to Rome was a clear setback: 10 per cent of agricultural production and civic revenues was paid to Rome; the payable amount was not estimated on an annual basis but for a period of five years, without considering fluctuations in supply. In the decades that followed the Aristonikos War, the province of Asia was the victim of ruthless economic exploitation. The complaints of the provincial population were addressed to the Roman senate and Roman magistrates, but when the complaints did not bring any noticeable change, the Greeks placed their hopes on the ambitious king of a rising kingdom: Mithridates VI, the king of Pontos. Mithridates' wish to expand his kingdom at the expense of Rome, combined with the dissatisfaction of the Greeks of Asia Minor and Greece, caused the Mithridatic Wars that lasted from 88 to 64 BC.

Pontos: from peripheral kingdom to international player

Located in the south-east corner of the Black Sea and originally part of the satrapy of Kappadokia, Pontos became an independent region during the Wars of the Successors. The first ruler was a Persian dynast of the city of Kios who, like his descendants, bore the name Mithridates. His son Mithridates Ktistes (the founder), declared himself king in 281 or 280 BC. In the following centuries the kingdom expanded along the south-eastern and eastern coast of the Black Sea (see Maps 3 and 5). With control of important ports such as Amastris, Sinope and Trapezous, and allies such as Chersonesos of Tauris in the Crimea and Odessos in modern Bulgaria, the kingdom of Pontos became a significant power in the Black Sea region. By allying his kingdom with Rome, Mithridates V (150–120 BC) profited from his display of loyalty and received additional territories in Phrygia. Under his rule the Hellenisation of his kingdom advanced and Greek mercenaries joined his army.

After his assassination, in unclear circumstances, the kingdom was ruled by his widow, Laodike, who favoured one of her sons, Mithridates Chrestos (the virtuous) over his brother Mithridates Eupator (the one of a good father). The young prince went into exile, to return with a vengeance in 113 BC. He killed his brother, imprisoned and later executed his mother, and radically transformed the traditionally pro-Roman policies of his kingdom. His early expansion was towards the East. He added Lesser Armenia to his kingdom through inheritance, conquered Colchis and won the loyalty of the Greeks in the Crimea by defending them against Scythian attacks.

After acquiring additional resources and manpower, taking control of important trade routes and consolidating his power, Mithridates expanded in Asia Minor at the expense of the neighbouring kingdoms. Paphlagonia was conquered and divided between him and King Nikomedes IV of Bithynia. Parts of Galatia were incorporated into his realm. In Kappadokia, his sister, who was married to King Ariarathes VI, engineered the king's murder in 116 BC and ruled the kingdom, until Mithridates placed his own son Ariarathes IX on the throne in 101 BC. The international situation favoured this expansion, since Rome was weakened by two long wars that had threatened its possessions in north Italy and North Africa: the wars against the Germanic tribes of the Cimbri and the Teutons in 113–101 BC and the war against King Iugurtha in Numidia, modern Algeria, in 112–105 BC.

But in 97 BC, Roman pressure became noticeable again and Mithridates withdrew from Kappadokia, where the senate installed Ariobarzanes as a king. But as soon as the Romans turned their attention to the conflict with their allies in Italy, who were demanding Roman citizenship, Mithridates returned to his policy of expansion. While his son-in-law and ally Tigranes the Great of Armenia invaded Kappadokia in 91 BC at Mithridates' instigation, Mithridates himself conquered Bithynia. But the deposed King Nikomedes IV regained his throne with Roman support. Although the Romans were still fighting the 'Social War' against their allies in Italy, they did dispatch an army to Asia in 90 BC and forced Tigranes to withdraw from Kappadokia.

This was not the end of the conflicts among these peripheral kingdoms. When Nikomedes plundered Mithridatic territories, Mithridates invaded Bithynia again in 89 BC, ignoring a Roman ultimatum. He could count on a large army – allegedly an infantry of 250,000 men, 50,000 cavalrymen and 130 scythed chariots – as well as the support of his allies and the dissatisfaction of the Greek population in Asia. He also hoped that the war the Romans were fighting with their allies in Italy would prevent them from sending many legions to the East. Such a window of opportunities begged for action, and Mithridates was a man of action. What he could not predict was that his expansion would also offer a window of opportunity to Roman generals thirsty for glory and power. In the next sixty years, the Greek and Hellenised East became a battlefield where Roman grandees won the laurels that would increase their power in Rome.

The First Mithridatic War and the rise of Sulla

The First Mithridatic War, which lasted from 89 to 84 BC, was accompanied by an uprising against Rome in Greece and Asia Minor and coincided with the first civil war in Rome. The Roman civil wars originated from the division between the *populares*, who were pressing for reforms to solve the social problems that had accumulated for decades, and the conservative *optimates*. While Marius, an experienced general and leader of the *populares*, and Sulla, the champion of the *optimates*, were fighting over who would command the war against Mithridates, the Pontic king succeeded in taking control of the largest part of the province of Asia.

In 88 BC, during his stay in Ephesos, Mithridates ordered the killing of the Roman and Italian settlers and entrepreneurs in Asia. About 80,000 Romans and Italians were killed in a single night. This atrocious deed, known as the 'Ephesian Vespers', reveals both the strong presence of Italians in Asia Minor and the hatred of the subdued population. A further massacre took place on Delos. The news of Mithridates' success aroused among the Greeks the hope of liberation from Rome. From Macedonia, Mithridates' army marched through Thessaly to central Greece. Only a few cities in Asia Minor and Rhodes, traditionally an enemy of pirates, who were Mithridates' allies, remained loyal to Rome. The period of peace that Greece had enjoyed after the conquest of 146 BC had not extinguished the desire for freedom. In Athens, Mithridates was welcomed as a liberator and a New Dionysus, and other cities were quick to follow. Within a year the rule of Rome in the East seemed to belong to the past.

The contemporary historian and philosopher Poseidonios (c. 135–51 BC), who at that time lived in Rhodes and regarded Rome as a force for stability, gives an account of how the philosopher Athenion encouraged the Athenians to take up arms against the rule of Rome. This description shows how rumours and exaggerations about Mithridates' power and success influenced decision-making:

Let me say things never expected, never dreamt before: King Mithridates is lord over Bithynia and Cilicia. The kings of Persia and Armenia are his royal attendants, his princely attendants are the princes of the Maiotic district and all round the Black Sea to a range of 30,000 miles. The Roman governor of Pamphylia, Quintus Oppius, has surrendered and follows in chains. The consular Manius Aquillius, who triumphed over Sicily, is dragged on a long chain, led by a Bastarnian warrior five cubits in height, the Roman on foot after the barbarian on horseback. The other Romans lie before their idols or have changed their togas into Greek clothes again, reclaiming their former countries. There is no town that does not honor him with more than human honors and welcome him as a God-king. Prophecies from all parts of the world promise him the sovereignty of the earth. Large armies are moving in the direction of Thracia and Macedonia and most countries of Europe are rushing to his side. Embassies not only from the Italian tribes but also from the Carthaginians are asking alliance in the war for the destruction of Rome.

Athenion's speech also gives us an impression of the expectations of the Athenians:

> What do I advise you? No longer to suffer the anarchy that the Senate of Rome inflicts upon us on the pretext of examining our constitution. No longer to tolerate our sanctuaries being closed, our gymnasiums uncared for, our theatres robbed of their public meetings, our courts silent and our Pnyx, which was given us by divine judgment, being withheld from the people. Let us no longer tolerate, citizens of Athens, that the holy cry of Iakchos is no more heard, that the sacred house of the goddesses is closed and that the schools of the philosophers are mute!

The Athenians enthusiastically elected him general, along with the men he nominated, and tolerated the relentless prosecution of those who resisted his policies.

The traditional political structures in Rome, created for the administration of a city and not of an empire, were unsuitable for such a crisis. The number of magistrates with *imperium* (military command) was limited and the processes of decision-making complicated and time-consuming. Weakened by wars and divided over the need for social and political reforms, the Romans were slow to respond. The two main opponents in Rome, Marius and the current consul Sulla, struggled for command in the war against Mithridates, amidst violent riots in the city. When Sulla did the unthinkable and marched on Rome with six legions, becoming the first general ever to cross the *pomoerium* (the city's border) with an army, Marius and his supporters were forced to flee, and Sulla secured the command for himself.

He landed in Epirus in 87 BC with five legions, not suspecting how fast the situation would change against him back in Rome. During his absence, Marius returned to the city, exiled Sulla and was elected consul for the next year. His death soon after his election left Rome under the control of his supporter Lucius Cornelius Cinna, who was scheming to relieve Sulla of his command. But Sulla's attention was devoted to the enemy of the Roman state and his Greek supporters. He marched through Boiotia to Athens and besieged the city. The Athenians defended their city for about a year, until the lack of food and manpower forced them to negotiate with him. Plutarch's report on the short negotiations can be read as a commentary on the contrast between past glory and present misery and between the traditional Athenian rhetoric and the pragmatism of a Roman general:

> When the envoys made no demands which could save the city, but proudly talked about Theseus, Eumolpos, and the Persian Wars, Sulla said to them: 'Go away, blessed men, and take these speeches with you; for I was not sent to Athens by the Romans to fulfill love of knowledge, but to subdue rebels.'

Athens capitulated in March 86 BC, but this did not save the city from brutal looting. In the meantime, Sulla's enemies in Rome had dispatched an army under Lucius Valerius Flaccus and Caius Flavius Fimbria to relieve him of his command. But as soon as the army reached Greece many of Flaccus' soldiers deserted to Sulla, and the ingenious general defeated Mithridates' troops first in Chaironeia and then in Orchomenos. While the remnants of the second Roman army operated in northern Greece against the Pontic troops and then moved into Asia Minor, Sulla took control of Greece, destroyed the cities that had resisted the Roman armies and occupied the Aegean islands.

Mithridates' power was also collapsing in Asia Minor. Although the Roman leadership was divided – Fimbria started a rebellion against Flaccus, who was captured and executed – Mithridates' troops could not resist the advance of the Roman legions. The Greeks began to realise that they had exchanged the rule of Rome for that of an Oriental despot who had no interest in respecting their traditions of civic autonomy. The inhabitants of Chios, whom the king suspected because of a strong pro-Roman faction, were first forced to deliver their arms and the children of the most influential families as hostages, then condemned to a fine and finally captured and transported to Pontos. When the cruelty of his general Zenobios became known to other cities, Mithridates was left with hardly any allies. He responded to the defection of his allies with an old populist recipe. He instigated popular unrest against the ruling elite by promising land to the dispossessed, cancellation of debts to the debtors and freedom to the slaves. His promises bought him some time but, under attack on two fronts, he realised that his best option was to negotiate. Also Sulla was eager to end the war as soon as possible in order to deal with his adversaries in Rome. For this reason the Roman general agreed to meet

Mithridates at Dardanos in 85 BC and to offer him lenient terms for peace. That Mithridates was required to evacuate all the territories that he had conquered since 88 BC was not a harsh term; Fimbria had reconquered these territories anyway. Mithridates also agreed to provide Sulla with a fleet and money, and in exchange he was allowed to keep his kingdom and to be accepted among the 'friends of the Roman people'.

Sulla was now free to deal with his enemies in Asia Minor, and he did this in a relentless manner that foreshadowed the massacres that were to take place in Rome a few years later. He attacked Fimbria in his camp, causing his army to desert and Fimbria to take his own life; he rewarded his veterans with permission to loot the rebellious cities of Asia and imposed large fines on the Greeks for their rebellion. The supporters of Rome were compensated with privileges, and Rhodes was given some territories in Caria. Sulla then returned to Rome, where a power vacuum occurred unexpectedly in 84 BC. During a badly organised campaign in Illyria, the consul Cinna was stoned to death by his own soldiers. In 83 BC, Sulla landed in Italy and after a bloody civil war he captured Rome in November 82 BC. Appointed by the senate as *dictator* 'for the making of laws and for the settling of the constitution' in 81 BC, he initiated reforms that significantly changed Roman provincial administration (see p. 272). After serving as consul for a year, he retired in 79 BC and died a year later, after finishing his memoirs, of which only a few quotations survive.

The Second and Third Mithridatic Wars and Lucullian ambitions

The Peace of Dardanos was short-lived. A Second Mithridatic War started in 83 BC, when Sulla's deputy Lucius Licinius Murena invaded Pontos, claiming that Mithridates was violating the peace and organising a new army to invade the province of Asia. Murena was defeated by Mithridates and at Sulla's orders the war ended in 81 BC. But if Murena suspected that Mithridates' expansionist ambitions had not died in Dardanos, he would be proved right a few years later. Nikomedes IV, king of Bithynia, died in 74 BC and bequeathed his kingdom to the Romans. The Roman senate accepted the will and established yet another province in Asia: Bithynia. Recognising an opportunity to make up lost ground, Mithridates occupied Bithynia in 73 BC, where he was welcomed by the local population, who preferred his rule to exploitation by the Roman *publicani*.

Lucius Licinius Lucullus, a Roman nobleman who had already served in the East under Sulla, was given a military command in the war against Mithridates. He was destined to become more famous for his dinners than for his military exploits, which in the early phase of the Third Mithridatic War were significant. Within three years he succeeded not only in recovering Bithynia but also in conquering Mithridates' kingdom of Pontos. In 70 BC, the defeated king was offered refuge by Tigranes, king of Armenia, the strongest ruler in the East.

In this period, Rome's foreign policy had become closely interconnected with the personal political interests of Roman aristocrats, with their competition for commands and with their need to offer spoils of war to their soldiers and land to their veterans. Roman expansion had also made the deficiencies of Roman political institutions evident. Lucullus' behaviour in the East after his victory can be explained in terms of these internal Roman conflicts. His task had been fulfilled with the defeat of Mithridates, but his ambitions had not been fully served. Lucullus needed to remain in command of legions. This was of vital importance at a time when other Roman statesmen were entrusted with military commands in a series of interconnected wars that were crucial for the survival of Roman power. Cnaeus Pompeius, later known as Pompey the Great, was celebrated as victor over the renegade governor of Spain, Sertorius, who had led a revolt of the oppressed population against Rome and created an independent state that existed from 83 until his murder in 72 BC. Closer to Rome, in Italy, Marcus Licinius Crassus had defeated the slave revolt of Spartacus, which had terrorised the Italian cities and countryside from 73 to 70 BC. And in 74 BC, Marcus Antonius – the father of the more famous Mark Antony – had received a command to fight the pirates whose raids of merchant ships had made traffic in the eastern Mediterranean hazardous. All these enemies of Roman order – Mithridates, Sertorius, the slaves and the pirates – were in contact. Their cooperation against Rome was at times closer than that of the Roman generals who were supposed to defeat them.

In order to prolong his command, Lucullus continued the offensive against Tigranes, under the pretext that the Armenian king refused to deliver Mithridates. But apart from his ambitions, Lucullus had other good reasons to continue the war. In view of Mithridates' past behaviour, it must have been clear to the Roman leaders that their possessions in the East would not be safe as long as the king was alive; and any statesman with foresight would have recognised the dangers emanating from the rise of the kingdom of Armenia, which under Tigranes the Great had annexed Mesopotamia, Cilicia and the greater part of northern Syria, replacing the Seleucid kingdom as the greatest power in the Near and Middle East.

In 70 BC, Lucullus won a great victory near Tigranokerta, Tigranes' capital, but was unable to capture Tigranes and Mithridates. Blinded by this success, he continued the campaign into regions where no Roman army had ever set foot, thus approaching the realm of the Parthians and making it difficult for his army to receive supplies. In addition to this, he aroused the enmity of the *publicani* and the Roman knights by his mild taxation of the provincial population, and the envy of his fellow *nobiles* by his success. In 69 BC, the Roman senate relieved him of his command in the province of Asia and then his command in Cilicia. In 67 BC, Lucullus had to halt his campaign in Armenia because of a revolt in his army. Tigranes recovered his kingdom and Mithridates succeeded in reconquering part of his old kingdom of Pontos. What Lucullus had achieved in six years of continuous war was to bring the Romans right back to the starting point of their war.

A change in Roman leadership occurred when Pompey was appointed as supreme military commander in the Mediterranean. It was a turning point in the history not only of Roman expansion but also of Rome's long march from republic to monarchy.

The wars against the pirates and the rise of Pompey

Because of Mithridates' cooperation with communities that traditionally made their living through naval raids, especially the Cretans and the Cilicians, the Third Mithridatic War was from the beginning closely connected with the Roman wars against the pirates. In the ancient Mediterranean, a very thin line – if any – separated maritime expeditions aiming to collect booty, what the Romans designated as piracy, from 'regular' warfare. Acts of reprisal, consisting of raids and the seizure of property, were often declared by one community against another for the satisfaction of grievances. Raids were also organised by privateers who exploited the chaotic conditions during wars, often accompanying an army and supporting its operations by attacking ships and coastal sites. But in certain regions, such as Illyria, Aetolia, Crete and Cilicia, raids were regularly launched against those who were not protected by means of a treaty of inviolability (*asylia*). The collection of booty – not unlike conquest – was regarded as legitimate profit that resulted from military superiority and was acquired with divine assistance. The profit from piracy and raids consisted primarily of valuables and prisoners, who were sold as slaves or ransomed by their families or their city. As soon as the raid was over, the pirates were transformed into merchants, approaching the next important harbour or returning to their home to sell their booty. The proverbial saying, 'The three worst *kappas* are Kappadokia, Krete and Kilikia,' derives from the notoriety of the inhabitants of these regions as pirates and bandits.

In the late second and early first centuries BC, frequent raids endangered the naval routes that connected Italy with the markets, grain suppliers and resources of North Africa, Greece, Asia Minor and the Near East. The rise of piracy was the result of various factors: the decline of Rhodes as a military power that had in the past contributed to the safety of the eastern Mediterranean, the cooperation between Mithridates and the pirates, the Cretans' need to compensate for their loss of employment as mercenaries in royal armies with an intensification of piracy, and possibly also an increased demand for slaves for agriculture and manufacture. Allegedly up to 10,000 slaves could be sold on a single day in Delos, and these people were often the victims of pirates.

Rome's first campaign against the pirates was launched in 74 BC, when the praetor Marcus Antonius was given a command to clear the seas from pirates. His campaign was a total failure and the requisition of resources from the provincial populations for his war increased the Greeks' dissatisfaction with Roman rule. Marcus Antonius died on Crete in 71 BC without achieving anything. He was remembered as Creticus, but instead of receiving this name as an honour for defeating the Cretans (the conqueror of the Cretans), it was given as an ironic reminder of his failure, as in Latin the word can be translated as 'the chalk-man'. Nevertheless, the Romans were determined to solve the problem of piracy.

When a delegation of the Cretan federation appeared in Rome in 70 BC to negotiate the terms of a peace agreement, the senate asked them to pay the enormous sum of 4,000 talents, to deliver their warships to Rome and to hand over 300 hostages, including their military leaders. The Cretans were divided: the older citizens were inclined to accept these demands but the young men, who were trained from childhood to fight and amass booty, prevailed. So 24,000 young Cretans fought the Romans under the leadership of Lasthenes of Knossos and Panares of Kydonia from 69 to 67 BC. The Roman forces were commanded by Quintus Caecilius Metellus, who swept the island from west to east, rewarding those who were willing to collaborate, razing pirates' strongholds, such as the harbour of Phalasarna, to the ground and inflicting extensive damage on cities such as Eleutherna and Knossos. At the end of this war, a social and political system that had persisted since the seventh century BC was abolished, and Crete received its first wave of Roman and Italian entrepreneurs.

In 67 BC, before the Cretan war was over, extensive powers were granted to Pompey to wage total war against the pirates. The *lex Gabinia*, the law that described the extent of Pompey's extraordinary command, decisively prepared the path for the establishment of monarchical rule four decades later. The command was superior to that of all other Roman commanders (*imperium maius*); it lasted for three years and gave Pompey control over sea and land for a distance of fifty miles from the coast. Such an *imperium* violated two fundamental principles of the Roman constitution: no office should exceed one year and every magistrate should have at least one colleague. Pompey was also given thirteen deputies (*legati*, or envoys), who foreshadowed the later *legati Augusti pro praetore* (see p. 272), the representatives of the emperor in the provinces where Roman troops were stationed. The opposition of conservative circles in the senate was ultimately overcome with the support of Caius Iulius Caesar and the plebeian tribune Aulus Gabinius, who proposed the law.

Pompey and his legates started with the systematic destruction of the pirates' strongholds and fleets from west to east. Within forty days, no pirate ship was left between Spain and Italy. Then the campaign moved to the two main centres of piracy: Crete, where Metellus was already operating, and Cilicia. With a combination of military operations and negotiations, Pompey forced the Cilician pirates to abandon their traditional occupation, and only a few pockets of piracy survived for another decade.

During his stay in Cilicia, Pompey seems to have developed a plan for a pacified East within the borders of the Roman Empire. He settled many pirates in the city of Soloi, which he renamed Pompeiopolis. This was a momentous decision, not only because of the lenient treatment of a former enemy, who was offered an alternative source of income – agriculture – but also because, for the first time, a Roman general had founded a city that was named after him, following the tradition of Hellenistic kings.

After this success in a war that was prepared in the winter, started in the spring and finished in the summer – in Cicero's words – Pompey was now asked to succeed where Lucullus had failed. His command was extended and he was assigned the war against Tigranes and Mithridates.

Pompey's vision for the Roman East

In the war against Tigranes, Pompey followed the principle of *divide et impera*. He established contact with the kingdom of the Parthians, who were threatened by Tigranes' expansion, and he recognised the River Euphrates as the Parthian border in the West. Thus Pompey defined an eastern limit for the expansion of the Roman Empire that was to dominate Roman policies for centuries. While the Parthians engaged Tigranes on the eastern borders of his kingdom, Pompey had a free hand to deal with Mithridates. The army of Mithridates was defeated near the northern course of the Euphrates, at a site where Pompey founded Nikopolis (the city of victory). Facing enemies on two fronts, Tigranes was forced to capitulate in 66 BC, withdrawing to his original kingdom of Armenia and abandoning all his conquests.

Mithridates managed to escape with the remains of his army to the northernmost part of his kingdom, the Kimmerian Bosporos, the northeast shore of the Black Sea. But despite the resistance of Caucasian tribes, Pompey continued the pursuit until he reached Colchis. In 65 BC, Mithridates occupied Crimea and, after putting his own son Machares to death, took the throne of the Bosporan kingdom. He was making plans to invade Italy following the course of the Danube when he realised that all had abandoned him, including his son Pharnakes, who led a rebellion against him. Besieged in Pantikapaion, the old king was unable even to take poison and commit suicide; for years he had been taking tiny amounts of various poisons and by increasing the dose he had made himself immune – this practice is called Mithridatism after him. Finally, a mercenary killed him at his request in 63 BC. His old kingdom was added to Bithynia to create a new province, Bithynia and Pontos. Pompey left on the throne of the Bosporan kingdom the son who had betrayed the father, Pharnakes, without suspecting that he had inherited Mithridates' ambition. In 49 BC, Pharnakes would use the opportunity offered to him by the civil war in Rome and annex Colchis and part of Armenia. His reign would have been without significance, if it were not for Caesar's quick campaign against him in 47 BC and a fast victory that made the Roman general write to a friend the famous phrase 'I came, I saw, I conquered' (*'veni, vidi, vici'*).

Having dealt with Mithridates, it was now time for Pompey to deal with Syria and the Middle East. If the Seleucid kingdom still existed, it was only at Rome's mercy. By 83 BC, most of its territories had been incorporated into the kingdom of Tigranes. The descendants of the various branches of the Seleucid dynasty continued the civil wars that for almost a century had divided the kingdom; they controlled only very small areas. Just one of them, Antiochos XIII, was recognised by the Roman senate as a king. When he was killed by an Arab dynast of Emesa in 63 BC, on Pompey's orders, the Roman general could finally settle matters west of the Euphrates. Now that Rome had common borders with the Parthians, it could not afford pockets of anarchy along the border. Syria became a Roman province in 63 BC. The Hasmonean kingdom of Judaea, divided by endemic civil wars, was also abolished; its king, Aristoboulos, was deposed and replaced by his son Hyrkanos II, who was given the titles of high priest and *ethnarches* (chief of the nation). Judaea was integrated into the province of Syria and became subject to the payment of tribute.

In less than five years, Pompey had reorganised the East in a radical manner. He had created the new provinces of Bithynia and Pontus, and Syria, and reorganised the province of Cilicia; he had added more territories to the Roman Empire than any other Roman commander; and he had fixed the borders of the remaining kingdoms – Armenia, Kappadokia, Bosporos and the Parthians. Unlike earlier expansions, the Pompeian order in the East seems to be the result of a unified concept concerning the future of the Roman Empire. Regions were conquered and annexed or given to neighbouring states with the aim of creating a continuous border for the empire. In this regard, Pompey's policy foreshadows that of Augustus.

The founding of new cities was part of the same policy of consolidation and organisation, gradually transforming former enemies and pirates into a loyal population of the empire. Pompey reorganised Cilician pirate harbours as *poleis* and renamed Soloi to Pompeiopolis. In the former realm of Mithridates VI, he restored Amastris, Sinope, Amisos and Phanagoreia to their old status as *poleis*, while several settlements were promoted to *poleis*: Abonou Teichos, which was later renamed Ionopolis, the 'Ionian city', Zela and Kabeira, which was renamed Diopolis, 'the city of Zeus'. More importantly, Pompey founded five entirely new *poleis* that commemorated his victories: Nikopolis, 'the city of victory', Megalopolis, 'the city of [Pompey] the Great', Magnopolis, 'the city of [Pompey] Magnus', a second Pompeiopolis and Neapolis, 'the new city'. The citizen body consisted of Roman military settlers in Nikopolis and Pompeiopolis in Paphlagonia, and of Greeks and natives in the other *poleis*.

When Pompey returned to Rome in 61 BC, he celebrated a triumph, but the senate received him with more suspicion than enthusiasm. His enemies opposed the ratification of the measures he had taken in the East and the reward of his veterans. In order to achieve what the senate was denying him, he joined forces with two other powerful men in a secret agreement known as the first triumvirate: Caius Licinius Crassus, the wealthiest man in Rome and the man who had saved Rome from the slave rebellion of Spartacus; and Caius Iulius Caesar, descendant of one of Rome's oldest families, a supporter of the *populares* and a successful officer in the war against Sertorius in Spain. What these men shared was limitless ambition; what all of them faced was the mistrust of their peers, who feared the concentration of power in the hands of a few individuals. In 60 BC, they supported legislation that favoured their immediate interests – election to office, military commands and land for their veterans. Their most eloquent opponents, the orator Cicero and the conservative statesman Cato the Younger, were exiled; Caesar received the command that allowed him the conquest of Gaul from 58 to 50 BC, while Crassus and Pompey secured for themselves the consulship of 55 BC.

This opportunistic alliance only postponed the breakout of civil war. When Crassus was killed in a war against the Parthians in 53 BC, the conflict between the two remaining triumviri was unavoidable. Riots in Rome between the *populares*, followers of Caesar, and the conservative *optimates*, for whom Pompey increasingly showed his sympathies, led to anarchy and the appointment of Pompey to the office of sole consul (*consul sine collega*). This was a direct violation of the constitutional order and a provocation towards Caesar. When reconciliation efforts failed and the senate expelled Mark Antony, Caesar's supporter in Rome, Antony fled to Caesar's camp near the River Rubicon, the border of his lawful military command. On 7 January 49 BC, the senate declared Caesar a traitor and a public enemy. The die was cast. Three days later, Caesar and his army crossed the Rubicon and marched against Rome, forcing Pompey and his supporters to flee to Greece. A new civil war had begun, this time closely linked with the only surviving kingdom of Alexander's successors: Ptolemaic Egypt.

The last Ptolemies: from rulers to clients of Roman patrons

Once the most powerful kingdom of the Hellenistic world, the Ptolemaic kingdom had been reduced by native revolts, dynastic conflicts, military defeats and limited revenues to a marginal power in the south-eastern corner of the Mediterranean. After losing all its external possessions in Asia Minor, Syria, the Aegean and Cyrenaica, it now consisted only of Egypt and Cyprus.

When Ptolemy IX Lathyros died in 81 BC without leaving a legitimate son as heir, a new dynastic crisis occurred. For the first time, a woman ascended the throne, Lathyros' daughter Berenike III, who had once been married to her uncle, King Ptolemy X Alexander, but was now a widow. Berenike was very popular among the population of Alexandria but did not enjoy the senate's trust. Rome could not afford a nest of troubles in a country that was an important supplier of corn. A new king had to be found. It is worth briefly looking at how this was done, because it shows the pitiable conditions in a once great kingdom, the part played by Rome and the population of Alexandria, and the relentless struggle for power within the dysfunctional Ptolemaic family.

A son of Ptolemy X Alexander – whose mother was possibly Berenike – now living in Rome was recruited by Sulla for this task. In 80 BC, Berenike was forced to marry her husband's (and her own?) son, known as Ptolemy XI. However, her new husband murdered her a few days after the wedding, only to be lynched himself by the population of Alexandria. Instead of solving a dynastic crisis, the short reign of Ptolemy XI had now caused a new one, one made more acute by the fact that, in accordance with Ptolemy XI's will, Egypt would become a Roman possession if he died without an heir. But an heir was found: Ptolemy IX Lathyros had bastard sons living in exile. The eldest was now placed on the throne and ruled as Ptolemy XII New Dionysus, but he was better known as Auletes (the piper) and Nothos (the bastard). His smartest move was to achieve through briberies his recognition as an ally of the Romans in 63 BC, thus securing his rule.

This did not prevent the Romans from proceeding with the annexation of Cyprus in 59 BC. The island, strategically important for the control of the eastern Mediterranean, was joined with Cilicia into a large province. An uprising of the population in Alexandria against Auletes gave his wife Cleopatra Tryphaina and his eldest daughter, Berenike IV, the opportunity to depose him, forcing him to flee to Rome together with his second daughter, Cleopatra. Continuing the long Ptolemaic tradition of family strife, Berenike IV successively poisoned her mother and her husband, and ruled alone from 57 to 55 BC, until a huge bribe convinced Gabinius, the governor of Syria, to restore Auletes to his throne. Berenike was beheaded on her father's orders, and 2,000 Roman soldiers, the so-called Gabiniani, were left in Alexandria for the king's protection but also to ensure Rome's supply of Egyptian corn. During this expedition a fourteen-year-old girl, the future Queen Cleopatra, allegedly caught the eye of Mark Antony, then a twenty-six-year-old cavalry commander in Gabinius' army. But their love affair, the stuff of a Shakespearean drama, a dozen movies and countless paintings, had to wait another sixteen years.

When Auletes died in 51 BC, he left a ruined kingdom and two teenage daughters and two sons to fight over it. The eldest daughter, eighteen-year-old Cleopatra, and her eleven-year-old brother, Ptolemy XIII, were placed on the throne, while the senate appointed Pompey as their guardian. But Pompey was far away and his attention was devoted to his conflict with Caesar. The beginning of the next Roman civil war, in January 49 BC, was soon followed by the final round of bloody dynastic struggles in Alexandria.

A Roman affair: Cleopatra and Caesar

Cleopatra VII had inherited from her predecessors an ambition to share power with no other, combined with an impressive education, a knowledge of the native language and customs, and charisma. Her extant portraits on coins do not do justice to her seductive power (see Fig. 13). They show a woman with a characteristically large nose – according to seventeenth-century physiognomists, an indication of strong character. This prompted Pascal's remark that the face of the world would be different if her nose had been shorter. After decades of weak kings, the power of the court in Alexandria had increased. As in many Oriental monarchies, it included eunuchs, who were thought not to present a threat to the dynasty, since they had been deprived of their procreative powers. Such a court did not look on the ambitions of an energetic monarch favourably. Soon after the beginning of the civil war in Rome, under the influence of a eunuch, Potheinos, the court deprived Cleopatra of her power and made Ptolemy

13. Coin with portrait of Cleopatra VII.

XIII sole ruler. Cleopatra sought refuge in Syria, where she organised her own army. Her younger sister, Arsinoe IV, also raised a claim to the throne, advised by another eunuch, Ganymedes.

The Egyptian civil war was only starting when the Roman war took a dramatic turn. After bringing the western provinces and Italy under his control, Caesar continued his campaign against Pompey in Epirus. In August 48 BC, he defeated Pompey at Pharsalos in Thessaly. Most of the senate defected to Caesar, but Pompey was still the guardian of the kings in Egypt. Pompey immediately escaped to Egypt, hoping to receive support from the kings. But as soon as he disembarked, he was killed on Potheinos' orders. The eunuch thought Caesar would be grateful for this deed, but he was wrong. When Caesar, elected dictator and then consul in 47 BC, arrived in Alexandria, he found no royalty but instead Potheinos, who presented Pompey's head and signet ring. For Caesar, who is said to have shed tears at the sight of his opponent's severed head, Pompey's killing was not the removal of an opponent but the assassination of a Roman citizen. At Caesar's invitation, Ptolemy XIII returned to Alexandria to discover that his exiled sister was standing at the Roman dictator's side. The ambitious queen had been smuggled into Caesar's chambers, hidden in a carpet, and had conquered the weathered general's heart.

Caesar's efforts to reconcile the royal family were doomed to fail. The unremitting plots of the eunuchs, the struggles between Ptolemy XIII, Cleopatra and Arsinoe for power, and the ambition of the commander of the Egyptian army, Achillas, resulted in an uprising in Alexandria in 47 BC, known as the *bellum Alexandrinum*. This was Caesar's last major military challenge. Besieged in the palace, he was confronted with an army larger than his. Receiving reinforcements from Pergamon and Judaea and taking advantage of the conflicts between his opponents, Caesar finally defeated the rebels. Ptolemy XIII drowned while he was trying to escape; Arsinoe, who led the uprising, was captured and decorated Caesar's triumph a year later. She was allowed to live as a suppliant in the Temple of Artemis in Ephesos, where she was killed at the orders of Cleopatra in 41 BC. The war's greatest victim was the famous library of Alexandria, which was burned down. Caesar placed Cleopatra on the throne, this time together with her younger brother Ptolemy XIV. In 47 BC, he left Egypt to return to Rome, just a few days before Cleopatra gave birth to his son, Ptolemy Kaisar, or Kaisarion (little Caesar). Four Roman legions were left behind, to re-establish order in the East.

In the next few years, from 47 to 44 BC, Caesar's attention was turned to the establishment of order in Rome, to political and other reforms, and to the preparation of a campaign against the Parthians. That Cleopatra decided to join him in Rome did neither her nor her lover any good. It aroused suspicion about Caesar's future plans; it offered his family reasons to worry, his enemies grounds for criticism and the populace a source of gossip. There were rumours that Caesar was drafting a law that would allow bigamy, in order to be able to marry Cleopatra and establish his own monarchical rule in Egypt, making Alexandria into the second capital of the empire. The fact is that in Caesar's will there was no reference to either Cleopatra or his only son, Kaisarion.

The dictator is dead. Long live who?

During a festival on 15 February 44 BC, the consul Mark Antony offered Caesar, now dictator for life, a diadem, a symbol of royal power. That

Caesar declined the offer did not deceive a group of suspicious senators. Caesar already had absolute power and the formal establishment of monarchy was just a matter of time. Led by Cassius and Brutus, about sixty senators jointly assassinated Caesar during a meeting of the senate on 15 March, only days before the beginning of the dictator's campaign against the Parthians. The assassins' hope that Caesar's death would automatically restore the Republic was as illusionary as George W. Bush's expectation that the fall of Saddam Hussein would automatically bring western democracy to the Middle East. Caesar's assassination only inaugurated a new round of civil wars.

The power vacuum persisted for months after Caesar's death. The senate resisted the creation of unconstitutional positions but at the same time was unable to deal with a crisis of this sort without the services of men with extraordinary authority. The position of the assassins was ambiguous. Some celebrated them as liberators; others hated them as the murderers of a popular figure, who was soon to be declared a god. The leadership of the Caesarian faction was disputed. Its natural leaders were the current consul Mark Antony and the experienced senator Marcus Aemilius Lepidus. Mark Antony, born in 83 BC, had spent his youth gambling, indiscriminately offering erotic pleasures to men and women, participating in a street gang, incurring debts and briefly studying oratory and philosophy in Athens. But in 57 BC, he joined the army as cavalry officer in the province of Syria, and he showed his military skill both during a rebellion in Judaea and later during Caesar's Gallic wars. In the years leading up to Caesar's assassination, he had been Caesar's closest assistant. Lepidus had served as consul together with Caesar in 46 BC and as Master of the Horse during his dictatorship. However, Caesar's will contained a surprise for both of them: the dictator had adopted his nineteen-year-old nephew Caius Octavius and made him heir of his vast fortune and network of clients. Under the name Caius Iulius Octavianus, the young man unexpectedly emerged as the primary candidate to succeed Caesar. Caesar's will gave him the right to claim a position of leadership, despite the fact that he lacked public office. Octavian is better known as Augustus, the name he received seventeen years later.

After a chain of violent conflicts, Antony and Octavian decided to put aside their differences and jointly face the champions of the senate, who were attempting to restore the Republic. Sextus Pompeius, the son of Pompey the Great, was given by the senate the command of the fleet in

Sicily; and Caesar's assassins Cassius and Brutus were appointed governors of Macedonia and Syria. With these appointments the entire eastern part of the empire was in the hands of Antony and Octavian's enemies. On 27 November 43 BC, Antony, Lepidus and Octavian, who had taken Rome by force and proclaimed himself consul, formed a triumvirate sanctioned by law. It was given the euphemistic name 'triumvirate for the restoration of the Republic', but the triumviri's sole task was to reunite the empire under their rule. After a massacre of their opponents in Rome between December 43 and January 42 BC, Antony and Octavian were ready to start their campaign in Macedonia and Thrace, where the 'liberators' were plundering cities in preparation for war. In two battles at Philippi in October 42 BC, Octavian and Antony defeated the 'liberators', who committed suicide while their army surrendered. Victorious, the triumviri divided the empire among themselves. Antony received Gaul – but gave it to Octavian in 40 BC – all the eastern provinces, and the task of leading an expedition against the Parthians, who had supported Cassius and Brutus; Lepidus received North Africa; Octavian controlled Spain and Gaul; Italy was under their joint responsibility.

Sextus Pompeius proved to be a tougher opponent than Cassius and Brutus. His resistance continued until 39 BC. Only when the Parthians, led by the Roman renegade general Labienus, invaded Syria and captured almost all of Asia Minor did Sextus Pompeius reach a peace with Octavian for the sake of Rome. When the Parthians were expelled from the Roman territories in 39 BC, the war against Sextus began again. He repeatedly defeated Octavian, until finally Octavian's friend Marcus Vipsanius Agrippa won a decisive victory in 36 BC. Sextus was arrested in Asia Minor and executed without trial in 35 BC. In 36 BC, Octavian removed Lepidus from power. The stage for the final showdown between the remaining triumviri was set.

The last Hellenistic drama: Antony and Cleopatra

After Caesar's murder, Cleopatra had no other option than to return to her kingdom. There, she put her brother-husband Ptolemy XIV to death, making Kaisarion her co-ruler, with the name Ptolemy XV. While her fleet participated in the war against Brutus and Cassius alongside the triumvirate, Cleopatra reorganised what was left of her kingdom. Unlike her immediate predecessors, who were primarily kings in Alexandria, Cleopatra understood herself as queen of Egypt. She was the first member of the Ptolemaic dynasty who spoke the local language; she supported the local cults; and the native population supported her. It is not a coincidence that one of her honorary attributes was *philopatris*, 'lover of her fatherland'. While the honorific attributes of her predecessors displayed affection towards members of the family (see p. 88), Cleopatra's attribute displayed her affection for a kingdom that she perceived as her fatherland. At a time in which the Parthian threat was re-emerging beyond the Euphrates and the client kings on the periphery of the empire felt the absence of Roman rule and had hopes for expansion, a strong personality was again on the Ptolemaic throne.

When Mark Antony was given the East, his assignment also included the task of stopping the Parthian expansion and securing the loyalty of the numerous client kingdoms and states in Anatolia and the Middle East. Therefore, Egypt acquired an important strategic position. From 42 to 41 BC, Antony spent time in Greece and Asia Minor, winning friends among the Greeks, rewarding the cities that were opposed to the 'liberators', pardoning exiled Roman senators, appointing friends as governors, collecting taxes and intervening in the dynastic affairs of client kingdoms. In 41 BC, he finally decided to deal with Egypt. The queen accepted an invitation to meet him at Tarsos in Cilicia. Well aware of the power of images and theatrical display, she prepared a show for the tough Roman soldier whom she regarded an easy game.

> She sailed up the river Kydnos in a barge with gilded stern, its purple sails spread, the rowers urging it on with silver oars to the sound of the flute blended with pipes and kitharas. She herself reclined beneath a canopy spangled with gold, adorned like Aphrodite in a painting, while boys like Erotes in paintings stood on either side and fanned her. Likewise also the fairest of her serving-maidens, dressed like Nereids and Graces, were standing, some at the rudder-sweeps, others at the reefing-ropes. Wonderful odors from countless incense-burners spread along the riverbanks.

Two dinners later, one in Cleopatra's extravagant tent, the other with characteristic Roman military austerity, Mark Antony had surrendered to the charms of the twenty-eight-year-old queen, a capitulation that all sources claim was based not on her physical beauty but on the strength of her personality.

As tensions between the triumviri increased, the war against the Parthians, already planned by Caesar, became of the greatest importance for Antony. A victory in the East would allow him to take control of the rest of the empire. But a successful campaign required resources and only Egypt had the capacity to provide them. Therefore, apart from Cleopatra's charms, political interests may have motivated Antony's decision to connect his fate with hers. In 37–36 BC, Antony proceeded with a territorial reorganisation that undermined Pompey's vision for the Roman East. Only three Roman provinces remained intact: Asia, Bithynia and Pontos, and Syria. The other provinces became client kingdoms, on whose throne Antony placed loyal friends. Judaea again became a kingdom, but under a new dynasty begun by Herod. The great winner of this reorganisation was Cleopatra, whose kingdom regained Cyprus and Cyrenaica, but also received the island of Crete and new territories in the Near East (the hinterland of Cilicia, parts of the Nabatean kingdom and the kingdom of Chalkis in Syria). Cleopatra's kingdom acquired a size unknown since the late third century BC.

Subsequent propaganda interpreted these measures as the result of the bad influence of an Egyptian seducer who made a Roman soldier commit treason. But we should consider the advantages that this arrangement had. Without losing any revenue, since Asia and Bithynia continued to pay tribute, Antony relieved Rome from the administration of mountainous and underdeveloped regions, leaving the difficult task of control to loyal client kings, who would support his campaign. By abolishing provinces, Antony could use the legions that were stationed there for his war; and by enlarging Egypt, he was enlarging not yet another client kingdom but a kingdom that would in the future be the base for a personal autocratic rule.

While Antony was in Antioch for the preparation of the war in 36 BC, he saw his twin children from Cleopatra, born three years earlier, for the first time. Their names, Alexander Helios (the Sun) and Cleopatra Selene (the Moon), had symbolical value not only for the Greek world and Egypt but also for the new enemy, since the title of the Parthian king was 'brother of the Sun and the Moon'. The war began in the same year; however, Antony's campaign in Armenia was not a great success. Octavian was supposed to contribute 20,000 soldiers but sent only 2,000. His propaganda in Rome criticised Antony as a traitor who, although married to Octavian's sister Octavia, had donated Roman possessions to his Egyptian concubine. Returning from his Armenian campaign, Antony was convinced that an understanding with Octavian was impossible and a war unavoidable. Sulla, Pompey and Caesar had already experimented with various versions of unrivalled personal power: Sulla as 'dictator for the making of laws and settling the public affairs' for a longer period than the six months that the constitution allowed, Caesar with the unconstitutional position of a dictator without time limit and Pompey with a series of extraordinary commands. Antony's new plan was more straightforward: monarchical rule in an empire in the East, with Alexandria as its capital. After his return from Armenia and the celebration of a triumph in Alexandria, he proceeded to declare Cleopatra and Kaisarion as Queen and King of all Kings. His three children were to be the rulers of three smaller kingdoms: Alexander Helios of Armenia and all the lands east of the Euphrates (i.e. the Parthian kingdom); Ptolemy Philadelphos of the lands west of the Euphrates, Syria and Cilicia; and Cleopatra Selene of Libya and Cyrenaica.

> ... and the Alexandrians thronged to the festival
> full of enthusiasm, and shouted acclamations
> in Greek, and Egyptian, and some in Hebrew,
> charmed by the lovely spectacle –
> though they knew of course what all this was worth,
> what empty words they really were, these kingships.
>
> (C. Cavafy, 'Alexandrian Kings', 1912)

These 'Alexandrian donations' were Antony's final break with Rome. The triumvirate, which had expired at the end of 33 BC, was not renewed and, after two years of propaganda against Antony in Rome, the Roman senate declared Antony an enemy of Rome in 31 BC and the last civil war of the Republic began. Octavian's greatest asset was his general Agrippa, who captured an important harbour in Greece, Methone, and then defeated the fleet of Antony and Cleopatra at Actium on 2 September 31 BC.

Defeated and despairing, Antony fled to Egypt, which in August 30 BC was invaded by Octavian's troops. Realising that resistance would be futile, Antony took his own life. A few days later Octavian arrived in Alexandria and arrested Cleopatra. After performing funerary rites for Antony and not wishing to be made a spectacle at Octavian's triumph, Cleopatra committed suicide, allegedly by letting an asp bite her on either her arm or her breast. The kingdom of Egypt was abolished and the land passed under the personal control of Octavian and the later emperors. Of Cleopatra's four children, Kaisarion, the only son of Caesar, was put to death by Octavian, the adopted son of Caesar. The advice of his teacher, the Stoic philosopher Areios Didymos, was hard to ignore: 'It is not a good thing to have many Caesars.' But the lives of Antony's three children were spared. They were brought to Rome and marched in Octavian's triumph. Instead of the diadems or royalty that their father had hoped for them, they carried golden chains so heavy that they could barely walk, arousing the spectators' pity. Cleopatra Selene was later married to King Juba in Numidia. Nothing is known about the fate of her brothers; they presumably died in Rome at a young age.

Whether on his last night Antony, who was called the New Dionysus, heard the noise and the music of Dionysiac revellers, as Cavafy describes it in his poem 'The God Abandons Antony', we do not know. But if for nothing else, we should be grateful to Antony for inspiring one of Cavafy's most beautiful poems.

When suddenly, at midnight, you hear
an invisible procession going by
with exquisite music, voices,
don't mourn your luck that's failing now,
work gone wrong, your plans
all proving deceptive – don't mourn them uselessly.
As one long prepared, and graced with courage,
say goodbye to her, the Alexandria that is leaving.
Above all, don't fool yourself, don't say
it was a dream, your ears deceived you:
don't degrade yourself with empty hopes like these.
As one long prepared, and graced with courage,
as is right for you who proved worthy of this kind of city,
go firmly to the window
and listen with deep emotion, but not
with the whining, the pleas of a coward;
listen – your final delectation – to the voices,
to the exquisite music of that strange procession,

and say goodbye to her, to the Alexandria you are losing.

The abolition of the last kingdom founded by one of Alexander's successors marks the end of the period that we traditionally call the Hellenistic Age. It also marks the end of continuous war and the unification of the Roman Empire under the rule of a single man in a political system that modern scholars call the Principate. Despite the great changes that the *pax Romana* and the monarchical rule of the *princeps* brought, all the major political, social and cultural developments in the Greek world in the two centuries that followed had their roots in the Hellenistic period.

11

A ROMAN EAST

Local Histories and Their Global Context
(30 BC– AD 138)

Earthly gods and heavenly kings

What millions of people consider the most important event in world history merits only a short note by the most important historian of the Imperial period. Tacitus, writing his *Annals* around AD 116, notes on Jesus' crucifixion:

> Christus ... suffered the extreme penalty during the reign of Tiberius at the hands of one of our procurators, Pontius Pilatus, and a most mischievous superstition, thus checked for the moment, again broke out not only in Judaea, the first source of the evil, but even in Rome, where all things hideous and shameful from every part of the world find their center and become popular.

Three or four years earlier, the governor of Bithynia and Pontos and personal friend of Emperor Trajan, Pliny the Younger, had only a very vague idea of what these Christians were. What he was told about their religious practices did not differ much from the cult practices of other religious groups: they gathered on fixed nights, sang hymns, bound themselves by oath to moral behaviour and partook of ordinary food. Neither Pliny nor Tacitus would have thought that the only events in the 150 years from Octavian's victory to their own times that would still be annually celebrated two millennia later around the globe would be Christ's birth and passion, events that had occurred in a small but troublesome province in the Roman East.

Five years before the date which historians of Christianity usually give for Christ's birth, the federation of the Greeks of the province of Asia issued a decree in honour of Octavian, who had been known by a new name since 27 BC: Augustus. The decree (see p. 261) establishes Augustus' birthday, 23 September, as New Year's Day:

> With his appearance Caesar exceeded the hopes of all those who had received glad tidings in the past, not only surpassing those who had been benefactors before him, but also extinguishing any hope of those who will come in the future that they might surpass him. The birthday of the god was the beginning of glad tidings on his account for the world.

For the largest part of the population in the Roman East, the key protagonist of public life in the centuries that followed Octavian's victory at Actium was the Roman emperor, a god on earth, mortal but with powers that could be compared to those of the immortals. His rule was ecumenical: that is, it stretched over the entire 'inhabited earth' (*oecumene*), or at least the part of it that mattered. One of the honorary titles attributed to Octavian/Augustus was 'supervisor of earth and sea'. The same title had already been given to Pompey, but in the case of Augustus it had a tangible meaning. Augustus was the sole ruler of an empire that stretched from the Iberian Peninsula and the provinces of Gaul (today's France, Belgium, Luxembourg and parts of Germany) to the Euphrates, comprised all of Europe south of the Danube, except for the allied kingdom of Thrace in modern Bulgaria, most of coastal North Africa, from Algiers to the Red Sea, including all of Cyrenaica and Egypt, most of Asia Minor, Syria and the coastal areas of the north shore of the Black Sea (see Map 7). Germany north of the Rhine was lost in AD 9, but Augustus added the territories of client kingdoms to his realm, Galatia in 25 BC and part of Judaea in 4 BC. His successors added new provinces (see pp. 245 and 253–4).

In his *Aeneid*, Virgil records a prophecy that Jupiter would give the

Romans an unlimited empire: *imperium sine fine*. In a luxurious house in Ephesos, occupied from the first to the mid-third century AD, someone wrote an acclamation on a wall that he must have heard in the streets of the city: 'Rome, ruler of all, your power will never perish!' Thanks to a book known as the Revelation, composed on the small Greek island of Patmos only two decades before the empire had reached its greatest extent, we know that there were groups within the empire that had other expectations: the destruction of the earthly realm and the coming of a heavenly kingdom. In one of the author's visions, an angel shows him Rome, likened to a whore seated on a seven-headed beast full of blasphemous names, the emperors' titles:

> The woman was dressed in purple and scarlet, and decked with gold and precious stones and pearls, having in her hand a golden cup full of abominations and the impurities of the sexual immorality of the earth ... When I saw her, I wondered with great amazement. The angel said to me, 'Why do you wonder? I will tell you the mystery of the woman, and of the beast that carries her, which has the seven heads and the ten horns. The beast that you saw was, and is not; and is about to come up out of the abyss, and to go into destruction ... The heads are seven mountains, on which the woman sits. They are seven kings. Five have fallen, the one is, the other has not yet come. When he comes, he must continue a little while ... The woman whom you saw is the great city, which reigns over the kings of the earth.'

The history of the Greek world under Augustus and the ten emperors who followed him is more than just the history of some great events that the Greeks observed as audiences of imperial history. It is also the history of collective feelings that range from the hope for peace and prosperity in this world to the hope for the coming of a divine saviour; it is the history of tensions between the dominant imperial ideology and those who challenged it; it is the microhistory of local communities striving to maintain a sense of identity and self-determination in a new world; and it is the history of the continuous reorganisation of the provinces and the client kingdoms and redefinition of the borders of the empire.

The Greeks as an audience of global history

Most of the wars of the Roman emperors from Augustus to Hadrian did not directly affect the lives of people in Greece, Asia Minor and Egypt. Locations in the Greek world were of only secondary importance in the course of major events. The Greek-speaking populations in the East had a sense of being part of major military enterprises only when they saw Roman legions crossing their territories on their way to a front that was beyond the borders of their world.

That military events rarely occurred close to Greece was a blessing for a region that was slowly recovering from the devastating wars of the second and first centuries BC. The modern concept of a *pax Romana*, which finds predecessors in ancient texts, is something that many Greeks would have accepted as a reality, especially if they were to compare their very limited exposure to war with the continuous and extreme violence in the decades before Actium. Philip of Pergamon, a Greek historian known only through an inscription on the base of his statue, introduced his work, composed roughly at the time of Augustus, with words that directly refer to the horrors of wars in the entire *oecumene*:

> With my pious hand I delivered to the Greeks the historical narrative of the most recent deeds: all sorts of sufferings and a continual mutual slaughter having taken place in our days in Asia and Europe, in the tribes of Libya, and in the cities of the islanders. I did this, so that they may learn also through us, how many evils are brought forth by courting the mob, love of profit, civil strife, and the breaking of trust, and thus, by observing the sufferings of others, they may live their lives in the right way.

Philip shares the uncompromised belief of historians of all times that people may learn from history. But if truth be told, the *pax Romana* was not the result of historical lessons. It was primarily the result of the violent extinction of all rivals to Octavian's monarchical power and the subjugation of those who challenged Roman rule. In the process, the Greek world was transformed from a troublesome area near the borders of the empire to a chain of provinces at a safe distance from barbarian enemies.

Official announcements and encomiastic orations for the emperors during festivals kept the Greeks informed about important events from afar. In AD 2, Augustus' grandson and heir, Caius Caesar, made peace with the Parthians on an island in the Euphrates. When the news arrived in Messene, a Roman magistrate,

> learning that Caius, the son of Augustus, fighting against the barbarians for the safety of all men, was in good health, had escaped danger, and had taken vengeance on the enemy, he, overjoyed at this best of news, directed everyone to wear wreaths and to sacrifice, being at leisure and untroubled, and he himself sacrificed oxen for Caius' safety and gave a variety of spectacles.

A representative of Roman authority instructed the population in Messene to display joy and loyalty for an incident in the distant East that had little bearing on their lives, despite the fact that Caius' campaign was declared to be a war 'for the safety of all men'. A peace treaty was celebrated as a military victory. Kos went one step further upon the announcement of the news: Caius was worshipped as a god and unofficially awarded the honorary title Parthicus: 'the victor over the Parthians'. A year later Caius died of his wounds in a battle in Armenia. For campaigns such as his, the Greek populations were a cheering audience at a safe distance. Imperial statues and monuments visualised Roman success (see Fig. 16); failures were conveniently forgotten.

The incorporation of the Greek world into the Roman Empire might give the impression that a separate 'Greek' history in a narrow sense – a Greek history whose agents were Greek communities and their political leaders – had come to an end. It may be true that Greek statesmen and monarchs were no longer the protagonists of major political developments as men and a few women such as Pericles, Demosthenes and Philip had been in the Classical period and Alexander, Ptolemy II and Arsinoe, Philip V, Antiochos III and Cleopatra VII in the Hellenistic period. The new protagonists and initiators of developments were emperors, senators and governors, and to a lesser extent Greek statesmen and intellectuals associated with them. Also in the field of culture and art, Rome was no longer merely the recipient of ideas, the savage victor who had been culturally conquered by the Greeks. In the late first century AD, the Greek philosopher Plutarch wondered: 'In our times, when the affairs of the cities do not offer the opportunity to undertake military leadership in wars, or to overthrow tyrannies, or to conclude alliances, how can one start a prominent and splendid political career?'

That the civic elites of Plutarch's time did not have the opportunities to prove their abilities in the leadership of their communities through wars and major diplomatic activities means neither the end of history nor the end of political life. In this period, political life and interstate relations were performed on multiple stages. On the local stage of the city, political and, more importantly, financial issues needed to be resolved. Although the initiative was in the hands of the elite, the pressure exercised by the people was significant (see p. 287). On the broader stage of regions and provinces, cities struggled for privileges and honours: the privilege to erect a temple for the cult of the emperor, the right to organise a fair or celebrate a contest, the inviolability of a sanctuary. Finally, the provincial populations and their leaders were called on to play certain roles on the even broader stage of the empire. These roles varied: suppliants for help after a natural disaster; protesters against oppressive behaviour by imperial officials; defenders of rights and privileges; a recruitment pool for the Roman administration and army.

In this chapter we shall examine a selection of historical events and processes that shaped the provinces of the Roman East and affected the lives of the Greek and Hellenised populations from Augustus to Hadrian.

Augustus and the shaping of the Principate

A few years after the coronation of Caesar's son in Alexandria (see p. 230), 'Kaisarion all grace and beauty' was dead and another son of Caesar, an adopted one, held in his hands the fortunes of the Roman Empire. Octavian had inherited Julius Caesar's wealth and political influence upon the dictator's murder; after his victory in 30 BC, the question arose as to what form the new rule should take. An answer was not given immediately. After a period of experimentation, a settlement was reached in 23 BC. Octavian, who was now referred to as Imperator Caesar Augustus, accumulated powers, titles and privileges that made him the *princeps*, the 'first man' in the empire. Modern historians, for lack of better alternatives, designate this form of government, which existed with small alterations until the end of the Antonine dynasty (AD 192), as the Principate. Augustus presented the new form of government to the Romans, who were obsessed with traditions, as a restoration of the old Republic: *res publica restituta*. The first *princeps* described this development in an account of his deeds

14. Augustus' temple in Ankyra and the Res Gestae.

(*Res Gestae Divi Augusti*). The final version, finished shortly before his death in AD 14, was inscribed in major provincial cities, either in the Latin original or in a Greek translation. An almost complete copy of both versions survives on the walls of the Temple of Roma and Augustus in Ankyra (modern Ankara; see Fig. 14). This is what the Greek translation communicated to Augustus' Greek subjects:

> In my sixth and seventh consulates [28 and 27 BC], after I had extinguished the fire of civil wars and had received absolute control of all affairs in accordance with the prayers of my fellow citizens, I handed it over from my power to the authority of the senate and the Roman people. On account of this, by decree of the senate, I was called Augustus [*Sebastos*, 'Revered']; the doors of my house were draped with laurel wreaths by public act; the crown that is made of oak-leaves and is awarded for the rescue of citizens was fixed over my door; and a gold shield, dedicated by the senate and the people in the senate-house, testifies through its inscription my virtue, mercy, justice, and piety. I exceeded all in rank/dignity [*axioma*], but I had no greater power than the others with whom I shared any magistracy.

Collegiality was an important principle of the Republican constitution: every magistrate shared power with at least one further colleague. By highlighting collegiality, Augustus tried to draw attention away from the violation of two other old Republican principles: no Roman citizen should accumulate many powers and no magistrate should serve continuously in the same office for more than one year. Of course, under the extraordinary circumstances of the civil wars, the Republican principles had repeatedly been disrespected; but now the accumulation of powers and the continuity of rule were institutionalised. Under the veil of the restored Republic, Augustus brought the process of transferring power from the senate to a single individual to a conclusion; later emperors, especially Vespasian (AD 69), made small modifications, but the Augustan form of government essentially remained unchanged until the late second century AD.

Augustus was the only man in Rome who held several powers at the same time and without interruption until his death. All of Augustus' powers originated in traditional Republican offices: the *tribunicia potestas*, the power of a people's tribune, gave him the right to convene the senate, propose laws, veto decisions of the senate and the assembly, speak first at the meetings and preside over elections. He also had the right to hold a *census* and thus determine who would be a senator. The *imperium proconsulare maius* made him governor of all provinces in which the Roman army was placed. From time to time, Augustus and his successors also occupied the annual office of consul, which was reserved for the most important senators, and also served as *pontifices maximi*, representing the highest religious authority. Originally, Rome had only two consuls, but the need to offer prestige to favoured senators or to acknowledge the service of loyal commanders and governors led to the election of additional 'suffect consuls'.

The singular position of the *princeps* was expressed by Augustus' name. Every Roman citizen had three names: a first name (*praenomen*); the name of the extended family to which he belonged by birth, adoption or manumission (*nomen gentile*); and the name under which he was known (*cognomen*). For identification purposes, official documents also included the name of the father or former master: for example, *Lucii filius* or *Publii libertus*, 'the son of Lucius' or 'the freedman of Publius'. The full name of Sulla was Lucius Cornelius Sulla, with an additional 'nickname' or *agnomen*: Felix. Octavian's original name was Caius Octavius – allegedly his cognomen was Thurinus. When Caesar was murdered in 44 BC, the nineteen-year-old Octavius was posthumously adopted by the murdered dictator on the basis of his will. *Caius Iulius Caii filius Caesar* became his new name, but he was also known as Octavianus, 'coming from the family of the Octavii'. When Caesar was declared a god in 42 BC, Octavian's name indicated his unique relation to a god and distinguished him from the thousands of other Iulii: he was *Caius Iulius Divi filius* (son of god) *Caesar*. Sometime later, between 38 and 31 BC, he replaced his *praenomen* and *nomen gentile* with names that no other Roman had: *Imperator*, a title that a victorious general received from his soldiers through acclamation, became his first name; *Caesar*, a name held in reverence, became his 'family' name. The name *Imperator Caesar Divi filius* unambiguously expressed Octavian's elevated position. Finally, on 6 January 27 BC, the honorary attribute *Augustus* became Octavian's third name, and the emperor was now known as *Imperator Caesar Augustus*. The names Caesar Augustus were adopted by Augustus' successors. When the emperors of the Flavian dynasty (AD 69–98) also added the name Imperator, *Imperator Caesar Augustus* became an integral part of every emperor's name and could be understood as a title.

Undergraduate students are surprised to learn that Imperator Caesar Augustus was not originally a position or a title but a personal name. What modern students (hopefully) understand after a moment of surprise, the population of the Greek-speaking provinces probably never comprehended. As we infer from the sometimes rather liberal translations of the names of emperors in Greek inscriptions, the names were understood as honorific titles. But even if the populations in the Greek-speaking provinces did not understand the technicalities of this new development, they knew that it affected their lives. Rituals of power, interventions of the emperor and his representatives in the administration of the provinces, and imperial benefactions to the cities and favours to members of the elite made clear that they were the subjects of a monarch.

Organising a Roman East: client kings and annexations

During the reign of Claudius and Nero a luxurious building complex was constructed in Aphrodisias, a free city in Asia Minor. Passing through a monumental gate, one reached a broad avenue flanked by three-storey porticoes that led to the temple of the emperors, which stood on a

15. The Sebasteion of Aphrodisias.

podium (see Fig. 15). The porticoes were decorated with 190 relief panels that represented cult scenes, themes connected with Roman and Greek mythology, and allegorical representations referring to the first Roman emperors and their victories (see Fig. 16). This decoration included representations of about fifty 'nations' on the fringes of Roman rule, from Spain to Arabia. Some are more familiar than others: for example, the Jews, the Egyptians and the Arabs. But even a specialist in ancient history might have difficulties in placing tribes such as the Piroustoi, the Andizetoi or the Trunpilinoi on a map. Such images gave an ancient visitor of this Sebasteion, 'the place dedicated to the Augusti', a visual impression of the extent of Roman power. The long list of tribes with their exotic names would fill him with awe, perhaps also with pride in being a free partner and ally of the Romans.

When the Sebasteion was completed, the process of annexation and creation of provinces had not yet come to an end. A series of client kingdoms formed a buffer zone between the empire and its potential enemies. The most important among them had existed for centuries and were ruled by local dynasties: the kingdoms of Pontos, Paphlagonia, Kappadokia and Galatia in Asia Minor, and the kingdom of Emesa in Syria. Additionally,

16. Relief panel from the Sebasteion of Aphrodisias: Claudius subdues Britain.

the collapse of Seleucid power in the second century BC and the chaotic conditions of the first century had produced a large number of small independent regions and cities ruled by dynasts or priests: for instance, the king in Hierapolis/Kastabala, the priestly rulers of Olba in Cilicia and Komana in Pontos, and a bandit turned dynast of Gordioukome in Mysia. In order to gain local support both in his planned war against the Parthians and in the civil war against Octavian, Mark Antony had intervened in the political geography of the East, putting his supporters – usually educated and wealthy Greeks – on the throne of traditional kingdoms, rewarding allied kings with additional territories, and either tolerating or supporting tyrants in cities and dynasts in small regions.

Augustus entered this minefield of personal ambitions and local conflicts with the necessary caution, removing some of Antony's supporters but tolerating others, judging each individual case as he saw fit. Client kings and dynasts offered indisputable advantages: they knew the local conditions and could fulfil administrative tasks that would otherwise have burdened the Roman administration. In a few cases, Augustus also rewarded his supporters by allowing them to establish a personal rule in

*17. Milestone of the Via Egnatia set up by the first
governor of Macedonia, Cnaeus Egnatius.*

their city. But knowledge of the local conditions could also be a threat. Too much power was undesirable, but so was too weak a buffer near the border of the empire. Since the rule of client kings depended entirely on imperial favour, it could be abruptly terminated. Once they had familiarised local populations with the Roman presence, client kings were dispensable. Whenever an opportunity was at hand, because of dynastic conflicts (e.g. Judaea), rebellions and raids (e.g. Thrace) or internal conflicts (e.g. Lycian League), the client states were annexed and added to the next Roman province or became a new province. This is a recurring pattern during the reign of Augustus and continued for about a century after his death, bringing most Greek and Hellenised regions under a unified administration.

Only the Greek cities in the Crimea and on the north-east coast of the Black Sea, Olbia, Chersonesos in Tauris, Pantikapaion and Phanagoreia, among others, were beyond the administration of the Roman Empire under Augustus. They were subject to the rule of the kings of the Bosporan kingdom. But here too the client kings proudly bore the name Tiberius Iulius, indicating that they were Roman citizens, and the title *philorhomaios* (friend of the Romans).

The incorporation of client states improved the defence of the Roman Empire and, therefore, the safety of the Greek areas, which were to

*18. A monument in Patara with measurements of the
roads that connected the cities of Lycia.*

experience an unprecedented period of peace. The Romans placed the
Greek and Hellenised populations under a unified administration, which
brought the burdens of taxation but also improved the infrastructure,
especially through the construction and maintenance of roads, and thus
also possibilities for communication. Milestones (see Fig. 17) indicating
the distance from important cities were a visible testimony of the empire's
unity. When Lycia was annexed under Claudius (AD 43), a monumental
pillar that probably supported a statue of the emperor was set up in Patara.
An inscription on three of its sides gives a list of all the cities of the new
province and measurements of the roads that connected them (see Fig.
18). By measuring and mapping their empire, the Romans created a sense
of order.

Revitalising Greece and Asia Minor

The wars of the second and first centuries BC had left open wounds in

Greece and Asia Minor. Even when a city had not been damaged by siege or looted after an attack, even when the fields were not burned and the slaves had not run away, it had generally still been forced to provide food, supplies, ships, pack animals and accommodation for foreign armies. After 146 BC, a continually increasing number of cities were also obliged to pay tribute to Rome. The wars had ruined the economy. They had also affected the relations between city and countryside, the population numbers, and the occupation and exploitation of the territory. Admittedly, the impact of war on demography and on the exploitation of the countryside was not uniform. In some areas – for instance, in Boiotia and Attica – archaeological surveys suggest a drop in the number of occupied sites in the countryside from around 200 BC onwards, but in other areas the decline in the occupation of the countryside started earlier and was followed by renewed growth after the Roman occupation. Similarly, it is not possible to speak of a general decline in population, such as the one described by Polybius in the mid-second century BC:

> In our time the whole of Greece has been subject to a low birth rate and a general decrease of the population; for this reason cities have become deserted and dearth of crops has occurred, although we have been befallen neither by continuous wars nor by epidemics ... For as men had fallen into such a state of arrogance, avarice and indolence that they did not wish to marry, or if they married to rear the children born to them, or at most as a rule but one or two of them, so as to leave these in wealth and bring them up to waste their substance, the evil rapidly and insensibly grew.

If such a dramatic demographic decline did occur it was a regional phenomenon, especially in areas of Greece where wars had caused extensive destruction of cities and their countryside. These areas, including Macedonia, the northern Peloponnese and parts of central Greece, were in urgent need of new inhabitants. On the periphery of the Greek world, the cities of the Crimea also suffered from loss of population. The personal names attested in Olbia, for instance, suggest that the city had to bolster its citizen body through the naturalisation of Hellenised Iranians and intermarriage.

In 39 or 38 BC, Octavian (Fig. 19), still cooperating with Mark Antony, received an envoy from Aphrodisias, 'the city of Aphrodite', in Asia Minor. The envoy painted a dramatic picture of his city's sufferings during the

19. Portrait bust of Emperor Augustus (Octavian).

invasion of Labienus. He knew that he would arouse Octavian's sympathy by adding that a golden statuette of Eros, dedicated to Aphrodite by Caesar, had been taken to Ephesos as war booty. Aphrodite, Eros' mother and Aphrodisias' patron goddess, was regarded as the ancestor of the family of Caesar (Aeneas, the founder of Rome, was Aphrodite's son and consequently Octavian regarded her as his remote ancestor). Octavian's letter to Ephesos gives us an impression of the atmosphere in these difficult years:

> Solon, son of Demetrios, envoy of the Plarasans and Aphrodisians, has reported to me how much their city suffered in the war against Labienus and how much property, both public and private, was looted ... I was also informed that out of the loot a golden Eros, which had been dedicated by my father to Aphrodite, has been brought to you and set up as an offering to Artemis. You will do well and worthily of yourselves if you restore the offering which my father gave to Aphrodite.

Octavian added, not without wit: 'In any case Eros is not a suitable offering when given to Artemis' – the virgin goddess Artemis would hardly have appreciated a statuette of the playful god of love. This was a nice gesture, but Aphrodisias and the other cities needed more than gestures. A few years later Octavian, now called Augustus, was the sole ruler of the *oecumene*. Even if the situation of the Greek cities was not as deplorable as the Greek envoys and his representatives imply, they were in urgent need of measures for their revival. Peace helped, but peace alone neither automatically filled the depopulated cities with inhabitants nor revived the economy. Augustus had to act.

Some of his early measures reveal the magnitude of the problems. Without the distribution of surplus grain to cities after his victory at Actium, many cities would have faced hunger. The *princeps* declared a general remission of public debt to Rome, probably expecting that the cities would also cancel debts owed by individuals to them. Rhodes, a wealthy city, was the only city to decline the offer; to most of the Greeks it brought temporary relief. But Greece needed more than such acts of generosity.

One of the most important measures for the revival of the Greek areas was the planned migration of population. Of course the motivation of Roman commanders for the resettlement of population was not the revival of the Greek landscape but their own urgent need to provide their veterans, dispossessed Italians, the poor urban population and the freedmen of Rome with land. Greece provided the necessary space. New foundations were also needed in Asia Minor – for instance, in Cilicia, Pontos and Paphlagonia – in order to promote urbanisation and with it acceptance of Roman rule. Pompey had already been a pioneer in this respect (see p. 220). Many of the cities founded or refounded by the Romans represent a legally distinct type of urban settlement: the colony of Roman citizens.

By founding colonies, Augustus applied a method that had contributed to the stabilisation of Roman rule in Italy and had already been practised by his adopted father, Julius Caesar. Caesar had founded colonies after his victory in 47 BC. One of them was in Corinth, on the site of a glorious city that had been abandoned for almost a century after its destruction in 146 BC. The colonies in Dyme in the Peloponnese, Bouthroton in Epirus and Sinope on the south coast of the Black Sea can also be attributed to Caesar's initiative, and possibly Parion in Asia Minor as well. There were also organised settlements of Roman citizens alongside the Greek population in several cities along the north coast of Asia Minor – for instance, in Herakleia, Kyzikos and Amisos.

This practice was continued by Octavian/Augustus, who turned many old cities into Roman colonies, including Dyrrhachion on the Adriatic coast of Illyria, Dion and Pella, the traditional sanctuary and the royal capital of the Macedonians respectively, Philippi in Macedonia, Patrae in the Peloponnese, Knossos in Crete and Alexandria Troas in north-west Asia Minor. The primary task of a dense network of colonies in Asia Minor was to secure Roman rule, especially in areas that were less Hellenised; besides providing the veterans with land, the new foundations secured the presence of a loyal population in recently acquired territories. Pisidia alone hosted six colonies – Antioch, Olbasa, Komana, Kremna, Parlais and Lystra. Colonies that can, in all likelihood, be attributed to Augustus also existed at Ninika in Cilicia, Germa in north Galatia and Apameia Myrleia (renamed Colonia Iulia Concordia) in Bithynia. There were also two Augustan colonies in Syria: Berytos and Heliopolis. More colonies were founded by the successors of Augustus, especially in Asia Minor and Judaea. Under Claudius, Seleukeia on the Kalykadnos in Cilicia became Claudiopolis; Vespasian promoted Caesarea Maritima to the status of a colony; in AD 130/131 Hadrian founded the *colonia Aelia Capitolina* in Jerusalem, at the side of the old city.

The foundation of a colony was a dramatic intervention of Roman authority into the traditional landscape, not only because of the arrival of a population that spoke a different language (Latin), worshipped different gods and had different cultural traditions, but also because the Roman colonies were given territory taken from pre-existing settlements, which either ceased to exist or became dependent villages. For instance, when in 28 BC Augustus founded his 'city of victory', Nikopolis, in Actium, he allocated to its territory most of southern Epirus and large parts of Akarnania and Aetolia, creating one of the largest civic territories and forcing the population of neighbouring cities and federations to settle in the new city. The Roman veterans coexisted with a Greek population that was not granted Roman citizenship but enjoyed the privileges of a civic community.

The Roman colonies had an impact on the local culture and society (see p. 282), contributed to the urbanisation or reurbanisation of areas that had suffered from wars and created new opportunities for manufacture and trade. Crete is a case in point. As soon as the conquest of the island was completed in 67 BC, Roman traders settled in the island's most important city, Gortyn, attracted by the trade in olive oil and wine. Around 27 BC, Augustus established a Roman colony in Knossos, which accommodated immigrants from Campania as well as veterans. From their country of origin, the new settlers and landowners were familiar with the possibilities and risks of a mode of agrarian production oriented towards exports. Within only a few decades, Cretan wines were widely exported throughout the Mediterranean; wine jars found in large numbers in Pompeii – destroyed by the eruption of Vesuvius in AD 79 – are inscribed with labels that reveal their Cretan origin. The integration of Crete into a pacified empire and the settlement of Italians turned an island whose agricultural production in the past had been mainly destined for local consumption and limited trade into an integral part of an international network of exchanges (see pp. 314–5). Similar developments can be observed elsewhere. In the Peloponnese and mainland Greece, the Augustan colonies in Corinth, Patrae and Nikopolis had close trade contacts with Italy across the Adriatic. The impetus given by Augustus' measures continued under his successors. Greece and Asia Minor did not turn into a paradise on earth; social tensions persisted and dissatisfaction with Roman rule occasionally led to riots. But most of the Greek and Hellenised areas were spared the terrors of war from Augustus to Hadrian.

Nero, the short-lived freedom of the Greeks and the long struggle of the Jews

In the pacified world created by Augustus, Achaea, the province that corresponds to Greece south of Macedonia, was a quiet province, not directly exposed to external threats. After Augustus' death, it was assigned to the governor of Moesia Inferior, but in AD 44 it became a separate province again. The first emperor to visit Greece after Augustus was Nero (AD 54–68). Towards the end of his reign, Nero made a grand tour in Greece, from September AD 66 to November 67. His ambition was to win in composition and singing at all four traditional festivals (Olympic, Isthmian, Nemean and Pythian). Since the festivals normally took place successively over a period of fours years and some of them did not include a competition of *kithorodoi* (singers who played the *kithara*), their programmes had to change and all four had to be squeezed into the period of one year.

Unsurprisingly, the emperor won all competitions and was cheered by enthusiastic crowds, if not for his talent then at least for his generosity. He invited all the Greeks to the Isthmian festival on 28 November AD 67 and declared Achaia's freedom and freedom from taxation in a speech that is preserved in an inscription:

> I make, oh men of Hellas, a gift that you would never have expected, though nothing is beyond hope from my great desire to help. I am making a gift so great that you never entertained the thought of asking for it. All ye who dwell in Achaea and especially in the land hitherto called the island of Pelops, receive freedom, immunity, which not even in your happiest hours you all had, for you were enslaved either to foreigners or to each other. Would that I were offering this gift when Hellas was at its peak, so that more might enjoy the favor! For this I blame Time, who anticipated me in expending the greatness of the favor. But even now I make the benefaction, not through pity of you but through goodwill, and I requite your gods, whose care of me I have ever experienced on land and on sea, because they afforded me the opportunity to make such benefactions. For other princes too have liberated cities, Nero alone has freed a province.

For his proclamation of freedom Nero chose the same venue as Flamininus 263 years earlier. But apart from the venue and the word *eleutheria*, nothing was the same. This was a declaration of freedom that expressed relations of dependence. Nero reminded the Greeks that even in their glorious days they 'were enslaved'. As lord of the entire world, assimilated with the Sun, Nero stressed the magnitude of his gift by drawing a comparison with the past and explaining his motivation in emotional terms: he acted not out of feelings of pity but with affection and gratitude towards the gods. To increase the emotional impact, Nero did not express joy at his gift but distress, because the demographic decline of Greece had decreased the number of the recipients of his gift. The historical circumstances had spoiled his joy and the Greeks were reminded of their decline.

Nero's gift was received with gratitude and enthusiasm. Epameinondas, a statesman of Akraiphia in Boiotia, formulated a decree in honour of the emperor, in which Nero is praised for restoring 'the freedom of the Greeks, which from the beginning of time has been indigenous and autochthonous, but had been taken away'. What for the emperor was a gift, for a self-conscious Greek was the restoration of ancestral status. Nero's proclamation caused his popularity to skyrocket and justified his assimilation with Zeus Eleutherios, the 'patron of freedom'. But the joy did not last long, either for him or for the Greeks.

While the Greeks in Achaia had reasons to celebrate, others did not. The troublesome client kingdom of Pontos was annexed in AD 64 (see p. 298). But the greatest troubles occurred in Judaea. The Jews had been ruled by a Roman governor (procurator) since AD 44. Provocations by Roman soldiers, heavy taxation and expressions of contempt towards the Jews radicalised even moderate Jews and increased the influence of a group with strong anti-Roman sentiments, the so-called zealots. When in AD 66 the governor, Florus, removed vast treasures from the Temple, the explosion was unavoidable; during the riots that followed, the Roman garrison was wiped out and soon Rome was at war with the Jews. Not only were the Jews confronted with the Roman troops; they also had to face their own deep divisions, with the zealots killing the moderate leaders. The great Jewish revolt lasted for four years.

But Nero had more problems at home. After the inferno in Rome on the night of 18 July AD 64, which destroyed a large part of the city, and the enormous expenses for extravagant building projects in the capital, the currency had to be devalued for the first time in Roman history. The senate and several governors were indignant at Nero's policies. Facing a rebellion in June AD 68, Nero saw no escape and asked his secretary to kill him. Although Nero was dead, his popularity in the Greek East lived on. For another twenty years after his death three impostors who claimed to be Nero exploited this popularity to lead short-lived rebellions in Asia Minor. With Nero's death, the Julio-Claudian dynasty founded by Augustus came to an end. It had reconciled the Romans and their subjects with the idea that the empire could be ruled only by a monarch.

A year of wars known as the 'year of the four emperors' followed. It saw the murder of one, Galba, the suicide of another, Otho, and the execution of a third, Vitellius. A fourth emperor, Vespasian, was acclaimed in Alexandria in AD 69. He succeeded in uniting the empire and founded the Flavian dynasty.

Integrating the Greeks into the imperial elite: the Flavians

Vespasian is known for his dictum *Pecunia non olet* (Money doesn't stink), when he introduced the taxation of public toilets. But apart from putting the finances of Rome in order, his priority was to re-establish order in the eastern provinces. Immediately upon securing the throne for himself, after a short civil war, he sent his son Titus to Jerusalem. It was only after a long siege that the city fell in the summer of AD 70. The Second Temple was destroyed and the treasures and religious symbols of the Jews carried to Rome. The resistance of a radical group of 960 people, the Sicarii, continued until AD 73 in the fort of Masada, a natural fortress near the Dead Sea. According to Josephus' report, which is not wholly corroborated by the archaeological data, the defenders committed suicide when, after several months of siege, the Romans constructed a ramp to bring a giant siege tower to the top of the mountain. As Jewish religion does not allow suicide, they allegedly drew lots and killed each other in turn, except for two women and three children, who survived hidden in a cistern.

Greece did not suffer from the Jewish revolt of AD 69–70 or the civil war of 69. But Vespasian recalled the grants of freedom to Achaea, Rhodes, Byzantion, Samos and perhaps Lycia. The Jewish revolt and the continuous threat from the Parthian Empire made clear that the defence of the eastern frontier needed improvement. Vespasian achieved this by annexing territories, reorganising the provinces and rearranging the legions along the frontiers to the Parthian kingdom. This had an impact on the administration of the easternmost Hellenised areas. In AD 72 or 73, the governor of Syria, Caesennius Paetus, annexed the client kingdom of Kommagene and added it to his province. The gap between Syria and Kappadokia, the two provinces with the greatest strategic importance in the East, was thus closed. The province of Kappadokia was joined with Galatia and territories in Armenia Minor; the new large province of Kappadokia and Galatia comprised the less urbanised and Hellenised Anatolian plateau. Another large province was created in south Asia Minor: Lycia et Pamphylia, which included parts of Pisidia and western Cilicia Tracheia. Cilicia Pedias, previously part of Syria, was joined with part of Cilicia Tracheia and became a new province. Some of these reforms were annulled by Trajan, who once more separated Kappadokia and Galatia, attaching Armenia to Kappadokia and Galatia to Paphlagonia.

These changes near the eastern frontier of the empire contrast sharply with the far more stable and peaceful conditions in Greece and the Hellenised part of Asia Minor. This part of the Roman East was also more rapidly and more strongly integrated into the empire under Vespasian (AD 69–79), Titus (AD 79–81) and Domitian (AD 81–96). Following a generous policy of granting Roman citizenship to wealthy and politically influential men in Greece and Asia Minor, the Flavian emperors recruited men of Greek descent for the ranks of Roman aristocracy. Nine men from the Greek East were admitted into the senate under Vespasian, thus rising to the highest levels of the imperial elite. Seven of them came from cities of Asia Minor, whereas the other two became senators after serving in the Roman army. Another eight senators from Asia Minor followed under Domitian. Profiting from a prolonged period of peace, the exploitation of natural resources, such as marble, the fertility of its soil and the supply of the Roman legions along the Danube and the Euphrates, Asia Minor experienced a period of growth. A sign of this growth is the fact that under the Flavians 300 of the roughly 500 cities of Asia Minor issued their own coins, promoting both a sense of identity and economic exchange. The Flavians can also be credited with the construction and upkeep of roads.

The Flavian dynasty came to an end when Domitian, unpopular among senators because of his autocratic rule but enormously popular in the eastern provinces, was murdered in a palace conspiracy. A new dynasty came into power with Nerva, an old and experienced senator. The most important decision in his short reign (AD 96–98) was to adopt a skilled general, Trajan, as his successor. This was the beginning of the dynasty of 'the adopted emperors' or the Antonines.

Consolidating the borders of the *oecumene*: Trajan and Hadrian

Under Trajan's rule (AD 98–117) the Roman Empire attained its greatest size (see Map 8). Trajan's campaigns in Dacia – modern Romania – in AD 101–6 added this troublesome kingdom to the empire; the kingdom of Nabataea, roughly equivalent to today's Jordan, was annexed in AD 107. The only serious enemy of the Roman Empire remained the Parthian kingdom. Both Rome and the Parthians struggled for influence in Armenia. Trajan's offensive in Armenia and Mesopotamia from AD 113 to 115 temporarily pushed Rome's frontiers to the Tigris and the Persian Gulf. Towards the end of his reign, in AD 115, Trajan faced a new revolt of

20. The odeon of Herodes Atticus in Athens.

the Jews that stretched from Babylonia and Syria to Egypt and Cyrenaica. The revolt was subdued with cruelty and nearly the entire Jewish population of Alexandria was killed. Trajan died in AD 117, shortly after he had given the empire its greatest expansion.

Following the Flavian policies, Trajan admitted many Greeks into the senate, from Asia Minor and now also from mainland Greece. One of them, Tiberius Claudius Atticus, was the father of Herodes Atticus, who was the wealthiest man in Greece in the second century, an important orator and the first Greek to become ordinary (not suffect) consul, in AD 143. Even today, visitors to Athens attend concerts and plays in the concert hall that he sponsored, the Herodeion (see Fig. 20).

When Trajan died childless in AD 117, Hadrian, his adopted son, ascended the throne at the age of forty-one. He was the son of a senator from Spain, Trajan's nephew and married to the emperor's grand-niece Sabina. Like his predecessor, Hadrian had military experience. Shortly before his accession he had been appointed governor of the most important province in the east, Syria. But he is better known for his love of Greek literature and philosophy, which earned him the nickname Graeculus (the little Greek; see Fig. 21). His other great passions were hunting and a beautiful young man from Bithynia, Antinoos. Upon ascending the throne, Hadrian terminated the war against the Parthians, abandoned Armenia and Mesopotamia, and spent most of his reign travelling his

21. Hadrian.

realm, subduing revolts and securing the empire's borders, from the wall in northern Britain that bears his name to the Euphrates. His long stays in the East made his impact on Greek affairs more significant that that of all his predecessors, including Nero.

During his first tour of the empire, from AD 121 to 125, he initiated the construction of Hadrian's Wall in Britain and dealt with a rebellion in Mauretania, before he had to move quickly to the East to prevent a new war with the Parthians. He stayed in Asia Minor in the winter of AD 123 and spring of 124, visiting numerous cities. On the occasion of his visit, Stratonikeia was renamed Hadrianopolis and a successful bear hunt in Mysia was commemorated with the foundation of the city of Hadrianou Therai (Hadrian's hunt). During this trip, a twelve-year-old boy from Mantineion in Bithynia was introduced to the emperor: Antinoos grew to become one of the most beautiful youths of his time and the emperor's favourite (see Fig. 22). In the summer of AD 124 Hadrian moved to Greece, visiting the most famous sites – Athens, Delphi and Sparta – and showing his love for Greece by serving

22. Antinoos.

as magistrate in Athens and being initiated in the Eleusinian mysteries. He saw to it that the Temple of Zeus Olympios, which had remained unfinished since the times of the tyrant Peisistratos in the late sixth century BC, was completed. In AD 125 Hadrian was back in Italy.

He returned to Greece in AD 128 after a journey to Africa, now holder of the honorific title *pater patriae* (father of the fatherland). In the East, he was greeted as the 'Olympian', assimilated with Zeus. In Athens, his arrival was regarded as the beginning of a new era. Hundreds of altars set up for his worship, both public and private, still attest to his popularity. From Athens he travelled once more through Asia Minor and Syria in AD 129–30. Arriving in Jerusalem in AD 130, the philhellene emperor took measures that rekindled Jewish opposition to Roman rule: he forbade circumcision, perhaps in an effort to promote the Hellenisation of the Jews. He also ordered the construction of a temple to Jupiter Capitolinus and founded a new city along the old city of Jerusalem, the *colonia Aelia Capitolina*.

In July AD 130 Hadrian and his entourage came to Egypt, where he spent some time debating with scholars in the Mouseion. A lion hunt in the Libyan desert together with Antinoos inspired a poem by the Alexandrian poet Pankrates. The imperial visit produced more poetry when the poetess Iulia Balbilla, Sabina's escort, commemorated the trip to Egyptian monuments in verses that can still be seen inscribed on the legs of the colossal statues of Pharaoh Amenhotep III in the Theban necropolis. At that time the statues were thought to represent the Ethiopian prince Memnon, who was killed by Achilles in the Trojan War. Damaged by an earthquake, they occasionally let out a sound at dawn, believed to be Memnon's song. Three times Memnon sang to Hadrian with a mighty roar:

> The emperor Hadrian then himself bid welcome to
> Memnon and left on stone for generations to come
> This inscription recounting all that he saw and all that he heard.
> It was clear to all that the gods love him.

These verses, composed in November, show not the faintest trace of a tragedy that had occurred only a few days earlier: the nineteen-year-old Antinoos had drowned in the Nile on 24 October. This occurred on the very day the Egyptians commemorated the death of their great god Osiris, who like Antinoos had drowned in the Nile. Whether this was accident, sacrifice or self-sacrifice, we will never discover. But his death gave Hadrian the opportunity to rival Achilles' lament for Patroclus and that of Alexander for Hephaistion. In myth, Osiris' sister and wife, Isis, resurrected Osiris. Hadrian could not resurrect Antinoos but he could and did make him a god. His beautiful image decorated temples in the eastern part of the empire, and in Athens the ephebes competed in the composition of poems and panegyrics for their deified fellow ephebe at the new festival Antinoeia. Only days after Antinoos' death, on 30 October, the new city Antinoopolis was founded, near the place of the accident and around the temple-tomb of Antinoos. Tax exemptions and other privileges attracted Greek settlers and Roman army veterans, and the city grew both as an important port and as a promoter of Hellenism in Egypt.

In the spring of AD 131, Hadrian started his long journey back to Rome by revisiting Syria, Asia Minor and Athens. His greatest achievement during his second trip was the foundation of the Panhellenion in AD 132. The idea was to create a council in which all Greek cities were to be represented. Continuing a tradition that reached back to the Persian Wars and the temporary unity of the Greeks, and combining it with the concept of religious centres – such as Olympia and Delphi – that claimed to represent the Greeks as a whole, Hadrian created an institution that united those cities that could plausibly prove their Hellenic origin. The foundation of the Panhellenion was an invitation to distant cities to present evidence for their Greek origins. This not only promoted local historiography, but also gave great impetus to the definition of Greek identity. The Panhellenion became a stage for the display of Hellenic identity and for competition between Greek cities.

The consequences of Hadrian's actions in Judaea did not leave him time to enjoy the creation of the new commonwealth of the Greeks. A great uprising in Judaea started under Simeon Bar Kochba in AD 132. The emperor summoned his best general, Sextus Iulius Severus, from Britain and troops from neighbouring provinces to fight the rebels. He returned to Rome in AD 133, but the war, which seriously threatened Roman rule in this area, went on until 135, when Judaea was integrated into the province of Syria and Palaestina. After the Roman victory the Jews were no longer allowed to enter Jerusalem.

Hadrian spent his last years in illness and the search for a suitable successor. When the designated successor, Lucius Aelius Caesar, died the choice fell on Aurelius Antoninus, remembered as the Pius. He owes this attribute to his insistence on having Hadrian deified despite the senate's opposition. Hadrian's final resting place is one of the best-known landmarks of Rome, Castel Sant'Angelo.

The Jewish revolt and Hadrian's health problems in his last years did not diminish his engagement with the Greeks. A continually increasing number of imperial letters found in inscriptions provides evidence for his interest in political and cultural issues in Greece. In AD 134, he composed three long letters with detailed instructions concerning the organisation of contests, the duties of the organisers, the money prizes to be paid to the winners and the establishment of a strict sequence of contests that would enable athletes and artists to travel from one venue to the next. Two other letters from his last years deal with the election of magistrates in the Macedonian Koinon and the erection of his temple in Pergamon, an honour that he declined. Just weeks before his death, Hadrian was still dealing with Greek disputes. Responding to an embassy from the small city of Naryx in central Greece, he confirms that Naryx had the status and the rights of a *polis*, displaying his erudition: 'And some of the most famous poets, both Romans and Greeks, have mentioned you as Narykeians; and they explicitly name some of the heroes as originating in your city.' Hadrian refers to the Lokrian hero Aias and references his deeds in the poetry of Callimachus, Virgil and Ovid. A short phrase in an inscription in Delphi in honour of 'Imperator Hadrian, the Rescuer', gratefully acknowledges that the emperor 'saved and nourished *his* Hellas' (*ten heautou Hellada*), a possessive phrase born not from forceful dominance but out of affection.

12

EMPERORS, CITIES
AND PROVINCES FROM
AUGUSTUS TO HADRIAN

(30 BC–AD 138)

The Divine Providence's gift to mankind: the Roman emperor

A decree of the assembly of the Greeks living in Asia Minor in 9 BC
declares Augustus' birthday to be 'the beginning of glad tidings for the
world'. Consequently, this day – 23 September – should be regarded the
first day of the year. The text's rhetoric leaves little doubt as to the emper-
or's position:

> Providence, which divinely disposes our lives, employing zeal and ardor
> has made the most perfect arrangement for life by producing Augus-
> tus. She has filled him with excellence for the benefit of mankind, and
> has given him to us and to our descendants as a god, to represent her.
> He brought war to an end and set an order.

The Greek population had no idea about Augustus' delicate negotiations with the senatorial aristocracy on which the emperor's power was
founded. But by the end of the Julio-Claudian dynasty (AD 68) this power

had taken a more or less clearly defined shape. In AD 69, a *lex de imperio Vespasiani*, issued by the senate for Vespasian, specified the powers of the emperor and their institutional basis: the *tribunitia potestas* and the *imperium proconsulare maius*. First, the emperor was directly and indirectly responsible for the government of the provinces. As proconsul he was the nominal governor of all provinces in which Roman legions were stationed. Large parts of the Balkans – under Hadrian, this meant Epirus, Thracia, Moesia and Dacia – most of the Near East and Egypt were thus under his direct authority. Since he was not personally present in all these 'imperial provinces', he governed them through important senators sent to the provinces as his representatives (see p. 272). No army was stationed in provinces that were under the direct authority of the senate (senatorial provinces). However, the emperor was involved in the selection of their governors too. And all governors turned to him for advice, support and authorisation, sometimes even for petty matters. The correspondence of Pliny the Younger, governor of Bithynia and Pontos, with Trajan shows the workload that a conscientious emperor might have to take upon himself, if he wished to provide advice. Usually, the emperor reacted to requests and problems as they arose, but some emperors, especially Vespasian, Trajan, and Hadrian, also implemented general policies with regard to the defence of the empire, the inclusion of the provincial elite in the aristocracy of the empire, the finances, building programmes and the reorganisation of provinces.

The emperors intervened in the life of provinces by formulating general rules in their edicts, sending letters (*epistulae*) with instructions to the governors or the provincial assembly, appointing supervisors of the finances (*correctores*) and responding to petitions concerning any conceivable matter: limitations on wine production, the fixing of fish prices, arbitration in civic conflicts and territorial disputes between cities, tax exemption and privileges, protection from abuses by the army and the organisation of contests. Augustus even had to deal with the death of a man in Knidos, who was hit by a chamber pot thrown at him by a slave. The victim deserved death, was Augustus' verdict, since he was attacking another man's home in the night. Usually, the emperor's response (*apokrima*) was written, often in his own hand, at the bottom of the letter (*subscriptio, hypographe*). Judging by a joke narrated by Plutarch, an emperor's response could be as ambiguous as Apollo's Delphic oracles – or simply express a certain sense of humour. Someone handed Augustus a *libellus* with the question: 'Is Theodoros of Tarsus a baldhead or a thief? What do you think?' Augustus answered: 'Yes, I think.'

The power of the emperor was perceived in different ways in the city of Rome and in Italy, in the western provinces and in those provinces of the Greek East that had a long tradition of monarchical power. For the Greek populations the emperor was an absolute monarch with an unprecedented universal claim on power, a ruler to whom the provincial population owed allegiance. The emperor's unique position of power was acknowledged through oaths of loyalty. The oath was taken only on occasion of a new emperor's accession to the throne by the population of a province – or its representatives – usually in the place where the imperial cult was practised. Also embassies visited the emperor to congratulate him. The population of the provinces indirectly demonstrated loyalty by invoking the emperor's fortune in ordinary oaths taken during transactions. Such rituals that were performed on a regular basis made clear to the Greek populations that the emperor was their ruler. He was more than the supreme representative of the Roman domination. He was a monarch who exercised a direct and absolute rule that no Hellenistic king could even have dreamed of. His power extended over the entire inhabited world. Augustus was praised as 'rescuer of the Greeks and the entire *oecumene*', Vespasian as 'rescuer and benefactor of the *oecumene*', Hadrian as 'the rescuer and founder of the *oecumene*' and 'the lord and rescuer of the *oecumene*', for whom 'the *oecumene* offers sacrifices and prays for his eternal preservation'. Nothing comparable is known for any Hellenistic king.

Although almost all emperors spent some time in the East before their accession, only Augustus, Nero, Trajan and Hadrian travelled in the Balkans, Greece and Asia Minor as emperors. Augustus spent some time in the eastern provinces between 22 and 19 BC. His successor, Tiberius, did not travel to Greece during his reign, but he had spent seven years in Rhodes, adopting Greek customs and dress. Nero was in Greece for his participation in contests in AD 67–8, Trajan in the Balkans, Asia Minor and Mesopotamia for his campaigns, and Hadrian toured the East twice. Some emperors developed particular relationships with single cities or provinces, either because they had friends there or because they had lived or studied there. For instance, Claudius was a great benefactor of the island of Kos, the fatherland of his doctor and friend Caius Stertinius Xenophon. That said, two of these emperors surpassed all others in the intimacy of their relations with Greek provinces and cities and the extent of their benefactions: Nero and Hadrian.

Even from a distance, almost all emperors had an impact on settlement history; they metaphorically became 'founders' (*ktistai*) of cities by donating funds for public works, enlarging territories, granting privileges and rebuilding cities whose outlook had suffered from earthquakes and other natural disasters, or from lack of funds. With the grant of an honorific title, such as 'temple warden' (*neokoros*) of the regional imperial cult, they triggered competition among the cities for rank and privileges, and thus, unintentionally, they did as much to promote local patriotism and identity as many a local statesman. Although the provincial populations hardly had any chance to see the emperor, the emperor was ritually and symbolically present in their lives.

Ruling from afar: the visibility of the emperor

In a famous passage in Mark's Gospel, Jesus takes a denarius in his hand and, pointing to the images that decorated its two sides, says: 'Render unto Caesar the things that are Caesar's, and unto God the things that are God's.' For a large part of the population in the Roman East, the most direct everyday contact with the Roman emperor was the use of coins that were decorated with his image (see Fig. 23). Engraved on the coins were inscriptions that glorified the emperor and transmitted important ideas about his position but also about the expectations his subjects could have: *aequitas, aeternitas, concordia, felicitas, fortuna, gloria, securitas* – impartiality, permanence, concord, joy, good fortune, glory, security. When coin users in the Greek-speaking East had difficulties in understanding the Latin legends, other media made the emperor and his powers ubiquitously visible.

Various forms of communication acquainted the population with the ruler of the empire: proclamations and announcements, festivals and contests, processions and sacrifices, hymns, encomiastic orations and images. Most people knew who ruled them and what he looked like. In a world without internet, it might take some time for the news of an emperor's death and the name of his successor to reach the most remote edges of the empire. A papyrus written on 17 November AD 54 preserves the draft of a proclamation on the occasion of Nero's accession to the throne. Since

23. Coin of Emperor Domitian.

Claudius had died on 2 October, the news about the new emperor reached Egypt more than a month later:

> The Caesar who was owed to his ancestors, god manifest, has gone to join them, and the Emperor whom the world expected and hoped for has been proclaimed, the good genius of the world and source of all blessings, Nero Caesar, has been proclaimed. Therefore we shall all wear wreaths and give thanks to all the gods sacrificing oxen.

Confusion was to be expected in times of usurpation, such as the 'year of the four emperors', and at least three Nero impostors are attested in the Roman East in the twenty years following the emperor's suicide.

A small number of Greeks from the Roman East were able to meet the emperor in person by travelling to Rome as envoys – one of the greatest services a member of the elite could offer his city or his province. Envoys had to face the usual risks of travel, the unusual dangers of an emperor's capricious mood and the fear of failing their community in advocating its requests. But successful service was not forgotten, and to be called *sebastognostos* (acquainted with the revered one) was a title of honour that gave both a man and his descendants great prestige. Envoys met the emperor with concrete requests but also simply in order to pay their respects and to congratulate him on his birthday, a victory or the occasion of a fifteen-year-old prince becoming an adult by receiving the symbol of manliness, the *toga virilis*. Such embassies became a tremendous financial burden on the cities: for example, Byzantion paid 12,000 sestertii annually – the price of six slaves – to dispatch an ambassador with an honorific decree to the emperor and another 3,000 for an envoy to the governor of Moesia, until

Pliny, with the approval of the emperor, saved them the money by ruling that the city should send the letter without an envoy. Some of the embassies were so large that Vespasian issued an edict that forbade the cities from sending more than three envoys. With some luck the envoys returned bearing a letter from the emperor with his recommendation that they should receive travel expenses, unless the envoys had promised to conduct the embassy on their own expense. Volunteers could be scarce in critical times, and so the city of Maroneia developed around the mid-first century AD a procedure that allowed any citizen to take the initiative to submit to the magistrates an application to go as an envoy to the emperor. Maroneia's decree also gives instructions as to how the envoy should behave:

> When the envoys come to the divine Caesar Augustus they shall embrace him on behalf of the city and, after expressing their joy for his and his entire family's health and for the excellent state of his affairs and the affairs of the Roman people, they shall explain to him and the sacred senate all the rights of the city and will request with all imploration and supplication that he preserves for us our freedom, our laws, our city and its territory as well as all the other privileges that our ancestors and we have, receiving them from them, so that we, who always and with no interruption preserved goodwill and trust toward the Romans, always enjoy their gratitude for these things.

One of the honorific attributes used for emperors from the early first century was *epiphanestatos*: that is, the one whose power is visibly present. Various media effectively insinuated their presence. Emperors often held ordinary civic and religious offices: for instance, Augustus served as *strategos* (general) of the Thessalian League, Trajan and Hadrian as prophets in the sanctuary at Didyma, Hadrian as chief magistrate in Delphi. Of course, they did not exercise the office in person but through a local representative.

In many cities or provinces, people signing and dating contracts used names of months that commemorated Augustus, members of his family or other emperors; in Kibyra, the first day of the month was called *sebaste* in honour of Augustus. In many cities the tribes, subdivisions of the citizen body, were given names to honour emperors, such as the tribe Hadrianis in Athens and Aphrodisias. Statues of emperors and members of their families were erected while they were alive and remained visible after their

24. Image of a high priest of the imperial cult on a sarcophagus from Aphrodisias.

death, except in rare cases of *damnatio memoriae*. Sometimes a new statue was dedicated on every birthday of an emperor. Portraits of the emperors decorated the crowns of high priests (see Fig. 24); busts were to be seen in public buildings and were ceremonially carried in processions. The statues of members of the imperial family acquainted the population of the provinces with them as well. Changes in the hairstyle of the members of the imperial family – including the facial hair of the men – were closely observed and imitated by all strata of the population. The elaborate hairstyle of Flavia Domitilla, Vespasian's wife, had the same impact on the heads of women from Egypt to Macedonia (see Fig. 25) as the colour and style of Lady Di's hair had on the heads of women in the West in the 1980s.

Encomiastic orations for the emperors and their house were regularly held in festivals of the traditional gods and were one of the disciplines in which orators and ephebes competed in some festivals. An emperor's accession was hailed with sacrifices if not in all, then at least in the major cities. On the emperor's birthday, hymns and orations praised him for his

25. Grave relief. The hairstyle of the man imitates that of Trajan, that of the girl next to him is modeled after the hairstyle of Faustina the Elder, wife of Antoninus Pius.

achievements. The imperial cult, typically performed on his birthday, was clearly the most important medium that not only associated the emperor with the provincial populations but also created a symbolic link among the populations of the empire.

Theoi sebastoi: the divinity of the emperors

In the Roman East, the cult of the emperor was deeply rooted in local traditions: in the offering of religious worship to the Hellenistic kings (see p. 108–15) and to the Roman commander Flamininus, in the cult of Thea Rhome – the personification of Rome – and in the occasional offering of divine honours to the personified Roman senate and to Roman governors. Following this model, many Greek cities established a cult of Julius Caesar after his death and then of Augustus and his successors during their lifetime. Usually, the civic cult of the emperor was connected with the worship of the goddess Rome or with the cult of a traditional god, often Zeus. Emperors were commonly given the name of a god as their honorary epithet, indicating that they possessed similar qualities. Augustus, Tiberius and

Claudius were called 'Zeus'; Augustus, Claudius and Nero were assimilated with Apollo; Claudius and Nero with Asclepius; Caius Caesar, Augustus' grandson, was honoured as Ares. Female relatives of emperors were associated with goddesses that protected fertility and motherhood: for instance, Julia, Augustus' daughter, was linked with Leto; Agrippina and Sabina with Demeter 'who brings fruit' (Karpophoros); Drusilla with Aphrodite. The most popular among the emperors, Hadrian, was honoured as a New Dionysus, a New Pythios (i.e. Apollo), 'patron of the council' (Boulaios), Olympian and 'Zeus who protects freedom' (Eleutherios).

A priest or high priest of the *sebastos* or the *sebastoi* was responsible for the civic cult of the current emperor. These civic priests were always members of the wealthiest and most respected families. They covered the expenses for the celebration and sometimes served in this office for life. They often held it together with a female member of their family, usually their wife, sometimes their daughter. In addition to the cities, federations (*koina*) that consisted of the cities of a geographical region, sometimes a district of a province, organised their own cult and celebrated annual festivals. These regional federations were presided over by a chairman whose title consisted of the name of the region and the suffix *-arches* (the chief magistrate): for example, Asiarches was the president of the federation of Asia, Makedoniarches the president of the federation of Macedonia, Lykiarches the chairman of the Lycians and so on. This magistrate also served as high priest (*archiereus*) of the imperial cult in his federation, together with his wife or closest female relative. He was assisted by an *agonothetes* (chairman of the contests). Sometimes, wealthy men occupied the role of both high priest and *agonothetes*.

One of the cities of the region or province, not necessarily the provincial capital, hosted the temple of the emperor and had the prestigious title *neokoros* (temple warden). The first *neokoreia* was established shortly after the Battle of Actium, when the federation of the Greeks of Asia requested permission to establish the worship of Octavian in 29 BC. The temple was erected in Pergamon and was dedicated to a joint cult of Octavian/Augustus and Rome. The Roman population of the province did not participate in the cult but instead established a cult of Julius Caesar and Rome in Ephesos. Other regions followed the model of Asia. In 25 BC, as soon as Galatia had been annexed by Rome, a cult of Rome and Augustus was established in Ankyra. After Augustus' death, in AD 23, the *koinon* of Asia requested the construction of a second temple, this time for the cult of Tiberius, his mother, Livia, and the senate; in this way, the Greeks of Asia wanted to express their gratitude for the prosecution of two corrupt governors. After a long dispute among eleven cities which claimed for themselves the right to host the temple on the basis of antiquity and loyalty towards Rome, this privilege was granted to Smyrna. By the time of the Flavian emperors it was an established practice for important cities to compete for the honour of the *neokoreia*, and sometimes this competition turned into bitter conflicts and enmities that lasted for decades.

Just like the cult of Hellenistic kings, the cult of the emperor comprised a combination of activities that derived directly from the cult of the gods: procession, sacrifice and athletic – sometimes also musical – contests. The Greeks consciously modelled the cult of the emperor after the cult of the gods. In Mytilene, for instance, the rituals for the birthday of Augustus were copied from 'the law concerning Zeus' (*Diakos nomos*), which regulated the rituals for the cult of Zeus. The emperor's birthday was usually the occasion for the celebration of the imperial festival. At both the civic and the regional levels there were also sacrifices for past emperors, as well as sacrifices on the day of every month that corresponded to an emperor's birthday: for instance, because Augustus was born on 23 September, in Pergamon sacrifices were offered on the twenty-third day of every month.

These celebrations were spectacular events. The priest and the *agonothetes* wore impressive garments, sometimes in purple, and a golden wreath on their heads decorated with the portraits of the emperor or emperors, sometimes also of a god who was associated with the celebration (see Fig. 24). 'The bearers of the images of the Augusti' (*sebastophoroi*) attended the procession, carrying shining images of the ruling emperor and earlier emperors, usually gilded or made of silver. The sacrifice to the emperor, often also to traditional gods, was accompanied by the singing of hymns. Associations of hymn singers (*hymnodoi*), consisting of the scions of prominent families, were responsible for the performance of the hymns, while *sebastologoi* (those who speak about the emperor) delivered encomiastic orations. The poet Publius Aelius Pompeianus Paion, honoured for his skills as 'the new Homer', had acquired fame for his melic and epic poems that sang the glory of the deified Hadrian (*melopoios kai rhapsodos Theou Hadrianou*).

The sacrifice was followed by a banquet, to which citizens and sometimes also foreigners and slaves were invited. An important component was the contest (*agon*), which was typically named after the emperor

– Sebasteia for Augustus, Hadrianeia for Hadrian and so on – and some-times also honoured a traditional god alongside the emperor. For instance, in Thespiai, the traditional contest for Eros additionally honoured Rome and Augustus (*Kaisareia Erotideia Rhomaia*). The celebration of the imperial cult was also a good occasion for the dedication of statues of the emperor and members of his family, although such a dedication could take place at any time during the year.

The imperial cult was based on reciprocity: the worshippers expressed their loyalty, expecting protection and care in return. For the wealthiest and noblest families that provided the high priests, the cult offered pres-tige – but sometimes turned into a financial burden that some men were not willing to accept. For the cities, it created an arena of competition in which they could display their past glories and their local identity. For the regions and provinces, the assembly of the representatives from the cities on the occasion of the annual festival provided an opportunity to discuss important issues connected with maladministration, heavy taxation and natural disasters.

Provincial administration

The development of Roman provincial administration was a slow process determined by two factors: the experiences that the Roman senate and the leading statesmen collected over the course of the Roman expansion; and the change of Roman society and institutions, especially after the destruc-tion of Carthage and the subjugation of Greece in 146 BC. Initially, the Romans did not have any institutions for the administration of provinces. *Provincia* described the responsibilities assigned by the senate to magis-trates with military command – the consuls and the praetors – and the geographical area in which they were to exercise their command for one year. When parts of Sicily and Sardinia were annexed in 241 and 238 BC, these new territories required direct and permanent administration; for this reason, they were placed under the responsibility of a magistrate with military command, becoming that magistrate's *provincia*. The senators who governed a province, usually with the title of praetor, were assisted by lower military commanders and financial administrators. A governorship secured them experience, wealth – through extortion and exploitation – and political contacts.

The population of the provinces was not entirely unprotected against reckless exploitation and bad management. First, the Roman system of patronage, whereby influential Roman senators promised their protection to dependent citizens, or *clients*, in exchange for political support, expanded beyond the city of Rome. This allowed provincial communities to declare a Roman statesman their *patronus*, obliging themselves to offer loyalty in exchange for support in times of need. Second, because of the competition among the Roman noblemen, accusations against a provincial official for corruption and mismanagement could be used by his rivals as a political weapon. And third, as much as the Roman senate during the Republic and the emperor during the Principate were interested in the regular flow of tribute from the provinces to the *fiscus*, they were also interested in avoiding revolts.

The most important reform of the provincial administration was the work of Sulla, during his dictatorship in 81 BC. Realising that the traditional number of magistrates with military command (*imperium*) – two consuls and four praetors – was not sufficient for the administration of an increased number of provinces, he introduced a system that essentially remained in place until Augustus. The number of praetorships was increased to eight. The rule was now that two consuls and eight praetors were elected for one year and exercised their function in Rome; after the end of the year, their *imperium* was extended and exercised in the provinces, not in Rome. As proconsuls and propraetors (substitute consuls and praetors), they were assigned the governorship of one of the then ten provinces and the command of the troops that were stationed there. This system proved to be insufficient, not only because the number of provinces increased but also because extraordinary commands became very common during the wars that followed. However, the basic idea that provinces should be governed by senators who had served in positions of high command did not change.

Augustus' Principate brought significant modifications to this system. The emperors continuously held the powers of a proconsul, combined with authority in the provinces that was greater than that of any other authority (*imperium maius*). As proconsuls, the emperors were the governors of all the provinces in which Roman troops were stationed. Under normal circumstances, the emperors were represented in the imperial provinces by their 'envoys', or *legati Augusti pro praetore* (envoys of Augustus with the powers of a praetor), who were personally appointed by the emperors. The emperors also appointed the governors of small, newly created provinces, as well as governors who were placed in charge of client kingdoms; these governors were not senators but knights, and had the title *praefectus* and later procurator.

Provinces without the army were under the authority of the senate, which appointed their governors or their proconsuls. The proconsuls were senators, former praetors, who were assigned a province by lot; only the proconsul of Asia was a former consul, because of the economic importance and prestige of this province. However, the emperor was involved in their selection, nominating candidates, and intervened in important matters of administration. There is no doubt that the lottery was manipulated. Otherwise we cannot explain why, from the mid-first century AD onwards, proconsuls originated in the provinces assigned to them more often than mere coincidence allows. The first senator to come from Asia, a certain Celsius Polemaianos, later became governor of Asia; soon after, Iulius Quadratus, another consul from Asia, also occupied the governorship in his province of origin. Experience from past service in the East, family traditions, personal connections and economic interests must have influenced such assignments.

Usually, the governor remained in his province for a year, unless special circumstances, such as a revolt, made an extension of his term necessary. The most important governorship was that of Syria, because of its proximity to the kingdom of the Parthians. Here, the imperial legate usually remained in office for three years. The governor received instructions (*mandata*) from the emperor and corresponded regularly with him. All governors received a substantial stipend that ranged from 100,000 sestertii for a procurator to 1 million for the governor of Africa in the late second century AD (for the sake of comparison, a legionary's annual salary in the late first century AD was 1,200 sestertii).

The governor was assisted by a small staff. The proconsul chose a deputy (*legatus*) from among the senators. The governors of large and important provinces such as Asia had three *legati*. The financial administration was the responsibility of a young senator, the quaestor. The governors were supported in their work by scribes, heralds and a personal guard. The lower-ranking personnel of the governor were recruited from among his slaves, the higher from among relatives and friends. Governors were also very keen to maintain relations with the elites of their province and accordingly recruited consultants from among their members. In the provinces in which the emperor had property or economic interests – lands, mines and so on – he was represented by a knight with the title of procurator.

In the Greek East, the development of provincial administration was a complex process, as new provinces were being created and reshaped until Trajan, and their status – or the status of individual cities – changed based on the empire's needs or as a result of privileges granted by the emperors. For instance, Rhodes lost its status as a free city in AD 43 and regained it in AD 55; Achaia was abolished as a province around AD 15 and was part of Macedonia until AD 44; in AD 67 Nero temporarily abolished it again and declared the cities free, but this measure was annulled after his death.

During the reign of Hadrian, when the borders of the empire had been consolidated, there were four provinces in the Balkans (see Map 8). Achaia, with Corinth as its capital, covered most of Greece, spanning the Peloponnese, central and west Greece, the Ionian Islands and most of the Aegean Islands. Macedonia, the oldest province on Greek soil, had Thessalonike as it capital and comprised Macedonia, Thessaly and Epirus. Thrace, heavily populated by non-Greek tribes, with the Greek population concentrated in several cities along the west coast of the Black Sea, was governed by a procurator. It became a province in AD 46, with Philippopolis as its capital. A few Greek colonies were also located in Moesia Inferior, further north; the old colonies on the north shore of the Black Sea were attached to this province. Thrace and Moesia Inferior, as well as the Latin-speaking Balkan provinces Dacia and Moesia Superior, were significant for the defence of the borders and were governed by imperial *legati*. In the south, the island of Crete formed a province with Cyrenaica, whose capital was Gortyn on Crete; the two parts of the province had very limited contact. The areas of Asia Minor that were dominated by Greek cities formed the province of Asia, with Ephesos as its capital. Bithynia and Pontos, in the more or less Hellenised north part of Asia Minor along the south coast of the Black Sea, was another imperial province governed by a proconsul, whose seat was Nikomedeia. Cyprus was likewise governed by a proconsul and lacked military presence. Cilicia had a complex history until around AD 74, when Vespasian merged Roman and semi-autonomous territories into a single province with Tarsos as its capital.

The rest of the Roman East was divided into imperial provinces, governed by imperial *legati*, who commanded armies of varying size, depending on the strategic significance of the province. Lycia, a province since AD 43, was joined with Pamphylia in AD 70; Attaleia was the capital. The other provinces in Asia Minor were rather superficially Hellenised: Galatia, with a mixture of Celtic, Greek, Roman and indigenous population, had Ankyra as its capital. Also Kappadokia, with Kaisareia as its capital, had a predominantly indigenous population that spoke their local language until the fourth century AD. In the south, Syria was the most important province, not only strategically, because of its proximity to the Parthian Empire, but also culturally and economically, because of an important network of Hellenistic foundations. Its capital, Antioch, was one of the most important urban centres of the empire. The presence of three to four legions made the legate of Syria, an ex-consul, one of the empire's most important governors. Judaea had a troubled history of endemic local conflicts and repeated uprisings against Rome; it was governed by a procurator, until the uprising of AD 66 made it necessary to place it under a *legatus*. The neighbouring province of Petraia Arabia, only added to the empire under Trajan, with Petra as its capital, was hardly Hellenised, although the Greek language was used for public and private inscriptions. Finally, Egypt, heavily colonised by the Greeks since its conquest by Alexander, was a peculiar province. Its importance for the corn supply of Rome and for the eastern trade, but also the conditions of its conquest by Octavian after Actium and the long tradition of personal, centralised rule, justified a different treatment. Egypt was governed not by a senator but instead by a member of the equestrian order with the title of prefect of Egypt. No senator was allowed even to set foot in Egypt without the emperor's permission.

The conditions in each province depended on a variety of factors, such as the degree of Hellenisation and urbanisation at the time of its creation, the homogeneity of the region with regard to culture and urban life, the presence of armed forces and the status of the provincial cities – former capitals of kingdoms, Roman colonies and free cities. Details concerning the individual provinces were contained in the 'provincial law' (*lex provinciae*). Only the content of the laws for Asia and Bithynia, drafted by Sulla and Pompey respectively, is indirectly known through references in literary sources and inscriptions. Among other things, the laws regulated electoral procedures in the cities, age requirements for service in offices and appointment to the council, and travel expenses for envoys. Despite the regional differences, the administration of the provinces shared common features.

The governor resided in the capital (*caput provinciae*). The provincial capitals were not new foundations but old important cities: capitals of abolished kingdoms – such as Alexandria, Antioch and Nikomedeia – important urban centres with access to the sea – such as Corinth, Thessalonike, Ephesos and Tarsos – or important cities of a region – such as Gortyn. The governor's palace (*praetorium*) was more than a luxurious residence with baths and ceremonial halls for receptions and trials. It hosted offices, archives, shrines and barracks for the guards. Depending on the size of the province, part of the administration took place in locations beyond the capital. The senatorial provinces were divided into districts, called *conventus*. Asia, a very large province, had thirteen districts; Macedonia had four. The governor visited the capitals of the districts at least once a year in order to administer justice. In large cities, such as Ephesos, he was continually represented by one of his legates. Roman citizens, the representatives of cities, but also ordinary people had the chance to present their case in front of the governor.

The main responsibilities of the governor were the administration of justice, taxation, public order, the defence of the province and arbitration in the conflicts between cities. The correspondence between Pliny and Trajan gives us important insights into the everyday life of a conscientious governor. The subjects that the governor might have to deal with were as diverse as the incidents that might occur during his governorship; they ranged from permission for the construction of public baths to the problems caused by a new religion, from fiscal problems to public order, and from territorial disputes between cities to requests from local magnates to be freed of duties. Often the governor simply responded to the requests of the cities and regional federations that approached him with their worries, but governors could also take the initiative, either out of interest or ambition, or because they had personal ties to the province. For their decisions they drew on precedent, referred to the rules laid out in the *lex provinciae*, sought the advice of local statesmen and intellectuals, or corresponded with the emperor to receive instructions.

An important task of the governor was the administration of justice. The principles that he would follow were explained in an edict, published at the beginning of his service. His edict often included regulations introduced by his predecessors. Many legal conflicts were resolved through arbitration; when arbitration was not possible, the cases were brought to magistrates or courts. The governor was confronted with only a very small proportion of the cases, especially those involving Roman citizens and influential individuals, or crimes that would incur the death penalty, such as homicide, sacrilege and adultery. Only the governor had the *ius gladii*, or 'the right of the sword': that is, the right to impose the death penalty. If condemned, Roman citizens had the right to appeal in front of the emperor. Whether the requests of individuals or cities to have their case judged by the governor were successful was dependent not only on the significance of the case but also on the connections of the individuals involved – and sometimes on the bribes paid. Overall, the governors, who were advised by a council (*consilium*), demonstrated flexibility and respected local traditions.

The governor had to show care for the cities regardless of their status. He had to make sure that the elected magistrates served in their office and covered the expenses connected with it, that the members of the city council did not neglect their duties, that buildings were repaired and aqueducts built and maintained. The governors initiated and carried out the construction of roads, which were important for trade, communication and military transports (see p. 183). A very important responsibility was the supervision of the civic finances. Because of the financial misman-agement of cities, the emperor occasionally appointed special overseers, even in autonomous cities. Control mechanisms that had in earlier times been in the hands of the people were now taken over by the emperor.

The cities that did not have the privilege of tax exemption (*immunitas*) were subject to the payment of a variety of taxes. In addition to a per capita tax, taxes also had to be paid on the agrarian production; exports and imports were subject to customs duties, and using harbours likewise incurred dues. Because of the protests of the provincial populations against the *publicani* (see pp. 190–1), their role gradually declined. In Asia, Caesar transferred the responsibility for the collection of taxes from the *publicani* to the cities, leaving the tax farmers responsible only for the collection of customs; by the second century AD their tasks had been taken over by representatives of the imperial government. The taxes were first collected by the civic authorities, which then paid the amount due either to the quaestor in the senatorial provinces or the procurator in the imperial provinces. The procurator was also responsible for the imperial revenues in those provinces in which the emperor possessed land, forests, quarries, mines and so on.

The successful administration of a province depended not only on the integrity and competence of the governor but also on his cooperation with the authorities of cities and regions and his consultations with the emperor. During the Republic and the early Principate, some governors of Asia, such as Quintus Mucius Scaevola, governor in 98/7 or 94/3 BC, and Sextus Appuleius, governor in 23–21 BC, were so successful in dealing with the various tasks that they received extraordinary honours. The festival Moukieia was celebrated in the major cities, and Appuleius was worshipped like a god in Alexandreia Troas. Soon after Trajan's enthronement, the proconsuls of Bithynia and Pontos, Africa and Baetica were accused of abuse of power. Various laws show the efforts of the emperor to limit corruption and extortion. Governors were not allowed to acquire land in their province during their governorship; marriages between a proconsul or his son and a woman from the province were not permitted; and when the behaviour of governors' wives came under scrutiny in accordance with a decision of the senate in AD 20, some governors chose – or found a good excuse – to leave their wives in Rome during their governorship.

The Roman governors, who had typically progressed through the stages of an equestrian or senatorial career for many years and had commanded troops and dealt with a variety of administrative tasks, were usually up to the demands of their office. But they had also enjoyed education in the art of persuasion, and sometimes their rhetorical training in sophistic arguments has left its traces in the way they thought and acted. Pliny was confronted with the following problem: although the law of the province did not allow a man to hold citizenship in two Bithynian cities simultaneously, this law had not been rigorously observed for 150 years, resulting in many councillors having dual citizenship. The censors, who regularly checked the members of the councils, now wanted to know how to deal with this situation. In his letter to the emperor requesting advice, Pliny does not conceal his preliminary response: 'It is true that the law forbids to admit in citizenship a citizen of another city, but it does not demand to expel him from the council for this reason.' The force of this argument did not come from stringent legal thinking but from pragmatism: too many cities would lose too many councillors if the law were to be strictly applied. Flexibility and realism made a good governor; Pliny knew that. But he also knew that it was better not to take the initiative but instead refer the matter to Trajan's judgement.

It is difficult to reach a balanced judgement on the success of Roman administration and the acceptance of Roman rule. Most of our sources – encomia, official Roman documents, public inscriptions formulated by members of the civic elites – are filtered and biased. But one cannot deny that the system of Roman provincial administration in the East was quite successful, at least until the late second century AD, in keeping the number of uprisings to a minimum and often providing solutions to pressing problems caused by natural disasters, financial shortages and security threats. A variety of factors contributed to this: governors and emperors mostly responded to administrative tasks with flexibility and pragmatism; they placed the main responsibility for the administration of municipalities – local jurisdiction, the maintenance of public order, the collection of taxes, the food and water supply, the erection and maintenance of public buildings – in the hands of civic magistrates and councils recruited from wealthy local elites; and the gradual creation of a 'supra-national elite', consisting of people from the provinces who had been accepted in the classes of senators and knights, contributed to the coherence of the empire.

In a memorable scene from the film *Monty Python's Life of Brian* a member of the People's Front of Judea asks the question: 'What have the Romans ever done for us?' A rhetorical question, one might think. The other members of the People's Front, however, present a list: the Romans have brought sanitation, irrigation, education, wine, security and peace; they have built streets, baths and aqueducts. Many of these Roman gifts were the result of good administration. One of its greatest achievements was to reconcile the subject population with the rule of Rome. The fact that around AD 200 priests in Lydia chose the words *senatus* (senate) and *praetorium* (the seat of the provincial governor) to designate the council of the gods and the temple shows that they did not associate something negative with two prominent institutions of Roman rule. Separate cultural identities flourished, as long as they were not perceived as a threat – as in the case of the Jews. And thanks to the 'soft' rule of considerate governors Roman imperial administration could co-exist with a pulsating public life in the cities.

The cities: traditional *poleis*, Roman colonies and political life

In his *Roman Oration*, the orator Aelius Aristides compares the Roman Empire with a city-state, with Rome serving as its urban centre and citadel and the civilised world as its territory:

What another *polis* is to its own boundaries and territory, this city is to the boundaries and territory of the entire civilized world, as if the latter were a country district and she had been appointed common town. It might be said that this one citadel is the refuge and assembly place of all *perioeci* or of all who dwell in outside demes.

For Aristides, as for large parts of the population of the Roman Empire, the city-state remained the only political reality of which they had direct experience. For the intellectuals, it offered the main framework of thought. For poets and novelists, it competed with idealised pastoral landscapes as a stage for their literary creations.

Although Aristides' praise is as exaggerated and one-sided as any encomiastic oration, the orator was right on one count: the Roman Empire indeed contained an unparalleled number of cities both large and small. In the western provinces and in North Africa this was the result of colonisation and urbanisation at the initiative of the Romans. In the Greek-speaking East, where urbanisation had a much longer tradition than in the West, some differentiation is called for. In mainland Greece, some islands and Asia Minor, numerous *poleis* disappeared in the course of the Hellenistic period, either through complete destruction or by losing their status as autonomous communities. But new cities came into existence and old cities were revived at the initiative first of Pompey, then of Caesar, Augustus and other emperors. The foundation of colonies under Augustus revived Greece and Asia Minor (see pp. 248–9). But also cities of the traditional *polis* type were promoted by the emperors. Trajan and Hadrian had an especially strong impact on Greek settlement history as founders of cities or promoters of settlements to the status of a *polis*, the former because of his campaigns in the Balkans, the latter because of his travels to the Greek East. Trajan founded Augusta Traiana, a large and prosperous *polis* in Thrace, and turned the fortress of Doriskos into Traianopolis. In Mysia, Hadrian founded Hadrianoi, Hadrianeia and Hadrianou Therai; and another four cities in Asia Minor and two in Greece were named Hadrianopolis after the same emperor. To commemorate his beloved Antinoos, Hadrian also founded Antinoopolis in Egypt (see p. 258). The coexistence of Greek cities and Roman colonies in the same regions contributed to mutual influences between Greek and Roman institutions. The colonies were miniatures of Rome, 'small likenesses and images', as Gellius has it (*'quasi effigies parvae simulacraque'*). Their political organisation copied

Roman institutions, and the religious offices were typically Roman. The citizens (*coloni*) had the full rights of Roman citizens and were exempt from the payment of tribute. They worshiped the gods of Rome, especially the Capitoline triad consisting of Jupiter, Juno and Minerva, and the 'spirit of the colony' (*genius coloniae*). For centuries after the establishment of a colony, Latin was used not only for the administration of colonial affairs but also as the common language of private communication. At least during the first centuries of a colony's life, the majority of the urban population, the *coloni*, was of Italian origin: army veterans and other settlers from Italy who possessed Roman citizenship, including freedmen. The population in the countryside, the *incolae* or *paroikoi*, consisted of the local Greek and Hellenised population. The colonies were governed by a council of *decuriones*, and a board of two 'mayors' (*duoviri*) and two supervisors of public space (*aediles*). Additional officials included the *augur*, responsible for divination on behalf of the colony, and a board of six men (*seviri*). Sometimes the colony appointed the emperor himself to the office of mayor; in those cases he was represented by a *praefectus Caesaris quinquennalis*, a prefect of the emperor, who served without a colleague and for a period of five years. This extraordinary honour was reserved for individuals of wealth and prominence.

The organisation of civic space was also Roman. Two avenues that crossed each other, the *ordo* and the *decumanus*, dominated the city plan (see Fig. 26). In Antioch in Pisidia, the districts of the city had exactly the same names as the districts (*vici*) of the city of Rome. The colonies with their elaborate baths and public toilets, fountains and aqueducts, theatres and concert halls contributed to the urbanisation of less Hellenised areas in Anatolia and the Near East and the reurbanisation of areas that had suffered wars. In Greece and Asia Minor, the Italian settlers arrived in places with a long tradition of self-government, advanced political structures, refined culture and widespread literacy, fully integrated into the common culture of the Hellenistic world. An intense exchange between the local population and the newcomers, not free of tensions or conflicts, gradually produced a new cultural and social profile. In most cases, the colonists were fully Hellenised two or three generations after their arrival – the ancestors of some colonists were Greeks from Italy – but in some cities, such as Philippi, for instance, Latin remained the predominant language until the third century AD.

The institutions of the Roman colonies indirectly influenced the

26. The main paved avenue in the Roman colony of Dion in Macedonia.

political institutions of the Greek cities. Roman administration and the rulings of governors also had a considerable impact on property and criminal law. Finally, direct Roman interventions enhanced and accelerated a process that had already started in the Hellenistic period (see pp. 137–43): the transformation of the Greek cities from moderate 'democracies' of sorts into oligarchies. In a letter to Trajan, Pliny asked the emperor for instructions concerning the following problem. According to the provincial law for Bithynia, only men older than thirty could serve in an office; thereafter, they were eligible for a seat in the council. However, Augustus had lowered the age requirement for less important offices to twenty-five. Does this, the provincial governor wondered, mean that these younger men could also enter the council – since they had served in a magistracy? And if such men, younger than thirty, could enter the council, does this mean that all other men between twenty-five and thirty were likewise eligible for the council, even though they had not occupied an office? This is one of the few detailed pieces of information that we have about how the *lex provinciae* affected the internal organisation of Greek cities. The provincial law in Bithynia contained dispositions with an immediate impact on political life: the criteria according to which a man could become a member of the council, the age required for an office, the amount of money to be paid by a newly elected member of the council and limitations on the right of a person to hold more than one citizenship. A combination of Roman interventions and the development of pre-existing trends anchored the power monopoly of an elite of 'notables'.

Wealth was the foundation of political rights. In order to determine the status of a citizen, a property census was regularly conducted, and it served as the basis for the exercise of citizen rights. For instance, in Sparta, 300 citizens had a privileged status; the thirty-two members of a board of magistrates (*synarchia*) were elected from their ranks. An inscription from Xanthos in Lycia from the second half of the second century AD distinguishes between various categories of citizens; only the wealthiest citizens could become members of the city council (*boule*) and a council of elders (*gerousia*), which did not have political significance but commanded a lot of social prestige; a second group consisted of the *sitometroumenoi* (those who are in a position to deal out portions of corn), who stood above 'the other citizens' and the foreign residents. Certain public functions were exclusively determined by wealth, not merit. For instance, 'the ten foremost' and 'the twenty foremost' (*dekaprotoi* and *eikosaprotoi*) were the wealthiest citizens, who undertook the most expensive *liturgies* and were elected, on the basis of wealth and prestige, to the leading civic offices. With their personal property they guaranteed the collection of direct taxes payable by the city to the imperial treasury but also supervised the collection of revenues by the city.

An important innovation in the Imperial period is the transformation of the council, which in traditional Greek constitutions was renewed every year, into a permanent body with life membership – similar to the Roman senate. The council continued to have the same function as in the past: to prepare proposals for the assembly and to cooperate with the magistrates on day-to-day political and financial matters; but its members now consisted of former magistrates. As in many cities the occupation of offices required the payment of money (*summa honoraria*), the council consisted of members of the elite who had reached the age required by law and served in a magistracy. This rule cemented the privileged position of the wealthy elite in the political leadership. It is telling that the word 'councillors' (*bouleutai*) designated not only those actually serving on the council, but also the entire property class of those allowed to do so. The purpose of regulations such as this is clearly stated by Pliny in a letter to Trajan: 'It is better to give access to the council to the sons of prominent families than to the sons of the people.' This was sometimes achieved when members of the elite shared an office with their sons or paid on behalf of their sons the expenses for a *liturgy*. A man in Nysa, in Asia Minor, who served as general, 'peacekeeper' (*eirenarches*, responsible for security), supervisor of the boys, treasurer, *dekaprotos* and supervisor of the market (*agoranomos*) four times, transferred the office of the *agoranomos* shortly before his death to his son, who was already serving as secretary of the city.

Many magistracies required expenses that would have quickly drained the city's limited coffers, including, for instance, the offices of the supervisor of the gymnasium and the agora (*gymnasiarchos, agoranomos*), but also the originally religious office of the *stephanephoros* (the wreath-bearer), who gave his name to the year during which he served. Consequently, such offices were occupied only by people of means; they alone could afford to be nominated and elected. As a result, the distinction between an office (*arche*), to which a man is appointed by election or lot, and a *liturgy* or *leitourgia*, a mandatory and honorific service to the community imposed on the propertied classes, became blurred. Three services were expected of the small circle of wealthy citizens: to occupy offices and priesthoods, to undertake *liturgies* and to serve in embassies.

At least in some cities, access to the assembly – or perhaps to certain meetings of the assembly – was not open to all citizens but only to those who met certain property qualifications. For instance, Pogla in Pisidia and Sillyon in Pamphylia had a group of citizens who were called 'those who [regularly] attend the assembly' (*ekklesiastai*); this implies that some citizens were excluded from certain meetings of the assembly. The same distinction may also be implied by the term *ekklesia pandemos*, 'assembly attended by the entire people'; some meetings of the assembly were apparently attended by only part of the citizen body. Similarly, groups such as 'the Five Hundred' in Oinoanda and 'the One Thousand' in Tlos, in Lycia, were groups of citizens who enjoyed privileges because of their wealth. Since wealth was hereditary, political privileges became hereditary as well. By the end of the second century BC the de facto hereditary rule of a wealthy elite had become the reality in most of the Greek world (see pp. 138–40).

Already in the late Hellenistic period the higher status of certain families was recognised. In the Imperial period this distinction was also formally connected with political privileges. The public inscriptions of the Imperial period use a series of terms that clearly separate a small group of families belonging to the wealthy elite from the rest of the people. These terms in part allude to the origin of their power – they are the *dynamenoi* or *dynatoi*, 'those who have [financial] power'. In part, they indicate their leading position – they are the 'first' (*protoi, proteuontes*). And in part, they express their self-esteem – they are the *aristoi*, the 'best', and the *endoxoi*, 'the ones with good reputation'.

The honorific inscriptions of the first and second centuries AD express this confluence of wealth, office and hereditary claim on political power by explicitly referring to the rank (*axioma*) of certain families. The rank was a combination of rights that were based on ancestry and obligations that derived from family traditions. In the advanced Imperial period an honorific inscription from Olbia on the north shore of the Black Sea, dating to around AD 200, nicely expresses the conflation of inherited wealth, family traditions and political power:

> Kallisthenes, son of Kallisthenes, has been a man of prominent ancestors, acquainted with the emperors, and who built the city and made benefactions during urgent times of crisis, men whose praise is hard to express with words but remains alive in memory in time. Originating in such ancestors, he not only inherited their property but also their virtue, adding more adornment to it. Not being forced by human necessity but educated by the providence of the gods, he possessed an inherent, incomparable love of wisdom. Upon adulthood he was engaged with public matters and became a trustworthy general, taking care of the guarding [of the city]; he also served four terms in the highest eponymous magistracies with modesty and justice. Making the best proposals and acting in an advantageous manner, he became father of the city.

In exactly the same way as the Roman emperor was 'father of the fatherland' (*pater patriae*), a man like Kallisthenes was 'father of the city', placed above the rest of the citizens and having an undisputed authority based on heredity. Honorific titles such as 'father of the city' and 'son/daughter of the city or the people' created the fiction of an intimate, indeed of a family, relation between the people and the elite. They established a relationship of mutual care and affection. The members of the elite were assimilated with adopted family members of the community: the elite assumed the responsibility to care for the community, exactly as a father cares for his children and children for their parents; and, in exchange, the community accepted the elite's authority. The members of the elite sat on special seats in theatrical performances and contests, and the decrees in their honour were read aloud at public gatherings. The honorific statues that decorated the public spaces and the inscriptions that listed offices and benefactions and recorded ancestral services made the elevated position of the elite visible and served as a model for future generations of elite benefactors. Acclamations during meetings of the assembly and festivals were another important medium for the enhancement of the elite's elevated position: 'Epameinondas is the one and only benefactor in all time!', 'Only Dion loves his city!', 'Long live he, who loves his fellow citizens, long live he, who loves moderation, initiator of good things, founder of the city!' Acclamations like these asserted gratitude and acceptance of leadership, but at the same time they expressed expectations. The Alexandrians in particular were such masters in acclamations that Nero brought to Rome some men from Alexandria to teach the Roman populace how to perform them.

When members of the elite died after having served their community, they could expect a public funeral, which again created the fiction of the city as a family. In AD 177, when Athens' wealthiest citizen, Herodes Atticus, died and his burial was being performed by his freedmen in Marathon, where he had his estates, the Athenian ephebes marched from Athens to Marathon, 'seized the body with their own hands', brought it back to Athens in procession and buried it near the stadium which Herodes had donated. Philostratus reports that all the Athenians attended the funeral, lamenting the death of their benefactor 'like children who have lost a good father'. Such demonstrations of gratitude and affection encouraged the elite to make even greater benefactions, while simultaneously establishing relations of dependence and dictating roles: the patronising role of the father for Herodes, that of dependent family members for the people.

This does not mean that the *demos* – the mass of the less-privileged citizen body – was politically irrelevant. It exercised influence and could put pressure on the elite, making political life in the Imperial Greek city a complex system of negotiations of power. First, proposals of magistrates had to be approved by the people's assembly. Judging by the occasional references to loud protests and even riots, there can be no doubt that some of the proposals made by the council and the magistrates met with opposition. Second, the assembly elected the magistrates. These two features – approval of decisions by the people's assembly and regular elections – along with the accountability of officials, were remnants of the old moderate democratic constitutions. But although all citizens voted, not all citizens were allowed to be nominated. We observe the political domination exercised by the elite in phenomena such as the accumulation of public functions, which was unusual in the Classical period, the repeated occupation of an office, which in Classical democracies was exceptionally allowed for military offices, the occupation of offices by close relatives and the monopoly of political initiatives in the council and the assembly.

Apart from its institutional power, through the assembly, the 'people' (*demos, plethos*) participated in political life by exerting pressure on the elite and making demands through acclamations and sometimes violent riots. We have substantial evidence for popular protests and riots especially from the early years of the Principate, when the opposition between the followers of Antony and Octavian was still fresh and the conditions unsettled. The geographer Strabo, who was roughly a contemporary of Augustus, and the orator Dio of Prusa in the late first century AD have a lot to say about the cities to which they travelled, recording not only myths of old and descriptions of landscapes and buildings, but also narratives of political controversies. Their writings show that Greek political life was alive and kicking in cities that were coming to terms with the new imperial rule but also maintained the freedom to fight relentlessly about things that mattered: the election of officials, spending public money, reducing the prices of grain, dealing with natural disasters or surpassing a neighbouring community in privileges and rank. Some protests were directed against the Romans, while some riots had an ethnic and religious background and targeted the Jews. A few examples may demonstrate what nourished public life and provided the 'people' with opportunities to show that they still mattered.

Tarsos was a city with a political life as vibrant as any fatherland of men with ambition and rhetorical skills. When the philosopher Athenodoros returned there during Augustus' reign, after he had spent some years in Rome educating the future emperor Tiberius, he found his city still controlled by the poet and demagogue Boethos, an old supporter of Antony (see p. 298). Strabo does not explain the causes of the political division, giving merely a blanket accusation – that Boethos' party abstained from no act of insolence. Using the authority given to him by Augustus, Athenodoros condemned Boethos and his followers to exile, probably not without having this decision somehow confirmed by a court or the assembly. Thereupon, Boethos' partisans wrote against him on the walls, 'Deeds are for the young, and counsels for the middle-aged, but farts for the old men.' Taking this inscription as a joke, Athenodoros asked for the phrase 'thunders for old men' to be added. But then someone who despised all decency and had a loose belly came in the night to his house and profusely bespattered the door and the wall. When Athenodoros brought accusations in the assembly against that faction, he said: 'One may recognize the city's illness and disaffection in many ways, and in particular from its excrement.'

Athenodoros could have considered himself fortunate to have his house just 'bespattered'. It is reported that in many cases mobs equipped with stones, sticks and torches attacked the houses of prominent men and set them on fire. One of the most prominent Thessalians during Augustus' reign, a certain Petraios, who had served twice as the 'general' of the Thessalian League, was burned alive in his house. Roman citizens are reported to have been crucified in Kyzikos under Tiberius and in Rhodes under Claudius; and during an uprising in Alexandria even the governor, the prefect Caius Petronius, was stoned to death. When a wealthy man in Aphrodisias, Attalos, established a foundation to fund the gymnasium and other things in the early second century AD, he knew that his initiative might meet with opposition, since the gymnasium was an elite institution. He wrote in his will that

> neither a magistrate nor a secretary nor a private person will have the authority to transfer part of or the entire capital or the interest or to change the account or to use the money for a different purpose, neither by organizing a separate vote nor through a decree of the assembly, a letter, a decree or a written declaration nor through violence of the mob nor in any other way.

The donor was worried about not only the potential intervention of non-civic (i.e. Roman) authorities but also the actions of local authorities, discussions in the assembly and pressure by the 'mob' – 'extra-parliamentary' opposition, we might call it today. Some people in Aphrodisias might have thought that storage of grain to sell at a cheap price – or perhaps gladiatorial shows – might be a better investment. The activities of the elite were closely scrutinised, as the orator Dio of Prusa knew from personal experience. When he bought public land in order to build shops on it at a time when his city faced rising grain prices, he had to face an angry and – in his view – envious assembly. On the other hand, spontaneous demonstrations are also attested in honour of members of the elite. For instance, after the death of benefactors, the people gathered in the streets to demand a public funeral or even snatched the corpse and transformed the private funeral into a public event, thus insinuating that the benefactor was a relative of the people.

The most significant political upheavals in the East did not have their origin in conflicts between Greeks or between Greeks and Romans but in cultural, religious and social tensions between Greeks and Jews. Alexandria, with a large Jewish population, was an important but not the only stage for riots. The Jewish community acquired a strong sense of identity when Augustus created a 'council of elders' as its governing body and assigned the Jews a specific civic duty: keeping the riverbanks clean. The fact that only Jews, who lived in a single quarter of the Nile Delta, had residential rights and tax exemption, and also that Jews were excluded from the gymnasium, contributed to the creation of a closed Jewish community, which continually antagonised the Alexandrian Greeks. The conflicts escalated under Caligula, when an initially minor incident triggered violent riots. In AD 38 Caligula sent the ruler of Galilee and his personal friend, Herod Agrippa, to Alexandria to check on the governor Flaccus, whom the emperor mistrusted. The self-confident appearance of a 'king of the Jews' enraged the Greeks, who were influenced by the demagogue Isidoros. Using as a pretext the alleged refusal of the Jews to offer cultic worship to the emperor, whose statues were placed in some synagogues, the Greek mob attacked Jews, desecrated synagogues and crucified thirty-eight elders, until the governor was recalled and the Roman army put an end to the riots. After Caligula's assassination in AD 41, envoys of both parties were sent to the Emperor Claudius, whose verdict satisfied neither side. The privileges of the Jews were restored, but it was strictly forbidden for them to attend the gymnasium or athletic contests; the request of the Alexandrians to have a council was rejected and two of their leaders, Isidoros and Lampon, executed. Papyri preserve fictionalised minutes of the encounter between the Greek notables and the emperor, presenting the Greeks as models of free speech, courage and patriotism, when facing an authoritarian emperor. The so-called *Acts of the Alexandrian Martyrs* is eloquent testimony to the value of freedom in a political community under Roman rule, to the defiance of imperial authority, but also to ethnic discrimination.

Similar outbursts with a religious background are randomly attested elsewhere. Around AD 55, during Paul's stay in Ephesos, a silversmith who made silver shrines of Artemis, to be sold to pilgrims, recognised a threat to his business from the spread of Christianity and instigated protests by the local guild of silversmiths. The incident, as described in the Acts of the Apostles, seems to have led to a spontaneous meeting of the assembly in the theatre:

> When they heard this, they were enraged and shouted, 'Great is Artemis of the Ephesians!' The city was filled with the confusion; and people rushed together to the theatre, dragging with them Gaius and Aristarchos, Macedonians who were Paul's travel companions ... Meanwhile, some were shouting one thing, some another; and most of them did not know why they had come together.

When a Jew attempted to address the assembly, the people shouted in unison for hours 'Great is Artemis of the Ephesians'. Only the secretary of the assembly, the city's highest official, managed to silence the gathered crowd, asking them to bring charges either to court or to a regular assembly and warning: 'We are in danger of being charged with rioting today.' More riots against Jews occurred in Greek cities during the great Jewish revolts of AD 68 and 115–17.

As valid as the notion of a *pax Romana* may be as a general characterisation of the early Imperial period, the Roman Empire was less homogeneous and pacified than encomiasts would allow. Disturbances of the peace and riots reveal a more complex picture, one not free of social and ethnic tensions.

13

SOCIO-ECONOMIC
CONDITIONS

From Greek Cities to an 'Ecumenical' Network

Reshaping social hierarchies: wealth, legal status and social position

If old habits die hard, the resistance of traditional social structures to change is harder. The conquests of Alexander and the avalanche of changes in the political geography of the eastern Mediterranean and Asia that it started had an impact on society and economy. Some changes occurred faster, especially changes triggered by migration and the new possibilities for trade; others became visible later, such as changes in the position of women and slaves. In this chapter, we will see the interplay of continuity and change in the expanded Greek world, as it was transformed in the centuries that followed Alexander's death and, again, during the long progress of its integration into the Roman Empire.

Continuities and changes are clear with regard to factors that determined the social position of an individual. Until the fourth century BC, the weight of two legal factors prevailed: freedom and citizenship. Of course, further criteria contributed to a finer differentiation among the citizens and the free people who lacked citizen rights. Wealth was the most important among them. But the social prestige of an individual very much depended on the source of his wealth – be it land, trade, manufacture, banking or raiding – as well as on his legal status. A freedman could be twice as wealthy as a citizen, but could nonetheless hardly ever reach a citizen's social standing. Other significant parameters of social stratification included family and ancestry, military achievements and education. The combination of such factors determined the position of an individual in the social structure of a community in pre-Hellenistic Greece. Social norms determined different roles for men and women, children, young men and girls, old men and old women. The impact of these factors varied depending on the size of a community, its geographical location and its institutions. But from the late fourth century BC onwards, the weight of these factors changed and new ones emerged.

Unsurprisingly, the contribution of wealth to a high social position did not change. What changed was the weight of wealth in the political life of communities by comparison with the fifth and fourth centuries BC. De facto, wealth had always been a requirement for political activity, but from the late Hellenistic period onwards it also became an institutional requirement (see p. 140). Wealth allowed an individual to maintain a social network by extending invitations to extravagant dinners, offering financial support and cultivating other forms of patronage. It also allowed an individual to gain the reputation of a good citizen by making benefactions and of a pious individual by making dedications. Another change can be observed in the increased number of women who possessed great wealth and could thus play an important part as benefactors (see p. 335). Finally, we observe a change in the social acceptability of different sources of wealth. Naturally, inherited wealth mattered and landed property remained the most respected source of wealth. But in the course of the Hellenistic period forms of wealth accumulation other than land ownership became more common and were not the object of social discrimination in the way they had been in the past in most cities. Such sources of wealth include trade, banking, manufacture, a successful career in entertainment as an actor, poet, orator or musician, expertise in a specialised profession – for instance, as a doctor or teacher of philosophy and oratory – prizes in athletic contests, mercenary service and, later, service in the Roman army. Naturally, the nouveau riche had a keen interest in investing his fortune in landed property, if not in his fatherland, then in another place. In the new cosmopolitan world, this could be achieved more easily than in the past. A man – sometimes also a woman – could establish a privileged relationship with a foreign community by being granted the title of a *proxenos* – a sort of friend of the state; the privileges associated with the *proxeny* usually included the right to purchase land and a house, inviolability from seizure (*asylia*) and expediency in legal business.

Also the significance of citizenship as a parameter of social position changed, first because acquisition of citizenship became easier; second, because the number of non-citizens in Greek cities increased; and third, because the rights of non-citizens were often protected through interstate agreements. The urban population was a very heterogeneous group, consisting of citizens, slaves and free residents who lacked citizenship. The latter had various origins: foreign immigrants, illegitimate children, the offspring of mixed marriages, freedmen and people who had lost their citizenship rights due to conviction in a court of law. Citizenship gave an individual the possibility to exercise political influence, the privilege to own land and the right to enjoy the protection of the law. After Alexander's conquests, the lack or loss of citizenship could be compensated for more easily than in the past. Those who lost citizen rights in their fatherland because of conquest, civil war or conviction migrated to a kingdom, expecting to be settled in one of the new foundations, or hoped to receive citizenship in another community, offering their good services there. Grants of citizenship or of privileges associated with citizenship – acquisition of land and a house, legal protection – became far more common than in earlier periods. Thanks to interstate agreements, the citizens of the partner cities were placed under the protection of the law. Hundreds of inscriptions attest individual grants of citizenship, usually to foreign benefactors, friends of kings, entertainers and doctors, but also to other professional specialists, traders and bankers. The naturalisation of larger groups, especially of soldiers, is less frequent, mainly attested in cities that faced population loss because of wars. Also the purchase of citizenship was practised, primarily on the periphery of the Greek world, in the cities of the Black Sea and in Magna Graecia, where the declining Greek population made the recruitment of additional defenders against barbarian threats necessary. On a far greater scale than ever before, people also came to possess several citizenships as a consequence of the honours they were granted by *poleis* other than their fatherland. This trend continued in the Imperial period. From the first to the third centuries AD, many athletes, entertainers and orators, people that lived an itinerant life moving from festival to festival, possessed multiple citizenships.

Due to the social complexity of the Hellenistic period, the free non-citizens were a heterogeneous category. An economically and politically significant group consisted of the foreign residents (*metics*). Thanks to services to a city or on the basis of interstate agreements, some foreign residents were privileged and assimilated with the citizens as regards legal rights – payment of taxes, exemption from certain customs, marriage rights, access to law courts and property rights. And thanks to the creation of private voluntary associations, foreign residents developed a sense of community and identity (see p. 323). The Roman conquest created a new type of privileged foreigner: Roman citizens. They were immigrants from Rome and Italy who lived in Greek cities, were organised in separate communities (*conventus*), were privileged because they possessed Roman citizenship and claimed special treatment. In the early period of Roman rule in Greece and Asia Minor, Roman citizens were sometimes the victim of attacks, the most notorious of which occurred in Ephesos in 88 BC (see pp. 210–1). But as the grants of Roman citizenship to Greeks became common, especially under the Flavians, and the manumission of slaves by Roman owners multiplied the number of Roman citizens, Roman citizenship gradually lost its importance as a mark of privileged position.

The least privileged free population in both cities and kingdoms were the inhabitants of the countryside. Those who lived on royal land, the *laoi* (see p. 99), were subject to the payment of tribute. Some cities in Asia Minor and the areas conquered by Alexander had large territories inhabited by a free population without citizenship, the *paroikoi* (those who live near the city). They had the right to own land but not the right of political participation, although they were obliged to contribute to the city's defence. Most of this population was indigenous but adopted the Greek language and culture in the course of the Hellenistic period. They continued worshipping local gods, usually under a Greek name, and practising local rituals. In the violent centuries of the Hellenistic period these *paroikoi* were often the victims of raids: for example, the raids of the Gauls in Asia Minor in the third century BC. During wars they faced captivity and the destruction of cultivated land and its facilities. Hellenistic cities made an effort to treat this population of the countryside as part of the *polis*. They were included in prayers for the salvation of the city and the territory and in complaints about raids and insecurity; they were invited to the civic festivals; and from the late Hellenistic period onwards, generous benefactors who funded public banquets occasionally also invited the *paroikoi* and other people of non-citizen status to attend. This was presented as an exceptional generosity; it allowed the population that did not share in the privileges of the citizens to feel part of the community. Such gestures contributed to concord without closing the legal and social gap between different population groups. If upward mobility was possible, it was thanks to education, skills or the proximity to power.

Men of learning: social enhancement through education and skill

Virtuosity in the performing arts (see p. 328), athletic skills (see p. 327) and education are three factors whose significance for the enhancement of social position continually increased throughout the Greek world from the fourth century BC to the establishment of the Principate. In the Hellenistic period, education, in many cities the privilege of the higher social strata that had the necessary leisure time, as well as literary and scholarly achievements acquired particular significance in political life and society. For poets, historians, mythographers and scientists it was a blessing that kings were genuinely interested in the promotion of arts and sciences, both for the direct profit they gained from technological discoveries and for the prestige that they accumulated by being surrounded by renowned artists and literary figures or being praised in their poems. The greatest Hellenistic poets, Theocritus, Callimachus and Poseidippos, were all closely associated with the court of Ptolemy II in Alexandria.

Although the 'universal scholar' was not unknown in the Hellenistic period, revolutionary advancement in the sciences was often connected with specialisation promoted by royal courts. The Mouseion was founded by Ptolemy I in Alexandria as a centre of knowledge, attached to the palace and home to the greatest library of the world. It assembled scholars representing all disciplines, from astronomy to zoology and from the study of Homer to medicine. The founders of the Alexandrian school of medicine, Herophilos (c. 331–280 BC) and Erasistratos (c. 304–250 BC), gave an impetus to medical research, especially through the practice of anatomy. Herophilos established that the brain is the centre of cognition and revolutionised knowledge of the vascular and nervous systems. Erasistratos, originally the doctor of Seleukos I who diagnosed Antiochos' love sickness (see p. 89), was an expert not only in affairs of the heart but also in its function. He studied the circulation of the blood, distinguishing between veins and arteries.

In the field of applied sciences, the military needs of Hellenistic kings attracted to their courts scientists and engineers. This royal patronage resulted in the invention of elaborate siege engines, such as the *helepolis* of Demetrios Poliorketes, an impressive lifting device, the *sambyke*, with which small detachments of soldiers were lifted to the wall, the torsion catapult, the repeating catapult and the flame thrower. The mathematician Archimedes (c. 287–212 BC) is the most famous scientist who flourished in close association with a royal court, that of King Hieron II of Syracuse on Sicily. During the siege of Syracuse by the Romans (214–212 BC) he put his genius and his inventions to work for his fatherland (see p. 159).

Orators, philosophers and the teachers of these disciplines were another group of people who could realistically expect advancement on the basis of education. In the moderate democracies of the Hellenistic cities, the people's assembly continued to be the source of all decisions. Even though the initiative for proposals was in the hands of members of the wealthy elite, the political leaders still required rhetorical training and persuasive skills in order to win the support of the citizens and represent the interests of a city in diplomatic contacts. Some orators and philosophers, who were at the same time also teachers in the art of persuasion, not only acquired fame and wealth but also became prominent political figures in their cities (see p. 298). Stoic philosophers often followed the example of the school's founder, Zenon of Kition, who in the late fourth century BC declined invitations to visit King Antigonos Gonatas, his admirer, in his court, as he also declined Athenian citizenship. Zenon laid the foundations of a philosophy of ethics that placed emphasis on living in accordance with reason and virtue, avoiding the negative emotions of desire, fear and pleasure, and was very influential throughout the Hellenistic and Imperial periods, admired especially by statesmen. But many philosophers placed themselves in the service of their cities as envoys and magistrates, and others won political influence through the friendship of kings, Roman statesmen and provincial governors.

Philosophers and orators occasionally managed to rise to power through demagogy or their proximity to power, especially in the troubled decades between the Mithridatic Wars and Actium, as the following examples show. In the early first century BC, the orator Metrodoros of Skepsis, 'a poor man, succeeded in a glorious marriage in Chalkedon because of his reputation, and acquired citizenship in Chalkedon'. He obtained a high position in the administration of justice in the kingdom of Mithridates VI but fell victim to the conspiracy of his opponents. The tumultuous years of the late Republic offered opportunities to men of humble origins to climb up the social ladder by using their intellectual abilities to impress and befriend Roman statesmen. In the city of Mylasa two skilled orators from different backgrounds became the leaders of their community in the first century BC. Euthydemos was a typical representative of the elite. He had inherited fortune and prestige from his ancestors, which he combined with dexterity in rhetoric to become an influential man in his city and in Asia Minor. His leadership in Mylasa resembled autocratic rule. During his funeral, the orator Hybreas famously praised him with the words: 'Euthydemos, you are the city's necessary evil. We can live neither with you nor without you.' This Hybreas, the second Mylasean orator and statesman, was a parvenu. Shortly after his death, his career was summarised by Strabo:

> As Hybreas himself narrated in his school, and as the citizens confirmed, his father had left him a mule that carried timber and the mule-driver. For a short time he made his living with these. But after he had been taught by Diotrephes of Antioch, he returned to the city and devoted himself to the service of the supervisor of the market. Wallowing in that dirt and making money for a while, he zealously turned to politics and started following those who frequent the market. Very fast his influence grew and he was admired, already during Euthydemos' lifetime, but especially after his death, taking control of the city.

Hybreas convinced his fellow citizens to remain loyal to Rome and oppose Labienus, the renegade general, and the Parthians in 40/39 BC (see p. 227). Because of his advice, the city was taken by force and plundered; Hybreas escaped to Rhodes and his luxurious house was looted. But when Labienus was defeated, Hybreas returned to his city and to power, and Mylasa's loyalty was rewarded by the Romans. He was granted Roman citizenship and after his death he was honoured as a hero. Although wealth was always required for political influence, sometimes it was not inherited but recently acquired, as the example of Hybreas shows. Although rhetorical skills alone did not suffice for a political career, they were important, because even the rule of the elites required legitimisation through the assembly.

When the empire was still divided between Octavian and Mark Antony and the East was in Antony's hands, a Tarsian poet and orator, Boethos, rose to power as a demagogue. Writing a poem in praise of Antony for his victory at Philippi, he gained the general's favour and tried to use it for Tarsos' benefit. The Tarsians were keen on having the typical feature of a Greek city: a gymnasium. As Strabo explains:

> Antony promised the Tarsians to create the office of the supervisor of the gymnasium; but instead he appointed Boethos, entrusting to him the expenditures. But Boethos was caught stashing the olive-oil, among other things. When his guilt was being expounded by his accusers in the presence of Antony he tried to lessen Antony's wrath, saying among other things that 'Exactly as Homer had sung the praises of Achilles, Agamemnon and Odysseus, so I have hymned you. Therefore, it is not right that I should be brought before you on such slanderous charges.' The accuser, however, laid hands on this statement responding, 'Yes, but Homer did not steal Agamemnon's oil, nor that of Achilles; you did. You shall, therefore, be punished.'

Boethos managed to escape punishment and continued to rule the city for a few years after Antony's defeat (see p. 287).

Zenon of Laodikeia is another orator who had risen to power thanks to his decision to support the Romans during the Parthian invasion of Labienus. The career of his son, Polemon, a man who would be king, surpassed those of other men in the troubled years of the late Republic and early Principate. Mark Antony made him king of Pontos, Colchis and Armenia Minor. Polemon's rule was not affected by Antony's fall. Although he lost Armenia Minor in 20 BC, when Augustus gave it to another dynast, he expanded his kingdom by marrying the queen of the Bosporan kingdom, Dynamis. After her death in 14 BC, he concluded another profitable marriage. His new wife, Pythodoris, came from a wealthy Greek family from Tralleis. Polemon and Pythodoris ruled together until Polemon's death in 8 BC. The influence of his family continued until the end of the Julio-Claudian dynasty. His firstborn son, Zenon, became king of Armenia; his second son, Polemon II, ruled Pontos until Nero annexed it around AD 64. His daughter Antonia Tryphaina, queen of Thrace through her marriage to King Rhoimetalkes II (AD 12–38), retired in the city of Kyzikos, where she excelled through her benefactions.

The importance of rhetorical, literary and scientific activity for imperial patronage and, therefore, social advancement continued into the Imperial period. The capital of the empire attracted numerous orators, philosophers, poets, historians, teachers and physicians, the most skilled of whom found patrons in the philhellenic circles of the senatorial elite. A few fortunate ones established close relations to Roman emperors and even won their friendship. The doctor Caius Stertinius Xenophon, for instance, the personal physician of Emperor Claudius, was the most important man in Kos in the mid-first century AD, and his descendants retained an influential position in their city. The philosopher Athenagoras of Tarsos was brought to Rome by Augustus as a teacher. As an old man he returned to Tarsos, sent the aforementioned Boethos into exile, ruled with absolute power until his death and reformed his city's institutions (see p. 287). He was succeeded by another philosopher, Nestor, the teacher of Augustus' nephew Marcellus.

Caius Iulius Nikanor, a poet from Hierapolis in Syria, came to Athens during Augustus' reign and used his great fortune to purchase on behalf of Athens titles to parts of the island of Salamis bought by some people during the civil wars. Giving back to Athens full control of the island that they associated with one of the most glorious moments in their history earned him the honorific title 'New Themistocles' – the former being the Athenian general who defeated the Persians in 479 BC. Whether Nikanor also deserved the title 'New Homer' we will never learn. None of his poetic works survived the test of time.

Proximity to power and social mobility

The single most important factor that promoted the social position of individuals in Hellenistic society and then during the Principate was the proximity to a representative of authoritarian rule: a Hellenistic king, a Roman commander with extraordinary power or the Roman emperor.

Military service afforded many Greeks the opportunity to acquire political influence as high commanders in armies, as friends and advisers of kings and as administrators. With some luck, they could retire to a Greek city and use royal patronage to acquire land and prestige. The kings were eager to repay loyalty and efficiency with honours, promotion and material rewards. At the lowest level, soldiers received land and less important military commanders received gifts and distinctions; but high-ranking officers and royal 'friends' could expect more, such as large estates and statues as visible testimony of royal patronage. After retiring to a city as a landowner, they continued to cultivate relations with the court, and such men henceforth belonged to the leading circles of their community.

Also Roman senators, commanders and governors needed Greek advisers with knowledge of local conditions. They found support among the well-off, educated citizens of Greek cities, who had strong sympathies with the Roman oligarchical form of government. Friends of Roman leaders include the historian Polybius, the Epicurean philosopher Philodemos, the teacher and friend of the governor of Macedonia Lucius Calpurnius Piso Caesoninus (57–55 BC), the polymath, philosopher and historian Poseidonios of Apameia, a friend of Pompey, and Theopompos, an influential man in Knidos and author of a compilation of myths, a friend of Caesar. If the dictator had listened to him, he would not have attended the meeting of the senate during which he was murdered. Theophanes of Mytilene is a good example of a highly educated and experienced man in the service of a Roman commander. He accompanied Pompey on his campaign against Mithridates. He used Pompey's support for the benefit of his city, achieving the recognition of its freedom. He not only received Roman citizenship but was also accepted into the Roman equestrian order. His services were not forgotten after Pompey's death: his city established his cult and his descendants retained an influential position for many decades. One of them, Pompeius Macer, was called to organise the imperial library in Rome; he rose to the rank of a Roman knight and served in Asia as procurator of the emperor. His son entered the senate as a praetor in AD 15. Such personal relations were profitable for both sides. The Roman commanders and governors could count on experienced advisers and loyal supporters. Their Greek friends were rewarded with patronage and sometimes with Roman citizenship. When they were able to use the patronage in order to achieve privileges for their city, this immediately increased their political influence and social prestige.

During the Roman civil wars, from 49 to 30 BC, some men, especially orators and philosophers, including men of humble origins, used Roman patronage to establish an almost monarchical rule in their cities, seen as political leadership by their friends and as tyranny by their enemies – Boethos in Tarsos (see p. 287), Hybreas of Mylasa (see p. 297) and Nikias in Kos (see p. 146) were such parvenus. The association of such men with the losing party could be fatal for their position, if not for themselves; some managed to change sides in time, others won the victor's trust. Those who had supported Octavian were rewarded for their service.

In the last phase of the Battle of Actium, when he realised that his allies, including Cleopatra, had abandoned him and the battle was lost, Mark Antony escaped aboard his ship. This ship was relentlessly pursued by a certain Eurykles of Sparta. Standing on deck, he shook his lance at Antony's ship. When Antony asked him who he was, he responded: 'I am Eurykles, son of Lachares, and follow the fortune of Caesar to avenge my father's death.' As Plutarch explains, Lachares had been executed by Antony for piracy and we may assume that piracy was also Eurykles' livelihood. He lived out his motivation to 'follow the fortune of Caesar' – that is, to support Octavian – and took his revenge not by attacking Antony's vessel but by capturing the second admiral's galley and another ship that contained Antony's most valuable possessions. This Eurykles and his descendants are an interesting, though not typical, case of social mobility in the Principate. Of obscure origins and probably not a member of Sparta's noble families that derived prestige and wealth from landed property, he and his father belonged to the last generation of buccaneers who took advantage of the chaotic conditions of the civil wars. He was rewarded by Octavian/Augustus with personal rule over Sparta. It is unknown if his nearly monarchical position was accompanied by a title: for example, leader (*hegemon* or *prostates*) or supervisor (*epistates*) of the Lakedaimonians. Eurykles was granted Roman citizenship and ruled Sparta, Lakonia and Kythera as a monarch until his abuse of power became too much for the local population and Augustus had to send him into exile in 2 BC. Nevertheless, his descendants remained the most important family in Sparta for generations.

Acquaintance with an emperor was the single most important factor in achieving social advancement. It often began long before an emperor's accession to the throne. Many future emperors spent some time in the East, as students, travellers, governors, army officers or exiles, thus coming into contact with Greeks representing a wide variety of different occupations and social strata. Greek families with 'imperial' *nomina* such as Iulius, Flavius or Aelius often owed Roman citizenship to the patronage of emperors or future emperors. A large number of people, almost exclusively men, interacted with the emperor as a result of their intellectual contributions as poets, orators, philosophers or historians, or impressed him with their artistic or athletic achievements. For instance, the lover of Emperor Titus, the conqueror of Jerusalem, was the Greek boxer Melankomas (the black-haired), undefeated by any opponent but defeated by death at a very young age during the celebration of the contest Sebasta in Naples in AD 82 or 86. Other examples of social advancement in the service of the emperor are provided by the Koan doctor Caius Stertinius Xenophon (see p. 299) and Flavius Arrianus or Arrian from Nikomedeia, whose literary prominence overshadows his long and successful administrative career. Having studied philosophy with Epictetus, a former slave who became the most influential Stoic philosopher in the late first and early second centuries AD, Arrian entered the imperial administration as a member of the equestrian order. Probably under Hadrian, he was admitted to the senate and sent as governor to Baetica (Spain) and Kappadokia (AD 131–7). After Hadrian's death he retreated to Athens, where he composed historical, geographical and strategic works, the best known of which is his history of Alexander the Great.

Another group of people with social prestige and wealth were the descendants of some of the client kings. They occupied leading positions and became benefactors of Greek cities. For instance, Philopappos (AD 65–116), the grandson of Antiochos IV, the last king of Kommagene, lived a glamorous life in Athens, using the title *basileus* (king), making benefactions, occupying high offices in the city and befriending philosophers. Under the emperors Trajan and Hadrian, he rose to the highest ranks of Roman society, becoming senator and suffect consul in AD 109. His sister Balbilla, a close friend of Hadrian, had a grave monument erected for Philopappos in Athens – still a prominent landmark opposite the Parthenon.

The social group of those who profited from proximity to the emperor included imperial slaves of Greek origin who succeeded in winning their master's trust. When they were manumitted, they automatically received Roman citizenship and could hold important positions. Such influential freedmen existed already in the late Republican period. Some of them were probably citizens of Greek cities who were enslaved as war captives; they were entrusted with important tasks because of their education, experience and skills. A certain Cornelius Epikados, for instance, was a manumitted slave of Sulla who completed his master's autobiography after Sulla's death. The number of slaves and freedmen with important positions in the imperial household and the imperial administration increased after the establishment of the Principate. In order to fulfil his various duties and maintain a high standard of living – but also to stay alive – the emperor required the service of personal doctors, secretaries responsible for the correspondence (*ab epistulis*) or the finances (*a rationibus*) and hundreds of slaves serving in the palaces and the villas.

One of the most remarkable imperial freedmen was Caius Iulius Zoilos, freedman of Augustus, who managed to obtain privileges for his native city of Aphrodisias, occupied the city's highest offices and was buried in an extraordinary funerary monument at its centre. Given the frequency of captivity during the wars of the first century BC, whose victims were people of every social position, it is possible that men like Zoilos belonged to respectable families in their cities before they were sold into slavery.

Other imperial slaves owed their power to education and skills. The three secretaries of Emperor Claudius, Kallistos, Pallas and Narkissos, were even wealthier than Crassus, the wealthiest man of the Republic. In order to reach their levels of wealth, 200 million sestertii, a man would have had to serve as provincial governor of Asia for 200 years. Another of Claudius' freedmen, Polybios, translated Homer into Latin and Virgil into Greek. A poem by the Roman poet Statius gives us some information about the life of an imperial freedman, the anonymous father of Claudius Etruscus. Born in Smyrna in AD 2, he was sold to the imperial household under Augustus, possibly as an exposed child. Under Tiberius, he was manumitted, receiving the *nomen* Claudius. Under Claudius he was one of the emperor's trusted men and married a woman of free birth. He survived Nero's rule, and when Vespasian ascended to the throne he became head of the imperial financial administration as *a rationibus*. His two sons, born free, met the property requirement for admittance into the equestrian order, and Vespasian bestowed this honour also upon the former slave. He was exiled by Domitian, but returned to Rome in his nineties, shortly before his death. His son Etruscus was wealthy enough to build a luxurious public bath.

For such people a personal relationship with the emperor could be a defining moment in their lives. But it also opened unique ways to use the emperor's favour not only for personal social advancement but also in order to help their country. Although many of the 'emperor's men' lived in Rome, they did not forget their place of origin and became agents through which an emperor could show his generosity. Publius Aelius Alkibiades, *cubicularius* (*epi tou koitonos*) or chamberlain of Hadrian, originated in

Nysa. Several inscriptions from his city, where he returned as a freedman and lived after the emperor's death, reveal his significant wealth, which he used for benefactions, receiving extravagant honours in exchange. His gilded statues were erected in the temples of the emperors in Asia Minor and in Nysa. No freedman would have ever dreamed of such a distinction in the Greek world before the Roman conquest.

Pressing problems and failed solutions in Hellenistic Greece

Around 320 BC, the philosopher Theophrastos, a disciple of Aristotle, portrayed in his *Characters* how people behaved in the private and public spaces of Athens. Some of the situations that he describes are intrinsically connected with the gap between the wealthy and the poor. He represents scenes in which Athenian men display extravagance and luxury: for instance, by owning a pet monkey and dice made of gazelle horns; by building a private palaestra and inviting sophists, military trainers and musicians to perform there; by purchasing a slave imported from Ethiopia; by hanging the skull of a sacrificial ox, the most expensive victim, near the house door for everyone to see. The wealthy supporter of oligarchy does not conceal his contempt towards the common people; to sit in the assembly next to a man of the working class, thin and sweaty, causes him disgust; he protests against financial contributions to the city's expenses. Lack of wealth is so embarrassing that a have-not would ostentatiously send his slave to the bank – no one must know that his deposits are not more than one drachma.

In late Classical Athens economic inequality was felt as the most visible and relevant expression of inequality. The social conditions that we see through the magnifying glass of an author writing in Greece's biggest urban centre existed with some differences in most of the Greek world around the time of Alexander's campaign, although they were more clearly visible in big cities than in smaller ones. Local peculiarities – for instance, the existence of serfs in Thessaly, Sparta and Crete, and special regulations concerning the legal status of traders and manufacturers in some cities – make the general picture more heterogeneous. But similar conditions existed on a different scale throughout the Greek world in the fourth century BC: the gap between those who could exploit the manpower of significant numbers of slaves in farming, manufacture and their households and those who struggled to make a living with their own labour and that of family members; the difference between the heirs to great fortunes and those condemned to toilsome work; the contrast between big and small landowners, lenders and debtors, givers and recipients of generosity. To judge from the existence of large numbers of men willing to risk their lives as mercenaries, from the numbers of exiles whose property had been confiscated and from the persistent controversy over the issue of debts and landownership, social and economic inequality was a widespread phenomenon that caused dissatisfaction. Whenever such dissatisfaction got out of hand, civil wars broke out and ambitious political leaders established autocratic rule in their deeply divided communities.

We often know of a civil war in the Hellenistic period only thanks to a reconciliation agreement preserved in an inscription; and we often know of a tyrant only because a source mentions how he came to power or how his power collapsed. That social tensions lie behind these violent disruptions of order is a good guess but no more. For instance, the unique and complex reconciliation process in the small Sicilian city of Nakone around 300 BC gives an impression of the deep division of the city but no clues as to its cause. After arbitration, the two opposing groups met in the assembly, each one presenting a list of thirty opponents. By drawing lots, they created 'brotherhoods', each consisting of members of the two opposing parties and neutral citizens – a process comparable to creating in Israel artificial families consisting of Israeli settlers, Hamas fighters and pacifists. The arbitrators hoped that these new artificial bonds of family might establish concord. In other cases, the conflicting parties were obliged not to remember past injuries and act upon them.

Unfortunately, the limited sources do not permit us to write a continuous social history of any Greek city. We have to collect isolated and sometimes exaggerated statements scattered in literary sources, inscriptions and papyri. But the repeated occurrence of a standard set of problems in very diverse regions, from Chersonesos in the Black Sea to Crete and from the Adriatic coast to Asia Minor, suggests that 'Old Greece' – that is, the world of the Greek *poleis* that had existed before Alexander's campaign – repeatedly faced social tensions caused by the indebtedness of significant parts of the population and by the existence of large groups of citizens who lacked landed property of sufficient size. If time and again well-meaning statesmen and demagogues alike – Agathokles in Sicily, Agis and Kleomenes in Sparta, Perseus and Andriskos in Macedonia, Kritolaos in Achaia and Aristonikos in Pergamon – exploited precisely these two problems, seeking the support of those who suffered under their burden, it is because the problems were very real and remained unsolved.

Only Kleomenes, who ruled as king of Sparta from 235 to 222 BC, implemented what seems to be a coherent and comprehensive reform to face the two problems of debt and the concentration of landed property in a few hands. After removing the board of the five *ephors* who oversaw the king's executive powers, he announced that 'the whole land should be common property, debtors should be set free from their debts, and foreigners should be examined and rated, in order that the strongest of them might be made Spartan citizens and help to preserve the state by their arms'. When all the private land was brought into common ownership, it was divided into parcels and assigned to each citizen. The recipients included Spartans who returned from exile and new citizens. The Spartan army, now 4,000-strong, learned new tactics, and the archaic traditions of military training for the youth and public messes for the citizens were revived. Kleomenes' reforms raised hopes in other cities in the Peloponnese as well, where people demanded the abolition of debt and redistribution of land, but the alliance of the Achaean League and the Macedonians crushed his army at the Battle of Sellasia in 222 BC, putting an end to his reforms. Though the Spartan reforms failed, the problems remained. Reactive measures to address the most pressing needs of the indebted and the poor were often taken, but not to provide real solutions. We can get an impression of the demagogical practices vaguely referred to in ancient sources by looking at the situation that Polybius describes for early second-century-BC Boiotia:

> Some of the generals would give allowances to the needy out of public funds. The masses learnt in this way to listen to and invest with high office those who would enable them to escape punishment for their crimes and unpaid debts, and to expect occasional gratuities from the public funds as a favor from the magistrates.

Polybius' report is not free of the clichés that one expects from a conservative mind. But inscriptions often refer to unpaid debts and to foreign judges who visited cities in order to deal with the chronic problems of legal disputes concerning debts. Also, the authors of decrees in many cities often lament the deplorable state of public finances and the heavy burden of public debt. Far less common are references to creditors who were willing to free their debtors from interest and debt. Indulgent courts and magistrates occasionally offered some relief but no structural change. With the exception of the Spartan experiment, a common response to the tensions triggered by debt and the lack of landed property was a war aiming at the conquest of a neighbour's territory. Such wars over contested borders were endemic in the Peloponnese, Asia Minor and Crete. A common result of civil war and economic crisis was the migration of the have-nots, sometimes only temporary – in order to serve as mercenaries – but often permanent, to territories in Asia and Egypt, as long as there were territories that could accommodate new settlers.

Ubi bene ibi patria: Hellenistic migrations

In the early third century BC, Theocritus presents in a poem the sufferings of Aischinas, a lovesick young man abandoned by his lover, Kyniska, for another man, contemplating mercenary service as a cure for his suffering: 'Simos, who fell in love with that brazen girl, went abroad and came back heart-whole – a man of my age. I too will cross the sea. Your soldier is not the worst of men, not yet the first, maybe, but as good as another.' Disappointment in affairs of the heart and fear of the revenge of cuckolded husbands have often caused men to run away from home and devote themselves to a martial occupation. But at the time of Alexander and his successors lack of land, debts and exile after a civil war, not broken hearts, were the main reasons for the availability of mercenaries.

The campaigns of Alexander the Great and the colonisation of the conquered areas offered temporary relief from the burden of debt and the shortage of land. The settlers in the newly founded *poleis* were soldiers in the army of Alexander and his successors, originating in Macedonia, mainland Greece, the Aegean islands and the old Greek colonies of Asia Minor; their number cannot be determined. The migration continued in the following decades, and gradually also mercenaries of non-Greek origin – Thracians, indigenous populations of Anatolia, Iranians, Gauls and Jews – were added to the Greek settlers, adopting Greek language and culture. In addition to bringing settlers to Egypt, the interior of Asia Minor, Syria and Mesopotamia, the kings also placed units in strategic places as garrisons. As late as 192 BC, Antiochos III brought Greeks from Euboia, Crete and Aetolia to Antioch; the same king settled 2,000 Jewish families from Mesopotamia and Babylonia in strongholds of his realm, especially in Asia Minor, where they were given land; and in the mid-second century BC, Attalos II founded Eukarpeia (the fruitful city) in Phrygia, settling soldiers and giving them plots of land. The devastations that followed Roman expansion in Macedonia probably added new impetus to migration to Asia Minor.

Rewarding military service with land became a common feature of the armies of the major Hellenistic kingdoms. Of course, the different structure of their territories resulted in local variations. In Ptolemaic Egypt, experienced soldiers and officers were given an allotment (*kleros*), which they exploited in exchange for military service whenever needed. The soldiers owned their weapons and armour, which they could bequeath in their will. Their families kept the original designation of ethnic origin or citizenship of the ancestor who had first been recruited (Cretan, Corinthian, Cyrenean, etc.), and we find these designations even generations after the original settlement of a man in Egypt. In the kingdom of the Seleucids, the mercenaries were usually settled in colonies with an urban character, some of which acquired the status of an independent *polis* at some point. In the Seleucid military colonies, the plot could be bequeathed by the colonist to close relatives and was returned to the king only when no one who could serve as a soldier was there to inherit it. An analogous system existed in Antigonid Macedonia. It is not unlikely that an early form of conditional grants of land to soldiers was devised by Alexander the Great or his father, Philip II. Both Philip and Alexander were city founders and had to deal with the problems connected with military settlers. Alexander is known to have given 'to the Macedonians' the city of Kalindoia in the Chalkidike, its territory and its villages; and already the first Successors, Kassandros and Lysimachos, made individual grants of land to soldiers and officers.

The prospect of the acquisition of landed property motivated thousands of men to seek employment as mercenaries. Often mercenaries were not hired individually but joined a foreign army either on the basis of a treaty between their city and a potential employer or as groups under the leadership of *condottieri*, experienced officers and generals. 'Soldier brokers' (*xenologoi*) received high rewards from kings and cities to travel to areas where they expected to find potential mercenaries. For instance, Pyrgopolynikes (the multiple conqueror of towers), the protagonist of Plautus' comedy *Miles gloriosus*, had his recruiting agency in Ephesos. A well-documented case of mass migration is that of mercenaries from Crete in the late third century BC. Having recently annexed land in the Maeander valley, in 234/33 and 229/28 BC, Miletos enfranchised more than 1,000 Cretan mercenaries and settled them together with their families in the new territory – an estimated total of more than 3,000 people. When the concentration of landed property in the hands of a few owners of large estates and the rising population numbers triggered a socio-economic crisis in Crete, citizens without land saw warfare as a profitable profession, engaging themselves in raids or serving as mercenaries. The fact that many of these mercenaries settled abroad, not only in Miletos but also in Kretopolis (the Cretan city) in Pisidia and in Egypt, suggests that what forced them to leave their island was the desire to own land. Poverty or the expectation of gain, in addition to military traditions, also motivated the population of other mountainous areas to seek employment as mercenaries: for example, the warlike Lycians, Pamphylians and Pisidians.

Depending on the conditions agreed with their employer, the soldiers received a rather good salary – at least in the third century BC, it was above the average pay received by other professionals. In addition to this, a mercenary expected food rations and, after a victorious battle, booty and gifts. The vital interest of many mercenaries was to receive what they lacked in their fatherland: land. Shortage of land persisted to varying degrees throughout the third century and for part of the second century BC; it was the main cause of social dissatisfaction in Greece. For mercenaries who were only temporarily employed, land ownership was a less realistic prospect than death in battle, captivity, disability or unemployment. Unemployed mercenaries (*apergoi*) are known to have gathered in the sanctuary of Hera in Samos, illegally acting as traders, most likely selling booty gained during their service.

The distribution of land in mainland Greece was a rare occurrence by comparison with Asia Minor and the Ptolemaic and Seleucid kingdoms. But when wars and migration resulted in the depopulation of areas rich in cultivatable fields, such as Thessaly, the distribution of land to new settlers was possible. For instance, in 214 BC Philip V advised Larisa in Thessaly to enfranchise the Thessalians and other Greeks who lived in the city, presumably soldiers, and to give them land that had been uncultivated in recent years. In the Greek cities, acquisition of land by foreigners was possible only as a privilege – called *enktesis* – that was granted to individuals in reward for their services or to whole communities on the basis of an interstate agreement of economic and political cooperation – called *isopoliteia*. The citizens of cities that signed a treaty of *isopoliteia* had 'equality of civic rights', if they chose to settle in the partner community.

The massive migration to new territories temporarily eased the tensions in Greek cities in the late fourth and third centuries BC and contributed to the urbanisation and integration of the areas in which the Greek troops were settled into large economic networks. But the continuous wars never ceased to create new problems. Mercenary service and raids may have responded to the economic needs of those who practised them but did not solve the accumulated social problems of the Greek cities. A mercenary's or raider's profit was another family's loss. In addition to this, the opportunities for mercenary service gradually declined in the course of the second and early first centuries BC, as the number of potential employers – the Hellenistic kingdoms – decreased. The Hellenistic wars recycled problems, they did not solve any. Only the pacification of the eastern Mediterranean brought about a significant change.

Professional specialisation and mobility

Except for the massive migration of soldiers to royal foundations, the political and economic networks that were gradually established after Alexander's conquests also increased the movement of individuals, families and groups of all kinds of professional specialists. Some of these professional specialists lived an itinerant life because their profession demanded it. By moving from city to city, from court to court, from festival to festival and from fair to fair, they had better chances of employment in activities in which demand was temporary. For instance, theatrical performances and concerts did not take place on a daily basis but only during major festivals and, irregularly, during extraordinary celebrations. By staying in one city, a specialised professional actor, poet or musician would be employed on just a few occasions a year; only constantly travelling to cities currently organising festivals guaranteed employment for a large part of the year. Another factor that contributed to the extensive travels of specialists is the fact that high-quality training in certain disciplines, such as medicine or sculpture, was not possible everywhere. It was only offered in large cities, and very often some cities developed local 'schools': for instance, Hellenistic Kos in medicine, Athens in oratory and philosophy, Rhodes – and in the Imperial period Aphrodisias – in sculpture and Sikyon in painting. Consequently, specialists from these cities were in demand far beyond their place of origin.

Famous specialists, especially in big cities, could afford to stay at home and wait for customers to knock on their door or invite them to offer their skills in a foreign place in exchange for a hefty fee. For instance, a certain Antipatros of Eleutherna in Crete, player of the *hydraulis* – an early form of the pipe organ that was invented in third-century-BC Alexandria and operated with the pressure of water – was such a specialist. In 94 BC, Delphi sent an embassy to invite him, together with his brother, who assisted him in the operation of this complex musical instrument, to give concerts and rewarded them generously. But only big cities offered possibilities for more or less continuous occupation in specialised arts and trades. So hundreds of entertainers – musicians, dancers, actors and singers – but also numerous artists, medical doctors and intellectuals – philosophers, orators and historians – spent significant parts of their life travelling. In the Hellenistic period, such itinerant specialists also included women (see p. 336). Only a few successful doctors or intellectuals could afford to offer their services for free. The reason we know about these people is their exceptional success; hundreds of their colleagues who struggled for a living are now lost to anonymity.

We know more about professional specialisation in the performing and visual arts only because of the greater visibility of their representatives. But specialisation, an important feature of urban economy and society, encompassed most economic activities, from agriculture and trade to pottery and perfume production, textile manufacture and metalworking. A late Hellenistic novelty is the organisation of representatives of the same occupation into voluntary associations. Especially for foreign residents in large trade centres, such as Athens, Rhodes and Delos, this form of organisation provided a sense of solidarity and identity, in addition to practical advantages (see pp. 322–4).

Specialisation in production is visible in the material evidence. That the origin of products such as wine jars, lamps or fine pottery can be determined simply by their shape and decoration was not something new; but it became more common than in any preceding period and encompassed the entire Greek world, as local products were being exported to distant markets on a much larger scale. The export of local wines from Thasos, Rhodes, Knidos, Kos and the Black Sea cities of Sinope, Chersonesos and

Herakleia is the best-known example, because the origin of the wine can be determined by a stamp that names the place and year of production, as well as by the shape of the jar – just as the bottle shape allows us today to distinguish a red Beaujolais from a white Pinot Grigio.

Professional specialisation combined with mobility and the spread of urban centres provided alternatives to agriculture and improved the possibilities of the dispossessed to seek employment. Although landed property remained the most esteemed source of wealth throughout antiquity, people who owed their wealth to their activities in manufacture, trade and banking could now attain high social standing and political influence in most cities, especially when they were willing to use part of their wealth for benefactions. The specialisation and mobility that started in the Hellenistic period reached their apogee in the pacified *oecumene* of the Imperial period.

Pax Romana: inherited tensions in a new context

Almost two centuries after the establishment of the Principate, the Greek world was largely pacified, but social problems continued to cause civil unrest (see p. 288). Around the time of Hadrian's reign, inscriptions that praise benefactors for their donations to the people reveal the urgent needs of part of the population and of cities unable to fund public projects. For instance, Opramoas of Rhodiapolis in Lycia, a great benefactor whose activity spans the last years of the reign of Hadrian and the reign of his successor, not only provided funds for temples, gymnasia, baths, markets and festivals in several cities, but also responded to the needs of the poor: he provided cheap grain, decent funerals for those whose families could not afford them and dowries for girls of limited means, covered the cost of education and nourishment of the children of citizens, and donated food to the poor.

The origin and nature of social problems and tensions did not radically change in the first centuries of the Principate: the gap between the poor and the wealthy was as visible as ever. The people of limited means, mostly the urban population, depended on benefactions to have access to cheap grain. Some of the dispossessed found no other resort than to expose their newborn children – the foundlings (*threptoi*) were usually raised as slaves –, sell themselves as slaves or turn to crime. Organised brigandage continued to be a problem, especially in Asia Minor, not only because old raiding habits in mountainous areas die hard, but also out of despair. In the early second century AD, Tillorobos terrorised the area around Mount Ida, in north-west Asia Minor, plundered the countryside and even attacked urban settlements: Arrian (see p. 302) wrote a history not only of Alexander the Great but also of Tillorobos.

If the main problems did not disappear, the responses were modified, since one traditional way of dealing with social pressure – the conquest of a neighbour's territory and the distribution of land and booty among the citizens – no longer existed. Territorial disputes between cities continued well into the Imperial period, but wars of conquest no longer presented a temporary answer to the pressing need for land. After Pompey, piracy and coastal raiding, important sources of income for the populations of Crete and Cilicia, largely disappeared from the eastern Mediterranean. Despite a famous scene in *Ben Hur* in which Roman ships are attacked by Macedonian pirates around the time of Augustus, pirates continued to play a significant part only in the novels of the Imperial period, whose plot is placed in earlier times, when pirates in the eastern Mediterranean were as abundant as dolphins.

One traditional response to pressure continued to exist in the Roman Empire: service in the army. Large-scale mercenary service in the royal armies was replaced on a smaller scale by military service in the Roman army; only the conditions of service had changed. Men from the eastern provinces who did not possess Roman citizenship (*peregrini*) could volunteer for service in the auxiliary units for a fixed period of twenty-five years. Around the time of Hadrian there were twenty-six units of archers, half of them from Syria and the rest from Thrace, Asia Minor and Crete. Men who possessed Roman citizenship – their number increased in the course of the first two centuries AD – were allowed to serve in the regular legions. As a result, army service continued to provide employment for those who did not own land or had no other attractive prospects.

The integration of the East into the Roman Empire also brought new opportunities. Already from the second century BC onwards new networks of exchange had emerged. Delos hosted a significant number of immigrants from Italy, mainly traders and bankers, soon after it became a free harbour in 167 BC. In other areas, in Macedonia, mainland Greece and Asia Minor, the presence of Italian and Roman entrepreneurs (*negotiatores*) and, to a much lesser extent, landowners (*enkektemenoi*) became noticeable only from the first century BC onwards. Roman colonies were the result of a one-time foundation, not of gradual growth and development. Consequently, the social stratigraphy of their population, which primarily consisted of former soldiers, freedmen, manufacturers, traders and urban plebeians who were given land, differed from that of old Greek cities. Attitudes towards sources of income other than landed property changed. For instance, the self-confidence with which Roman and Italian tradesmen presented themselves with monuments and dedications in the international harbour of Delos in the late second and early first centuries BC is without parallel in most Greek cities. The Roman colonists could establish and promote networks of economic cooperation that crossed the boundaries of cities and regions. Various branches of the same Roman family could be resident in different cities and mutually support economic activities and work towards their social advancement. For these reasons, Italian newcomers had a momentous impact on the economy. In the late first century BC and the first century AD, the Roman colonies brought life to areas that had suffered during the wars. Corinth and Patrae, for instance, on the east and west end of the Corinthian Gulf respectively, facilitated traffic with Italy and thus contributed to economic growth. The pottery industry of Corinth supplied Greece, Asia Minor, North Africa and Italy with clay lamps.

In Asia Minor, the establishment of Roman provinces and, consequently, the integration of large areas under a unified administrative model, the construction and maintenance of highways, and the new possibilities for mobility of traders and entrepreneurs across the borders of cities and provinces gave an unprecedented impetus to trade with specialised commodities – for instance, textiles – and raw materials – especially with marble. Large estates, in which agricultural production was organised not only to meet the needs of local markets but also to export specialised products such as olive oil and wine, were a common occurrence in Asia Minor and Macedonia, and to a lesser extent in other areas. Some of these estates were now owned by Roman senators and Greeks who had been accepted into the equestrian order. Wealthy men – and some women – sometimes owned land within the territory of cities other than their own. Large estates were managed by slaves and freedmen, who served as the stewards (*oikonomoi*) of the owners.

Crete is a good example of the impact that conquest and pacification had on the economy (see pp. 249–50). As soon as the Cretans, who used to make a living through raids and mercenary service, recovered from the shock caused by their conquest in 67 BC, they exploited the advantages that the integration of their fertile island into the trade networks of the empire offered. In addition to the massive export of wine, there is also evidence for trade in olive oil and medicinal plants; large fish tanks from the Imperial period reveal a new type of food production; and Crete excelled in the production of lamps that were exported to Asia Minor and North Africa. The impulse for the production of clay mould lamps came from Italian immigrants from Campania. In the mid-second century AD, the great doctor Galen reported another profitable export, unattested before the Roman conquest:

> Every year, in the summer, many medicinal plants come from Crete to Rome. The emperor keeps on the island herbalists, who deliver not only to him but to the entire city baskets full of medicinal plants. Crete exports these herbs to other regions, too, because this island does not lack herbs, fruits, corns, roots, and juices. All the other products are pure, but some juices are adulterated, although this does not happen often. The variety of plants on Crete is so huge, that the herbalists do not really need to cheat their customers.

The provincialisation of the Greek world by the Romans was a slow process. The Roman authorities responded to challenges as they arose; they did not follow a plan. This does not mean that they were not aware of some of the long-term impacts that their measures would have. In the Greek East, especially in the Greek or strongly Hellenised provinces with their strong urban traditions and high levels of culture, they did not seek to 'Romanise'. They did not uproot local traditions. They did not impose specifically Roman culture, customs, legal institutions or values. But the creation of a pacified geographical zone under a unified administration and with relatively clear and stable borders had tremendous integrative power. By the time Hadrian toured his eastern provinces for the second time, women were imitating the hairstyle of his wife and men his beard; people with the imperial name Publius Aelius, owing Roman citizenship to Hadrian, could be found in every corner of the empire; Latin words had been adopted by the Greeks; columns from the quarries of Mons Claudianus in Egypt were shipped to Rome to be used in the Pantheon; ships regularly sailed from Berenike and Ptolemais in Egypt to reach the ports of Arabia and India; baskets full of Cretan medicinal plants reached Rome and other cities; caravans from Mesopotamia and Arabia were connected to the empire via Palmyra in Syria and Petra in Jordan, while the trade routes were protected by Roman garrisons such as Dura-Europos. In AD 155, Aelius Aristides, in a panegyric for Rome that he delivered in the capital of the empire, sketches a picture of prosperity and affluence. The exaggerations of a professional encomiast aside, his speech still reflects the possibilities for advanced economic exchange that more than a century of uninterrupted peace had offered most Greek regions:

> The [Mediterranean] Sea resembles a sort of a belt in the middle of the inhabited earth and your empire alike. The great continents around it are inclined towards it, always bringing you something in affluence. For whatever the seasons grow and each country produces, and the rivers, the lakes, and the arts of the Greeks and the barbarians, is being brought to you from every earth and sea. If someone would like to inspect all this, he should either travel in the entire oecumene to see them, or he can just come to this city. For there is no way that there is shortage here of anything that grows or is made in any country at any time ... If you desire loads from India or Arabia Felix, you can see so many that you will suspect that their trees have now been left naked and that if they need something, they will now have to come here to ask you for some of their own products.

Aristides' perspective, that of an educated landowner from Asia Minor whose family had received Roman citizenship under Hadrian and had profited from Roman rule, was certainly not shared by the Jews, whose last revolt had been suppressed twenty years earlier. And it must have been incomprehensible to those who had to struggle to pay the tribute on which Rome's splendour – as that of Periclean Athens six centuries earlier – was based.

14

SOCIAL AND
CULTURAL TRENDS

Benefactors, Confrères, Ephebes,
Athletes, Women and Slaves

Detecting trends and innovation

An inscription in Metropolis in Asia Minor, written some time in the first
or second century AD, records the names of those who made donations to
a gymnasium, a place of athletic training and leisure. Their names are listed
under the following heading:

> For good fortune and for the salvation of the emperors and their
> entire household, when Alexandros, son of Alexandros, grandson of
> Rheximachos, was priest, on the second day of the month Dystros. In
> accordance with the decree of the older citizens and when Alexandra
> Myrton, daughter of Asklepiades, was supervisor of the gymnasium,
> the following individuals consecrated donations for the emperors and
> the older citizens.

The gymnasium was dedicated to the imperial family and placed under its
protection. Those who would use it would be citizens over sixty years old

(*presbyteroi*). Most contributors pledged to fund a *triclinum*, a set of three beds used in banquets. The old men of Metropolis went to their gymnasium not only to train their bodies but also – or more likely – to spend some time reclining on these beds, drinking and conversing. Only one of the sponsors was 'one of the *presbyteroi* himself'; the numerous men who contributed must have done so for the sake of elderly family members and for their own future use.

There is nothing unusual in all this; on the contrary, this text is typical of three important trends of the Hellenistic and Imperial periods: benefactions, conviviality in voluntary associations, and the social and cultural importance of the gymnasium. But there are two striking features that would have been unthinkable before the third century BC. First, a woman appears as a holder of an important civic function, that of the *gymnasiarchos*, the supervisor of an exclusively male institution. She held this function solely because of her wealth; as a matter of fact, she appears among the contributors who pledged significant amounts (630 denarii). Second, among the contributors we find three individuals who certainly were not allowed to set foot in the gymnasium: two women and one public slave. They donated because they had the means and could freely dispose of them, and because they expected to receive public recognition for their contribution.

This seemingly ordinary inscription from Metropolis is not the result of a revolution but of gradual changes that affected society and culture. We shall briefly look at trends that have one thing in common: they all started in the Hellenistic period, roughly in the third century BC, and continued without dramatic changes into the Imperial period. They thus reflect the unity – neither uniformity nor homogeneity – of the 'long Hellenistic Age'.

'Euergetism': benefactions, social prestige and political power

The Greek cities did not have an advanced system of income and property tax. Of course, there was a variety of taxes and revenues: proceeds from the leasing of public land, public pastures, mines and quarries; customs and sales taxes, fines, war booty, revenues from the sale of priesthoods and so on. Because of the endemic lack of funds, important regular expenses, such as the funding of festivals and the maintenance of a fleet, had to be covered by wealthy citizens through a system of *liturgies*, whereby such responsibilities were delegated on the basis of property. There remained the important problem of irregular expenses: for instance, for building projects, defence measures or the purchase of a stock of cheap grain. In such cases, the citizens were required to make extraordinary payments (*eisphorai*) or voluntary contributions through public subscriptions (*epidoseis*). But even this was not sufficient. Because of frequent wars, sometimes the expected revenues did not come, even as needs became more pressing: for the payment of mercenary soldiers, provisions for the troops and the repair of city walls.

When their expenses were higher than the available funds, the Greek cities did what most governments still do today: they took loans, sometimes under unfavourable conditions, unless patriotic citizens were willing to lend money without interest. However, the moneylenders' principal motivation was precisely a high interest rate. During the Roman war against the pirates in 71 BC, no creditor was willing to lend Gytheion, south of Sparta, the money that the small city required. Two Romans, the Cloatii brothers, agreed to a loan but at an extremely high interest rate of 48 per cent. Even so, they were honoured as benefactors, because they ultimately renounced a large part of the interest, when Gytheion (unsurprisingly) was unable to repay the debt. Gytheion's case is extreme, but relatively high interest rates of 12 per cent or more and unrepaid loans were a common occurrence in the second and first centuries BC. Sometimes, the cities solicited donors, but in extreme cases there was no other solution than to place a mortgage on the entire public territory. Many honorific inscriptions of the Hellenistic period were set up for men who had given loans with low interest or no interest at all – or who had accepted a 'haircut' on the loan, as we might say today.

In modern societies, sponsors or donors are usually not promised anything in return for their generosity. The donors' expectations do not go beyond the naming of a building, a street or an award after themselves – and even that often happens posthumously; not uncommonly, donors wish to retain their anonymity. In Hellenistic Greece and in the Imperial period, there was no such thing as the anonymous sponsor, and generosity was part of a system of reciprocity with a dramatic impact on political life (see p. 139). Donations were public performances, organised as displays of patriotism. The purpose and date of a public subscription were announced and honours promised to the contributors. During the subscription, the assembled people made loud demands of citizens whose wealth they suspected, and every pledge was publicly announced and greeted with cheers and acclamations, motivating wealthy citizens to commit themselves to greater donations – or making them wish to disappear unnoticed. The contributions were publicly commemorated. Often, they were not registered according to volume – with the largest amounts first – but in the sequence in which they were made. Pledging was a sort of competition, and those who were first to volunteer received the greatest honour. Not only were the names of those who contributed commemorated, but also the names of those who did not keep their promises and were exposed to the contempt of their fellow citizens.

In the case of subscriptions, the purpose was determined by the assembly. With voluntary benefactions, the benefactors took the initiative to determine a project, often responding to real needs – a public building, olive oil for the gymnasium, funds for the maintenance of a public office – but sometimes guided by personal interests and inclinations, such as in the funding of a new festival. The increased visibility of benefactors (*euergetai*) and their social and political role are designated in modern scholarship as 'euergetism'. Euergetism was based on reciprocity. A good and simple definition of reciprocity is found in Mama's song in Fred Ebb's musical *Chicago*:

> Got a little motto,
> Always sees me through:
> When you're good to Mama,
> Mama's good to you.

With voluntary contributions, local benefactors displayed their willingness to offer part of their private property to the community. However, this willingness was combined with the expectation that the community would accept their political leadership. In exchange for the donations and *liturgies* provided by wealthy families, the *demos* acquiesced to their power monopoly. This reciprocal relation permitted cities in the late Hellenistic and Imperial periods to maintain some moderate democratic institutions and the illusion of popular sovereignty, despite the oligarchic features that political life accrued.

Local benefactors were honoured with statues in prominent places, golden crowns and public announcements of their donations; they were invited to prominent seats in theatrical performances and athletic contests, or to dine together with the magistrates; and the buildings that they funded – town halls, public baths, gymnasia – were named after them. When they died, they could expect a public funeral and sometimes the extraordinary honour of a funeral within the city walls. In exceptional cases, they received cultic honours after death. These honours made the benefactors visibly present in their city. More importantly, the benefactions were not forgotten. Honorific inscriptions for prominent citizens often mention the fact that their ancestors had contributed to subscriptions or had made donations. Benefactions strengthened the social prestige and the political influence not only of the benefactors but also of their families, for decades.

The benefactors were not only great landholders or members of the elite. As their social backgrounds were increasingly diverse – including women, foreigners, freedmen and even slaves – benefactions became a significant means of upward mobility. Foreigners who made significant money contributions to a *polis* could expect preferential treatment there, and their privileges were sometimes hereditary. The benefactor was usually rewarded with the privileges of a *proxenos* (see p. 293) and in some cases with citizenship. The dependence of Greek cities on the contributions of wealthy benefactors had become clearly visible by the second century BC. This trend culminated in the Imperial period. A new form of benefactions were endowments left to the city for the expenses of offices like those of the *stephanephoros*, the *agonothetes* and the *gymnasiarchos*. In years in which no citizen was willing to undertake these offices, the endowment covered the expense and the benefactor bore the title of the office. Such endowments – called 'eternal *stephanephoria*', 'eternal *agonothesia*' and 'eternal *gymnasiarchia*' – allowed an individual to nominally occupy an office even posthumously.

In the early Hellenistic period, the title of *euergetes* was often given to people for their heroism in battle or for their political services to their city. They were respected as patriots. In that period, wealthy men who excelled in generosity succeeded in becoming the first among fellow citizens; but as an increasing number of public and religious activities were funded through *liturgies* and voluntary benefactions, the extraordinary treatment of the *euergetai* elevated them above their fellow citizens. This development becomes clear in the language of decrees in honour of benefactors – for instance, in the praise of a certain Hermogenes in Aphrodisias around 50 BC:

one of the foremost and most illustrious citizens, a man who has as his ancestors men among the greatest and among those who built the community together and have lived in virtue, love of glory, many promises of benefactions, and the fairest deeds for the fatherland; a man who has been himself good and virtuous, a lover of the fatherland, a constructor, a benefactor of the polis, and a savior; a man who has shown benevolence and prudence in his conduct towards the entire people and towards each one of the citizens; a man who has always shown the utmost reverence towards the gods and the fatherland; who has adorned the fatherland, most generously fulfilling the most noble promises and making dedications ...

In such encomia (cf. p. 285), men like Hermogenes of Aphrodisias appear as a city's beloved leaders. We cannot expect that public inscriptions state what many people must have privately thought: that these benefactors were a city's necessary evils. Herodes Atticus, Athens' greatest benefactor during Hadrian's reign, must have felt this. He had terrible curses inscribed on the bases of the statues that he dedicated, addressed to those who might destroy them. Benefactors knew what they might expect from their fellow countrymen: not gratitude but envy.

Voluntary associations

Before Alexander's campaigns, the population of foreign residents was significant only in major urban centres, especially in Athens and a few other cities with commercial activities. The presence of foreigners in most Greek cities continually increased in the course of the Hellenistic period. These included permanent foreign residents (*metics*), merchants and bankers, exiles, members of garrisons and mercenaries. The presence of foreigners reached a climax in the first two centuries after Augustus.

While in newly founded cities the immigrants were immediately integrated into the community and shared a new civic identity with other settlers of different origins, the situation was very different in the old Greek cities of Greece and Asia Minor. Here, the foreign residents were and remained a distinct minority. Admittedly, they were largely treated in the same way as citizens with regard to legal rights, they had military and financial obligations, they made financial contributions and under certain conditions they were allowed to own landed property, but they did not have political rights. Their gradual assimilation with the citizens did not change the fact that the citizens cultivated a separate identity, based on an elaborate system of 'patriotic' education (see pp. 329–33). Foreigners could feel that they belonged to a group by joining a voluntary association. Beyond a common ethnic origin, associations could also be based on family relations, a shared profession or religious beliefs.

Voluntary associations (*eranos, thiasos, koinon*), resembling modern 'clubs', already existed in the sixth century BC. But their number increased tremendously from the fourth century BC, for three main reasons. First, greater mobility increased the numbers of foreign residents, especially in important harbour towns and centres of trade, culture and manufacture. Expatriated people formed associations as a form of community. When, in the second century BC, the migration of Italian tradesmen to Greece and Asia Minor began, associations became an important locus for the organisation and celebration of Roman festivals, especially in economic centres such as Delos. Second, cults that promised a close and privileged relationship between a worshipper and a deity increased in number; especially popular were cults that required the initiation of members in secret rites and doctrines; they were organised on the basis of exclusive groups of devotees or initiates who celebrated the rites on certain dates in the clubhouses (see p. 373). Prayer houses and synagogues of the diaspora Jews were also a form of voluntary organisation – *synagoge* is in fact a Greek term for a club. Finally, clubs offered people of lower social status the possibility to reproduce a form of conviviality that in the past characterised the elite and that in the Hellenistic period was practised in the royal courts: the symposion. These associations organised gatherings in club-houses, celebrated feasts for patron gods in shrines and offered interment for members in their own burial plots.

Independent of the origin of their members or their primary activity, associations were always placed under the patronage of a divinity. In most cases, a club's name derived from the god or gods worshipped by its members. The Apolloniastai were under the patronage of Apollo, the Hermaistai under that of Hermes and so on. The voluntary associations reproduced, on a smaller scale, the institutions of the *polis*: they had their statutes, assemblies, magistrates, decrees, common property and finances. Membership of voluntary associations resembled citizenship and, to a certain extent, it replaced citizenship as a foundation of community and identity. Associations usually admitted people as members without regard to their status: citizens, foreign residents, freedmen, often women and sometimes also slaves. Devotion to certain deities and acceptance of ethical principles and religious beliefs were the basis of communality, not origin, gender or status. In this way, clubs contributed to a loosening of the strict legal boundaries that dominated earlier Greek society; to a degree, they facilitated increased interaction between different social groups.

A very specific type of voluntary association, and at the same time a characteristic expression of mobility and cosmopolitanism, was the association of theatre artists, the so-called 'artists of Dionysus' (*Dionysiakoi technitai*). Founded for the first time in the late fourth or early third century BC in Athens, it contributed to the organisation of festivals, represented the interests of its members (who were continually on the move in dangerous times), established close relations with kings and exercised political influence. Through the course of the Hellenistic period, local associations existed in many places in Greece, Asia Minor, Egypt, Cyprus and Sicily. The local chapter of Dionysiac artists in Teos established such a close connection with the city that the Teians dedicated their entire city and its territory to the god Dionysus. This association resembled a state within a state, even issuing its own currency to be used for the funding of festivals.

By contributing to the creation of social networks within a city and by building bridges between social groups, the voluntary associations were a motor for social change and a marker of the cosmopolitan character of the Hellenistic cities. Their importance continued under Roman rule. Because of the rising popularity of mystery cults, the number of religious clubs increased. Furthermore, professional associations became more common, exercising economic, social and political influence; streets, public squares and city quarters were named after them. In the Imperial period, the elderly members of the elite formed a 'club of elders' (*gerousia*) with significant social prestige and some political influence.

The shared interests that brought people together in an association had no limits. We know of clubs of lovers of jokes (*philopaiktores*), of joy and exuberance (*kalokardioi, eutherapioi*) and of gladiatorial shows (*philhoploi*). Also, the athletes and the representatives of the performing arts who competed in international festivals were organised in 'ecumenical associations', whose leaders had close contacts with the emperor. Voluntary associations in many ways reflect the international and cosmopolitan character of the world that emerged from Alexander's conquests.

Agonistic culture and international stars in sport and entertainment

The Greeks organised athletic and musical competitions from the earliest periods of their recorded history. These took place in connection with civic and federal festivals, rites of passage and funerals of important people – and later, in connection with military victories. A contest (*agon*) usually attracted competitors from a single city or the members of a federation, but by the sixth century BC four festivals – in Olympia and Nemea in honour of Zeus, in Delphi in honour of Apollo Pythios and at the Isthmus near Corinth in honour of Poseidon – had acquired a Panhellenic reputation. They took place on four successive years, thus forming a four-year cycle, the *periodos* (circuit). The Greeks were invited by means of sacred envoys (*theoroi*) and a truce was declared for the period of the competition.

From the Hellenistic period onwards, the number of contests increased tremendously. New contests were founded by kings, old and new cities, federations and private sponsors. They were established in order to commemorate a military victory or the liberation of a city, to honour newly introduced gods, kings, local benefactors, statesmen, generals, deceased family members and, from 196 BC, Roman commanders and governors. Federations enhanced their unity through contests, cities used them to support their efforts to be recognised as inviolable, and sponsors hoped to increase their own prestige and that of their families. Every time a new *agon* was established in a city, this motivated an envious neighbour to establish or augment its own. This trend continued and expanded in the Imperial period, when contests were founded in honour of emperors. As the cities acquired oligarchic features, the number of wealthy individuals who established a public contest (*themis*) honouring deceased family members increased, as did the number of contests founded by and named after benefactors, such as the Demostheneia in Oinoanda.

Important new festivals in the third century BC include the Ptolemaia in Alexandria in honour of Ptolemy I (see pp. 74–5), the Soteria in Delphi commemorating the victory over the Gauls, the Didymeia in Miletos in honour of Apollo, the Asklepieia in Kos and the Leukophryena in Magnesia on the Maeander in honour of Artemis. The establishment of the Principate added two further festivals of international reputation: the Sebasta in Naples in honour of Augustus and the Aktia in Nikopolis commemorating Octavian's victory at Actium. Nero attempted to introduce a Greek-style *agon* in Rome, with his Neroneia; these, however, did not outlive their founder. By contrast, the *agon Capitolinus*, founded by Domitian in Rome in AD 86 in honour of Jupiter Capitolinus, ranked alongside the four old festivals. The Panhellenia in Athens, connected with the foundation of the Panhellenion under Hadrian (see p. 258), never reached the same prestige, despite the emperor's support. It has been estimated that by the second century AD there were about 500 *agones* in the eastern provinces, but this is a rather moderate number. Because of the proliferation of agonistic festivals, Hadrian intervened in AD 134, establishing a strict sequence for the most important contests, so that competitors could move from one competition to the next in a timely manner. The agonistic culture from the late third century BC to the early third century AD finds no precedent in any earlier period; it can only be rivalled by competitions in sport and the performing arts after the Second World War.

In order to increase the appeal of their contests, cities and federations expanded the programme to include musical and dramatic competitions. The most prestigious contests were those that awarded crowns as prizes – made of wild olive at the Olympic games, laurel at the Pythia, celery at the Nemea and celery (and later pine) at the Isthmia. Some contests gave prizes with material value: shields, gold crowns, tripods and cash. However, the *hieronikai*, the 'victors in a sacred contest', in which the prize was a crown, expected more than the glory and social prestige that came with the victory. Depending on the rank of the festival, their hometown bestowed upon them a variety of honours ranging from an honorary position in a procession and a seat of honour to cash prizes and free food at public meals. When a festival was recognised as of equal rank with the Pythia of Delphi (*isopythios*), the victorious athlete expected to receive the same rewards from his city as the winner at the Pythia. The winners of *iselastic* contests were honoured with *eiselasis*, a ceremonial entrance into the city, and received prize money.

Most contests were athletic events to which contestants belonging to different age groups – boys, ephebes and men – were admitted. The programme usually included the 'classical' disciplines of ancient sport: races of various distances, sometimes of armed men, wrestling, boxing, pentathlon (discus, standing jump, javelin, *stadion* race, wrestling) and *pankration* – a sort of kickboxing. In addition, various *agones* included exceptional events. A race in full armour took place at the Eleutheria of Plataiai, commemorating the victory of the Greeks over the Persians in 478 BC. The contestants had to run from the trophy of the battle to the altar of Zeus Eleutherios – around 2,500 metres. The victor received the honorary title 'the best of the Hellenes'. Races for girls are attested in rare cases. Equestrian events were less common, but popular and prominent in areas with a tradition of horse breeding: races of single young and adult horses, war horses, pairs of horses, pairs of mules, mounted torch races, competitions in throwing the javelin while on horseback, and races of chariots drawn by young and adult horses. Participation in the equestrian disciplines was the privilege of the wealthy classes that could afford a horse and its training. Women took part in equestrian events as owners of horses.

For the audiences, athletic contests were spectacular and thrilling events. A victory without competition was very prestigious, especially when a boxer achieved it due to his fame, strength or skill at scaring all potential contestants away from the competition. The boxer Melankomas, the lover of Emperor Titus (see p. 302), owed his extraordinary fame to the fact that he had never been hit by an opponent. He did not defeat his opponents by knocking them down but by exhausting them. There were cases of undecided competitions, because both opponents withdrew or the *agon* was interrupted by the trainers; in such cases, the award was dedicated to the god. Sometimes both opponents were declared victors, on account of time constraints or because the opponents agreed to share the victory and the awards. Athletes who were victorious in their discipline in all four great festivals were known as *periodonikai*, the 'circuit winners' – the equivalent of the winners of the Grand Slam in modern tennis. In the case of prestigious contests, even to have been accepted into the competition could be regarded as an honour.

Music competitions have ancient roots, as old as those of athletic contests. The most widespread were competitions among choruses of boys, girls and men representing the civic subdivisions of the *polis*. Under the influence of Athens, dramatic festivals spread throughout the entire Hellenised world. Dionysiac festivals that included choral, musical and dramatic *agones* are attested in nearly every city. Musical and dramatic – or *thymelic* – contests were also added to the programme of traditional athletic festivals. The contestants competed in the presentation of new plays and the production of 'classics', in poetry, music and dance accompanied by song, and in the vocal performance of heralds. Gradually, a more or less standardised schedule of competitions developed, allowing for local variations. Common contests were those for trumpeters, heralds, encomium writers, poets, musicians (oboists, kithara players), tragic choruses, comedians and tragedians. The adult kithara singer received the highest cash prize. Although performances of mimic dancers (*pantomime*) were very popular, they were not included in agonistic festivals until the late second century AD. Some cities had *agones* in peculiar disciplines, connected with local traditions. For instance, we know of a contest of sculptors in Aphrodisias, a contest of doctors in Pergamon and beauty contests in Lesbos.

The agonistic festivals were usually connected with a market fair that attracted foreign visitors and merchants. There were also additional paid concerts, as well as a variety of cultural performances, such as epideictic orations and lectures. Agonistic festivals also hosted political and social events. Important announcements were made: magistrates and honoured individuals were invited to take a seat of distinction and honours were announced.

The participants in athletic competitions were often the scions of elite families, who had the leisure to train in the gymnasium; provided that they had the physical capabilities, they started participating in competitions as early as boyhood. For such people, athletic victories were only a further component of their family's prestige. The statues of victorious boy athletes joined those of their relatives who had excelled in benefactions or public service.

Entertainers were a socially diverse group – as diverse as the music, literary and dramatic disciplines that they represented – from the epic poet to the mimic dancer. Since virtuosity and success required extensive training – which in antiquity was often offered in the family setting – musicians, dancers, acrobats and comedians often belonged to families of entertainers and were trained in a discipline from a very early age. Their professional specialisation is often reflected in their names: Areskousa and Terpnos (the one who pleases), or Apolaustos (the enjoyable). For a talented man or a woman of humble origin, success in musical victories brought wealth and social prestige.

Agonistic culture not only increased the unity and mobility of the Hellenistic and Hellenised world, but also created new opportunities for artists and athletes to specialise in their disciplines and to make a living simply by competing for prizes.

Shaping civic values and civic identity: the *ephebeia* and the gymnasium

Public education – which focused on military training and the transmission of civic values, local customs and historical traditions – was a requirement for the incorporation of a young individual into the citizen body and the society of the *polis*. Education separated not only citizens from foreign residents but also members of the elite from the mass of the people and, of course, men from women. In addition to their training in affairs of the household, girls usually received some elementary education in writing and reading, music and poetry; depending on the wealth and education of their family, the literary training of girls could be substantial, and from the Hellenistic period on we find a significant number of female poets. Girls performed in choruses in religious festivals and this duty familiarised them with the traditions and values of their city. In exceptional cases, women received advanced education in the philosophical schools. The education of boys took place both in their homes, with private teachers (usually slaves), and in public schools in those cities that had funds for public instructors. Typically, their education focused on reading and writing, rhetoric and mythology, the recitation of excerpts from Homer and other poets, and some music. In the Hellenistic period, the importance of the training that boys and young men received under the supervision of the civic authorities increased. Two related institutions promoted the 'patriotic' training of a city's youth: the *gymnasion* and the *ephebeia*.

The *gymnasion* – literally, the place where men train their naked bodies – was the main locus of male training. Its supervisor, the *gymnasiarchos*, was usually a respected and wealthy man between thirty and sixty years of age. He was elected to this office, but because of the expenses involved, in the Hellenistic and Imperial periods the *gymnasiarchia* became one of the most important *liturgies*; occasionally, it was even assumed by wealthy women who covered the associated expenses. The *gymnasiarchos* made sure that discipline and the opening hours were kept, and that different age classes trained separately. He supervised the trainers (*paidotribai*), procured the necessary funds for the purchase of the olive oil used for anointing athletes' bodies, organised competitions and paid for the prizes that were given to the winners.

Hermes and Heracles were the patron gods of the gymnasium. At the festival of the Hermaia, young men competed in the areas of discipline (*eutaxia*), endurance (*philoponia*), manly behaviour (*euandria*) and good physical condition (*euexia*); the younger members of the gymnasium competed in torch races. The prizes were shields. In some Hellenistic gymnasia, the athletic competitions included – in addition to the 'classical' disciplines (races, wrestling, boxing, *pankration* and torch race) – military disciplines, such as the use of the catapult, javelin, archery and fighting with shield and lance. Depending on the idiosyncrasies of the *gymnasiarchos*, unusual contests could also take place, such as literary contests.

In the later part of the Hellenistic period, lectures – especially by philosophers and historians – took place in the gymnasium. Men continued to attend the gymnasium as adults to train their bodies and socialise. Cities with means and large populations had more than one gymnasium, not only in different locations but also reserved for different age groups. Slaves and freedmen, as well as the descendants of freedmen, were typically excluded from the gymnasium; other prohibited persons included male prostitutes, in some cities traders, drunks and people who were regarded as insane. In Alexandria, the Jews were denied access to the gymnasium under Claudius (see p. 289). Thus the gymnasium was an expression of social hierarchies and remained so throughout the Imperial period.

In the Hellenistic period, the gymnasium was more than just a place of athletic and, indirectly, of military training. It was a centre of social interaction among citizens; outside mainland Greece, it also became a symbol of Hellenic culture and one of the most important external features of a *polis*. Gymnasia existed in every major Greek city, as far as today's Afghanistan. In fact, one of the largest gymnasia has been excavated in Ai-Khanoum (Alexandria on the Oxus) in Bactria (see Fig. 27). In the early second century BC, what distinguished the Jewish Hellenisers in Jerusalem from those who remained faithful to the Jewish law was that the former attended the gymnasium. When Tyriaion in Phrygia raised a claim to the status of an independent *polis*, what it requested from King Eumenes II was a gymnasium, in addition to a council and laws. This perception remained alive throughout the Imperial period. In the late second century AD, the traveller Pausanias was surprised that the town of Panopeus in Phokis counted as a *polis*, despite its lack of a gymnasium, a theatre and a marketplace.

The term *ephebeia* designates the training of a group of young men, usually between eighteen and twenty years old, under the supervision of

27. *The gymnasium at Ai-Khanoum (second century* BC*).*

state authorities. Archaic forms of training that had declined during the Classical period were revived in the Hellenistic period both for military reasons and as an expression of civic sovereignty. For instance, the *agoge*, the archaic training of the Spartans that had been one of the requirements for citizenship, had lost its importance by the fourth century BC. It was revived by King Kleomenes III in 228 BC as one of the foundations of his reforms, but abolished again in 188 BC by Philopoimen. Only in very conservative places, such as Crete, did old forms of training survive apparently unchanged. In the Cretan cities, the young men were organised into 'herds' (*agelai*) under the leadership of another youth of high social status; they trained in fighting, wrestling, boxing, running, hunting and dancing in full armour. In Macedonia, another conservative region, ephebic rituals and contests – races and horse races – survived until the Hellenistic period.

In Athens, the political turbulence of the late fourth century BC led to a decline of the *ephebeia* as an obligatory martial training of the young men, those between eighteen and nineteen years old, of citizen status. During the regime of Demetrios of Phaleron (317–307 BC), the ephebic training was a privilege of the sons of citizens with property worth a minimum of 1,000 drachmas; between around 306–268 BC, participation in the *ephebeia* was not obligatory, and the training lasted only one year instead of two. Only after the end of the Macedonian monarchy, when Athens regained some of its overseas possessions and as foreign residents were allowed to register as ephebes, did the number of ephebes increase again, to between around 100 and 180 men. The great interest shown by the community in training the offspring of the elite can be seen in the large number of honorary decrees praising, year after year, those volunteers who had successfully finished their education in a manner demonstrating the virtues that the Athenians expected from their future citizens and soldiers: diligence, endurance, obedience, discipline, piety and respect towards ancestral traditions. The Athenian *ephebeia* was a combination of athletic activities, military training and police duties in the countryside, participation in the customary religious rituals, attendance of commemorative anniversaries and preparation for civic duties. The institution of the *ephebeia* existed in many other cities and regions which often adopted the Athenian model. The Greek settlers also brought these institutions to Anatolia, the Near East and Egypt.

Under Roman dominion, the Greek cities preserved the institution of the *ephebeia*. An inscription from Amphipolis in Macedonia dating to 24/23 BC but recording a law of the early second century BC shows the continuing importance of ephebic training for Greek cities. The ephebes were primarily trained in athletics, to a limited extent in the use of weapons (bow, sling, javelin) and, where horse breeding had a long tradition, also in cavalry. Members of the elite supervised the ephebes and the 'chief ephebe' (*ephebarchos*) was sometimes a close relative of the supervisor. The ephebes still had the task of policing the civic territory and protecting it from bandits. However, the main function of the *ephebeia* in the Imperial period was to construct a sense of identity through religious rituals, to promote local patriotism through the transmission of historical memory, to propagate loyalty towards the emperor and to forge relations among the members of the propertied classes whose sons could afford to devote one or two years to this training.

Until the third century AD, the institution of the *ephebeia* remained a characteristic feature of Hellenic culture, even in the heart of the Roman Empire, in Italy. Shortly before his death, Augustus, while in Neapolis (today's Naples), watched how the ephebes of this Greek city exercised following the ancestral traditions. And in the early third century AD, the small Boiotian city of Tanagra still had more than sixty ephebes divided into two 'regiments' (*tagmata*). The young men competed during eight festivals in various disciplines evincing an obsession with tradition. One of the competitions was the simulation of a sudden attack of infantry and cavalry (*prosdromai*), a relic from a time when the *ephebeia* aimed at training soldiers. Another discipline required the carrying of an ox for a certain distance (*boarsion*), an old contest among young men. The *ephebeia* remained, at least until the early third century AD, an important medium of socialisation that prepared the scions of elite families for the leadership of their communities.

New marriage patterns and the visibility of women

In his funeral oration for the fallen Athenians in 430 BC, Pericles had little to say about women: 'To a woman not to show more weakness than is natural to her sex is a great glory, and not to be talked about for good or for evil among men.' The position of women in early Greece cannot be adequately summarised by Pericles' ideologically loaded statement. His words certainly do not do justice to the visibility and influence of his own spouse, Aspasia. The roles of women in family, society, economy, religion and culture were complex and varied greatly from place to place. But, generally, women were kept under the tutelage of their closest male relative (*kyrios*, lord): when unmarried their father or brother, when married their husband, when widowed their son. In most communities, they could not inherit property in their own right. They did not hold public offices, except for priestly ones. Women born into a citizen family transferred citizenship to their offspring, since in most cities only marriages between citizens were regarded as legitimate; however, they themselves were excluded from political participation. Naturally, some women could influence their husbands. And sometimes, women of low social position but engaged in professional activities – nurses, laundresses, cooks and courtesans – had more freedom of movement and the freedom to use their property (e.g. by making dedications) than the wives and daughters of the propertied classes. The life of women in Greece before Alexander is too complex to be regarded simply as a life in the shadow of men.

The new world that emerged after Alexander's conquests brought significant changes. Migration was a very important trigger of change. The increased number of immigrants in the urban centres made marriages between men and women of different citizenship more common than ever before. Agreements between two communities could make intermarriage (*epigamia*) possible. In cities that insisted on requiring citizenship from both partners for the legitimacy of the marriage, the children produced by mixed marriages were still regarded as illegitimate. But as innumerable Greeks found themselves away from their cities, with little prospect of ever returning there and limited possibilities of finding a partner from the same city while abroad, they did not object to a Greek wife who had different citizenship. However, those who served in remote garrisons had no alternative to an indigenous wife. Already Alexander realised the consequences of these circumstances and organised a mass wedding between his soldiers and Iranian women.

A marriage contract from Egypt, where such documents have been preserved on papyri, illustrates this new state of affairs. Dated to 311 BC, the contract concerns the marriage of a man from Temnos in Asia Minor and the daughter of a man from Kos. Both men, as well as the witnesses who came from Temnos, Gela, Cyrene and Kos, must have been mercenaries in the service of Ptolemy I, now permanently settled in Egypt.

> Herakleides takes as his lawful wife Demetria from Kos, both being free by birth, from her father Leptines from Kos and her mother Philotis; she brings her clothing and jewelry with a value of 1000 drachmas. Herakleides shall provide Demetria with all that is proper for a free wife. We shall live together wherever it seems best to Leptines and Herakleides conferring together in common counsel. If Demetria is discovered damaging in any way the shame of her husband Herakleides, she shall be deprived of all that she brought into the marriage, but Herakleides must prove whatever he alleges against Demetria before three men approved by them both. It shall not be allowed to Herakleides to bring home another wife to the insult of Demetria nor to have children by another woman nor to wrong Demetria in any way, on any pretext. If Herakleides is found doing any of these things and Demetria proves it before three men whom they both approve, Herakleides shall give back to Demetria the dowry of 1000 drachmas that she brought and pay an additional fine of 1000 drachmas of the silver coinage of Alexander ...

Some elements in this contract correspond to old Greek traditions: both partners were free; the bride was represented by the closest male relative; she brought into the marriage a dowry that was returned to her in the case of divorce; the contract protected the honour of both husband and wife. But we also see local influences: the explicit prohibition of a second wife or concubine must be attributed to Egyptian influence. The most novel feature in this contract, however, is the fact that husband and wife had different citizenships. The important issue was not whether their children would have citizenship in a city that they would probably never see but the legitimacy of children and inheritance.

As the rules concerning the legitimacy of marriage became more flexible and citizenship was deemed unnecessary for the acquisition of property, the possibilities for women to acquire and govern their own property gradually increased. In the Classical period, an heiress was obliged to marry her closest male relative, because she could not inherit property in her own right; she could only transfer it to her children. This law, which still played an important part in the plot of Hellenistic comedies and their Latin adaptations, gradually lost its significance. Women inherited property in their own right, as daughters or widows; they owned workshops, large estates and slaves; and they also earned property as professionals. Women were active in many professions, from trade to medicine, although entertainers, such as musicians, actors and poetesses, are best represented in the sources.

When women used their wealth for benefactions, their social visibility increased. The most important group of female personalities in the Hellenistic period – queens aside – were wealthy women known for their largesse. They usually came from wealthy families, and this endowed them with a social network, wealth and the capability to make benefactions. If we know about them, it is because of inscriptions in their honour that record their donations and endowments. Such women overshadow the thousands who remain anonymous, unless a gravestone was set up in their memory.

Women benefactors also played a major part in the cities in the Imperial period. On the basis of their wealth, they adorned their cities with buildings and statues; they were charged with *liturgies*, undertaking functions that would have been unthinkable before the third century BC, such as the 'eponymous' office of the 'crown bearer' (*stephanephoros*) and the supervisor of the gymnasium. Two such extraordinary women give an impression of the possibilities opened by wealth. The first is a certain Epikteta in the third century BC. She was a wealthy widow from the island of Thera who had inherited property but had also acquired additional land herself. Following the instructions of her late husband and son, she completed the construction of a sanctuary of the Muses, where statues of her relatives were erected. She also created a club of family members that was to meet in that shrine once a year to offer commemorative sacrifices to Epikteta, her husband and her sons; the sacrifices were funded through an endowment. The fact that she left a will shows that she could freely dispose of her property.

The second extraordinary woman is Archippe of Kyme in the late second century BC. Born into a family with prominent ancestors, Archippe used her inherited property to pay for the construction of a council hall and to provide funds for a feast for the entire free population. In exchange, she was honoured with a statue; next to it stood a statue of the personification of the People placing a crown on her head. She received a crown at the celebration of the Dionysiac festival during the competition of boys' choruses: that is, when the largest number of spectators was expected. She was to receive a golden wreath during her funeral. In order to expedite the construction of her statue, the assembly asked her brother to pay for it, without the expectation of repayment. When Archippe recovered from a serious illness, the city publicly offered a thanksgiving sacrifice to the gods, exactly as children would have done for the salvation of a mother.

Apart from the female benefactors, another group of women with great social visibility were the itinerant female entertainers. This too was a development generated by increased mobility, but also by the frequency of festivals and the demand for performers. Poetesses, musicians and other entertainers travelled extensively in the Greek world, alone or accompanied by a male relative. The most successful among them received honours for their performances and acquired wealth and fame. An early example of such a woman is the female trumpeter Aglais, around 270 BC. Her very name, inspired by the Muse Aglaia, suggests that she had been raised as an artist, possibly as a member of a family of performers. She was known for her great appetite, which increased her abilities in playing an instrument that required strong lungs; allegedly, she ate up to twelve pounds of meat accompanied by four pounds of bread, and drank three litres of wine a day. A real 'star', she was praised for the vigour of her performance in processions and celebrations for victorious athletes. Her most notable day was when she performed during the procession at the Ptolemaia in Alexandria, wearing a wig and a crested helmet.

The harpist Polygnota of Thebes is another instructive example. In 86 BC, while the Delphians were preparing to celebrate the Pythian games, Sulla's campaign in Greece made travel hazardous and the contest had to be cancelled. Nonetheless, Polygnota – more courageous than her colleagues – arrived in Delphi together with her cousin and gave a series of concerts with spectacular success. She was honoured for her piety and good professional conduct. In addition to various important privileges, including the right to purchase landed property in Delphi, she also received an honorarium of 500 drachmas – more than a mercenary soldier earned in a year.

The visibility of women also increased in religious celebrations. Already in earlier periods, girls and women participated in public events and processions, and they had their own, exclusively female festivals. However, from the third century BC onwards, the frequency of festivals increased, and with them also the occasions on which women went outdoors, as spectators of processions, and fulfilled religious functions. Additionally, new festivals exclusively for women were founded, such as the Eisiteria in Magnesia on the Maeander, which commemorated the dedication of the statue of Artemis Leukophryene in her new temple. If we believe a literary topos, it was during processions or festivals that girls lost their mind, heart and virginity.

An indication of the increased mobility of women is also the fact that they appear among the members of voluntary associations, especially in the cities of the Imperial period. Partly under Roman influence and partly imitating male corporate bodies, such as the assembly, the council of elders and clubs of young men, women had corporate organisations of their own, consisting of the wives of Greek and Roman citizens; they are attested in Dion in Macedonia, in Stratonikeia in Caria and in Akmoneia in Phrygia. They probably held their separate assemblies during women's festivals. One of their activities was to set up honorific statues; since this was an expensive business, these women's organisations administered their own funds.

Whenever women in traditional societies acquire some influence, defenders of tradition are likely to react. The office of 'the supervisor of women' (*gynaikonomos*), introduced in some Hellenistic cities, was a response to the challenges – the protection of women, decorum and male domination – that a changed world had produced.

Shades of grey: slavery in the Hellenistic world and the Roman East

Slavery is one of the oldest Greek institutions, attested already in documents of the fourteenth century BC. Its definition is simple: a slave is an individual who is the property of another individual or of a group of individuals – a public slave or a slave of an association. Often simple legal definitions shelter a very complex social reality. The position and life of slaves depended on their ethnic origin, the conditions of their enslavement, their training and their occupation. There were people who were born as slaves, exposed children raised as slaves and people captured in North Africa, Asia Minor and the northern Balkans and sold in slave markets, but also people who lost their freedom as war captives or victims of pirates, or because of unpaid debts. Slaves who were employed in the civic administration (e.g. in archives or as security forces) and in the household were in a far better position than those who worked en masse in mines. Slaves who served their owners in trade, manufacture and banking could acquire significant wealth; those employed in agricultural production sometimes enjoyed some form of independence.

The history of Greek slavery – and of any slavery, for that matter – is not only or even primarily the history of legal norms and socio-economic practices, but also the history of interpersonal relations and individual experiences. Individual experiences do not easily add up to a general picture. On the one hand, there are stories of eponymous slaves: Epikles, the son of a Cretan mercenary in Cyprus, captured and sold by pirates, liberated and naturalised in Amphissa; the eunuch Krokos, educator of a Cilician princess; the public slave Philippos, who had enough means to make a donation to the gymnasium in Metropolis (see p. 317); and Epaphroditos, a slave of Trajan and Hadrian and contractor in the stone quarries of Egypt. These lives may be contrasted, on the other hand, with the fate of the 10,000 anonymous people who are said to have been sold on a daily basis in Delos, the thousands of rowers in ships, the gladiators who placed their hope of liberation in the killing of their opponents, and the workers in mines and quarries. In the first century BC, Diodorus painted a dark picture of work in the goldmines of south Egypt, with people bound in chains, working day and night, with lamps bound on their foreheads. The physically strongest broke the quartz rock with iron hammers, then boys carried it through the tunnels out into the open, where it was to be ground by old men and women, compelled to work by blows until they died:

> And since they cannot care for their body and even lack the garments to cover their shame, no man can look upon the unfortunate wretches without feeling pity for them because of the magnitude of

their suffering ... Because of their severe punishment, these unfortunate people believe that the future will always be more terrible than the present and therefore look forward to death as more desirable than life.

Fascinating as individual stories may be, in this chapter we only have space for general trends. Although Hellenistic intellectuals – especially Epicurus in the early third century BC and his contemporary Zeno, the founder of the Stoic school of philosophy – criticised slavery, attributing its existence not to nature but to human convention, what brought changes to slavery was not philosophy but war. First, wars offered slaves who lived in the countryside an opportunity to escape. Second, in desperate situations cities increased their military manpower by liberating and sometimes even naturalising slaves, expecting them to fight to protect their new status. Third, and most important, the ubiquitous wars from Alexander to Actium, in addition to piracy and raids, increased the numbers of slaves who changed masters and of free people who were sold into slavery. While captives of citizen status could be ransomed by their families and return home, non-Greek slaves were usually sold abroad. A slave could achieve a price of 100–300 drachmas; the ransom for a free person was at least twice as high. Pirates turned merchants and slave-traders, who followed the armies in their campaigns, regularly supplied the main slave markets of the Aegean – Rhodes, Delos, Crete and Ephesos. Although the ancient sources provide numbers of women, children and other captives sold in slavery, especially in the period of the Roman expansion, these numbers should be taken with a grain of salt. Allegedly, 50,000 *perioikoi* – that is, free, non-citizen inhabitants of Lakonia – were enslaved by the Aitolians during a single campaign in 240 BC, as were 150,000 Epirotans in 167 BC by the Romans. Such numbers, exaggerated as they may be, still indicate that there was an increased supply of slaves who were not born in the household. This not only affected the economy in Italy, where slaves were used on a massive scale in agricultural production and manufacture; it also had an impact on the frequency of manumissions. It was profitable for slave-owners to manumit a slave, receiving compensation that roughly corresponded to the price of a slave and using this to buy a new one.

The manumission of slaves was practised already in the Classical period, especially in large urban centres such as Athens. Some of the enquiries of worshippers at the oracle of Zeus in Dodona in the late third and early second centuries BC were made by slaves anxious to learn whether they would be freed; manumission was, therefore, a realistic prospect, especially when a slave had some savings to pay the ransom for the manumission. But freedom could be a challenge. Only slaves with some training had the necessary perspective to stand on their own feet; many slaves must have hoped to continue working for their former masters, offering paid services. Freedmen were sometimes obliged to stay in the former master's household until his death and continue some services. For some slaves this obligation, called *paramone* (obligation to stay near), was a blessing. In one of the Dodona tablets, around 300 BC, a slave asks the god what he should do with regard to his manumission in order to have the right to stay with his master.

In central and northern Greece, manumissions often took the form of a dedication or a sale to a divinity. A manumission record from Physkos in central Greece in the second century BC is a characteristic example:

... Anthemo and Ophelion sold to Athena, the one who is in the city of the Physkeis, a slave boy, born in the household, who has the name Soterichos, for the price of three mnai, under the following conditions: Soterichos shall stay with Anthemo fulfilling Anthemo's orders as long as Anthemo lives. If he does not stay or does not fulfill her orders, then Anthemo or someone else, whoever is asked by Anthemo, shall have the power to punish Soterichos in whatever manner she wishes. But if Anthemo dies, then Soterichos shall be free.

Since freedmen were not granted citizenship and did not enjoy the legal protection connected with it, dedication to a god protected their new status. By becoming 'property' of a god, the former slaves were safe from seizure, since anyone attempting to enslave them would be seizing divine property. Manumissions, whether they were determined by the will of an owner or took the form of a transaction or of a dedication to a god, were recorded in documents and registered in the public archive. From the third century BC, it became increasingly common to inscribe manumission records in stone in sanctuaries. Thousands of manumission records survive from the late third century BC to the third century AD. The largest group from the Hellenistic period comprises around 1,250 manumissions in the sanctuary of Apollo in Delphi. One might argue that the number of manumissions did not increase from the late third century BC, but that only the habit of recording them in stone was new. But we have more evidence, such as gravestones and dedications of freedmen, showing that manumissions were more frequent in the late Hellenistic period than before. This may have been influenced by Roman manumission practices and the large supply of slaves. Manumissions continued to be common during the Imperial period.

Another important factor in the development of slavery in the Hellenistic period was the concentration of land in the hands of a small number of landowners. This trend reached a peak after the establishment of the Principate, when large estates were the most important assets of the elite. References to stewards (*oikonomoi*) who run the large estates, as well as honorific inscriptions set up by groups of slaves for the landowner, confirm their existence. Also, Roman senators and the emperor owned large estates in the eastern provinces, using slave labour for their exploitation.

The establishment of the Principate brought further changes. Slave markets continued to thrive in cities such as Ephesos, Sardis and Thyatteira. Not only landowners but also entrepreneurs employed agents (*pragmateutai*) who operated with a large amount of initiative and enjoyed substantial freedom of movement. The freedmen of Roman citizens and emperors acquired Roman citizenship and this opened the possibility of social advancement, if not for themselves then for their offspring. Many magistrates in Roman colonies were freedmen or the descendants of freedmen. Slaves now regularly appear among the members of cult associations.

Other categories of slaves that are more visible in the Imperial period are exposed children, found and raised in another family (*threptoi, trophimoi*), and sacred slaves (*hieroi, hierodouloi*). But not every *threptos* was a slave, and some 'sacred slaves' were free according to the secular law, designated as 'sacred' because they had been manumitted through dedication to a god. An entirely new category of slaves is formed by the gladiators. Although there were gladiators of free status, they were usually slaves and convicts. Groups of gladiators (*ludi*) were owned, trained and exploited by entrepreneurs, and sometimes by members of the elite, who organised gladiatorial shows in connection with the imperial cult.

The Imperial period seems to have increased the heterogeneity of slavery and the range of the activities of slaves. Public slaves served as guards, scribes and as personnel in archives; private slaves were employed in agricultural activities, manufacture and banking, in the household, and as the schoolteachers and supervisors of children. Female slaves served in the household as housemaids and wet nurses. Female dancers, musicians,

28. The grave monument of Timotheos, a former slave who became a slave merchant.

acrobats, mimic dancers and prostitutes, as well as a few female gladiators, were often of slave status. A Greek slave-trader in Rome, Marcus Sempronius Neikokrates, had a speciality commemorated on his epitaph: 'trader of beautiful women'.

In the Imperial period, there was no legal marriage between slaves or slaves and free individuals; the children of slaves were regarded as illegitimate. However, slaves who were employed in the household or in agriculture could have a family life and set up epitaphs that do not differ from those of the free. In some cases, we even see signs of affection between slaves and their masters. Freedmen could rise to wealth and power. But how did the experience of slavery affect the life of a freed slave? Caprilius Timotheos, a freedman from Amphipolis living around AD 100, chose to commemorate on his funerary monument not only that he was a freedman but also that he became a slave-trader himself (see Fig. 28). He visualised his occupation in two reliefs: marching captives in chains in the lower register show the source of his wealth; a scene in the upper register, showing the production of wine, suggests that these slaves, possibly captured in Thrace, were employed in viticulture in Macedonia. Is this an expression of Timotheos' pride and joy that he had escaped the fate of those to whom he owed his later wealth? Is it a kind of overcompensation for the humiliation he had suffered? This we do not know. What we do know is that in the rare cases in which the personal voices of slaves reach us, they present slavery as the worst human fate. A certain Menandros expresses this in the epigram he wrote for his brother Hyllos, a slave and schoolteacher in first-century-AD Ephesos: 'Fortune weeps for you, unbearable Necessity mourns for your status as a slave, which Fate has spun for you.' Neither philosophical discourses nor legislation made this fate any better.

15

FROM CIVIC WORSHIP
TO MEGATHEISM

Religions in a Cosmopolitan World

Global trends, individual experiences

In his metrical mime 'Women Celebrating Adonis', the poet Theocritus, born in Syracuse but living in Alexandria in the early third century BC, describes how two women from Syracuse experienced a festival in Alexandria. Gorgo invites her friend Praxinoa to join her on a visit to the palace for the celebration of the festival of Adonis:

'Let's go and see the Adonis in our rich King Ptolemy's palace. I'm told the Queen is giving a fine show.' – 'Everything's grand in grand houses.' – 'What you've seen you can talk about, when you've seen it and another hasn't.'

Fighting their way through the crowd, the two women get into the palace:

'Praxinoa, come here and look first at the tapestries, how fine they are and how lovely – fit for gods to wear, you would say.' – 'Lady Athena, what workers they must have been that made them, and what artists that drew the lines so true! The figures stand and turn so naturally they're alive not woven. What a clever thing is man! And look at him; how marvelous he is, lying in his silver chair with the first down spreading from the temples, thrice-loved Adonis, loved even in death.'

This mime, with all the exaggerations inherent in this genre, epitomises some central aspects of religious experience in the cosmopolitan world that emerged after Alexander's conquests. We notice the urban and 'international' character of worship: the protagonists of the mime are two women from Sicily; they attend the festival of a god of Oriental origin, a newcomer to Egypt. Praxinoa is fascinated by the illusion created by the images. Under the strong impression left by the decoration of the chair on which the image of the god appears, she uses the ritual acclamation 'thrice-loved Adonis' – an emotional expression of devotion. We recognise the importance of royal agency in this spectacular celebration. Finally, a festival is perceived as an aesthetic experience. The two women attended the festival as the audience of a staged spectacle about which they would be able to talk later. Such features more generally characterise religious experience in the Hellenistic world and, later, in the Roman Empire.

Processes of religious transformation sometimes require an examination across long periods of time, even if this unavoidably leaves little space for the study of local differences and short-term developments. From roughly the late fourth century BC to the mid-second century AD, the entirety of the Greek world was affected by the same trends, but to different degrees. One should be aware of regional differences: for example, in the Greek cities of the north shore of the Black Sea, religious practice involved the merging of Greek, Thracian, Scythian and Iranian gods, while the villagers of Anatolia continued to perform rituals originating in the Bronze Age and to worship local gods under a Greek guise.

Interspersed through this long period, there were significant turning points. In the first decades after the conquests of Alexander, as a result of the migration of Greek colonists to Egypt and the East, familiarity with foreign religions increased, new cults were established, the worship of living and dead kings arose and private cult associations became very common in urban centres. In the following phase, roughly from the celebration of the Ptolemaia in Alexandria shortly after 280 BC (see pp. 74–5) to the conquest of mainland Greece by the Romans in 146 BC, one observes how Greek cities reorganised and upgraded old festivals, founded new contests and promoted local cults that were important for the expression of identity and the acquisition of privileges. Many diplomatic missions for the recognition of the inviolability (*asylia*) of sanctuaries take place in this period, as do decrees concerning the more spectacular celebrations of traditional festivals. The main trends of the previous phases culminate in a third phase, from the establishment of Roman provincial administration in Greece to the beginning of Augustus' rule – that is, from 146 to 27 BC: the cult associations became an important venue of worship and the significance of mystery cults increased. Expressions of private devotion were far more common and elaborate than in previous periods. These trends continued under the conditions of peace and mobility in the fourth phase – the first two centuries of the Principate, from around 27 BC to the reign of Marcus Aurelius (AD 161–180). In addition to the imperial cult, which became one of the most important occasions for sacrifices and contests in cities and regions (see pp. 268–71), old local cults were revived and sumptuous celebrations organised. Local patriotism, competition between cities and the display of generosity by the elite enhanced this process. Mystery cults and cult associations offered expatriates, including soldiers, traders, freedmen and slaves, the possibility to belong to a community – a community of worshippers. The need for divine protection strengthened the attachment of individuals to cults beyond or in addition to the traditional cults of cities. The Jewish diaspora, very important already in the Hellenistic period but intensifying after the failed Jewish revolts in Judaea and Cyrenaica, contributed to an exchange between religious groups. Eschatological quests and the desire for a powerful and continual connection between mortals and the divine had been until this time satisfied by cults that required strong, almost exclusive, devotion to one god. In the first century AD, Christianity offered a new answer. The mobility of ideas in the Roman Empire facilitated the cross-fertilisation of religions, as wandering philosophers, 'holy men' and early Christian proselytisers became an important factor in this movement of ideas.

What is 'Hellenistic' about the religions of the 'long Hellenistic Age'?

One might argue that little changed in Greek religion in the centuries after Alexander the Great. The Greeks continued to worship their old gods. Admittedly, they added a few more, such as Sarapis and Mithras, but this can hardly be seen as a new phenomenon. They had often done so in the past. For instance, the cult of the Thracian Bendis was introduced to Athens in the late fifth century BC; Anatolian and Near Eastern gods such as Cybele and Adonis were worshipped even earlier. Greek gods continued to be assimilated, identified or jointly worshipped with foreign gods, as happened with Artemis and the Persian Anahita, Hermes and the Egyptian Thot, and Zeus and the Anatolian Sabazios. The form of worship remained unchanged, with processions, sacrifices, libations, the singing of hymns, the performance of prayers and the organisation of athletic and musical competitions. To be sure, new rituals were introduced under the influence of foreign religions. The lighting of lamps in the temples of traditional and new gods imitated an Egyptian practice. But such new rituals did not fundamentally change the character of worship. Oracles continued to give their ambiguous answers to frustrated enquirers. And while philosophers persisted in speculating on the nature of the divine, as they had been doing since the sixth century BC, men and women of all social strata went on practising magic, hoping in this way to protect themselves and to make the lives of their opponents miserable. Mortals continued to have uncertain knowledge as to what happens after death, compensating this ignorance with very elaborate and often contradictory imaginings of an afterlife, and basing their hopes for a pleasant life after death on initiation into mystery cults, as they had done for centuries. Myths, sanctuaries and cults had always been the objects of political and diplomatic exploitation, and this did not change after Alexander's conquests. In the Hellenistic period, mortals, kings and benefactors were worshipped as gods, sometimes after their death but also during their lifetime; after 196 BC, they were joined by Roman generals and later by the Roman emperors. The attribution of divine honours to mortals is not a Hellenistic innovation. So, is there anything essentially new about religion and cult from the late fourth century BC to the mid-second century AD other than the many new festivals and a few divine newcomers? In order to answer this question, we need to consider something more abstract: the zeitgeist, or spirit of the times. How do religious practices and conceptions from the late fourth century BC onwards correspond to the general contemporary mentality?

One way to approach the zeitgeist of the Hellenistic period and the early Principate is through the study of a specific vocabulary: that is, of expressions often used in contemporary documents. Every historical period has its own buzzwords that reflect contemporary concerns and priorities – in our day, for instance, 'sustainability', 'transparency', 'social networks' and so on. We can recognise such words in the period under discussion in public documents, especially decrees of the assembly and works of contemporary historians. Words that appear either for the first time or with greater frequency than before give us significant clues about the values and concerns of the intellectual and political elite that influenced discourses, revived old customs, introduced new practices, set priorities and responded to demands.

Several words and expressions reflect the contemporary religious mentality. *Spoudé* (eagerness) and *zelos* (emulation of glory) express a trend towards intense and visible displays of piety. *Epauxanein* (to increase, to enlarge) corresponds to quantitative changes in celebrations: almost nothing was new in religion after the fourth century BC, but everything was bigger than ever before. The formulation 'so that it becomes visible to everyone that a community shows gratitude', a phrase that concludes honorific decrees, reflects the trend towards the theatrical display of feelings. The word *paradoxon* reveals the careful registration of contrasts and a fascination with the opposition between expectation and sudden change, between hope and the stroke of fate. Finally, laudatory epithets used in acclamations and in eulogies of gods express attitudes towards the divine. The epithets *epekoos* (the one who listens to prayers), *soter* (rescuer), *megas* (great) and *heis* (genitive: *henos*, one, singular) reflect the desire of mortals to receive divine protection from dangers and to establish a personal connection with one god. The modern terms 'soteriology', 'henotheism' and 'megatheism', referring to the strong personal devotion to one god and the popularity of divinities and cults that promised safety in this world and salvation in the next, derive from these epithets (see p. 365).

A second method to approach 'Hellenistic' traits in religion is to consider the factors that shaped the world in this period and consequently influenced religion and religious feeling. First kingship and then the establishment of imperial power had a visible impact on religious practices. In addition to the ruler cult and the cult of the emperor (see pp. 108–15 and 268–71), the institution of monarchy influenced religious worship through its interest in the display of luxury. The festivals that were celebrated in the royal capitals became trendsetters. The kings served as religious agents in various ways. They promoted cults that were connected with their houses – Ptolemy I, for example, promoted the cult of Sarapis.

They favoured sanctuaries with their patronage and gifts, competing to display their power in traditional sanctuaries such as Delphi and Delos. They actively intervened in religious matters – for instance, the translation of the Torah from Hebrew to Greek was made possible through the sponsorship of Ptolemy II. Finally, their soldiers transferred the religious traditions of their homelands to their places of service.

Second, the creation of large multi-ethnic kingdoms and the unification of the eastern Mediterranean and the Near East under Roman rule increased the mobility of populations, thus contributing to the dissemination of religious ideas and cult practices. The participation of foreigners and foreign residents in the public cults of cities became more common, and the activities of private cult associations increased religious diversity. Religious mobility was also enhanced through the intensive diplomatic contacts between cities, federations, kings and the Roman authorities. War was another factor of paramount importance, not only because it contributed to mobility but also because it strengthened the belief that humans' safety and well-being depended on their successful communication and good relations with the gods.

In the cities, further factors that had an impact on religion included the increased visibility and power of women; the agency of men of strong faith in religious innovation (along with a few such women); the support offered to cults and sanctuaries by benefactors; and the contribution of the elite to the development of religion – by establishing new cults, organising spectacular celebrations and reviving old rites and introducing new ones.

Festivals

The geographer Strabo, writing in the first century BC but drawing on an earlier source, claims that in Taras the state festivals were more numerous than the working days. A similar claim about Athens is made by the Hellenistic traveller Herakleides. What a visitor to the city would encounter in the third century BC would be 'festivals of all sorts; intellectual enjoyment and recreation through all sorts of philosophers; many opportunities for leisure; spectacles without interruption' (see p. 123). Although such claims cannot be taken at face value, celebrations were a more frequent phenomenon in Hellenistic and later cities than in earlier periods. In Kos, a calendar of celebrations held in the local gymnasium around 150 BC lists eight civic sacrifices and festivals, in the month of Artamitios alone, in which the participation of the young men of the gymnasium was mandatory: the festival of Poseidon on the 4th, a procession for King Eumenes II on the 6th, the festival of Apollo and processions to the sanctuaries of Apollo Kyparissios and the Twelve Gods on the 7th, the festival of Zeus Soter, endowed by Pythokles, on the 10th, a sacrifice for Dionysus on the 12th, a procession to the sanctuary of Apollo Delios on the 15th, a procession in honour of the Muses on the 19th and a procession for King Attalos II on the 26th. Three of these processions had been added in the Hellenistic period: two to honour Hellenistic kings and one sponsored by a benefactor. The number of celebrations continually increased, especially after the mid-second century BC. More than 500 agonistic festivals – festivals combined with athletic and/or musical contests – were celebrated in Greece and Asia Minor in the second century AD.

Many factors contributed to the explosion of a festival culture. The new cities had to establish their own festivals; political events, usually military victories, led to the creation of new festivals; the members of the local elites used the celebration of festivals as one of the arenas of competition among themselves, making donations for more luxurious celebrations, establishing foundations, revitalising old traditions or serving as officials responsible for festivals and contests. In addition to the new public festivals, there emerged a novel phenomenon almost unknown in pre-Hellenistic Greece: the foundation of privately sponsored festivals, often in commemoration of deceased members of elite families. A new form of celebration was the ritualised reception of kings, foreign envoys, Roman magistrates and, later, emperors and their family members in cities. Institutionalised theatrical contests, a rarity in the Classical period, were a common phenomenon in the Hellenistic period, attested in almost every city that had a considerable number of inhabitants. Finally, another significant factor was the diffusion of gymnasia. These were not only places of military and athletic training and education; they were also places of regular competitions and celebrations.

Ancient sources usually refer to a festival with the paraphrase 'procession, sacrifice and contest' (*pompe kai thysia kai agon*), thereby highlighting three important components of religious celebrations: the sacrifice was the most important cultic element; the athletic and musical competitions constituted the most spectacular part of the festival; the procession required the active participation of large numbers of citizens and non-citizens and thus could easily be subject to detailed 'staging directions'. An inscription from Mallos (Antioch on Pyramos) in Cilicia exemplifies the combination of tradition and innovation evident in the new festivals. In the mid-second century BC, a festival was established in this city to honour the personification of Concord (Homonoia) and to commemorate the end of a conflict with Tarsos (Antioch on Kydnos). An altar was dedicated to Homonoia and

> on the day on which the altar will be founded, a procession shall be held, as beautiful and glamorous as possible, from the altar of the council to the sanctuary of Athena. The procession will be led by the *demiourgos* [chief magistrate] and the *prytaneis* [councillors]. They will offer a sacrifice of a cow with gilded horns to Athena and to Homonoia. The priests, all the other magistrates, the winners of the games, the supervisor of the gymnasium with all the ephebes and the young men, and the supervisor of the children with all the children shall participate in the procession. This day will be a holiday; all the citizens shall wear garlands; all shall be released from work; the slaves shall be released from chains ...

The officials were invited to employ taste, imagination and money, or to copy models observed in other festivals, in order to make the celebration 'as beautiful and glamorous as possible'. Three main aspects emerge from contemporary discourse around festivals and processions: size, aesthetics and political overtones.

The increase in the size of festivals – duration, expenses and number of participants – is the most immediately striking trend. The festivals organised by the kings created new standards. As festivals were an important aspect of monarchical self-representation, they were planned and performed in a sumptuous way in order to have a great effect and demonstrate power. This was imitated on a smaller scale by the cities, and even by private persons. The organisers of civic festivals could not compete with royal celebrations such as the Ptolemaia of Alexandria (c. 274 BC; see pp. 74–5), but they did try to surpass their predecessors and other cities. Cities upgraded their contests and the prizes given to victorious athletes. Measures were taken to increase the number of participants, priests, magistrates, victors, ephebes, citizens and foreign residents. Size mattered. What also mattered was beauty and good order.

Processions have always been the subject of careful staging, because they reflect social and political structures, but also because aesthetics was one of the strategies employed by mortals to attract the interest of the gods. From the mid-fourth century BC onwards, we observe heightened attention given to aesthetics and stage directions. Sacred regulations not only elaborate on questions of religious rites, but also concern themselves with exact staging directions for the active participants, as well as with the preparation, arrangement, decoration and performance of the procession: the cleaning of processional roads, the purchase of implements and objects carried during the procession, the dress of the magistrates and the popula-tion, the sequence of the sacrificial animals according to their beauty, the participation of horsemen, the musical accompaniment and the arrange-ment of the participants into groups according to tribes, age groups, hierarchy, prestige or duties. A cult regulation concerning a mystery cult in Andania, near Messene, in the early first century AD does not reveal anything about the initiation rituals but provides plenty of informa-tion on a spectacular procession that started in Messene and arrived at the sanctuary of the Great Gods in Andania probably three hours later. Mnasistratos, the man responsible for the reorganisation of the cult, led the procession and was followed by the sacred officials, flute players, the 'sacred girls' who accompanied the wagons on which the sacred objects of the mysteries were carried, the woman who organised the banquet for Demeter and her assistants, the 'sacred women' who impersonated god-desses, the 'sacred men' and the sacrificial animals. Great attention was given to solemnity, decency and order. The regulations stipulated the exact garments to be worn by the functionaries and the worshippers: wreaths for the 'sacred men', white hats and long robes for the 'sacred women', a tiara for the 'chief initiates' at the beginning of the initiation and a laurel wreath at the end, white robes and bare feet for the initiates. The female initiates were not allowed to wear transparent clothes, clothes with wide borders, jewels, extravagant coiffures or make-up. Decrees in honour of individu-als responsible for the successful organisation of festivals place the beauty of the processions in the foreground. A decree from the Macedonian city Kalindoia in AD 1 honours a local benefactor for organising a procession that was 'artful/colourful' and 'worth seeing'. The responsible magistrates were honoured because they had offered a pleasing and beautiful spectacle.

Several historical and cultural factors determined such a strong inter-est in the aesthetic aspects of the worship of the gods. The ubiquity of elaborate theatrical performances increased the interest in the staging of celebrations. As the possibilities for travel grew, information concerning innovative and spectacular celebrations was disseminated, motivating one cult community to emulate or surpass what another had offered. A festival in one city could easily become the talk of the town in another. But there was also an additional factor at play: the desire to experience the presence of the divine. The words *enargeia* (vividness) and *enarges* (vivid), which in rhetoric and literature refer to the skill of an orator or an author to make the audience feel they are witnessing what is described in words, are very often used in religious contexts. They refer to manifestations of divine power that had a strong emotional impact on the individuals or groups present. The staging of celebrations was one of the ways used in order to make divine power 'more vividly manifest' (*enargestera*), in order to maintain the illusion of the presence of the god and to arouse the appropriate emotions.

Another reason why festivals were so important throughout this era was for the political advantages that they offered. They provided a *polis* the opportunity to undertake a diplomatic mission, to attract visitors, to demonstrate loyalty towards a king or emperor, to organise a fair, to represent itself, to transmit traditions to the youth, to strengthen its cohesion and to distract the attention of the poor from their problems.

Because of the fear of war and raids, cities were very keen on having their inviolability from raids (*asylia*) recognised by other communities. Very often, the dispatch of envoys to cities, federations and kings with the request of *asylia* coincided with the reorganisation of a festival and the invitation to other Greek communities to participate. Kos requested the *asylia* of the sanctuary of Asclepius in 242 BC, and Tenos that of the sanctuary of Poseidon and Amphitrite, as well as the entire island, around the same time; these were followed by Magnesia, which declared the whole of its territory inviolable when it upgraded the festival of Artemis Leukophryene in 208 BC, and Teos, which dedicated its territory to Dionysus in 203 BC. The embassies sent by Kos, Magnesia and Teos to the entire Greek world are the best-documented diplomatic enterprises that we know from Greek antiquity. The declarations of *asylia* became so common – and a cause of problems, as criminals exploited the *asylia* of sanctuaries to escape punishment – that in AD 22 the Roman senate re-examined, case by case, all claims to inviolability and ended up rejecting most of them.

All the festivals that were founded in the Hellenistic period, and many of the new festivals of the Imperial period, had a political and secular background. They were founded in order to commemorate a recent political event – such as victory in a war, the removal of a foreign garrison or the restoration of freedom and democracy – to honour a king or an emperor, or to commemorate a benefactor. In such festivals, religious rituals were embedded in an explicit political context. When the Athenians celebrated the Panathenaia from the sixth century BC onwards, they honoured Athena; when the Aitolians introduced the Soteria in the third century BC, they honoured Apollo Pythios and Zeus Soter. But the Athenians commemorated the victory of Athena over Poseidon, whereas the Aitolians celebrated *their* victory over the Gauls. Not to take note of the difference would be to ignore the secular function that was assigned to the new festival by the agents who created it.

A good example of the political functions of festivals is provided by a decree that concerns one of the oldest Athenian festivals: the Thargelia. The predominant rituals of this celebration were the offering of first fruits to Apollo Patroos, the patron of the ancestors, and a scapegoat ritual. When it was reorganised in 129/128 BC, it became a patriotic festival that highlighted the achievements of the forefathers. The man who drafted the decree explains:

> It is a norm of the forefathers and a custom of the Athenian demos and an ancestral tradition to show the greatest care for piety towards the gods. It is for this reason that the Athenians have achieved the fame and the praise of the most glorious deeds both on land and at sea through many campaigns on land and on board of ships, always beginning all their activities with a homage to Zeus Soter and with the worship of the gods. There also exists Apollo Pythios, who is an ancestral god of the Athenians and an interpreter of good things, at the same time a savior of all the Greeks, the son of Zeus and Leto.

Measures were taken to 'increase the sacrifices and the honours in a beautiful and pious manner'. This text combines the main aspects that characterise Hellenistic festivals: augmentation, beauty and political overtones.

Shifting popularities of the old gods

A puzzling story is narrated by Plutarch in his work 'On the Obsoles-
cence of Oracles'. As a certain Thamos was sailing past the small island
of Paxoi on his way to Italy during the reign of Tiberius (AD 14–37), he
heard a voice urging him to proclaim the news: 'Pan is dead!' Ancient gods
did sometimes die, but they died with a purpose: they were periodically
reborn, representing the annual cycle of nature – this is believed to be the
case with the Cretan Zeus; or their death and return to divine life became
the foundation of a mystery cult, as in the case of Dionysus and Osiris; or
it was part of a special arrangement – the Dioskouroi, inseparable siblings,
spent every other day in the underworld; or the death was re-enacted every
year in the context of rituals, as in the case of Adonis. Greek gods did not
die qua gods, at least not until the spread of Christianity – and according
to an early episode of *Star Trek*, they only retreated to Pollux IV, unable to
maintain their power without mortals' love.

It is not clear what we are to make of Pan's alleged death. But it is certain
that the cults of individual gods had their ups and downs. Time and again,
inscriptions mention the fact that a certain cult had to be restored at the
initiative of a pious worshipper, priest or magistrate. Sometimes the reason
was simply the lack of funds for the continuation of worship. In some Hellenistic cities, priesthoods were offered at public auction, to ensure the
constant presence of a citizen who would oversee the regular performance
of the rites and take care of the sacred places. Sometimes the worship of
a particular god declined as the popularity of another divinity increased.
The constellation of gods worshipped in any given Greek city – we usually
call this the 'pantheon' of a *polis* – continually changed.

Admittedly, the worship of certain gods remained unaffected by such
shifts. The first position among them was taken by the almighty Zeus, followed by Athena, the defender of citadels, and Demeter, the goddess of
fertility, whose secret rites were annually celebrated by women all over the
Greek world. Other key divinities included Dionysus, not only the god of
the theatre but also a god associated with orgiastic rites and the guarantor
of a blessed afterlife to those who were initiated into his mysteries; Apollo,
god of music, oracles, purity and healing; the huntress Artemis, protector
of women, especially during childbirth; Aphrodite, goddess of love, also
worshipped as patron of magistrates; Hermes, the patron of journeys and
transactions; and Hestia, the protector of a city's public hearth. From the

29. The grave relief of Kotys, a 'new hero', decorated with an image of the Thracian Rider.

fifth century BC, Asclepius, the god of healing – originally worshipped in only a few places – became one of the most popular divinities. Although Heracles was not one of the traditional Olympians, he was the god invoked by many people in times of need.

Even prior to Alexander's conquests, the contacts of the Greeks with foreign religions resulted in the assimilation of foreign gods with their Greek counterparts, as well as the introduction of gods worshipped under foreign or Greek names: the Thracian huntress Bendis, the Anatolian Great Mother Cybele, the Near Eastern god Adonis, the Egyptian Amun and Isis, and others. The introduction of cults from Asia and North Africa intensified, of course, after the campaigns of Alexander; moreover, the Roman conquest of Greece and the foundation of Roman colonies brought several Italian gods to the Balkans, Asia Minor and the Near East. These included the Capitoline triad – Jupiter, Juno and Minerva, assimilated with Zeus, Hera and Athena respectively – and the patron of the woods, Silvanus.

In many places, the most important divinities were local gods of very ancient origin, such as Diktynna and Britomartis in Crete, or those traditionally associated with a city, such as the Nemeseis in Smyrna. The non-Greek populations in the northern Balkans and Asia continued to worship their traditional indigenous gods. Sometimes we get written evidence about these deities only after the literacy levels of the indigenous populations had risen along with the diffusion of the Greek language as lingua franca. As the number of dedications written in Greek increased, the names of the deities that had been worshipped for centuries but had left little if any trace of their popularity are now mentioned, often as assimilated with Greek gods. For instance, a popular deity in Thrace was the so-called 'Thracian Rider', usually associated with Apollo and Asclepius and represented as a young horseman approaching an altar and a tree with a snake coiling around its trunk (see Fig. 29). He was worshipped as a 'hero', a rescuing god (*soter*) and a god who listens to prayers (*epekoos*).

The popularity of gods is often indicated by the laudatory epithets with which they were invoked in prayers and acclamations. Such epithets display affection, devotion and the belief that the gods respond to human needs and requests. 'Rescuer' – *soter* for gods, *soteira* for goddesses – is one of the most common among them, also used for a number of Hellenistic kings and deified mortals. A god who was invoked and praised as *soter* was expected to offer protection in all sorts of life-threatening situations: disease, earthquakes, bad weather, crime and war. Gods such as Zeus, his warrior daughter Athena, worshipped as Polias (patron of the citadel) and Nikephoros (the bearer of victory), Artemis, the Dioskouroi, protectors of sailors and soldiers, and Heracles, associated with fair victory (Kallinikos), owed their popularity to their status as patrons of war. But soldiers and the defenders of cities could invoke the protective power of most gods, from Pan, the god of panic, and Ares, the traditional god of war, to Aphrodite Stratia, the leader of armies, Hermes, the defender of city gates (*propylaios*) and Hekate, the goddess of crossroads, magic and the night. In the Imperial period, this protective function was also attributed to the Roman emperor.

In the time of the empire, under the conditions of relative peace that prevailed in most parts of the Greek world, the protection sought by individual worshippers and communities involved relief from other problems: food shortages, fiscal problems, the deterioration of cityscapes, brigandage and, above all, illness. This explains the popularity of Apollo, his son

Asclepius and his sister Artemis. But a whole host of old and new gods served similar functions: mother goddesses such as the Mother of the Gods (Meter Theon), an old Anatolian deity assimilated with Leto (the mother of Apollo and Artemis), the new healing god Glykon New Asclepius (see pp. 379–82) and other deities of diverse origins whose cults spread through the extensive networks of contacts and mobility. The worship of Egyptian gods, the cult of Theos Hypsistos, Oriental and mystery cults, and Christianity are worthy of special mention here.

Egyptian and Egyptianising cults

The Greeks were acquainted with Egyptian cults long before Alexander conquered Egypt. Amun, identified with Zeus, was worshipped as early as the fifth century BC, and Egyptian immigrants and traders had brought the cult of the great moon goddess Isis, the sister and wife of Osiris, to Athens by the fourth century BC. But this cult transfer cannot be compared with the massive diffusion of Egyptian cults from the third century BC onwards, and especially after the Roman conquest. Isis, Osiris and Sarapis were worshipped alone or together with other divine beings with Egyptian names and unfamiliar forms of representation: the jackal-faced Anubis and the child god Harpokrates.

With royal support, Sarapis' cult was widely diffused in areas that were under the influence of the Ptolemies. It most likely originated in Egypt's traditional capital, Memphis, where Apis, a sacred bull, was venerated. After his death, the bull was identified with Osiris as Oserapis. Ptolemy I promoted a version of this god under the name Sarapis or Serapis, presumably in order to give his vast and multicultural kingdom some coherence through shared worship; thus the Greek settlers in Egypt could worship a local god that did not seem entirely unfamiliar and barbaric. The god's image (see Fig. 30), an artificial mélange of heterogeneous elements, combined features of Zeus, the healing god Asclepius and Plouton, the god of the underworld. Sarapis became a patron of divination, healing, fertility and the afterlife. Facilitated by the mobility of Ptolemaic soldiers, administrators and envoys, the cult spread first in the Ptolemaic possessions and the areas where the Ptolemies exercised political influence – in the Aegean islands and Asia Minor – and then around the entire Mediterranean. Amulets, statues and statuettes, inscriptions and personal names

30. Statue of Sarapis.

(Sarapion, Serapas, Serapammon, etc.) attest to Sarapis' popularity into late antiquity. In Delos, the cult first had to overcome the resistance of the priests of the traditional cult of Apollo. When it did, this was interpreted by Sarapis' priests as the god's miracle, further contributing to the cult's appeal to worshippers. The narration of miracles was an essential part of Sarapis' worship. There were regional differences in the worship of Sarapis. For instance, it was only in his principal sanctuary at Memphis that his devotees spent large periods of time in seclusion (*enkatochoi*).

The cult of Isis (see Fig. 31) originated in Egyptian myths and rites but was enriched with additional elements. An important aspect of her cult was the celebration of mysteries, which promised the initiates that they would receive her favour in this world and a blessed destiny in the next. According to an Egyptian myth, Osiris was killed by the god of the desert, Seth, and dismembered. Isis succeeded in collecting the parts of her brother's mutilated body. After bringing him back to life, she took him as her husband, giving birth to their son Horus. This myth of death, rebirth and

31. Votive relief from Dion with representation of Isis with sceptre and ear corns.

eternal life offered consolation to the initiates, encouraged them to seek an afterlife in Osiris' realm and gave them hope to face the adversities of life. The sacred ceremonies included dramatic representations of Isis' suffering performed by cult personnel. A relief in Thessalonike shows a priest impersonating the god Anubis (see Fig. 32). Under the strong emotional impression left by such cultic dramas, the initiates performed a ritual that insinuated their own death and rebirth. Because of the importance of the water of the Nile in Egyptian rituals, miniature 'Niles' were recreated in the sanctuaries of the Egyptian gods, whether in Dion in Macedonia or in Tivoli near Rome, symbolically bringing initiates to the birthplace of Osiris and strengthening the illusion of close connection with the Egyptian god. In the Imperial period Isis was celebrated as a patron of seafaring. A festival of Isis marked the beginning of the seafaring season on 5 March.

The worship of Isis required a higher level of devotion and emotional attachment than the traditional public cults. Religious texts, hymns, narratives of miracles and accounts of Isis' powers, the so-called 'aretalogies',

*32. Funerary relief from Thessalonike with the representation
of a priest impersonating Anoubis.*

contributed to the construction of her profile as a powerful and caring
goddess. One such aretalogy, allegedly the copy of an inscription in an
Egyptian temple, was reproduced in several of her sanctuaries. It presents
the goddess as speaking herself ('I am Isis') and revealing her powers. Such
texts filled the communities of worshippers with the hope of salvation.
The aretalogies were probably recited by priestesses impersonating the
goddess. A few passages from a copy of the inscription set up in Kyme in
the first century BC give us an impression of the impact this divine self-
revelation might have had on worshippers:

> I am Isis, the ruler of the whole land ... I am she who invented crops for
> humans ... I divided earth from heaven. I appointed the paths of the
> stars. I regulated the passage of sun and moon. I invented fishing and
> seafaring. I made justice strong. I coupled woman and man ... I ended
> the rule of tyrants. I ended murders. I forced women to be loved by

men. I made justice stronger than gold and silver ... I am mistress of war. I am mistress of the thunderbolt. I calm and agitate the sea. I am in the rays of the sun. I accompany the passage of the sun. Whatever I decide is actually accomplished.

Isis' qualities were so diverse that she could easily be assimilated with other goddesses: with Artemis Lochia, as patron of childbirth; with Demeter, as protector of agriculture; with the moon goddess Hekate; with Aphrodite and innumerable other Greek and Oriental goddesses. The elevation of Isis above other divine beings and her connection with initiation into a mystery cult are significant religious developments of the late Hellenistic and Imperial periods.

Mithras

Although very different in content, the cult of Mithras, the Iranian god of light, had similarities with other mystery cults in the staging of ceremonies, the existence of seven different grades of initiation and the expectations held by the initiates. This cult was already important in the Hellenistic kingdoms with Iranian populations, especially Pontos and Kommagene. But around the first century BC, in unclear circumstances, it was transformed into a mystery cult with questionable, if any, affinities to its Iranian origins. The initiates met in underground temples with artificial caverns (*speleum*, *antrum*), where they celebrated feasts. Although almost nothing is known about the cult's sacred texts, the iconography of Mithras gives some clues about his properties as a victorious god who protects life. He is usually represented as being born from a rock or in the act of killing a bull, accompanied by two torch-bearers; he may also be seen sharing a meal with the sun god, or ascending to the heavens in a chariot. In scenes where Mithras kills the bull, a scorpion seizes the animal's genitals, and a dog and a snake reach up towards the blood; ears of wheat sprout from the bull's tail or his wound (see Fig. 33). It seems that only men were admitted into these mysteries, and usually those of low standing – mainly soldiers, but also considerable numbers of freedmen and merchants. Until the late second century AD, the cult was not widely spread in the Greek-speaking provinces, except for those where the Roman army had a strong presence, especially Syria.

Because of the coherent iconography and the widely attested

33. A Mithras relief from Dura-Europos.

designations of seven grades of initiation (possibly connected with the planets), it is possible to argue that despite local variations there may have been some homogeneity in the myths, rituals and religious ideas connected with this cult. But we know nothing about the man or men who formulated its founding principles, shaped its standard mythical narratives, wrote the scriptures that were used in the ceremonies, invented the ordeals required of the initiates and developed the models for the scenes that were copied innumerable times in Mithraea as the cult spread throughout the empire. A gradual evolution cannot be excluded, but it is more likely that the Mithraic mysteries, in the form in which they spread in the Roman Empire, were the work of a religious reformer who remains anonymous – a man like Alexander of Abonou Teichos, who founded the cult of Glykon, or Paul, who significantly shaped Christianity.

The Highest God, Jewish influences and monotheistic trends

The idea that there is one single divine being known under many names is found in the work of Greek intellectuals as early as the fifth century BC. An almighty god could easily be accommodated in a tolerant polytheistic system; the worship of one supreme divine being could coexist with the worship of other gods; and sometimes, two or even three originally separate gods could be merged into one – for instance, Zeus Helios Serapis was regarded as one single and singular god. A particular expression of this trend towards the worship of one god within a polytheistic system was the cult of Theos Hypsistos. His epithet is ambiguous. It literally means the 'highest god', but it can also mean the 'god of the heights' and 'the god who is exalted'. The epithet Hypsistos was often used for Zeus, already before the Hellenistic period, but in the Imperial period it was attributed to one anonymous god, who was simply called Theos, 'god'. In areas where Jewish communities existed – in Greece, Asia Minor and the Black Sea region – the cult of Theos Hypsistos was influenced by Judaism. In the area of the Bosporan kingdom, Theos Hypsistos was often the name under which the Jews worshipped their god in prayer houses. The worshippers of Theos Hypsistos (Hypsistarii, Hypsistiani) are sometimes designated as *theosebeis* (god-fearers); at least some of the god-fearers were Gentiles who attended the Jewish synagogue.

It is doubtful that all references to Theos Hypsistos refer to one single god with a homogeneous theology, but it is certain that the cult was already significantly diffused in the first two centuries AD. An oracle of Apollo Klarios may be a reference to this god:

> Born of itself, untaught, without a mother, unshakeable, not contained in a name, known by many names, dwelling in fire, this is god. We, his angels, are a small part of god. To you who ask this question about god, what his essential nature is, he has pronounced that aether is god who sees all. To him you should pray at dawn, gazing on him and looking towards the sunrise.

This oracle allowed for the traditional gods to be integrated, as angels, into this worship of the one god. Also quoted by Christian authors, the oracle had an impact on worship in Asia Minor and beyond.

The conception of the divine revealed by this oracle has sometimes been associated with early, pagan monotheism, but the term monotheism – which implies the exclusive worship of one single god – is inadequate to describe the religious phenomena of this period, with the exception of Judaism and Christianity. Non-Jews and non-Christians could be devoted to one deity without denying the existence of other gods. Believers of this sort tended to assimilate gods of different origin and to regard them as different hypostases of one single divinity; acclamations in praise of such gods use the word *heis* (genitive: *henos*), hence the term henotheism: that is, the assimilation of different gods and the attribution of supreme divine properties to them. *Heis* was also used in the sense of singular (not 'single'). But in many cases, the devotees of a specific god only recognised their preference and acknowledged their deity's great power by using the attribute *megas* (for gods) and *megale* (for goddesses): 'great' (or, in the superlative, *megistos*). Any god could be acclaimed as 'great' by an individual who had experienced his power, but Zeus, Apollo and Artemis among the Olympians, and Serapis and Mes among the gods of foreign origin were most commonly addressed with this epithet expressing particular devotion. The presence of the gods was connected with their efficacy, which is what the epithet *megas* expressed. The acclamation *megas theos* (god is great) or *megas* followed by the name of a god (— is great) is found in hundreds of inscriptions, amulets and literary texts, reflecting the contemporary trend to show devotion to those gods who had visibly demonstrated their power. Because of this use of *megas*, megatheism has been suggested as the term for this affective, almost exclusive worship.

The physical presence of a god (*parousia, epiphaneia*), the power revealed by the efficacy of his intervention (*arete, dynamis*) and his willingness to listen to prayers (*epekoos*) constitute a triad of interconnected capacities that played a significant part in religiosity. References to divine epiphanies reflect the same longing for the presence of the gods. Divine epithets such as *epidemos* (the one who is present) and *epiphanestatos* (the one whose power is most visible) insinuated the tangible, continuous and effectual presence of the gods in the world of mortals. Narratives of miracles provided the evidence for divine power.

An age of miracles

Evidence for the manifestation of divine power or *arete* was provided by inscriptions that recorded miracles, both healing or rescuing and punitive. The collections of healing miracles set up in sanctuaries of Asclepius in Epidaurus, Lebena on Crete, Kos and Rome illustrate the experience of pilgrims in these sanctuaries. After the performance of rituals, the worshippers slept in a dormitory or incubation room next to the temple, expecting to see the god in a dream and be cured. The largest collection, that from Epidaurus, contains healing narratives that defy rational explanations: 'A man had a stone in his penis. He saw a dream. It seemed that he was having sex with a beautiful boy and as he had an orgasm in his sleep, he ejected the stone, and picking it up, he departed with it in his hands.' Some of those who practised incubation – that is, spending the night in a sanctuary and expecting the god to appear in a dream and give advice or cure – did believe that they were cured. The incubation did not remove the disease but it changed its subjective perception by the patient. Some patients were *malades imaginaires*, hypochondriacs. Being in the sacred space and listening to the narratives about miracles, they were prepared to believe that the god had blessed them too. If he had performed so many and such incredible cures, how could he not cure them? Other patients continued to suffer but could not admit it. That the god had ignored them might be regarded as the consequence of sin. Consequently, some patients must have claimed that their pain was gone in order to save face. Patients whose illness was of a psychosomatic origin found relief through autosuggestion. Finally, many cures occurred naturally, without the intervention of a doctor. A certain Artemisia in Ephesos was cross-eyed in her left eye due to the temporary paralysis of a nerve, as one can recognise on the votive tablet that shows her sick eye (see Fig. 34). When Artemisia's affliction suddenly disappeared and she could again see properly, she attributed the cure to the god to whom she had prayed. Thanks to such undeniable cures, few as they may have been, the inscribed collections of miracles became credible and aroused hope. For those who might still have doubts or might attempt to cheat the god and not offer the obligatory dedication, stories such as the following served as a warning:

> A man who was paralyzed in all his fingers except one came as a suppliant to the god. When he was looking at the plaques in the sanctuary, he didn't believe in the cures and was somewhat disparaging of the inscriptions. Sleeping in the shrine, he saw a vision. It seemed he was playing the knucklebones below the temple, and as he was about to

34. The anatomical votive of Artemisia who suffered from an eye disease.

throw them, the god appeared, sprang on his hand and stretched out his fingers one by one. When he had straightened them all, the god asked him if he would still not believe the inscriptions on the plaques around the sanctuary, and he answered no. 'Therefore, since you doubted them before, though they were not unbelievable, from now on,' he said, 'your name shall be "Unbeliever".' When day came, he left well.

Texts reflecting the same religious mentality and the belief in communication between mortals and gods are continually found in the Greek and Roman East. A very important group consists of records of divine power, both healing and punishing, found in sanctuaries in Asia Minor from the first to the third century AD. They owe the somewhat inaccurate designation 'confession inscriptions' to the fact that some of those who set them up confess their own transgressions or describe the sins of ancestors or relatives. Sometimes the gods appeared in dreams giving instructions or offering help, but often the communication of their will required agents: priests and oracles. An inscription from Silandos dating to AD 235 illustrates this. Theodoros, a sacred slave at Silandos, had repeatedly violated the obligation of sexual abstinence and had even committed adultery. When his sight was afflicted, he went to the sanctuary. Kept in custody there, he received instructions concerning the rituals through which he could propitiate Mes, the Iranian moon god who had punished him. The inscription does not give a continuous narrative of the events, but presents Theodoros' confessions, followed by divine utterances and ritual instructions:

> I have been brought to my senses by the gods, by Zeus and the Great Mes Artemidorou ... I had sexual intercourse with Trophime, the slave of Haplokomas, the wife of Eutychis, in the *praetorium* ... While I was a slave of the gods of Nonnos, I had sexual intercourse with the flutist Ariagne ... I had sexual intercourse with the flautist Aretousa.

The gods' declarations and the instructions to remove the sins by transferring them to triads of animals (see p. 399) were probably given by priests who impersonated the gods. Theodoros was fortunate; he claims: 'I had Zeus as my advocate [*parakletos*].' Interestingly, here he uses the same word and concept as the author of the First Epistle of John, who asserts that 'if anyone does sin, we have an advocate [*parakletos*] with the Father, Jesus Christ the righteous.' With Zeus' advocacy, the council of the gods in a heavenly court entreated Mes to forgive Theodoros. Finally, Mes restored Theodoros' sight.

The epigraphic culture of the Hellenistic and Imperial periods did not create the expectation of divine protection and the fear of divine justice, but it certainly enhanced them. It is this dynamic exchange between display and feeling that brought changes in religiosity. Increased mobility made the circulation of ideas and stories possible, facilitated the introduction of new cults and increased the impact of trendsetters.

Whoever came to a sanctuary ready to believe the narratives of miracles demonstrated that he trusted the power of a god; by showing piety, he earned the god's attention. Narratives of divine power constructed the image of a mighty god willing to understand, to assist, to be present. The popularity of certain gods in the Hellenistic and Imperial periods was closely connected with this image, which also characterises the Christian God and his son on earth. Gods who mattered were those 'who listened to prayers', gods with whom worshippers could establish direct communication.

Lend me your ears: personal communication with the divine

Religious worship is dominated by the three feelings of fear, hope and gratitude: fear of punishment for transgressions, hope for assistance in times of need, gratitude for manifestations of divine help. These feelings are enhanced by the belief that gods and mortals can communicate with each other. The desire to receive divine protection was not felt for the first time by people in the Hellenistic period; it was as old as Greek religion. What was truly new after Alexander's campaigns was the diffusion of an epigraphic culture across the entire Greek world. Dedications, exaltations of gods, narratives of miracles and analogous texts inscribed in stone and attesting divine interventions became more numerous and were no longer limited to a few larger cities and sanctuaries. And such an increased display of successful communication with the gods had an impact on contemporary religious feeling and on the perception of the divine. Although philosophical schools, especially the Epicureans, claimed that even if the gods existed, they were irrelevant to the lives of mortals, the visitors of sanctuaries found themselves surrounded by textual and visual evidence that the gods had rescued people in need and avenged evil deeds. Their hope that their prayers might be heard increased, as did their fear of divine punishment. And precisely because of the ubiquitous display of evidence for manifestations of divine power, epithets underlining the presence, might, justice, holiness and protective power of gods were more extensively used to characterise the divine than they were before the third century BC. For these reasons, personal communication between mortals and gods can be regarded as a significant, albeit not unique, feature of religiosity in the centuries between Alexander and Hadrian.

In the Greek world, the channels of this communication were diverse – oral and written, linguistic and visual. The mortals voiced their requests with prayers. With concomitant vows, they promised rewards. They asked for advice by submitting oracular enquiries orally and in writing. They propitiated the gods for their transgressions, but also for the transgressions of relatives and ancestors. In some regions of Roman Asia Minor, they publicly confessed their sins. With curse tablets – deposited in the graves of people who had suffered premature or violent death – they delivered their enemies to the wrath of the underworld gods. With magical substances, they tried to win the heart of the man or woman they desired; with incantations and incubation in sanctuaries of Asclepius, they sought healing

35. *Dedication to Dionysus with the ears of the epekoos theos.*

from disease. They hoped to receive advice from gods in their dreams. And when they felt that they had suffered injustice, they turned to the gods with 'prayers for justice'. When a wish was fulfilled, the worshippers believed that the gods had listened to their prayer, accepted the vow and responded. A common epithet of gods in the 'long Hellenistic Age' is the word *epekoos*: 'the one who listens'. The ears represented on votive reliefs of the Imperial period (see Fig. 35) allude precisely to the willingness of gods to listen to prayers. The gods were also thought to respond through signs, such as the movement of birds, the barking of dogs, a sudden storm or a peal of thunder.

More elaborate forms of communication were oracular responses in prose or in verse, addressed to individuals and communities. They usually concerned practical matters, but from the first century AD oracles giving instructions on the form of worship and rituals, and even revealing the nature of the divine (see p. 364), became very common. Appearances of gods in dreams and visions were probably no more common than before Alexander, but they were now often recorded in inscriptions; people were keen to mention that they had communicated directly with a god and had received divine instructions. Incubation was already practised in the fifth century BC in a few sanctuaries of Asclepius, certainly in Athens and Epidaurus; in the Hellenistic period, however, it became far more common and was practised in the sanctuaries of other gods, especially Serapis. Communication was not only individual, as signs were also observed by larger groups. During critical battles, combatants claimed to have seen heroes fighting among them; in second-century-AD Miletos, there seems to have been a massive intrusion of gods into the dreams of humans, making Alexandra, a priestess of Demeter, wonder: 'The gods had never been so apparent through dreams – both in the dreams of girls and in those of married women, in the dreams of men and in those of children – as from the day she received the priesthood. What is this? And is it auspicious?'

To understand the importance of communication for Greek worship, we need to consider a basic but often overlooked truth about Greek gods: they could only be in one place at a time. The presence of a god in a certain place was the result of his or her personal choice and was therefore subject to competition. When people narrated a miracle in an inscription, made a dedication in fulfilment of a vow or claimed that their dedication was made in accordance with a divine command, they asserted that they had successfully communicated with a deity and thus established, if only temporarily, a privileged relationship with the divine. In Epidaurus in the late fourth century BC, a certain boy named Isyllos described his experience with the healing god Asclepius in a hymn. While Sparta was under attack by a Macedonian army, Isyllos implored the god to cure him from a disease; in his vision, the god responded: '"Take courage. I will come to you in due course of time. You stay here while I ward off disaster from the Spartans ..." Thus he went on his way to Sparta.' While Asclepius was in Sparta, he could not cure the boy in Epidaurus; he performed his epiphanies one after the other. The presence of a god should therefore be negotiated. Around 100 BC, an anonymous orator in Maroneia in Thrace wrote in praise of Isis, reminding the goddess of the fact that she had cured his eyes and requesting her presence:

Isis, exactly as you listened to my prayers concerning my eyes, now come to listen to your praise and come to fulfill a second prayer ... I am convinced that you will certainly be present. For if you came when you were invited to save me, how can you not come in order to be honored?

By inviting Isis to receive the appropriate honour, the author also asked her to listen to yet another prayer. This need to approach the gods was connected with concrete expectations: protection, health, wealth, longevity. The altars set up by a private cult association at Philadelpheia around 100 BC were dedicated to a conglomerate of personifications and deities connected not only with spiritual qualities but also with material advantages: the benevolent Zeus, Bliss (Eudaimonia), Wealth (Ploutos), Virtue (Arete), Health (Hygeia), Good Fortune (Tyche Agathe), Good Spirit (Agathos Daimon), Remembrance (Mneme), the Graces, Success (Nike). This association required from the worshippers moral qualities, purity and the performance of initiatory rituals. Initiation into a mystery cult was expected to establish a personal relationship between devotee and deity.

Traditional mystery cults

Konkurrenz belebt das Geschäft is a German proverbial saying: competition invigorates business. The diffusion of the mystery cult of Isis responded to needs that were also addressed by traditional mysteries – especially the Eleusinian mysteries, the oldest initiatory cult in Greece, and the Dionysiac-Orphic mysteries that started spreading from the sixth century BC. The myth of the abduction of Persephone or Kore (the Maiden) by Plouton, the god of the underworld, provided an aetiology or explanation for the mysteries that were celebrated in Eleusis, near Athens. After a desperate search, Demeter – Persephone's mother – reached an agreement with Plouton, according to which Persephone spent only part of the year in the underworld. To reward the king of Eleusis, who had offered her hospitality, Demeter gave him the gift of agriculture. The myth of a divine child, Iakchos (identified with Dionysus), was already associated with this cult at an early stage. Things said, done and shown (*legomena, dromena, deiknymena*) played a central part in the ceremonies of this initiation, about which little is known. The initiation, originally accessible only to speakers of Greek, was connected with ideas of fertility and concepts of the afterlife. Since, according to myth, agriculture was first introduced by Demeter on Athenian territory, the Athenians requested from all the Greeks to make first-fruit offerings to Eleusis. This custom was neglected in periods of Athenian decline, but sporadic attestations in the first century BC and the second century AD indicate that there were periodic revivals. The association of the mysteries with ideas of purity and the initiation of Romans, usually prominent statesmen and emperors, are two important innovations in this conservative cult.

The association of mysteries with moral ideas, and their appeal to Romans, can also be observed in the mysteries of the Great Gods of Samothrace. Having profited from the royal patronage of Arsinoe II and Ptolemy II, the sanctuary of the Great Gods developed from a regional cult centre into an international sanctuary that attracted regular festive embassies (*theoriai*) from many cities, and initiates from places as distant as Asia Minor, Syria, Egypt, Sicily and Rome. These mysteries were very popular among slaves and freedmen, the crews of ships and Roman military personnel.

Another important mystery cult existed in Andania, near Messene. A long inscription – the most detailed cult regulation surviving from Greece, probably dating to AD 24 – gives instructions for the staging of the procession and the celebration of the festival, without, however, revealing anything about the religious ideas connected with the cult of the Great Gods and their mysteries.

These mystery cults, as well as many others of minor significance, took place in specific locations. On the contrary, the mysteries of Dionysus, exactly as the Egyptian mysteries, could be performed wherever a cult association (a *thiasos* or *bakcheion*) existed; we find these associations in every corner of the Greek world. We need not assume that all Dionysiac associations followed the same doctrines in the celebration of their mysteries from the third century BC to the late third century AD. Occasionally we can get a glimpse into their rituals through random references to different grades of initiation, shrines with vaulted corridors, subterranean chambers and artificial caves, cult officials who carried statues, ritual objects, phalluses and other sacred symbols, and torch-bearers, presupposing nocturnal ceremonies. Designations such as 'chief shepherd' and 'silenos' suggest the use of costumes.

The Dionysiac mysteries were of very ancient origin. By the late sixth century BC, if not earlier, they were connected with eschatological ideas. Although we do not have the sacred texts of the Dionysiac initiates, texts placed in their graves provide some information on their ideas about the afterlife, a subject of fundamental importance for religions in the 'long Hellenistic Age'.

Afterlife

A grave epigram in Perinthos from around 100 AD presents a deceased eighteen-year-old student of oratory from Ephesos as speaking from the grave and asserting: 'I dwell in the sacred house of the heroes, not that of Acheron [the river of the underworld]; for this is the end of life for the wise men.' To manipulate the voice of a dead individual and to present him or her as speaking from the grave, describing good prospects in the afterlife for those who deserve it – the wise, the pious, the just and those who died young with a pure conscience – was a common practice, usually a strategy of consolation for the bereft. The same device was used around the mid-third century BC by the Alexandrian poet Callimachus, but this time the dialogue between a dead man and someone who stopped in front of his grave limits the reader's expectations: '"How is it down there?" – "Very gloomy." – "Any roads leading up?" – "That's a lie." – "And Plouton?" – "A myth." – "I am lost!" – "My words are true. But if you prefer sweet words, then you should know that a large ox only costs a penny in Hades."' What the poet in Perinthos and Callimachus have in common is that they do not speak from personal experience. Although conceptions of the afterlife and the underworld are the work of the imagination of the living, they are often presented as reports from mortals who went to the underworld and returned – for instance, Odysseus or Orpheus – or of deceased individuals who appear in the dreams of loved ones and describe the realm that they now call home. For instance, a girl of Thyatteira in the Imperial period speaks from the grave:

> I immediately appeared to my revered mother in the darkest night explaining thus: 'Melitine, my mother, stop the lament, stop the woe, and think of my soul, which Zeus, who takes delight in thunders, made to be immortal and eternally young; he snatched it away and brought it to the starry sky.'

Greek conceptions of the afterlife and the underworld have a long and complex history. They ranged from the complete denial of life after death to the view that death is an eternal sleep, and from elaborate imaginings about the geography of the underworld to the view that the deceased join the aether or become stars. An epitaph in Smyrna is agnostic: 'If there is rebirth, then sleep will not hold you for long. But if there is no way to come back, then eternal sleep holds you.' A contemporaneous epigram from Amorgos presents a young man addressing his mother: 'Mother, do not cry over me, what is the use? Now that I have become a star in the night sky, among the gods, show reverence to me.' Such diverse and often contradictory conceptions are very well reflected in grave inscriptions from the sixth century BC all the way to late antiquity. One may observe some significant trends in the Hellenistic and Imperial periods.

According to an old and widespread idea, death is a journey that brings the deceased to a dark area under the earth. Only a very few people have a different destination – the island of the Blessed or the Elysian Fields, where an eternal life of joy awaits them. According to another widespread view, the soul of the dead was united with the aether. Already in the Classical period, a good afterlife was associated with an initiation into a mystery cult, the mysteries of Eleusis and the Dionysiac mysteries. We have gleaned some information about the afterlife of these initiates through the discovery of inscribed golden tablets placed in graves, often on the mouth of the dead, and also through literary sources concerning the sects of the Orphics and the Pythagoreans, which were associated with the figure of Dionysus.

The Dionysiac mysteries were rooted in the supposed dichotomy between the mortal body and the immortal, divine soul. Moral conduct in life, the study of ritual and sacred texts, and the following of ritual prescriptions concerning purity guaranteed that the initiate escaped reincarnation – the destiny of ordinary mortals – and joined the gods at an everlasting banquet. Initiation into the mysteries made the initiates conscious of the divine origin of their soul and prepared them for the journey to the underworld. Short texts, inscribed on golden tablets and placed in the graves of the initiates, have been found in Hellenistic Macedonia, Thessaly, the Peloponnese and Crete, evincing the continuous popularity of these mysteries. Some texts give instructions to the deceased about the path they should follow in the underworld, advising them to avoid drinking from the fountain of oblivion and revealing what to say upon encountering the guardians of the underworld or Persephone herself: 'I am the son of the Earth and the starry Sky', 'Dionysus himself has released me.' If the initiate remembered the doctrines of the cult in the moment of death, he or she – the initiation of women was permitted – would reach the place reserved in the underworld for the blessed and pious.

But initiation alone was not sufficient. A blissful afterlife required a pious life. This emphasis on values and not actions corresponds to an important change of attitude towards rituals that was already emerging in the late fifth century BC. According to an increasingly influential view, first expressed by intellectuals such as Euripides and later attested among ritual experts, the efficacy of rituals does not only depend on the correct performance of a script but also requires justifications and adherence to values. Supplication was not automatically accepted when a suppliant reached the altar; instead, measures were introduced to exclude criminals from asylum. The authors of curses did not simply rely on the use of the correct curse formulas; they also justified themselves, thus creating a distinct category of curses known as 'prayers for justice'. The ritual of purification no longer focused on the purity of the body alone, as it did until the fifth century BC; it also required a pure heart. The worship of the gods demanded verbal expressions of devotion, not just sacrifices. Similarly, mystery cults started to require commitment to moral values in addition to initiation. The statutes of a cult association in Philadelpheia from around 100 BC (see p. 372) are preoccupied with the moral conduct of the initiates, forbidding deceit, the use of poisons or potions, extramarital relations and abortion; they condemn not only those who violated the rules but also those who simply had knowledge of misconduct and took no action against it. In the Hellenistic and especially in the Imperial periods, references to justice and piety as requirements for a blissful afterlife become common.

Another important trend is the heroisation of mortals. Attested already in early periods – for war dead and founders of cities – it became common in the Hellenistic period due to the predominant position of political leaders and then benefactors. Under the influence of the heroisation of public figures, this practice spread in Hellenistic society, with wealthy people elevating deceased family members to the status of heroes and establishing cults for them.

Religious innovation: cult founders, missionaries and 'holy men'

New sanctuaries and cults were often founded in the fifth and fourth centuries BC at the private initiative of individuals. The cult of the healing god Asclepius owes its great diffusion in the late fifth and fourth centuries BC to the initiative of missionaries and devotees; the tragic poet Sophocles was one of them, hosting Asclepius' cult in his house. Such private cult foundations burgeoned tremendously in the Hellenistic period. This trend, which becomes very clear in the third century BC, especially with the foundation of sanctuaries of Sarapis by devotees, continued into the Imperial period. The motivation of the agents of such religious innovations varied. Some were expatriates guided by their gratitude to the gods who had helped them, people who believed that they had been given a mission by a god, and 'holy men' who claimed a special relationship with the divine. Others were civic benefactors wishing to associate their name with a public celebration, or conservative people wanting to revive forgotten traditions, or men and women who wished to keep alive the memory of deceased family members and so established commemorative cults. Royal agency was also very important. Ptolemaic soldiers contributed to the diffusion of the Sarapis cult. In the mid-third century BC, the Mauryan king of India, Ashoka – a zealous Buddhist – issued an edict renouncing war and propagating Buddhist ethical principles. He had this text translated into Greek and inscribed in public places, and dispatched monks to the west. Although his inscription claims that Greeks in the Hellenistic kingdoms converted to Buddhism, this is only attested in the areas that were later ruled by the Graeco-Bactrian and Graeco-Indian kings. And in the late first century AD, King Antiochos I of Kommagene – famous for his sanctuary and grave at Nemrud Dağ in Turkey – introduced religious reforms based on a mélange of Hellenistic practices around the ruler cult and Zoroastrian religious concepts, Greek and Iranian rituals, and Greek, Iranian and Armenian gods.

Cult foundations by ordinary people were far more common than such elaborate religious reforms. Artemidoros, originally a citizen of Perge in Pamphylia, is an early example of a devoted cult founder. After serving in the armies of the Ptolemies (c. 285–245 BC), Artemidoros settled as an old man of means on the island of Thera. There he restored the temple of the Egyptian gods; after a dream in which the personification of Concord appeared to him and recommended the foundation of her altar, he founded a precinct for her cult, in which he also established the cults of several other divinities, mostly of foreign origin. What they had in common was their protective powers: the Dioskouroi Soteres, the saviour gods of sailors and soldiers; the Great Gods of Samothrace, perceived as protectors of individuals in need; the local deities Zeus Olympios, Apollo Stephanephoros, Poseidon and Hekate Phosphoros; the god of fertility Priapos; Tyche, the personification of Fortune; and the heroines. An altar was also dedicated to the cult of Artemis of Perge, the goddess of Artemidoros' fatherland and his personal saviour (Soteira).

Very often, a new foundation was less elaborate than the divine constellation created by Artemidoros. For instance, when a certain Menophilos experienced an epiphany of Zeus, he founded an altar; the god to whom sacrifices were offered at this altar was henceforth known as the 'Great Zeus of Menophilos'. In rare cases, a new cult acquired regional popularity. A shrine founded by the otherwise unknown Artemidoros in the Lydian city of Axiotta was dedicated to 'Mes of Artemidoros of Axiotta'; from Axiotta, the cult spread throughout other areas of Lydia and Phrygia. The inscribed narratives of Mes' healing and punishing miracles made him known as a powerful god who requested continual praise from his worshippers.

The introduction of a new cult or festival usually required the endowment of funds. For festivals that commemorated their sponsor, the funds were limited and the celebration modest: a sacrifice, accompanied by a banquet, sometimes a choral performance or an athletic competition. But in the Imperial period, the growing competition among benefactors led to extravagant festivals such as the one sponsored in Ephesos in AD 104 by Caius Vibius Salutaris, a wealthy local citizen and a Roman knight. Salutaris provided the funds for the creation of a golden statue of Artemis and twenty-eight silver statues – eight of them representing the goddess and the remaining representing Emperor Trajan and his wife Plotina, the Roman senate and the Roman people, King Lysimachos (the founder of the Hellenistic city) and personifications that commemorated Roman and Ephesian institutions and places significant to local identity. From Artemis' temple, the statues were carried in procession to the theatre during public events and were displayed there. Salutaris' endowment glorified the local goddess, displayed loyalty to Rome and transmitted elements of local history and civic values.

A particular type of a religious agent in the early Imperial period was the 'holy man', an itinerant preacher with theological and philosophical interests. Philostratos, an author of the early third century AD, narrates the life of such a man: Apollonios, born in Tyana in Kapaddokia, was a follower of Pythagorean philosophy; moreover, he was a philosopher himself who lived an itinerant life and travelled as far as India in pursuit of the source of wisdom. He acquired a reputation as a man of extraordinary capacities and the ability to perform miracles: for instance, it was said that about midday on 18 September AD 96, Apollonios announced in Ephesos that he had just witnessed the assassination of Emperor Domitian in Rome, praising this deed as the killing of a tyrant. Most of this is fiction. That he followed the Pythagorean doctrines of a division between mortal body and immortal soul, reincarnation and escape from reincarnation through a life in justice is plausible – after all, these Pythagorean ideas gained in popularity in the Imperial period. It is also very likely that Apollonios spent most of his life travelling in Asia Minor and adjacent regions, such as Syria and Crete – such an itinerant life was very common among philosophers. His criticism of sacrifices and his view that god, as pure intellect, does not respond to prayers and sacrifices but to a spiritual worship by the human intellect are ideas to be expected in the Imperial period. An oracle of Apollo of Didyma in the second century AD presents the god as claiming that the immortals are not interested in sacrifices; what fills Apollo with joy are hymns, the older the better. Because of the similarity of the narratives of Apollonios' miracles with those of Jesus, in the late third and in the fourth centuries AD, Apollonios became the object of admiration by the worshippers of the traditional gods and the target of Christian attacks. Long after Christianity had become the state religion of the Roman Empire, cities in the East still believed in the protective power of talismans attributed to Apollonios.

New cult foundations are surpassed in sophistication by a cult that was introduced, shortly after Hadrian's death, by a certain Alexander into his hometown of Abonou Teichos on the Turkish coast of the Black Sea. Apollonios of Tyana was his mentor. In his 'Alexander or the False Prophet', the satirist Lucian presents Alexander as a crook who, looking for the best method of gaining money and power, realised that human life is governed by hope and fear, and consequently by the desire to foretell the future. With material profit in mind, he persuaded his fellow citizens to undertake the construction of a temple of Asclepius. He then convinced them that a snake of uncommon size and beauty, Glykon (the Sweet One), was the New Asclepius. The temple became the centre of divination, miraculous healing and a mystery cult. Coins, statuettes and inscriptions confirm the cult's diffusion around Asia Minor. Even the Roman provincial governor of Kappadokia, Rutilianus, is said to have consulted the oracle; his daughter married the cult's founder. A genuine innovation was that oracles were given by the snake-god with a human voice. According to Lucian, Alexander seated himself on a couch in a dark chamber, with majestic clothes, holding Glykon in his bosom. Coiling the snake about his neck and letting its long tail stream over his lap and drag on the floor, he kept its head hidden under his arm; instead, he showed a linen head to which cranes' windpipes were attached. A collaborator answered the questions by speaking into this tube, giving the impression that the voice was the snake's.

Influenced by Pythagorean ideas concerning metempsychosis, Alexander preached that a correct and pure way of life releases an individual from the cycle of rebirths. One's way of life and moral qualities determined the fate of one's soul after death: rebirth in the body of an animal, a king or a slave, or liberation from the cycle of rebirth and the joining of the blessed and the gods. For the masses of worshippers, Alexander established a ritual of initiation copying the model of the mysteries of Eleusis, the oldest and most prestigious of Greek mystery cults. Lucian's description of this ritual, despite the exaggerations that are to be expected from a satirical author, gives us an impression of the part played by 'sacred dramas', sound and light, costumes and chanting in a mystery cult:

> On the first day, there was a proclamation, as in Athens, as follows: 'If any godless or Christian or Epicurean has come to spy upon the rites, he should go away. Those who believe in the god may perform the mysteries, with good fortune.' Then, the 'expulsion' took place, immediately at the beginning. He started by saying, 'Out with the Christians,' and the crowd chanted in response, 'Out with the Epicureans.' Then the childbed of Leto, the birth of Apollo, his marriage to Koronis, and the birth of Asclepius were represented; on the second day, the epiphany of Glykon and the birth of the god; on the third day, the marriage of Podaleirios [the son of Asclepius] and Alexander's mother. This day was called the Day of Torches, and torches were lighted. Finally, the love of the moon goddess and Alexander was represented, and the birth of Rutilianus' daughter. Alexander, the new Endymion [the mythological lover of the Moon], served as torch bearer and mystical expounder. While he lay as if he were asleep, there came down to him from the roof, as if from heaven, not the moon goddess but a certain Rutilia, a most beautiful woman, wife of one of the emperor's stewards, who was truly in love with Alexander and he with her. And before the eyes of that rascal, her husband, they engaged in kisses and embraces in public. And if there had not been that many

36. Statue of Glykon New Asclepius.

torches, very quickly copulation would have occurred. After a short time, Alexander entered again, wearing the costume of the expounder of the mysteries, amid profound silence. In a loud voice he said, 'Hail, Glykon,' and some Paphlagonian imitators of the Eumolpids and the Heralds [of the Eleusinian mysteries], who followed him in brogues, chanted in response 'Hail, Alexander,' belching out garlic sauce.

An essential component of Alexander's success was that his sanctuary provided, in a single place, everything worshippers usually had to seek in separate holy places: healing from disease, foretelling of the future and liberation from the anxiety of death through initiation into a cult that guaranteed a blessed afterlife. Like many other priests, Alexander operated with tricks, illusions and staged performances of ritual dramas. In the celebration of the mysteries, costumes, torches, light effects and the dramatic contrast between silence and loud cries were instrumental in arousing the feeling of awe among worshippers. Another important element in this cult was the physical presence of the divinity in the sanctuary. Glykon was presented as being continually concerned with the worries of his worshippers and attentive to their requests. In statues and amulets, the snake-god is represented with distinctively big ears – an allusion to his willingness to respond to prayers (see Fig. 36). Finally, Alexander placed emphasis on the emotional interaction of the worshippers. The expulsion of the cult's adversaries was shaped as an event of ritualised aggression that separated the worshippers of Glykon from 'the others', strengthening their sense of solidarity and thus also their almost exclusive devotion to this one god.

Other contemporary sources confirm the main features of the religiosity that the above examples of religious innovation show: the strong desire to achieve a personal communication with the divine; an emphasis on the aesthetic, performative and theatrical aspects of religious celebrations; strong emotionality during worship; and personal devotion.

Christianity and the beginnings of religious intolerance

Monty Python's Life of Brian populates Judaea in the early decades of the first century AD with myriad prophets, preachers, missionaries and ascetics, all eager to show the right path to whomever is willing to listen. This is a rather accurate representation of the religious quests and religious plurality that were typical of the time. In Judaea, heated discussions among the main sects of the Essenes, the Sicarii, the Zealots, the Pharisees and the Sadducees revolved around the interpretation of the Torah and the will of God, as well as the coming of the Messiah, morality and purity, the correct performance of rituals, sin and redemption, and resurrection and the afterlife. If these quests do not explain the birth of Christianity, they certainly explain its spread: people of different ethnic and religious origins asked similar questions, and different religions gave answers that were, to a certain extent, similar. Despite its uniqueness and its distinct profile, Christianity could not have seemed so extraordinary to a contemporary observer, except for its demand for the exclusive worship of one god. The Christians not only claimed that their faith was the one true faith, they regarded it as incompatible with any other religious practice, including the performance of acts of worship addressed to the emperor.

The historical Jesus and his teachings have been the subject of debate for centuries, and this is not the place to summarise them. It is not the origin of Christianity that is of relevance to the history of the Greek world, but its spread from the mid-first century AD onwards. Both the Jewish sects and the early Christian movement shared some of their concerns with earlier and contemporary cults, especially those that had a soteriological background: the proper definition of purity and the sources of pollution; the purity of the mind or the heart; the regulation of sexual codes of behaviour and food restrictions; the importance attributed to the recognition of sin and repentance; the belief in a superior god who communicates with the mortals through angels and to whom lesser gods advocate the concerns of the humans; the form of worship and the efficacy and appropriateness of animal sacrifice. Aspects of Judaism were well known in areas beyond Judaea because of the existence of significant diaspora communities in major cities (e.g. in Alexandria), but also in many smaller cities in Asia Minor, Crete, some Aegean islands and the Bosporan kingdom. The failure of the Jewish revolts in the first and second centuries AD gave a new impetus to the involuntary diaspora and increased the numbers of Jews and their synagogues in the Greek world. Unlike Judaism, which reluctantly accepted proselytes, early Christianity did not keep any strict boundaries defined by ethnicity, origin or social status. On the contrary, zealous proselytising was, from the beginning, a characteristic feature of Christianity.

Since Christians are usually invisible in the epigraphic record and hardly ever mentioned in the literary sources of the first and second centuries AD, we do not have enough unbiased information about their mission. There are only a few indisputable things known about the message of early Christianity: the belief in the resurrection of Jesus as the long-expected Messiah; the expectation of the resurrection of the dead; the love of one's neighbour; the condemnation of avarice and material pleasures. Even the governor of a province had only a vague idea about who they really were. Eager to find out what this new form of religious worship was, Pliny, the governor of the province of Bithynia and Pontos, conducted an investigation in AD 112, and this is what he found out and communicated to the emperor:

> They asserted that the sum and substance of their fault or error had been that they were accustomed to meet on a fixed day before dawn and sing responsively a hymn to Christ as to a god, and to bind themselves by oath, not to some crime, but not to commit fraud, theft, or adultery, not falsify their trust, nor to refuse to return a trust when called upon to do so. When this was over, it was their custom to depart and to assemble again to partake of food – but ordinary and innocent food.

There is nothing in Pliny's report about Christian practices that might have seemed a strange novelty. Meeting on fixed days is attested for numerous cult associations. The singing of hymns was a popular form of worship – a more spiritual substitute for animal sacrifice. The obligation, under oath, to follow moral standards and the condemnation of certain crimes, especially perjury, find exact parallels in religious inscriptions of Asia Minor from the late second century BC to the early third century AD. Finally, the joint consumption of ordinary food – obviously wine and bread – and the nocturnal celebrations were anything but an exclusive feature of Christian worship. For instance, at midnight on certain days, bread was distributed among the members of a cult association dedicated to the worship of Dionysus in Thessalonike around the same time Pliny was writing his letter. So how can we explain the enmity towards the Christians?

A distinctive feature of early Christianity that explains both its success and the enmity it aroused is the missionary spirit – the strongly felt obligation of the early Christians to spread the word to the Gentiles, even to the extent of persecution and death if need be. This missionary zeal is of course connected with the faith in one and only one true god, whose worship cannot be reconciled with the performance of religious rituals honouring other gods, including the emperor. There had been missionaries of cults in the past – especially zealous devotees of Asclepius and Serapis – but they had never shown intolerance towards other gods and they never opposed the cult of kings or emperors; their devotion to one particular god did not prevent them from participating in the public cults or even from assuming priestly offices in cults of gods other than the one to whom they were devoted.

The Christian missionaries, a new type of 'holy men', become a distinctive feature of Christianity. The best known among them is Paul. Information about his travels, his teachings, his occasional violent conflicts with both Jews and Roman civic authorities, his temporary imprisonment in Philippi and finally his death in Rome in AD 64 derives from the Acts of the Apostles and his genuine and 'deutero-Pauline' epistles. His preaching took place in public spaces, such as Jewish synagogues and the meeting place of the Athenian council of the Areopagus, opposite the Acropolis. His audience consisted of Jews, Gentiles and sympathisers of Jewish religious ideas known as the god-fearers or *theosebeis*. From Palestine, Christianity spread to Egypt and Cyrenaica, north Syria (Antioch), Asia Minor, Crete and, as we learn from the few genuine letters of Paul, also to large cities in Greece such as Philippi, Thessalonike and Corinth. The early loci of Christianity were urban centres, with complex social stratification and often a Jewish community, usually on important routes of traffic and trade. Christian communities and sects also existed in the countryside of Asia Minor: for instance, in Phrygia.

These missionaries often met with a violent reaction from the Jewish mob. Roman law did not outlaw Christianity as such, but it did prosecute troublemakers, and the Christians were sometimes regarded as agitators, especially when they got into conflict with Jews. The great fire in Rome in July AD 64 was attributed by Nero to the Christians and led to violent persecution. The populace was eager to believe that the followers of this hated new sect, whose rites and beliefs were only inaccurately known, were responsible for the crime, and greatly enjoyed the execution of those who were arrested. By the mid-second century AD, the Christians were such an important and visible religious group that Alexander of Abonou Teichos regarded them, along with the atheistic Epicurean philosophers, as the greatest enemies of his newly founded cult of Glykon New Asklepios (see p. 380).

Christianity was born in the eastern Mediterranean in the religious atmosphere sketched in this chapter. It responded to the same needs that brought worshippers to the sanctuaries of 'great gods' and to mystery cults. Despite the novelty of the answers that it provided, the early Christian proselytisers expressed their message in terms familiar to the Jews and pagans of the time. According to the Acts of the Apostles, when Paul arrived in Athens in the winter of AD 51/52, he started his preaching by pointing to the fact that there existed in the city an altar for the 'Unknown God' (Agnostos Theos). The Greeks, for centuries seeking effective divine protection, were open to new suggestions.

16

THE GREEKS AND
THE *OECUMENE*

Six degrees of separation: an ancient 'globalisation'

The film *Babel*, released in 2006, shows how the fate of a handful of people in Morocco, Japan, Mexico and the US – people who are strangers to one another – is connected because of certain circumstances. This drama, directed by Alejandro González Iñárritu and written by Guillermo Arriaga, is one of many films, plays and TV series that are based on the theory that everyone is six or fewer steps away, by way of relationships or acquaintances, from any other person in the world. This concept was first formulated by the Hungarian author Frigyes Karinthy in his 1939 short story '*Láncszemek*' ('Chains'). It became known through the work of the social psychologist Stanley Milgram, author of 'The Small World Problem', published in *Psychology Today* in 1967. In the words of a character in the 1990 play *Six Degrees of Separation* by John Guare: 'Six degrees of separation between us and everyone else on this planet. The President of the United States, a gondolier in Venice, just fill in the names.' In the age of the internet, Facebook and Twitter, this concept seems archaic.

It cannot be seriously claimed that when Alexander ascended the throne of Macedonia in 336 BC there were six degrees of separation between him and any individual living in the areas that would, ten years later, comprise his empire. By contrast, it is not unreasonable to assume that when Hadrian ascended his throne 453 years later there were six, or fewer, degrees of separation between the emperor and any individual in his empire and in the adjacent states. Even a simple fellah in south Egypt knew a village secretary, who communicated with the village chief, who had a contact with the governor of the district, who knew the prefect of Egypt, who had been appointed by the emperor. The developments that Alexander's campaigns set in motion ultimately led to the creation of a complex network of political, administrative, economic and cultural connections that came close to the modern phenomenon of globalisation. Of course, this network did not extend over the entire globe, but it did cover the region that contemporaries knew as the *oecumene*, 'the inhabited earth'. One might more appropriately speak of ecumenisation.

The conquests of Alexander destroyed the Persian Empire but did not create a lasting empire to replace it. Nonetheless, they did engender a huge political network of kingdoms, semi-independent dynasts and *poleis* extending from the Adriatic Sea to Afghanistan and from the north shore of the Black Sea to Ethiopia. These states also had relations with Italy, the Greek *poleis* of Magna Graecia and Rome, the Greek colonies in the south of France, Carthage in North Africa and the Mauryan Empire in India. Thus the world of Alexander's successors constituted a network that comprised the entire known world, with the exception of East Asia. But if we also consider various population movements – for instance, the migration of the Gauls into Greece and Asia Minor in the early third century BC, the invasion of the Yuezhi and other nomadic tribes into Bactria in the second century BC and the repeated raids of Scythians and other tribes into the territories of the Greek cities – the world of Alexander's successors was also connected with central Europe, central Asia and the western borders of China. The Roman expansion from the late third century BC onwards gradually enlarged the borders of this network of interconnected regions to include the Iberian Peninsula, central and western Europe, Britain and north Africa. By the time of Hadrian's death, a large part of the *oecumene* was within the borders of one single empire.

Of course, the great Greek colonisation from the eighth to the sixth century BC had broadened the perspective of the Greeks, but it is in no way comparable to what we encounter after Alexander's campaigns. This process affected various Greek regions in different ways. Traditional hegemonic powers such as Athens, Sparta and Thebes were surpassed in political importance by the Hellenistic kingdoms and the federal states, and also by regional powers such as Rhodes. The Roman conquest boosted the economic weight of provincial capitals and Roman colonies. In the pacified Roman Mediterranean, Crete was no longer an island on the periphery of the Greek world, but a nexus point with a central position in the traffic of the eastern Mediterranean. In this concluding chapter, we shall briefly examine the changing geographical setting of the Greeks and the factors that determined their new position in the *oecumene*: connectivity, mobility and multiculturalism.

Connectivity: a small world

At about the same time that Alexander attempted to surpass Heracles by conquering Aornos – the rock that the hero had failed to take in his easternmost adventure – another Greek undertook a daring enterprise at the place marking Heracles' westernmost deed: the Pillars of Hercules, or modern Gibraltar. Around 325 BC, the geographer and mariner Pytheas of Massalia embarked on an expedition to explore the western Ocean. After breaking the Carthaginian blockade of the Straits of Gibraltar, he sailed along the coast of Portugal in an attempt to circumnavigate Europe. In the course of his journey, he discovered the British Isles, possibly reached Norway or Iceland – depending on where one locates the place the ancients called Thule – and sailed deep into the Baltic Sea. Although it is unlikely that Alexander ever learned of Pytheas' enterprise, it is not by chance that these adventures were more or less contemporary. Both Pytheas and Alexander were motivated by the same inquisitive spirit and fascination with the unknown. Around this time, in the more comfortable venue of the Athenian Lyceum's shady gardens, Aristotle and his pupils were pursuing a plan to map, analyse and classify the entirety of the visible world and all aspects of human behaviour. Pytheas in the West, Alexander in the East and Aristotle in Greece's intellectual centre are parallel culminations of decades of Greek scientific exploration, which in the late fourth century BC was breaking new paths.

After Alexander had opened up new horizons in the East, others followed, guided by plans or fortune. The universal scholar Poseidonios, while visiting Gades (modern Cadiz in Spain) and studying the tides on the Atlantic coast in the early first century BC, heard about the adventures of a certain Eudoxos of Kyzikos a few years earlier. His work *On the Ocean* is lost, but an account of Eudoxos' expeditions is preserved in the *Geography* of Strabo:

> In the reign of Ptolemy Euergetes II [c. 145–116 BC], Eudoxos came to Egypt as a sacred envoy and herald for the contests of the festival of Kore. He joined up with the king and his court, most particularly in his voyages up the Nile, for he was a man naturally curious of strange places, and not untutored in them. It so happened that an Indian was brought to the king by the garrison of the Red Sea, who reported that they had found him half-dead, shipwrecked and alone; but who he was or where he had come from they had no idea, as they could not understand his language. He was handed over to people to teach him Greek. Once he had learned it, his story was that he was sailing from India when he happened to lose his way and ended up safely after his fellow sailors had died of starvation. He was taken at his word and promised to act as guide for the route to India to a crew selected by the king. Eudoxos was one of them. So he sailed off with presents and returned with a cargo of perfumes and precious stones ... But Eudoxos was deceived in his hopes. King Euergetes appropriated the whole cargo.

What Eudoxos learned from the Indian sailor was the use of the monsoon winds that permitted a direct journey from Ethiopia to India through the Indian Ocean, avoiding the long, expensive and dangerous journey along the southern coast of Arabia and through the Gulf of Oman. In 116 BC, the king died and, sometime later, the queen Cleopatra III sent Eudoxos on a new expedition, which again filled his ship with luxuries – probably spices, perfumes and precious stones. The return journey was adventurous; the ship was stranded somewhere between Cape Guardafui in Somalia and Zanzibar. Eudoxos managed to return to Alexandria, only to see his cargo confiscated by the new king. Then Eudoxos tried his luck in the West. He went to Gades in Spain, with the plan to circumnavigate Africa and reach India through an alternative route. He failed, and the king of Mauritania delivered him to Sulla. He attempted a fourth journey, from which he never returned. The way this story is narrated by Poseidonios (and Strabo) corresponds to Hellenistic taste: Fortune stages an encounter between a shipwrecked Indian, a curious Greek and an avaricious king. And as in many Hellenistic stories, there are unexpected twists of fate and thwarted expectations. The adventures of Eudoxos exemplify, to an extreme level, the new possibilities that the Hellenistic world created for trade in exotic products and the dissemination of information. This was in part endorsed by royal patronage, unknown before Alexander.

A travel handbook known as the *Circumnavigation of the Erythraean Sea* (*Periplous Maris Erythraei*), probably composed in the mid-first century AD, provides detailed information about the harbours, trading posts and products to be found along the coasts of the Red Sea, the Persian Gulf and the Indian Ocean. For instance, merchants interested in importing frankincense from the Arabian Peninsula learned that

> after Arabia Felix there is a continuous length of coast, and a bay extending two thousand stadia or more, along which there are Nomads and Fish-Eaters living in villages. Just beyond the cape projecting from this bay there is another market-town by the shore, Kana, of the Kingdom of Eleazos, the Frankincense Country; and facing it there are two desert islands, one called Island of Birds, the other Dome Island, one hundred and twenty stadia from Kana. Inland from this place lies the metropolis Sabbatha, in which the King lives. All the frankincense produced in the country is brought by camels to that place to be stored, and to Kana on rafts held up by inflated skins after the manner of the country, and in boats.

This text shows in the most impressive way how far knowledge of these regions had advanced since the time of Nearchos, the admiral of Alexander who travelled from India to the Persian Gulf in 327 BC. Under Nero, when the Roman emperor enjoyed diplomatic relations with rulers in Arabia, his subjects – motivated by the expectation of profit – risked trading journeys along the coast of the Arabian Peninsula and as far east as India and Sri Lanka. Trading activity with these regions was quite diverse. For instance, the important harbour of Barygaza in north-west India was a place where Roman and Greek traders could profitably sell wine, textiles and silver vessels, as well as singing boys and beautiful girls for the king's harem, receiving in exchange semi-precious stones, herbs, spices and exotic animals.

A certain Sophytos, a man who died in Alexandria Arachosia (today's Kandahar) in the late first century BC, may be one of the traders who visited Barygaza. In the elaborate grave epigram that he composed for himself, he gives an account of his achievements. His ancestral fortune having been lost, Sophytos sought ways to raise the ancestral home high again. He took a loan and left his city, determined to return only as a rich man: 'With this aim I sailed on merchant ships to many cities and obtained great wealth without causing harm.' His maritime enterprises must have been in the Indian Ocean. From Kandahar he could have easily reached the harbour of Barygaza, and from there his trips may have brought him as far as Egypt. He returned a wealthy man, rebuilt the ancestral house, erected a new grave for his ancestors and himself, and composed a poem in Greek for the Greek population that must have still been living in Alexandria Arachosia. The archaeological exploration of harbour sites in southern India and the discovery of Roman coins and wine jars there corroborate the advancement of Greek trade with these areas in the early Imperial period.

The impetus for such connections came from Alexander. His campaign was the 'big bang' of Hellenistic 'globalisation', as it were. Alexander decided to make the limits of the world, rather than the limits of the Persian Empire, the destination of his campaign. He settled his soldiers in strategic places along his way to the Indian Ocean and he scientifically explored all the regions that he visited.

People on the move

The development of a network of interconnected regions – at times engaged in wars, at times united under a single authority – was accompanied by an unprecedented movement of populations. As we have seen in previous chapters, this ranged from the voluntary movements of mercenaries, artists, merchants, entertainers, itinerant orators and educators, students of oratory and philosophy, pilgrims journeying to sacred places and athletes to the forced migration of exiles after civil wars, captives, slaves and diaspora Jews. Some movements were periodical, as in the trips of the 'sacred envoys' (*theoroi*), who announced Panhellenic festivals, the visits of audiences to the great athletic contests in Olympia and Delphi, and the maritime journeys through the Indian Ocean that were determined by the monsoon winds. More often, they were determined by ad hoc needs, such as the trips undertaken by ambassadors to cities, kings, Roman authorities and emperors. Movements could be massive, as with the settlement of Hellenistic new city foundations or Roman colonies, the Gallic invasions of Greece and then of Asia Minor, or the resettlement of

Jews after their revolts. The movement of large groups was usually permanent, resulting in dramatic changes in the ethnic composition of the
population and contributing to cultural diversity. At the same time, the
individual and temporary movements of people, especially of traders and
scholars, had a significant impact on culture.

The trips of intellectuals are a case in point. Orators, philosophers and
historians who travelled around the Greek world, giving lectures in major
cities and sanctuaries, are already attested in the fifth and fourth centuries
BC. Due to the increased connectivity of the world from the third century
BC onwards, as well as the frequency of large festivals, the advancement
of education, historiography, oratory and philosophy, and the existence
of royal courts (followed by the imperial court in Rome), these lectures
became far more common than ever before. *Akroasis* (public lecture) is the
word that designates the main activity of the itinerant scholars: visiting
a city, a sanctuary or a court, staying there for a few days or months, and
giving lectures in gymnasia, theatres, town halls, and palaces. The content
of the lectures was very diverse: the reading of excerpts from historio-
graphical works, the presentation of philosophical questions, encomia
that praised a city – making references to its myths, historical achievements, buildings, famous men and the beauty of its landscape – eulogies
of emperors, orations offering advice on social and political issues, such as
concord within a city or reconciliation between cities, and the provision
of evidence for the 'kinship' between two cities or two regions, originating
in the kinship of particular gods or founding heroes.

Polemon of Ilion is one of the best-known polymaths of this period. He
travelled around, collecting information on local history and local cults
and lecturing on these subjects, for instance in Delphi and Athens in the
170s BC. From the second century BC onwards, eulogies that praised the
Romans became increasingly common, and as the influence of the senate
on Greek affairs increased, the city of Rome was added to the favourite
destinations of intellectuals. Some of them came to Rome as ambassadors
of their cities, others as friends of Roman statesmen and yet others tried
their fortune in the new metropolis of the world. A turning point in this
respect was the 'embassy of the philosophers' of Athens to Rome in 155 BC,
which was sent to appeal against the decision of the senate to impose a fine
on the city. The lectures of Karneades, one day focusing on the defence of
justice and the next against it, became famous; although Cato the Elder, a
conservative Roman senator, made sure that the philosophers left the city

immediately, their influence remained, and in the following decades the number of Greek intellectuals visiting Rome multiplied.

The activities of itinerant historians, orators, grammarians and philosophers – or scholars who combined expertise in these fields and were known as 'sophists' – continued into the Imperial period, culminating in a time known as the 'Second Sophistic', lasting roughly from the reign of Nero to the early third century AD. The orations of Dio of Prusa, who flourished under the Flavians and Trajan and is known as Chrysostomos (golden-mouthed), are the best-preserved specimens of such lectures from this period. They were often dedicated to important political and moral subjects, such as ideal kingship, slavery and freedom, but they also included playful exercises in rhetorical skill, such as his 'Praise of Hair'. Expressing an opinion, however, can be a dangerous business in times of autocratic rule. Philosophers were expelled from Rome under Vespasian for corrupting students and Dio was exiled under Domitian. But, generally, the second century AD was a golden age for itinerant scholars, whose teachings and lectures contributed significantly to the homogenisation of culture and the transmission of ideas and literary and rhetorical styles.

'Go east' was the advice for most of the Greeks under those who succeeded Alexander, and with few (if important) exceptions – such as Pyrrhos' campaigns in Italy and Sicily – it remained so for centuries. As Rome consolidated its position at the centre of the *oecumene* and the *pax Romana* made journeys relatively safe, individuals and groups from Greece and the Hellenised provinces found their way to Rome, Italy and the western provinces. Men of letters, actors and athletes were a minority of such people, over-represented in our sources; most were slaves, traders, artists and skilled workers. Occasionally, grave inscriptions tell these people's stories, such as the sad case of Hyle from Thessalonike, who died alone in Bonn around AD 200: 'Thessalonike was my fatherland and Hyle was my name. Aisos, the son of Batallos, conquered me with love potions, although he was a eunuch. And so my wedding bed was ineffectual. And now I lie here, so far away from my fatherland.' In the small world of the Roman Empire, a woman from Thessalonike who followed her husband to Germany could still think of her fatherland with nostalgia.

Movement in the 'long Hellenistic Age' involved not only the movement of people, but also the movement of objects. Looted works of Greek art decorated Roman houses and villas, and Roman clay lamps lit the

37. The epitaph of a wandering pig.

houses of Asia Minor. Isolated objects of Greek and Roman manufacture even reached China, Thailand and Korea, suggesting contacts, if not regular trade.

Finally, we should not forget the movement of animals: horses and dogs from areas renowned for their special breeds, but also exotic creatures displayed in processions and triumphs or killed in the arena. The grave epigram of a travelling pig gives us an unusual insight into the mobility of this era. Probably trained to perform acrobatic tricks in festivals, the pig came all the way from Dyrrhachion on the Adriatic Sea to Edessa in Macedonia to attend a Dionysiac procession. But during a festival it was run over by a wagon (see Fig. 37).

> Here lies 'the Pig', beloved by all, a young quadruped, having left the land of Dalmatia, brought as a present. I reached Dyrrhachion and wishing to see Apollonia I crossed every land with my own feet, alone, undefeated. But now I have left the light because of the violence of the

wheels. I wished to see Emathie and the wagon of the phallus, but now here I rest, although I was too young to pay my tribute to death.

It is not possible to think of an earlier period in recorded human history in which movement was so intense, massive and wide-ranging. However, the gradual political and cultural convergence of the *oecumene* that started with Alexander and continued advancing under the Roman emperors never uprooted local identities and allegiances.

Cultural convergence and local traditions

An altar or pedestal was set up near a temple in the Bahariya Oasis during Alexander's stay in Egypt or shortly thereafter. On the front, a hieroglyphic text mentions Alexander with his pharaonic titles, such as King of Upper and Lower Egypt, son of Amun, Beloved by Amun-Ra. On the left side, a Greek text, probably written by an Egyptian mason unfamiliar with Greek letters, declares: 'King Alexander dedicated this to Ammon, his father'. It may well be the earliest surviving text that shows Alexander adopting the local traditions of a conquered region, presenting himself as the son of a local god, exactly as any pharaoh would have done before him. Alexander also adopted the royal traditions of the Persian Empire. His successors followed his example, both in Egypt and in the Seleucid kingdom.

The merging of Greek and local traditions has been recognised as one of the most important cultural phenomena of the Hellenistic period. It took different forms and had different levels of intensity. Greek-style visual art and architecture became predominant in the Seleucid Empire, less so in most of Egypt, and exercised strong influence beyond its borders, in the areas of the Graeco-Bactrian and Graeco-Indian kingdoms. This influence was profound in Pakistan and northern India, as demonstrated by reliefs from Mathura dating to the second century BC (see Fig. 38) and stone palettes with mythological subjects from first-century-BC Pakistan. It remained visible until the second century AD, as we can see in the Buddhist sculpture of Gandhara.

The best-attested form of cultural convergence is the use of the Greek language in the kingdoms of Egypt and Asia. Greek was used not only by the administration, but also by the local populations: for instance, in dedications and building inscriptions. Although the language was Greek,

38. Relief from Mathura with scenes from the wanderings of Buddha. The artist was influenced by Hellenistic sculpture.

the ideas and customs that it expressed were mostly indigenous, gradually mixing with practices, values and beliefs of the Greek settlers. Typical Greek social institutions, such as athletic training, contests and dramatic performances, were introduced into the conquered territories, and vice versa; the Greek settlers increasingly adopted local customs, identified indigenous gods with theirs, and adapted their dress and their diet to local conditions – in Egypt, for instance, wearing garments made of linen instead of wool. The most important representatives of indigenous traditions in the areas of the Hellenistic kingdoms were the local priests; they not only defended their communities' privileges through negotiations with the kings, but also preserved customs through their interaction with the indigenous populations, continued composing documents in the local languages and sustained the memory of the local past. Manetho, allegedly a priest of Heliopolis under Ptolemy II, wrote a history of Egypt, which survives only in fragments but was an important source for the Greeks' knowledge of the Egyptian past.

Below the level of administration, the Greeks and the local populations were engaged in continuous processes of exchange. These were not free from conflicts. The conservative Jews in Jerusalem rejected the Greek institution of the gymnasium, and in Egypt petitions that are preserved in papyri occasionally refer to ethnic tensions. In 218 BC, a certain Herakleides describes, in a petition, his conflict with an Egyptian woman in Magdola:

> As I was passing by her house, an Egyptian woman, whose name is said to be Psenobastis, leaned out of a window and emptied a chamber pot of urine over my clothes, so that I was completely drenched. When I angrily reproached her, she hurled abuse at me. When I responded in kind, Psenobastis in her own right hand pulled the fold of my cloak in which I was wrapped, tore it and ripped it off me, so that my chest was laid quite bare. She also spat in my face, in the presence of several people whom I called to witness ... I therefore beg you, O King, if it please you, not to ignore my being thus – for no reason – manhandled by an Egyptian woman, whereas I am a Greek and a visitor.

But papyri in the same period also show how Greek settlers gradually built mixed families by marrying Egyptian women. A man named Dryton and his family have left us a large group of documents that provide insights into the life of Greeks and Egyptians. Dryton, probably the son or descendant of mercenaries from Crete, was born around 195 BC as a citizen of the Greek city of Ptolemais. As we can infer from the Cretan name of his father-in-law, Esthladas, his first wife, Sarapias, was of Cretan descent; thus Dryton first married within his own ethnic group. After Sarapias' death or divorce, Dryton married again around 150 BC. His second wife, Apollonia, also called Senmouthis, was much younger, did not have citizen status and was not Cretan. Her family had probably immigrated to Egypt, by the mid-third century BC at the latest, from Cyrene. After three or four generations of living in the Egyptian countryside, the members of this family had to a great extent adopted Egyptian culture and Egyptian names. This Apollonia, her four sisters and her five daughters all had double names, a Greek one and an Egyptian one. The convergence between the two cultures becomes more evident in the generation of Dryton's children. Two of his daughters are known to have married – and then divorced – Egyptian men.

Similar changes occurred in mainland Greece and the Greek colonies of Asia Minor when Italians settled there from the mid-second century BC onwards. Mixed marriages – but also simply coexistence in the same area – promoted cultural convergence. Roman law and institutions also had a great impact. For instance, around AD 100, Chersonesos in Tauris (modern Sebastopol) reformed its court system, adopting the Roman principle of *reiectio iudicum*: that is, the right of the adversaries to reject up to five judges.

The most important effect of Roman colonisation was its impact on culture. The Latin language was not only the official language in the Roman colonies, but also the spoken language of the population. In many colonies, Latin was gradually replaced by Greek and was only used for official documents or public inscriptions. But there were also colonies, such as Philippi and Dion in Macedonia, Patrae in Achaia and Alexandria Troas in Asia Minor, where Latin remained the main language of communication until the late second or third centuries AD. Roman gods, festivals and rituals were also introduced, and their impact did not remain limited to the colonies. An early example of cultural convergence is the introduction of the Roman festival of the Compitalia in Delos in the late second century BC. It was celebrated in neighbourhoods where Italian families lived, in front of the houses, with sacrifices offered to the Roman family gods, Lares, as well as to Mercury (assimilated with the Greek Hermes) and Hercules. Although the festival was an official celebration of the community of the Italici, it was also adopted by the freedmen of Italian families. The athletic competitions (*ludi*) and the sacrifices were part of the original tradition, but the custom of erecting altars in front of the houses was a Greek practice adopted by the Italian settlers.

The Roman funerary ritual of the *rosalia* is another case in point. The annual adornment of graves with roses took place on the occasion of the Roman festival of the Rosalia in May, devoted to the commemoration of the deceased. It was first brought to the Balkans by Roman and Italian settlers and was soon adopted by the local populations under the name *rhoda* or *rhodismos*, because it could easily be associated with the traditional custom of bringing flowers to the graves. From the Balkans, it spread further east, to Asia Minor. Artistic influence travelled in the opposite direction, from Greece to Italy, Rome and the western provinces. The agonistic culture of the Greeks was also not unknown in the West. Around the time of Hadrian's death, a certain Caius Valerius Avitus built a villa in Tarraco in Spain. Painted inscriptions in Greek on a wall fresco commemorated victories – most likely those of a family member – at two agonistic festivals in Greece: the Nemea and the Aktia.

Under the more or less uniform culture that we call the *koine*, local traditions persevered. Sometimes we know of them only because the spread of literacy allowed indigenous populations to produce inscriptions attesting to rituals that must have been practised for centuries without leaving any earlier trace in the written record. In Lydia, it is only in the second and third centuries AD that inscriptions mention a unique ritual whereby a sin was transmitted to triads of animals representing different spaces such as the earth, the sky, the underground and the rivers – the *triphonon* (animals of three voices) and the *enneaphonon* (animals of nine voices) – expecting the animals to carry the sin away. This ritual transmission of sin to animals finds parallels in Hittite rituals of the second millennium BC, according to which various creatures – birds, fish, mice – were released in order to remove evils and sins; the ritual was accompanied with incantations. The survival of such traditional rituals through the centuries in the local sanctuaries, rather than an artificial revival, seems the most likely explanation. In Tralleis, inscriptions of the second and third centuries AD mention the otherwise unattested ritual service of the 'concubine' (*pallake*) and 'those who do not wash their feet' (*aniptopodes*). We might be inclined to regard these cult peculiarities as artificial revivals or 'inventions of traditions', if the texts did not state that these functions were transmitted for generations within the same family. Another Lydian ritual that appears to be a survival of a long tradition is described by Pausanias, who saw it in sanctuaries of the 'Persian Artemis' in Hierokaisareia and Hypaipa in Lydia in the mid-second century AD. In these sanctuaries, there were altars onto which a *magus*, a Persian priest, wearing a tiara, placed dry wood. 'He then sings to some god or other an invocation in a foreign tongue, unintelligible to Greeks, reciting the invocation from a book', expecting the wood to burst into flames without the use of fire.

While in Capri, only months before his death in AD 14, Augustus distributed Greek dress to Romans and Roman garments to Greeks, and encouraged the two groups to speak each other's language. The Imperial period was a time of osmosis. Precisely this confrontation of the Greeks with different cultures made the educated among them conscious of their cultural traditions, triggering a great interest in Greek antiquities and history. The 'long Hellenistic Age' is the golden age of historiography, at least as far as quantity goes; it is also the golden age of commemorative anniversaries, historical monuments and mythography. The Greeks struggled to retain a broader Greek identity, often in addition to a local, civic or regional one, in a cosmopolitan world. *Hellenarch*, 'the chief magistrate of the Greeks', was the title of one official in Tanais, at the entrance to the Sea of Azov, in the second century AD.

Even in times when assimilation into the Roman Empire, especially linguistic, was strong, the memory of Greek origins never faded. In one of his 'Hidden Poems', Cavafy, animated by a passage in the work of the second-century-AD author Athenaios, expresses, with his characteristic historical sensitivity and perspicacity, this persistence of memory:

> The Poseidonians forgot the Greek language
> after so many centuries of mingling
> with Tyrrhenians, Latins, and other foreigners.
> The only thing surviving from their ancestors
> was a Greek festival, with beautiful rites,
> with lyres and flutes, contests and wreaths.
> And it was their habit toward the festival's end
> to tell each other about their ancient customs
> and once again to speak Greek names
> that only a few of them still recognised.
> And so their festival always had a melancholy ending
> because they remembered that they too were Greeks,
> they too once upon a time were citizens of Magna Graecia;
> and how low they'd fallen now, what they'd become,
> living and speaking like barbarians,
> cut off so disastrously from the Greek way of life.

REFERENCES AND SOURCES

Abbreviations

BCH: *Bulletin de Correspondance Hellénique*

CIG: *Corpus Inscriptionum Graecarum*, Berlin, 1825–77

F.Delphes: *Fouilles de Delphes*

FdXanthos VII: A. Balland, *Inscriptions d'époque impériale du Létôon. Fouilles de Xanthos* VII, Paris, 1981

FgrH: F. Jacoby et al., *Die Fragmente der griechischen Historiker*, Berlin and Leiden, 1923–

I.Didyma: A. Rehm, *Didyma, II: Die Inschriften*, edited by R. Harder, Berlin, 1958

I.Ephesos: H. Wankel et al., *Die Inschriften von Ephesos* (*IGSK*, 11–17), Bonn, 1979–81

I.Erythrai: H. Engelmann and R. Merkelbach, *Die Inschriften von Erythrai und Klazomenai*, I–II. (*IGSK*, 1–2), Bonn, 1972–73

IG: *Inscriptiones Graecae*, Berlin, 1873–

IGR: *Inscriptiones Graecae ad res Romanas pertinentes*, Paris, 1911–27

IGSK: *Inschriften griechischer Städte aus Kleinasien*, Bonn, 1972–

IGUR: L. Moretti, *Inscriptiones Graecae Urbis Romae*, Rome, 1968–90

I.Iasos: W. Blümel, *Die Inschriften von Iasos* (*IGSK*, 28, 1/2), Bonn, 1985

I.Knidos: W. Blümel, *Die Inschriften von Knidos,* I (*IGSK*, 41), Bonn, 1992

I.Kyme: H. Engelmann, *Die Inschriften von Kyme* (*IGSK*, 5), Bonn, 1976

I.Metropolis: B. Dreyer and H. Engelmann, *Die Inschriften von Metropolis. Teil I. Die Dekrete für Apollonios: Städtische Politik unter den Attaliden und im Konflikt zwischen Aristonikos und Rom* (*IGSK*, 63), Bonn, 2003

I.Olympia: W. Dittenberger and K. Purgold, *Inschriften von Olympia*, Berlin, 1896

IOSPE I²: V. Latyshev, *Inscriptiones antiquae orae septentrionalis Pontis Euxini Graecae et Latinae. Vol. 1. Inscriptiones Tyriae, Olbiae, Chersonesis Tauricae*, 2nd edn, St. Petersburg, 1916

I.Pergamon: M. Fraenkel, *Die Inschriften von Pergamon*, Berlin, 1890–95
I.Perinthos: M. H. Sayar, *Perinthos-Herakleia (Marmara Ereğlisi) und Umgebung: Geschichte, Testimonien, griechische und lateinische Inschriften*, Vienna, 1998
I.Priene: F. Hiller von Gaertringen, *Inschriften von Priene*, Berlin, 1906
ISE: L. Moretti, *Iscrizioni storiche ellenistiche*, I–II, Florence 1967ʒ5
I.Side: J. Nollé, *Side im Altertum: Geschichte und Zeugnisse. Band II (IGSK, 44, 2)*, Bonn, 2001
I.Smyrna: G. Petzl, *Die Inschriften von Smyrna (IGSK, 23–4)*, Bonn 1982–90
I.Tralleis: F. B. Poljakov, *Die Inschriften von Tralleis und Nysa.* Volume I: *Die Inschriften von Tralleis (IGSK, 36, 1)*, Bonn, 1989
JHS: *Journal of Hellenic Studies*
JRS: *Journal of Roman Studies*
LSAM: F. Sokolowski, *Lois sacrées d'Asie Mineure*, Paris, 1955
Milet VI.1: *Inschriften von Milet. Teil 1: A. Inschriften n. 187–406 (Nachdruck aus den Bänden I.5–II.3) von A. Rehm, mit einem Beitrag von H. Dessau; B. Nachträge und Übersetzungen zu den Inschriften n. 1–406 von P. Herrmann*, Berlin and New York, 1997
OGIS: W. Dittenberger, *Orientis Graeci Inscriptiones Selectae*, Leipzig, 1903–5
P.Eleph.: O. Rubensohn, *Ägyptische Urkunden aus den Königlichen Museen in Berlin: Griechische Urkunden, Sonderheft. Elephantine-Papyri*, Berlin, 1907
P.Enteux.: O. Guéraud, *Enteuxeis: Requêtes et plaintes adressées au Roi d'Égypte au IIIe siècle avant J.-C.*, Cairo, 1931–2
P.Oxy.: *Oxyrrhynchus Papyri*, London, 1898–
REG: *Revue des études grecques*
SEG: *Supplementum Epigraphicum Graecum*, Leiden, 1923–
Staatsverträge III: H. H. Schmitt, *Die Staatsverträge des Altertums*, III, Munich, 1969
Steinepigramme I: R. Merkelbach and J. Stauber, *Steinepigramme aus dem griechischen Osten. Band I: Die Westküste Kleinasiens von Knidos bis Ilion*, Stuttgart and Leipzig, 1998
*Syll.*³: W. Dittenberger, *Sylloge Inscriptionum Graecarum*, 3rd edn, Leipzig, 1915–24
TAM: *Tituli Asiae Minoris*, Vienna, 1901–
ZPE: *Zeitschrift für Papyrologie und Epigraphik*

All translations of Cavafy's poems are by Edmund Keeley and Philip Sherrard.

1 How It All Began

Further reading: A. B. Bosworth, *A Historical Commentary on Arrian's History of Alexander*, Oxford, 1980–95; Bosworth, 1988; A. B. Bosworth, *Alexander and the East: The Tragedy of Triumph*, Oxford, 1996; P. Cartledge, *Alexander the Great: The Hunt for a New Past*, London, 2004; A. W. Collins, 'The Royal Costume and Insignia of Alexander the Great', *American Journal of Philology* 133, 2012, 371–402;

Errington, 1992; P. M. Fraser, *Cities of Alexander the Great*, Oxford, 1996; N. G. L. Hammond, *Sources for Alexander the Great: An Analysis of Plutarch's 'Life' and Arrian's 'Anabasis Alexandrou'*, Cambridge, 1993; N. G. L. Hammond, *Alexander the Great: King, Commander and Statesman*, 2nd edn, Bristol, 1994; Hammond and Walbank, 1988; M. B. Hatzopoulos, 'Philippe II fondateur de la Macédoine nouvelle', *REG*, 125, 2012, 37–53; W. Heckel, *The Conquests of Alexander the Great: Key Conflicts of Classical Antiquity*, Cambridge, 2008; W. Heckel and L. A. Tritle (eds.), *Alexander the Great: A New History*, Malden, MA, 2009; W. Heckel and J. C. Yardley, *Alexander the Great: Historical Sources in Translation*, Malden, MA, 2004; A. J. Heisserer, *Alexander the Great and the Greeks: The Epigraphic Evidence*, Norman, OK, 1980; F. L. Holt, *Into the Land of Bones: Alexander the Great in Afghanistan*, Berkeley, 2005; R. Lane Fox, *Alexander the Great*, London, 1973; Lane Fox (ed.), 2011; J. Roisman (ed.), *Brill's Companion to Alexander the Great*, Leiden, 2004; H.-U. Wiemer, *Alexander der Grosse*, 2nd edn, Munich, 2015; Worthington, 2014; I. Worthington (ed.), *Alexander the Great: A Reader*, London, 2003.

Sources mentioned: *Arrian on Philip*: Anabasis, 7.9.2. *The palace at Aigai (Vergina)*: A. Kottaridi et al., *The Palace of Aegae 2007–2009: The Commencement of a Major Project*, Thessaloniki, 2009. *Isocrates' letter to Philip*: Letter 5.16. *Demosthenes and Philip*: Aeschines, 2.34. *The peace treaty after Chaironeia*: Staatsverträge, III, 403. *Alexander in Troy*: Arrian, *Anabasis*, 1.11.6–8. *Correspondence between Alexander and Darius*: Arrian, *Anabasis*, 2.14. *Alexander's campaign plans*: M. B. Hatzopoulos, 'Alexandre en Perse: la revanche et l'empire', *ZPE*, 116, 1997, 41–52. *Alexander and the Iliad*: Plutarch, *Alexander*, 7. *The exiles decree*: S. Dmitriev, 'Alexander's Exiles Decree', *Klio*, 86, 2004, 348–81. *The cult of Hephaistion*: SEG, XL, 547. *Droysen on Alexander*: J. G. Droysen, *Alexander der Große* (reprint), Frankfurt-Leipzig, 2004, 1. *Aristotle on Greeks and barbarians*: Politics, 1285a19–22.

2 The Successors

Further reading: E. M. Anson, *Eumenes of Cardia, a Greek among Macedonians*, Leiden, 2015; R. A. Billows, *Antigonos the One-Eyed and the Creation of the Hellenistic State*, Berkeley, 1990; A. B. Bosworth, *The Legacy of Alexander: Politics, Warfare and Propaganda under the Successors*, Oxford, 2002; Bouché-Leclercq, 1913–14; Bowman, 1996; P. Briant, *Antigone le Borgne: Les débuts de sa carrière et les problèmes de l'assemblée macédonienne*, Paris, 1973; S. N. Consolo Langher, *Agatocle: Da capoptre a monarca fondatore di un regno tra Cartagine e i Diadochi*, Messina, 2000; W. M. Ellis, *Ptolemy of Egypt*, London, 1994; Errington, 1992; J. D. Grainger, *Seleukos Nikator: Constructing a Hellenistic Kingdom*, London, 1990; Habicht, 1997; Hammond and Walbank, 1988; Hauben and Meeus (eds.), 2014; W. Heckel, *The Marshals of Alexander's Empire*, London, 1992; Hoelbl, 2000; J. Kobes, *'Kleine Könige': Untersuchungen zu den Lokaldynastien im hellenistischen Kleinasien (323–188)*, St Katharinen, 1996; C. Lehmler, *Syrakus unter Agathokles und Hieron*

II: Die Verbindung von Kultur und Macht in einer hellenistischen Metropole, Frankfurt, 2005; P. Lévêque, *Pyrrhos*, Paris, 1957; H. S. Lund, *Lysimachus: A Study in Hellenistic Kingship*, London, 1992; Martinez-Sève, 2011; A. Meeus, 'Kleopatra and the Diadochoi', in P. Van Nuffelen (ed.), *Faces of Hellenism: Studies in the History of the Eastern Mediterranean (4th Century BC–5th Century AD)*, Leuven, 2009, 63–92; L. O'Sullivan, *The Regime of Demetrius of Phalerum in Athens, 317–307 BCE: A Philosopher in Politics*, Leiden, 2009; J. Seibert, *Das Zeitalter der Diadochen*, Darmstadt, 1983; Sherwin-White and Kuhrt, 1993.

Sources mentioned: *Kassandros and the statue of Alexander*: Plutarch, *Alexander*, 74.6. *Eumenes and Alexander's throne*: Diodorus, 18.60.6. *Alexander's last words*: Diodorus, 17.117.4. *Demades on Alexander's death*: Plutarch, *Phokion*, 22. *'Hellenic War'*: *IG*, II², 467. *The royal proclamation of Antigonos*: Plutarch, *Demetrios*, 17. *Demetrios in Athens*: Demochares, *FgrH*, 75, F 2; Duris, *FgrH*, 76, F 13; Plutarch, *Demetrios*, 12, 34; Herodianus, 1.3.3. *Demetrios' cloak*: Duris, *FgrH*, 76, F 14. *Pyrrhos, a new Alexander*: Plutarch, *Pyrrhos*, 8. *Pyrrhos and Kineas*: Plutarch, *Pyrrhos*, 14. *Hannibal on Pyrrhos*: Plutarch, *Pyrrhos*, 8.2.

3 'Old' Greece in the Short Third Century

Further reading: A. J. Bayliss, *After Demosthenes: The Politics of Early Hellenistic Athens*, London and New York, 2011; K. Buraselis, *Das hellenistische Makedonien und die Ägäis: Forschungen zur Politik des Kassandros und der drei ersten Antigoniden im Ägäischen Meer und in Westkleinasien*, Munich, 1982; Cartledge and Spawforth, 1989; Errington, 1992; J. J. Gabbert, *Antigonus II Gonatas: A Political Biography*, London, 1997; Gray, 2015; Habicht, 1997; Hammond and Walbank, 1988; H. Heinen, *Untersuchungen zur hellenistischen Geschichte des 3. Jahrhunderts v.Chr. zur Geschichte der Zeit des Ptolemaios Keraunos und zum Chremonideischen Krieg*, Wiesbaden, 1972; Koehn, 2007; S. Le Bohec, *Antigone Dôsôn, roi de Macédoine*, Nancy, 1993; McKechnie and Guillaume (eds.), 2008; G. Nachtergael, *Les Galates en Grèce et les Sotéria de Delphes: Recherches d'histoire et d'épigraphie hellénistique*, Brussels, 1977; Oliver, 2007; K. Scherberich, *Koinè symmachía: Untersuchungen zum Hellenenbund Antigonos' III. Doson und Philipps V. (224–197 v. Chr.)*, Stuttgart, 2009; F. W. Walbank, *Aratos of Sicyon*, Cambridge, 1933.

Sources mentioned: *The miracle at Delphi*: Pausanias, 10.23.1–10; cf. Iustinus, 24.8. *The small Attalid Group*: Pausanias, 1.25.2. *Antigonid garrisons as fetters of Greece*: Polybius, 18.45. *Glaukon and Plataiai*: SEG, LXI, 352. *The decree of Chremonides*: *IG*, II², 687; Austin, 2006, no. 61; Bagnall and Derow, 2004, no. 19. *Polybius on the Achaean League*: 2.38.6. *The treaty of the Lycians with Caesar*: SEG, LV, 1452.

4 The Ptolemaic Golden Age

Further reading: Bowman, 1996; K. Buraselis, M. Stefanou and D. J. Thompson (eds.), *The Ptolemies, the Sea, and the Nile: Studies in Waterborne Power*,

Cambridge, 2013; D. L. Clayman, *Berenice II and the Golden Age of Ptolemaic Egypt* (Women in Antiquity), Oxford, 2014; Fraser, 1972; Grainger, 2010; Harris and Ruffini (eds.), 2004; Hoelbl, 2000; McKechnie and Guillaume (eds.), 2008; Manning, 2010; J. G. Manning, 'Hellenistic Egypt', in Scheidel et al. (eds.), 2007, 434–59; R. Strootman, *The Birdcage of the Muses: Patronage of the Arts and Sciences at the Ptolemaic Imperial Court (305–222 BCE)*, Leiden, 2016; Weber, 1991.

Sources mentioned: *Theocritus on Ptolemy II*: 17.77–97 and 104–105. *The procession at the Ptolemaia*: Athenaios, V, 202a–203b. *Aratos on Egypt*: Plutarch, *Aratos*, 15. *The ship 'Isis' in Nymphaion*: SEG, L, 696. *The inscription of Ptolemy III in Adulis*: OGIS, 54; Austin, 2006, no. 268; Bagnall and Derow, 2004, no. 26. *The Battle of Raphia*: Polybius, 5.82.5–86.6. *The rebellion of the Egyptians*: Polybius, 14.12.4.

5 Kings and Kingdoms

Further reading: Allen, 1983; G. G. Aperghis, *The Seleukid Royal Economy: The Finances and Financial Administration of the Seleukid Empire*, Cambridge, 2004; Bagnall, 1976; B. Bar-Kochva, *The Seleucid Army: Organisation and Tactics in the Great Campaigns*, Cambridge, 1976; J. Bauschatz, *Law and Enforcement in Ptolemaic Egypt*, Cambridge, 2013; Bikerman, 1938; Billows, 1995; Bouché-Leclercq, 1913–14; D. Bonneau, *Le régime administratif de l'eau du Nil dans l'Égypte grecque, romaine et byzantine*, Leiden, 1993; Bowman, 1996; Capdetrey, 2009; Chaniotis, 2005, 57–77; A. Chaniotis, 'The Ithyphallic Hymn for Demetrios Poliorcetes and Hellenistic Religious Mentality', in P. P. Iossif, A. S. Chankowski and C. C. Lorber (eds.), *More Than Men, Less Than Gods: Studies in Royal Cult and Imperial Worship*, Leuven, 2011, 157–95; Fischer-Bovet, 2014; Fraser, 1972; J. D. Grainger, *The Cities of Seleukid Syria*, Oxford, 1990; C. Habicht, *Divine Honors for Mortal Men in Greek Cities*, translated by J. N. Dillon, Exeter, 2017; Hansen, 1971; Hatzopoulos, 1996; M. B. Hatzopoulos, *L'organisation de l'armée macédonienne sous les Antigonides: Problèmes anciens et documents nouveaux*, Athens and Paris, 2001; Hoelbl, 2000; W. Huss, *Der makedonische König und die ägyptischen Priester: Studien zur Geschichte des ptolemäischen Ägypten*, Stuttgart, 1994; L. Koenen, 'The Ptolemaic King as a Religious Figure', in A. Bulloch et al. (eds.), *Images and Ideologies: Self-definition in the Hellenistic World*, Berkeley, 1993, 25–115; Kosmin, 2014; A. Lichtenberg, K. Martin, H.-H. Nieswandt and D. Salzmann (eds.), *Das Diadem der hellenistischen Herrscher: Übernahme, Transformation oder Neuschöpfung eines Herrschaftszeichens*, Münster, 2012; Ma, 2002; J. Ma, 'The Attalids: A Military History', in Thonemann (ed.), 2013, 49–82; Manning, 2003 and 2010; H. Melaerts (ed.), *Le culte du souverain dans l'Égypte ptolémaïque au IIIe siècle avant notre ère*, Louvain, 1998; A. Monson, *Agriculture and Taxation in Early Ptolemaic Egypt: Demotic Land Surveys and Accounts (P. Agri)*, Bonn, 2012; Monson, 2012; L. Mooren, *La hiérarchie de cour ptolémaïque: Contribution à l'étude des institutions et des classes dirigeantes à l'époque hellénistique*, Leuven, 1977; K. Mueller,

Settlements of the Ptolemies: City Foundations and New Settlement in the Hellenistic World, Leuven, 2006; Préaux, 1939; P. Sänger, 'Das *politeuma* in der hellenistischen Staatenwelt: eine Organisationsform zur Systemintegration von Minderheiten', in P. Sänger (ed.), *Minderheiten und Migration in der griechisch-römischen Welt*, Paderborn, 2016, 25–45; I. Savalli-Lestrade, *Les philoi royaux dans l'Asie hellénistique*, Geneva, 1998; Scholz, 2015; C. Schuler, 'Landwirtschaft und königliche Verwaltung im hellenistischen Kleinasien', *Topoi*, 6, 2004, 509–43; Sherwin-White and Kuhrt, 1993; Strootman, 2014; Thompson, 1988; P. Thonemann, 'The Attalid State', in Thonemann (ed.), 2013, 1–48; P. Van Nuffelen, 'Le culte royal de l'Empire des Séleucides: Une réinterpretation', *Historia*, 52, 2004, 278–301; Versnel, 2011, 439–492; B. Virgilio, *Le roi écrit: Le correspondance du souverain hellénistique, suivie de deux lettres d'Antiochos III, à partir de Louis Robert et d'Adolf Wilhelm*, Pisa, 2011; Weber, 1991; Welles, 1934.

Sources mentioned: *Definition of kingship*: Suda, s.v. *basileia*; Austin, 2006, no. 45. *Kassandros as 'king of the Macedonians'*: Hatzopoulos, 1996, II, no. 20. *Royal proclamation of Demetrios the Besieger*: Plutarch, *Demetrios*, 37.2–3; cf. Justin, 16.1.9 and 18. *The enthronisation of Antiochos IV*: IG, II³, 1323. *Antiochos I and Stratonike*: Plutarch, *Demetrios*, 38. *The dossier of cover letters from Philomelion*: SEG, LIV, 1353. *Brigandage in the 'amnesty decree'*: Austin, 2006, no. 290. *The trial of Phokion*: Plutarch, *Phokion*, 34; Diodorus, 18.66–67. *The Achaeans 'bridled like a horse'*: Plutarch, *Aratos*, 38.10. *Philip's letters to Larisa*: Austin, 2006, no. 75; Bagnall and Derow, 2004, no. 32. *Philip V's theatrical behaviour*: Polybius, 10.26.1–2. *Demetrios and the old woman*: Plutarch, *Demetrios*, 42. *Theocritus' praise of Ptolemy*: 17.105–6. *Alexander's blood*: Plutarch, *Alexander*, 28. *Continuation of Alexander's cult*: LSAM, 26, L. 9; I.Ephesos, 719; I.Erythrai, 64. *The cult of Seleukos I and Antiochos I in Aigai*: SEG, LIX, 1406 A. *The cult of Antiochos III in Teos*: SEG, XLI, 1003; A. Chaniotis, 'Isotheoi timai : la divinité mortelle d'Antiochos III à Téos', *Kernos*, 20, 2007, 153–71. *The hymn for Demetrios*: Demochares, FgrH, 75, F 2; Athenaios, VII, 253 D–F. *Dio Cassius on godlike honours*: 52.35.5. *Prusias I in Rome*: Polybius, 30.18–19. *The theatricality of Demetrios the Besieger*: Plutarch, *Demetrios*, 28, 34, 41, 44–45, 53. *Diotogenes on kingship*: Stobaeus, 4.7.62. *The teatricality of Philip V*: Polybius, 10.26.1–2. *Polybius on Antiochos IV*: 26.1.5. *The sons of Attalos I in Kyzikos*: Polybius, 22.20.5–7.

6 The City-state in a World of Federations and Empires

Further reading: Beck and Funke (eds.), 2015; R. Behrwald, *Der lykische Bund: Untersuchungen zu Geschichte und Verfassung*, Bonn, 2000; Berthold, 1984; Billows, 1995; Brun, 1996; Cartledge and Spawforth, 1989; Chaniotis, 2005; Cohen, 1978, 1995 and 2006; Couvenhes and Fernoux (eds.), 2004; Dmitriev, 2005; Fernoux, 2004; Fröhlich, 2004; Fröhlich and Müller (eds.), 2005; Gabrielsen, 1997; Gauthier, 1985; Grainger, 1999; V. Grieb, *Hellenistische Demokratie: Politische*

Organisation und Struktur in freien griechischen Poleis nach Alexander dem Großen, Stuttgart, 2008; Habicht, 1997; P. Hamon, 'Le conseil et la participation des citoyens: les mutations de la basse époque hellénistique', in Fröhlich and Müller (eds.) 2005, 121–44; Hamon, 2007; Harding, 2015; Labarre, 1996; C. Mann and P. Scholz (eds.), *'Demokratie' im Hellenismus. Von der Herrschaft des Volkes zur Herrschaft der Honoratioren,* Mainz, 2012; Migeotte, 1992; K. Mueller, *Settlements of the Ptolemies: City Foundations and New Settlement in the Hellenistic World,* Leuven, 2006; Quass, 1993; Roubineau, 2015; Sartre, 1995; Sherwin-White, 1978; Wörrle and Zanker (eds.), 1995.

Sources mentioned: *Herakleides on the cities of Greece*: F. Pfister, *Die Reisebilder des Herakleides,* Vienna, 1951. *Polybius on the Achaian League*: 2.37.11. *Cities in the Roman Empire*: Aelius Aristides, *Orations,* 26.93. *Tyriaion becomes a polis*: SEG, XLVII, 1745. *The garrison at Kyrbisos*: SEG, XXVI, 1306, 8–11. *The Achaean League as a democracy*: Polybius, 2.38.6. *Diokles of Kos*: SEG, XLVIII, 1104. *Eurykleides and Mikion*: *IG*, II², 834, 1705; C. Habicht, *Studien zur Geschichte Athens in hellenistischer Zeit,* Göttingen, 1982, 179–82. *Helikon of Priene*: I.Priene, 19. *Philippides of Athens*: *IG*, II², 657. *Protogenes of Olbia*: IOSPE, I², 32; Austin, 2006, no. 115. *Strabo on Rhodes*: 14.2.5. *Mummius and oligarchic constitutions*: Pausanias, 7.16.9. *Kondylis on populism*: P. Kondylis, *Niedergang der bürgerlichen Denk- und Lebensform,* Frankfurt, 1991, 200. *Quintilian's advice to orators*: Institutio oratoria, 11.3.147. *Bush's campaign*: E. Burns, *Theatricality: A Study of Convention in the Theatre and in Social Life,* London, 1972, 34. *Alketas*: Diodorus, 18.46.1–47.3. *Tyrannies in Sikyon*: Plutarch, *Aratos,* 2.1–2. *Eugnotos of Akraiphia*: J. Ma, 'The Many Lives of Eugnotos of Akraiphia', in B. Virgilio (ed.), *Studi ellenistici,* 16, Pisa, 2005, 141–91. *Diodoros Pasparos*: C. P. Jones, 'Diodoros Pasparos and the Nicephoria of Pergamon', *Chiron,* 4, 1974, 183–205. *Chairemon, Pythodoros and their family*: C. P. Jones, 'An Inscription Seen by Agathias', *ZPE,* 170, 2011, 107–15. *Nikias of Kos*: *IG,* XII.4, 682–711; Buraselis, 2000, 30–65, 131–33. *Diodoros of Adramyttion*: Strabo, 13.1.66. *Lysias of Tarsos*: Athenaios, V, 215b–c.

7 Entanglement

Further reading: Berthold, 1984; Eckstein, 2006; R. M. Errington, *Philopoemen,* Oxford, 1969; Errington, 1992; Grainger, 1999, 2010, and 2015; Ferrary, 2014; Gruen, 1984; Hammond and Walbank, 1988; Hansen, 1971; Harris, 1979 and 2016; Hoyos (ed.), 2013; Koehn, 2007; Ma, 2002; R. Pfeilschifter, *Titus Quinctius Flamininus: Untersuchungen zur römischen Griechenlandpolitik,* Göttingen, 2005; J. B. Scholten, *The Politics of Plunder: Aitolians and their Koinon in the Early Hellenistic Era, 279–217 BC,* Berkeley, 2000; Sherwin-White and Kuhrt, 1993, 188–216; Wiemer, 2002.

Sources mentioned: *Polybius on symploke*: 1.3.1–4. *Polybius on Teuta*: 2.4.8–9. *Pliny on the Roman Empire*: Pliny, *Natural History,* 3.39. *The speech of Agelaos in*

Naupaktos: Polybius, 5.104. *The impact of Cannae*: Polybius, 3.117.2; Livy, 22.54.7. *The treaty between Philip V and Hannibal*: Polybius, 7.9. *The siege of Syracuse*: Plutarch, *Marcellus*, 14–19. *The treaty between Rome and the Aetolians*: *Staatsverträge*, III, no. 536. *The freedom declaration in Isthmia*: Polybius, 18.46; Plutarch, *Titus*, 10.3–6. *Antiochos III's speech in Lysimacheia*: Polybius, 18.51. *Cicero on the mission of Rome*: Polybius, 18.51. *Hannibal's last words*: Livy, 39.51. *Philopoimen, 'the last of the Greeks'*: Plutarch, *Philopoimen*, 1. *Pausanias on Philopoimen*: 8.52.

8 The Greek States Become Roman Provinces

Further reading: Bernhard, 1985 and 1998; Camia, 2009; Cartledge and Spawforth, 1989; G. Champion, 'Empire by Invitation: Greek Political Strategies and Roman Imperial Interventions in the Second Century BCE', *Transactions of the American Philological Association*, 137, 2007, 255–75; Eckstein, 2006; Ferrary, 2014; Gruen, 1984; Hansen, 1971; Harris, 1979 and 2016; J. Hopp, *Untersuchungen zur Geschichte der letzten Attaliden*, Munich, 1977; Hoyos (ed.), 2013; P. Kay, *Rome's Economic Revolution*, Oxford, 2014, 59–83; Magie, 1950; Martinez-Sève, 2011; Z. Yavetz, 'Towards a Further Step into the Study of Roman Imperialism', in E. Hermon (ed.), *Gouvernants et gouvernés dans l'imperium romanum* (*Cahiers des Études Anciennes* 3), Québec, 1991, 3–22.

Sources mentioned: *Perseus monument in Delphi*: *SEG*, XLVIII, 588. *The Roman accusations against Perseus in Delphi*: Bagnall and Derow, 2004, no. 44; Austin, 2006, no. 93. *Decree of Abdera*: *Syll.*³, 656. *Horace on the cultural impact of expansion*: *Epistles*, 2.1.156–7. *Antipatros of Sidon on the sack of Corinth*: *Greek Anthology*, 9.151. *Attalos II's letter to Pessinous*: Welles, 1934, no. 61; Bagnall and Derow, 2004, no. 50. *The honorific inscription for Attalos III*: *I.Pergamon*, 246. *The honorific inscription for Apollonios of Metropolis*: *I.Metropolis*, 1. *The lex de portorii Asiae*: M. Cottier et al., *The Customs Law of Asia*, Oxford, 2008. *Mark Antony on the taxation of Asia*: Appian, *Civil Wars*, 5.1. *Tiberius Gracchus' journey through Etruria*: Plutarch, *Tiberius*, 8.7. *Gracchus' speech*: Gellius, *Noctes Atticae*, 11.10.3. *Cicero on the publicani*: *De imperio Cnaei Pompeii*, 17. *The impact of taxation*: Diodorus, 34/35.25.

9 Decline and Fall of the Hellenistic Kingdoms in Asia and Egypt

Further reading: B. Bar-Kochva, *Judah Maccabee: The Jewish Struggle Against the Seleucids*, Cambridge, 1989; C. R. Benjamin, *The Yuezhi: Origin, Migration and the Conquest of Northern Bactria*, Turnhout, 2007; E. J. Bickerman, *The Jews in the Greek Age*, Cambridge, MA, 1988; Bouché-Leclercq, 1913–14; Bowman, 1996; Braund, 1984; Chauveau, 2000; Coloru, 2009; F. Daubner, *Bellum asiaticum: Der Krieg der Römer gegen Aristonikos von Pergamon und die Einrichtung der Provinz Asia*, 2nd edn, Munich, 2004; Eddy, 1961; Ehling, 2008; C. Feyel and L. Graslin-Thomé (eds.), *Le projet politique d'Antiochos IV*, Nancy, 2014; Grajetzki, 2011; E.

S. Gruen, *Heritage and Hellenism: The Reinvention of Jewish Tradition*, Berkeley, 1998; Hoelbl, 2000; F. L. Holt, *Thundering Zeus: The Making of Hellenistic Bactria*, Berkeley, 1999; S. Honigman, *Tales of High Priests and Taxes: The Books of the Maccabees and the Judean Rebellion against Antiochos IV*, Berkeley, 2014; O. Hoover, 'A Revised Chronology for the Late Seleucids at Antioch (121/0–64 BC)', *Historia*, 56, 2007, 280–301; Hoyos (ed.), 2013; A. Jördens and J. F. Quack (eds.), *Ägypten zwischen innerem Zwist und äußerem Druck: Die Zeit Ptolemaios' VI. bis VIII.*, Wiesbaden, 2011; Kallet-Marx, 1995; J. D. Lerner, *The Impact of the Seleucid Decline on the Eastern Iranian Plateau: The Foundations of Arsacid Parthia and Graeco-Bactria*, Stuttgart, 1999; Martinez-Sève, 2011; P. F. Mittag, *Antiochos IV. Epiphanes. Eine politische Biographie*, Berlin, 2006; Schwartz, 2001 and 2014; Sherwin-White, 1984; Sherwin-White and Kuhrt, 1993, 217–29; A.-E. Véisse, *Les 'révoltes égyptiennes': Recherches sur les troubles intérieurs en Egypte du règne de Ptolémée III Evergète à la conquête romaine*, Leuven, 2004.

Sources mentioned: *Heliodoros in the Temple of Jerusalem*: Maccabees 2.3. *Inscriptions mentioning Heliodoros*: *SEG*, LVII, 1838; LX, 1723; H. M. Cotton, A. Ecker and D. Gera, 'Juxtaposing Literary and Documentary Evidence: A New Copy of the So-Called Heliodoros Stele and the Corous Inscriptionum Iudaeae/Palestinae (*CIIP*)', *Bulletin of the Institute of Classical Studies*, 60, 2017, 1–15;'. The *'day of Eleusis'*: Polybius, 29.27.1–10. *Antiochos IV's parade in Daphne*: Athenaios, V, 194c–195f. *Inscription praising King Euthydemos*: *SEG*, LIV, 1569. *Inscription from Mathura*: R. Salomon, 'The Indo-Greek Era of 186/5 BC in a Buddhist Reliquary Inscription', in O. Bopearachchi and M.-F. Boussac (eds.), *Afghanistan, ancien carrefour entre l'est et l'ouest*, Turnhout, 2005, 373. *Inscription from Bahrain*: P. Kosmin, 'Rethinking the Hellenistic Gulf: The New Greek Inscription from Bahrain', *JHS*, 133, 2013, 61–79. *The Rosetta stone*: *OGIS*, 90. *Scipio Aemilianus on the riches of Egypt*: Diodorus, 33.28b. *The Ptolemaic amnesty decree*: Austin, 2006, no. 290.

10 A Battlefield of Foreign Ambitions

Further reading: S.-A. Ashton, *Cleopatra and Egypt*, Oxford, 2008; S. Benne, *Marcus Antonius und Kleopatra VII.: Machtausbau, herrscherliche Repräsentation und politische Konzeption*, Göttingen, 2001; Bernhard, 1985 and 1998; H. Börm, 'Hellenistische Poleis und römischer Bürgerkrieg. Stasis im griechischen Osten nach den Iden des März (44 bis 39 v. Chr.)', in H. Börm, M. Mattheis and J. Wienand (eds.), *Civil War in Ancient Greece and Rome*, Stuttgart, 2015, 99–125; Braund, 1984; Chauveau, 2000; De Souza, 1999; Ferrary, 2014; Gruen, 1984; Habicht, 1997; Hoelbl, 2000; Kallet-Marx, 1995; Magie, 1950; A. Mayor, *The Poison King: The Life and Legend of Mithradates, Rome's Deadliest Enemy*, Princeton, 2010; B. C. McGing, *The Foreign Policy of Mithridates VI Eupator King of Pontos*, Leiden, 1986; A. Niebergall, 'Die lokalen Eliten der griechischen Städte Kleinasiens und Mithridates VI Eupator zu Beginn des ersten römisch-pontischen Krieges', *Hermes*,

139, 2011, 1–20; H. Pohl, *Die römische Politik und die Piraterie im östlichen Mittelmeer vom 3. Jahrhundert bis zum 1. Jahrhundert v. Chr.*, Berlin and New York, 1993; D. W. Roller, *Cleopatra: A Biography*, Oxford, 2010; F. Santangelo, *Sulla, the Elites and the Empire: A Study of Roman Policies in Italy and the Greek East*, Leiden, 2007; Sherwin-White, 1984; R. D. Sullivan, *Near Eastern Royalty and Rome: 100–30 BC*, Toronto, 1990; Syme, 1939.

Sources mentioned: *Athenion's speech in Athens*: Poseidonios, *Histories*, fragment 247 (ed. Theiler); *FgrH*, 87, F 36, 51; Athenaios, V, 212b–213c. *Sulla in Athens*: Plutarch, *Sulla*, 13. *Mithridates' treatment of the Chians*: Appian, *Mithridatic Wars* 12.46–47. *Cicero on Pompey's war against the pirates*: In Defence of the Manilian law, 12.35. *Veni, vidi, vici*: Plutarch, *Caesar*, 50.3; Suetonius, *Divus Iulius*, 37.2. *Cleopatra's show in Cilicia*: Plutarch, *Antony*, 26.

11 A Roman East

Further reading: M. Adak and M. Wilson. 'Das Vespasianmonument von Döseme und die Gründung der Doppelprovinz Lycia et Pamphylia', *Gephyra*, 9, 2012, 1–40; Alcock, 1993; J. Bergemann, *Die römische Kolonie von Butrint und die Romanisierung Griechenlands*, Munich, 1998; Birley, 1997; Bowersock, 1965; Braund, 1984; Cartledge and Spawforth, 1989; Champlin, 2003; Drexhage, 2007; Eck, 2003; Galinsky, 2012; Galinsky (ed.), 2005; Goldsworthy, 2014; Halfmann, 1979; C. P. Jones, 'The Panhellenion', *Chiron*, 26, 1996, 29–56; T. Kaizer and M. Facella (eds.), *Kingdoms and Principalities in the Roman Near East*, Stuttgart, 2010; C. Katsari and S. Mitchell, 'The Roman Colonies of Greece and Asia Minor: Questions of State and Civic Identity', *Athenaeum*, 96, 2008, 221–49; Levick, 1967 and 2010; Magie, 1950; F. G. B. Millar, 'The Roman Coloniae of the Near East: A Study of Cultural Relations', in H. Solin and M. Kajava (eds.), *Roman Eastern Policy and Other Studies in Roman History*, Helsinki, 1990, 7–58; T. Opper, *Hadrian: Empire and Conflict*, London, 2008; Raaflaub and Toher (eds.), 1993; A. D. Rizakis, 'Roman Colonies in the Province of Achaia: Territories, Land and Population', in Alcock (ed.), 1997, 15–36; D. Rousset, 'The City and its Territory in the Province of Achaea and "Roman Greece"', *Harvard Studies in Classical Philology*, 104, 2008, 303–37; Syme, 1939; Veyne, 1999; S. Zoumbaki, 'The Colonists of the Roman East and Their Leading Groups: Some Notes on Their Entering the Equestrian and Senatorial Ranks in Comparison with the Native Elites', *Tyche*, 23, 159–79.

Sources mentioned: *Tacitus on Jesus*: Annals, 15.44. *Pliny on the Christians*: Letters, 10.96. *Imperium sine fine*: Virgil, *Aeneid*, 1.279. *Acclamation for Rome in Ephesos*: SEG, LIII, 1290. *Rome in the Apocalypse*: John, *Apocalypse*, 17.4–18. *The historian Philip*: IG, IV².1, 687; *FgrH*, 95, T 1. *Celebration in Messene for Caius Caesar*: SEG, XXIII, 206. *Honours for Caius Caesar in Kos*: IG, XII.4, 105. *Plutarch on political life*: Moralia, 805a. *The reliefs in the Sebasteion of Aphrodisias*: R. R. R. Smith, '*Simulacra gentium*: The *ethne* from the Sebasteion at Aphrodisias', *JRS*, 78,

1988, 50–77. *Polybius on demographic decline*: 36.17.5. *Octavian's letter to Ephesos*: Reynolds, 1982, no. 12. *Nero's speech in Isthmia*: *IG*, VII, 2713; Oliver, 1989, no. 296. *Epameinondas of Akraiphia*: *IG*, VII, 2713. *Balbilla's poem*: *SEG*, VIII, 715. *Hadrian's letters on the organisation of contests*: *SEG*, LVI, 1359. *Hadrian's letter to Naryx*: *SEG* LI, 641. *Hadrian's honours in Delphi*: *Syll*.³, 835 A.

12 Emperors, Cities and Provinces from Augustus to Hadrian

Further reading: Bekker-Nielsen, 2008; G. Boulvert, *Domestique et fonctionnaire sous le Haute-Empire romaine: La condition de l'affranchi et de l'esclave du prince*, Paris, 1974; Bowersock, 1965; B. Burrell, *Neokoroi: Greek Cities and Roman Emperors*, Leiden, 2004; Cartledge and Spawforth, 1989; M. Coudry and F. Kirbihler, 'La lex Cornelia, une lex provinciae de Sylla pour l'Asie', in N. Barrandon and F. Kirbihler (eds.), *Administrer les provinces de la République romaine*, Rennes, 2010, 133–69; Dmitriev, 2005; M. Dräger, *Die Städte der Provinz Asia in der Flavierzeit*, Frankfurt, 1993; Drexhage, 2007; F. K. Drogula, *Commanders and Command in the Roman Republic and Early Empire*, Chapel Hill, NC, 2015; W. Eck, 'Administration and Jurisdiction in Rome and in the Provinces', in M. van Ackern (ed.), *A Companion to Marcus Aurelius*, Malden, MA, 2012, 185–99; B. Edelmann-Singer, *Koina und Concilia: Genese, Organisation und sozioökonomische Funktion der Provinziallandtage im römischen Reich*, Stuttgart, 2015; Fernoux, 2004 and 2011; G. Frija, *Les prêtres des empereurs: Le culte impérial civique dans la province romaine d'Asie*, Rennes, 2012; T. Fujii, *Imperial Cult and Imperial Representation in Roman Cyprus*, Stuttgart, 2013; S. Gambetti, *The Alexandrian Riots of 38 C.E. and the Persecution of the Jews: A Historical Reconstruction*, Leiden, 2009; R. Haensch, *Capita provinciarum: Statthaltersitz und Provinzialverwaltung in der römischen Kaiserzeit*, Mainz, 1997; Halfmann, 1986; Hamon, 2007; A. Heller, '*Les bêtises des Grecs*': *Conflits et rivalités entre cités d'Asie et de Bithynie à l'époque romaine (129 a.C.–235 p.C.)*, Bordeaux, 2006; Jones, 1971; Lintott, 1993; B. Levick, 'Some Augustan Oaths', in S. Cagnazzi et al. (eds.), *Scritti di storia per Mario Pani*, Bari, 2011, 245–56; Magie, 1950; O. Meyer-Zwiffelhoffer, *Politikos archein. Zum Regierungsstil der senatorischen Statthalter in den kaiserzeitlichen griechischen Provinzen*, Stuttgart, 2002; Millar, 1992; S. Mitchell, 'The Administration of Roman Asia from 133 BC to AD 250', in Eck (ed.), 1999, 17–46; A.-V. Pont, 'L'empereur "fondateur": enquête sur les motifs de la reconnaissance civique', *REG*, 120, 2007, 526–52; Price, 1984; Raaflaub and Toher (eds.), 1993; G. Salmeri, 'Reconstructing the Political Life and Culture of the Greek Cities of the Roman Empire', in van Nijf and Alston (eds.), 2011, 197–214; C. Samitz, 'Die Einführung der Dekaproten und Eikosaproten in den Städten Kleinasiens und Griechenlands', *Chiron*, 43, 2013, 1–61; Sartre, 1995; A. N. Sherwin-White, *The Letters of Pliny: A Historical and Social Commentary*, Oxford, 1985 (corrected edn); Syme, 1939; Varga and Rusu-Bolindeţ (eds.), 2016; Zuiderhoek, 2009.

Sources mentioned: *The decree of the Greeks of Asia for Augustus*: Sherk, 1969, no. 65; *SEG*, LVI, 1233. *Augustus' letter to Knidos*: *I.Knidos*, 34. *Augustus on Theodoros of Tarsos*: Plutarch, *Moralia*, 207b–c. *The emperor as rescuer of the oecumene*: *I.Olympia*, 366; *I.Iasos*, 602; *IG*, VII, 1840 and 2497; *I.Smyrna*, 594. *The announcement of Nero's enthronement in Egypt*: *P.Oxy.*, 1021. *The decree of Maroneia*: *SEG*, LIII, 659. *The imperial cult in Mytilene*: *IGR*, IV, 39. *Monthly sacrifices in Pergamon*: *IGR*, IV, 35 (*emmenos genesios tou Sebastou*). *Publius Aelius Pompeianus Paion, 'the new Homer'*: *I.Ephesos*, 22; *I.Side*, 70. *The lex provinciae of Bithynia in Pliny's letters*: *Letters*, 10.79, 112, 114. *The cult of governors (Scaevola, Appuleius)*: G. Thériault, 'Remarques sur le culte des magistrates romains en Orient', *Cahiers des Études Anciennes*, 37, 2001, 85–95; G. Thériault, 'Culte des évergètes (magistrats) romains et agônes en Asie Mineure', in K. Konuk (ed.), *Stephanèphoros: De l'économie antique à l'Asie Mineure. Hommages à Raymond Descat*, Bordeaux; 2012, 377–88. *Roman terms (senatus, praetorium) used by Lydian priests*: SEG, XXXVIII, 1237; LVII, 1186. *The Roman Empire as a city*: Aelius Aristides, *Orations*, 26.61. *Gellius on Roman colonies*: *Noctes Atticae*, 16.13.9. *Categories of citizens in Xanthos*: *FdXanthos* VII, 67. *Ekklesiastai*: *IGR*, III, 409. *Kallisthenes of Olbia*: *IOSPE*, I², 42. *Acclamations*: *P.Oxy.*, I 41. *The funeral of Herodes Atticus*: Philostratus, *Lives of the Sophists*, 15.20. *Political conflicts in Tarsos*: Strabo, 14.5.14. *Petraios of Thessaly*: Plutarch, *Moralia*, 815d. *The foundation of Attalos in Aphrodisias*: B. Laum, *Stiftungen in der griechischen und römischen Antike*, Leipzig and Berlin, 1914, no. 102. *Dio of Prusa*: Jones, 1978, 19–25. *Riots in Ephesos*: Acts 19:23–41.

13 Socio-economic Conditions

Further reading: Alföldy, 2011; Z. Archibald, J. Davies and V. Gabrielsen (eds.), *The Economies of Hellenistic Societies*, Oxford, 2011; Z. H. Archibald, J. Davies and V. Gabrielsen (eds.), *Making, Moving, and Managing: The New World of Ancient Economies, 323–31 BC*, Oxford, 2005; J. Bartels, *Städtische Eliten im römischen Makedonien*, Berlin, 2008; Bekker-Nielsen, 2008; A. Bielman, *Retour à la liberté: Libération et sauvetage des prisonniers en Grèce ancienne*, Paris, 1994; Billows, 1995; Bowersock, 1965 and 1969; Brélaz, 2005; C. Brélaz, 'Les "pauvres" comme composante du corps civique dans les *poleis* des époques hellénistiques et impériale', *Ktèma*, 38, 2013, 67–87; Brun, 1996; P. Brun (ed.), *Économies et societés en Grèce classique et hellénistique*, Toulouse, 2007; Cartledge and Spawforth, 1989; Chaniotis, 2005; A. Chaniotis, 'What Difference did Rome Make? The Cretans and the Roman Empire', in B. Forsén and G. Salmeri (eds.), *The Province Strikes Back: Imperial Dynamics in the Eastern Mediterranean*, Helsinki, 2008, 83–105; Chauveau, 2000; Cohen, 1978, 1995 and 2006; Couvenhes and Fernoux (eds.), 2004; De Souza, 1999; M.Domingo Gygax, *Benefaction and Rewards in the Ancient Greek City: The Origins of Euergetism*, Cambridge, 2016; Fernoux, 2004; J. Fournier, *Entre tutelle romaine et autonomie civique: L'administration judiciaire dans les provinces hellénophones de l'empire romain (129 av. J.-C.–235 ap. J.-C.)*, Athens, 2010; Fraser, 1972; Fröhlich and Hamon (eds.), 2013; Gabrielsen, 1997; Gauthier, 1972 and 1985; Gray, 2015; T. Grünewald, *Räuber, Rebellen, Rivalen, Rächer: Studien zu Latrones im römischen Reich*, Stuttgart, 1999; M. Haake, *Der Philosoph in der Stadt: Untersuchungen zur öffentlichen Rede über Philosophen und Philosophie in der hellenistischen Polis*, Munich, 2007; Harris and Ruffini (eds.), 2004; Harding, 2015; J. Hatzfeld, *Les trafiquants italiens dans l'Orient hellénique*, Paris, 1919; A. Heller and A.-V. Pont (eds.), *Patrie d'origine et patries électives: Les citoyennetés multiples dans le monde grec d'époque romaine. Actes du colloque international de Tours, 6–7 novembre 2009*, Bordeaux, 2012; Jones, 1978; Kuhn, 2012; Labarre, 1996; Launey, 1987; F. Lerouxel and A.-V. Pont (eds.), *Propriétaires et citoyens dans l'Orient romain*, Bordeaux, 2016; Lewis, 1986; Y. Le Bohec, *The Imperial Roman Army*, translated by R. Bate, London, 1994; Ma, 2013; C. Müller and C. Hasenohr (eds.), *Les Italiens dans le monde grec: IIe siècle av. J.-C.–Ier siècle ap. J.C. Circulation, activités, intégration*, Athens and Paris, 2000; K. Mueller, *Settlements of the Ptolemies: City Foundations and New Settlement in the Hellenistic World*, Leuven, 2006; M. Niku, *The Official Status of the Foreign Residents in Athens, 322–120 BC*, Helsinki, 2007; Oliver, 2007; Papazoglou, 1997; Perrin-Saminadayar, 2007; Peachin (ed.), 2011; Puech, 2012; Quass, 1993; G. Reger, 'Hellenistic Greece and Western Asia Minor', in Scheidel et al. (eds.), 2007, 460–83; Rizakis and Touratsoglou (eds.), 2013; Rizakis and Lepeniotis (eds.), 2010; Rostovtzeff, 1941; Roubineau, 2015; Sartre, 1995; C. Schuler, *Ländliche Siedlungen und Gemeinden im hellenistischen und römischen Kleinasien*, Munich, 1998; E. Stavrianopoulou, 'Die Bewirtung des Volkes: Öffentliche Speisungen in der römischen Kaiserzeit', in Hekster et al. (eds.), 2009, 159–80; G. Steinhauer, 'C. Iulius Eurycles and the Spartan Dynasty of the Euryclids', in Rizakis and Lepeniotis (eds.), 2010, 75–87; Thompson, 1988; Thonemann, 2011; Varga and Rusu-Bolindeţ (eds.), 2016; A. V. Walser, *Bauern und Zinsnehmer: Politik, Recht und Wirtschaft im frühhellenistischen Ephesos*, Munich, 2008; Wörrle and Zanker (eds.), 1995; Zuiderhoek, 2009; A. Zuiderhoek, 'Sorting out Labour in the Roman Provinces: Some Reflections on Labour and Institutions in Asia Minor', in K. Verboven and C. Laes (eds.), *Work, Labour, and Professions in the Roman World*, Leiden, 2017, 20–35.

Sources mentioned: *Archimedes' devices during the siege of Syracuse*: Plutarch, *Marcellus*, 15–17. *Metrodoros of Skepsis*: Strabo, 13.1.55. *Boethos of Tarsos*: Strabo, 14.5.14. *Nikanor in Athens*: C. P. Jones, 'Julius Nicanor Again', *ZPE*, 178, 2011, 79–83. *Euthydenos and Hybreas of Mylasa*: Strabo, 14.2.24. *Eurykles of Sparta*: Strabo, 8.5.5. *Melankomas*: Dio of Prusa, *Orations*, 28 and 29. *Caius Stertinius Xenophon*: *IG*, XII.4, 712–79; Buraselis, 2000, 66–110. *Zoilos of Aphrodisias*: R. R. R. Smith, *The Monument of C. Julius Zoilos*, Mainz, 1993. *The father of Claudius Etruscus*: Statius, *Silvae*, 3.3; P. R. C. Weaver, 'The Father of Claudius Etruscus: Statius, Silvae 3.3', *Classical Quarterly*, 15, 1965, 145–54. *Alkibiades of Nysa*: *I.Ephesos*, 22; *SEG*, I, 417, 441; IV, 417, 418; *CIG*, 2947, 2948; *I.Tralleis*, 17. *Theophrastus on wealth and poverty*: *Characters*, 5, 21, 23, 24, 26. *The reconciliation in Nakone*: E. Lupu, *Greek Sacred Law: A Collection of New Documents*, Leiden, 2005, 347–358 no. 26. *The reforms of Kleomenes*: Plutarch, *Kleomenes*, 10–11. *Social conditions in Boiotia*: Polybius, 20.6. *Foreign judges*: P. Hamon, 'Mander des juges dans la cité: notes sur l'organisation des missions judiciaires à l'époque hellénistique', *Cahiers du Centre Gustave Glotz*, 23, 2012, 195–222. *Public debt*: Migeotte, 1984. *Theocritus on a love-sick man*: *Idyll*, 14.50–56. *Grant of land in Kalindoia by Alexander*: *SEG*, XXXVI, 636. *Royal land donations in Macedonia*: Hatzopoulos, 1996, nos. 20, 22. *Cretan migration to Miletos*: *Milet* VI.1, 33–38. *Unemployed mercenaries in Samos*: *IG*, XII.6, 169. *Antipatros of Eleutherna*: *Syll.*[3], 737. *The benefactions of Opramoas*: *FdXanthos*, VII, 67; C. Kokkinia, *Die Opramoas-Inschrift von Rhodiapolis: Euergetismus und soziale Elite in Lykien*, Bonn, 2000. *Export of Cretan medicinal plants*: Galen, *On Antidotes*, XIV p. 9 (ed. Kühn). *Aelius Aristides on economic exchange in the Roman Empire*: *Orations*, 26, 11–12.

14 Social and Cultural Trends

Further reading: Alföldy, 2011; S. Aneziri, *Die Vereine der dionysischen Tech-niten im Kontext der hellenistischen Gesellschaft: Untersuchungen zur Geschichte, Organisation und Wirkung der hellenistischen Technitenvereine*, Stuttgart, 2003; R. S. Bagnall, *Everyday Writing in the Graeco-Roman East*, Berkeley, 2011, 54–74; Bowersock, 1965; Brun, 1996; E. Bauer, *Gerusien in den Poleis Kleinasiens in hel-lenistischer Zeit und der römischen Kaiserzeit: Die Beispiele Ephesos, Pamphylien und Pisidien, Aphrodisias and Iasos*, Munich, 2012; S. Bussi, *Economia e demografia della schiavitù in Asia Minore ellenistico-romana*, Milan, 2001; Cartledge and Spaw-forth, 1989; Chaniotis, 2005 and 2011; R. Cribiore, *Gymnastics of the Mind: Greek Education in Hellenistic and Roman Egypt*, Princeton, 2001; I. Dittmann-Schöne, *Die Berufsvereine in den Städten des kaiserzeitlichen Kleinasiens*, Regensburg, 2001; J. C. Eule, *Hellenistische Bürgerinnen aus Kleinasien: Weibliche Gewandstatuen in ihrem antiken Kontext*, Istanbul, 2001; Fernoux, 2004; Fraser, 1972; Fröhlich and Hamon (eds.), 2013; V. Gabrielsen, 'Brotherhoods of Faith and Provident Plan-ning: The Non-Public Associations of the Greek World', *Mediterranean Historical Review*, 22, 2, 2007, 176–203; Gauthier, 1985; P. Gauthier and M. B. Hatzopoulos, *La loi gymnasiarchique de Beroia*, Athens, 1993; L.-M. Günther, *Bürgerinnen und ihre Familien im hellenistischen Milet: Untersuchungen zur Rolle von Frauen und Mädchen in der Polis-Öffentlichkeit*, Wiesbaden, 2014; Hamon, 2007; Harris and Ruffini (eds.), 2004; Jones, 1978; D. Kah and P. Scholz (eds.), *Das hellenistische Gymnasion*, Berlin, 2004; Kuhn, 2012; B. Legras, *Néotês: Recherches sur les jeunes grecs dans l'Égypte ptolémaique et romaine*, Geneva, 1999; Lewis, 1986; Ma, 2013; N. Massar, *Soigner et servir: Histoire sociale et culturelle de la médecine grecque à l'époque hellénistique*, Paris, 2005; Migeotte, 1984 and 1992; T. Morgan, *Literate Education in the Hellenistic and Roman Worlds*, Cambridge, 1998; H. Mouritsen,

The Freedman in the Roman World, Cambridge, 2011; C. Müller, 'Évérgetisme et pratiques financières dans les cités de la Grèce hellénistique', *Revue des Études Anciennes*, 113, 2011, 345–63; D. Mulliez, 'Les actes d'affranchissement delphiques', *Cahiers du Centre G. Glotz*, 3, 1992, 31–44; Peachin (ed.), 2011; Perrin-Saminadayar, 2007; Pomeroy, 1984; Quass, 1993; M. Ricl, 'Legal and Social Status of *threptoi* and Related Categories in Narrative and Documentary Sources', in Cotton et al. (eds.), 2009, 93–114; Robert, 1940; Rostovtzeff, 1941; E. Stavrianopoulou, '*Gruppenbild mit Dame*': *Untersuchungen zur rechtlichen und sozialen Stellung der Frau auf den Kykladen im Hellenismus und in der römischen Kaiserzeit*, Stuttgart, 2006; E. Stephan, *Honoratioren, Griechen, Polisbürger: Kollektive Identitäten innerhalb der Oberschicht des kaiserzeitlichen Kleinasien*, Göttingen, 2002; Thompson, 1988; P. Thonemann, 'The Women of Akmoneia', *JRS*, 100, 2010, 163–78; van Bremen, 1996; O. van Nijf, 'Athletics and *paideia*: Festivals and Physical Education in the World of the Second Sophistic', in Borg (ed.), 2004, 203–27; Vatin, 1970; Velissaropoulos-Karakostas, 2011; A.-M. Vérilhac and C. Vial, *Le mariage grec: Du VIe siècle av. J.-C. à l'époque d'Auguste*, Paris, 1998; A. Weiss, *Sklave der Stadt: Untersuchungen zur öffentlichen Sklaverei in den Städten des Römischen Reiches*, Stuttgart, 2004; U. Wiemer, 'Von der Bürgerschule zum aristokratischen Klub? Die athenische Ephebie in der römischen Kaiserzeit', *Chiron*, 41, 2011, 487–537; R. Zelnick-Abramovitz, *Not Wholly Free: The Concept of Manumission and the Status of Manumitted Slaves in the Ancient World*, Leiden, 2005; Wörrle and Zanker (eds.), 1995.

Sources mentioned: *Donations to the gymnasium in Metropolis*: SEG, XLIX, 1522. *The Cloatii in Gytheion*: IG, V.1, 1146. *Hermogenes of Aphrodisias*: SEG, LIV, 1020. *Tyriaion*: SEG, XLVII, 1745; Bagnall and Derow, 2004, no. 43. *Panopeus*: Pausanias, 10.4.1. *The hunters of Heracles Kynagidas*: SEG, LVI, 625. *Augustus and the ephebes in Neapolis*: Suetonius, *Augustus*, 98.3. *The ephebarchical law of Amphipolis*: M. B. Hatzopoulos, 'Loi ephebarchique d'Amphipolis', *Archaiologike Ephemeris*, 154, 2015, 46–8. *Ephebes in Tanagra*: SEG, LIX, 492. *Pericles on women*: Thucydides, 2.45.2. *Marriage contract*: P.Eleph. 1; D. Thompson, 'Hellenistic Families', in Bugh (ed.), 2006, 93–4. *Epikteta of Thera*: IG, XII.3, 330. *Archippe*: I.Kyme, 13. *Aglais*: Athenaios, X, 415a–b. *Polygnota*: F.Delphes, III.3, 249. *Epikles*: Syll.³, 622 B. *The eunuch Krokos*: J. Strubbe, *Arai epitymbioi: Imprecations Against Desecrators of the Grave in the Greek Epitaphs of Asia Minor. A Catalogue*, Bonn, 1997, no. 393. *Goldmines in Egypt*: Diodorus, 3.12–13. *Tablet from Dodona*: SEG, LVII, 536.14. *Manumission record from Physkos*: SEG, LVI, 572. '*Trader of beautiful women*': IGUR, 1326. *Caprilius Timotheos*: SEG, XXVIII, 537. *Hyllos in Ephesos*: SEG, LIX, 1318.

15 From Civic Worship to Megatheism

Further reading: C. Bonnet and A. Motte (eds.), *Les syncretismes religieuses dans le monde méditerranéen antique*, Rome, 1997; Bricault, 2005; P. Bruneau, *Recherches sur les cultes de Délos à l'époque hellénistique et romaine*, Paris, 1970; A. Busine, *Paroles d'Apollon: Pratiques et traditions oraculaires dans l'Antiquité tardive (IIe–VIe siècles)*, Leiden, 2005; A. Chaniotis, 'Ritual Performances of Divine Justice: The Epigraphy of Confession, Atonement, and Exaltation in Roman Asia Minor', in Cotton et al. (eds.), 2009, 115–53; A. Chaniotis, 'Megatheism: The Search for the Almighty God and the Competition of Cults', in S. Mitchell and P. van Nuffelen (eds.), *One God: Pagan Monotheism in the Roman Empire*, Cambridge, 2010, 112–40; Chaniotis, 2011; A. Chaniotis, 'Processions in Hellenistic Cities: Contemporary Discources and Ritual Dynamics', in R. Alston, O. M. van Nijf and C. G. Williamson (eds.), *Cults, Creeds and Contests*, Louvain, 2013, 21–47; S. G. Cole, *Theoi Megaloi: The Cult of the Great Gods at Samothrace*, Leiden, 1984; N. Deshours, *L'été indien de la religion civique*, Bordeaux, 2011; H. Engelmann, *The Delian Aretalogy of Sarapis*, Leiden, 1975; Fraser, 1972; F. Graf, *Roman Festivals in the Greek East: From the Early Empire to the Middle Byzantine Era*, Cambridge, 2015; F. Graf and S. I. Johnston, *Ritual Texts for the Afterlife: Orpheus and the Bacchic Gold Tablets*, London and New York, 2007; C. P. Jones, *New Heroes in Antiquity: From Achilles to Antinoos*, Cambridge, MA, 2010; Lane Fox, 1986; B. Legras, *Les reclus grecs du Sarapieion de Memphis: Une enquête sur l'hellénisme égyptien*, Leuven, 2010; J. Lieu, J. A. North and T. Rajak (eds.), *The Jews among Pagans and Christians in the Roman Empire*, London, 1992; MacMullen, 1981 and 1984; J. D. Mikalson, *Religion in Hellenistic Athens*, Berkeley, 1998; S. Mitchell, 'The Cult of Theos Hypsistos between Pagans, Jews, and Christians', in P. Athanassiadi and M. Frede (eds.), *Pagan Monotheism in Late Antiquity*, Oxford, 1999, 81–148; Nock, 1933; J. A. North and S. R. F. Price (eds.), *The Religious History of the Roman Empire. Pagans, Jews, and Christians*, Oxford, 2011; R. Parker, *Polytheism and Society at Athens*, Oxford, 2005; É. Perrin-Saminadayar, 'L'accueil officiel des souverains et des princes à Athènes à l'époque hellénistique', *BCH*, 128/129, 2004–5, 351–75; S. Price, 'Religious Mobility in the Roman Empire', *JRS*, 102, 2012, 1–19; E. Rice, *The Grand Procession of Ptolemy Philadelphus*, Oxford, 1983; K. J. Rigsby, *Asylia: Territorial Inviolability in the Hellenistic World*, Berkeley, 1996; Y. Tzifopoulos, *Paradise Earned: The Bacchic-Orphic Gold Lamellae of Crete*, Washington, DC, 2010; H. S. Versnel, *Ter unus: Isis, Dionysos, Hermes. Three Studies in Henotheism*, Leiden, 1990; Versnel, 2011; U. Victor, *Lukian von Samosata, Alexander oder Der Lügenprophet: Eingeleitet, herausgegeben, übersetzt und erklärt*, Leiden, 1997; H. Wendt, *At the Temple Gates: The Religion of Freelance Experts in the Early Roman Empire*, New York, 2016; Wörrle, 1988.

Sources mentioned: *Theocritus: Adoniazousai. Festivals in Taras*: Strabo, 6.3.4. *Festivals in Kos*: *IG*, XII.4, 281. *Festival in Antioch near Pyramos*: *LSAM*, 81. *The Procession of the Ptolemaia*: Athenaios, V, 196a–203b. *The cult regulation of Andania*: L. Gawlinski, *The Sacred Law of Andania: A New Text with Commentary*, Berlin, 2012. *Inscription of Kalindoia*: *SEG*, XXXV, 744. *Thargelia in Athens*: *SEG*, XXI, 469 C. *The death of Pan*: Plutarch, *Moralia*, 419b–d. *The aretalogy of Kyme*:

Bricault, 2005, no. 302/0204. *The oracle of Apollo Klarios*: SEG, XXVII, 933. *The healing miracles of Epidaurus*: L. LiDonnici, *The Epidaurian Miracle Inscriptions: Text, Translation and Commentary*, Atlanta, 1995. *Artemisia of Ephesos*: R. Merkelbach, 'Aurelia Artemisia aus Ephesos, eine geheilte Augenkranke', *Epigraphica Anatolica*, 20, 1992, 55. *The confession of Theodoros*: G. Petzl, *Die Beichtinschriften Westkleinasiens* (*Epigraphica Anatolica*, 22), Bonn, 1994, no. 5. *Dreams in Miletos*: *I.Didyma*, 496. *The hymn of Isyllos*: W. D. Furley and J. M. Bremer, *Greek Hymns*, Tübingen, 2001, I, 227–40. *The praise of Isis in Maroneia*: Y. Grandjean, *Une nouvelle arétalogie d'Isis à Maronée*, Leiden, 1975. *The cult association in Philadelpheia*: *TAM*, V.3, 1539. *Grave epigrams with ideas concerning afterlife*: *I.Perinthos*, 213; Callimachus, *Epigrams*, 13 (ed. Pfister); *TAM*, V.2, 1108; *Steinepigramme* I 05/01/63; *IG*, XII.7, 123. *The cult foundation of Artemidoros in Thera*: *IG*, XII.3, 421–2, 464, 863, 1333–50, 1388. *The 'Zeus of Menophilos'*: SEG, LVI, 1434. *The foundation of Salutaris*: *I.Ephesos*, 27. *The mysteries of Glykon*: Lucian, *Alexander*, 38–9. *Pliny on the Christians*: *Letters*, 10.96. *Bread distribution at midnight*: *IG*, X.2.1, 259.

16 The Greeks and the *Oecumene*

Further reading: J. Boardman, *The Greeks in Asia*, London, 2015; Bowersock, 1969; Goldhill (ed.), 2001; J.-C. Couvenhes and B. Legras (eds.), *Transferts culturels et politique dans le monde hellénistique: Actes de la table ronde sur les identités collectives (Sorbonne, 7 février 2004)*, Paris, 2006; F. De Romanis and M. Maiuro (eds.), *Across the Ocean: Nine Essays on Indo-Mediterranean Trade*, Leiden, 2015; Jones, 1978; C. P. Jones, *Kinship Diplomacy in the Ancient World*, Cambridge, MA, 1999; M. Pitts and M. J. Versluys (eds.), *Globalisation and the Roman World: World History, Connectivity, and Material Culture*, New York, 2015; Puech, 2002; Veyne, 1999; Whitmarsh (ed.), 2010.

Sources mentioned: *Eudoxos of Knidos*: Strabo, 2.2.3. *Trade with Arabia*: L. Casson, *The Periplus Maris Erythraei: Text with Introduction, Translation, and Commentary*, Princeton, 1989, Ch. 49. *Sophytos*: SEG, LIV, 1568; J. Lougovaya, 'Greek Poetry in a Post-Greek Milieu: The Epigram of Sophytos from Kandahar Contextualized', in P. Sänger (ed.), *Minderheiten und Migration in der griechischrömischen Welt*, Paderborn, 2016, 185–201. *The epitaph of Hyle*: *IG*, XIV, 2566. *The grave of the 'Pig'*: SEG, XV, 711. *Alexander's dedication in the Bahariya Oasis*: SEG, LIX, 1764. *The petition of Herakleides*: *P.Enteux.*, 79. *The archive of Dryton*: J. Mélèze-Modrzejewski, 'Dryton le crétois et sa famille, ou Les marriages mixtes dans l'Égypte hellénistique', in *Aux origines de l'Hellénisme: La Crète et la Grèce. Hommage à Henri van Effenterre*, Paris, 1984, 353–76. *The courts in Chersonesos in Tauris*: SEG, LV, 838; LXI, 607. *The villa of Avitus in Tarraco*: SEG, LXI, 832. *Triphonon and enneaphonon*: Petzl, 1994, nos. 6 and 55; SEG, LVII, 1172 and 1222. *Pallake and aniptopodes in Tralleis*: *I.Tralleis*, 6–7. *Rituals in Hypaipa*: Pausanias, 5.27.5–6.

BIBLIOGRAPHY

Ager, S. L., *Interstate Arbitrations in the Greek World, 337–90 BC*, Berkeley, 1996

Alcock, S. E., *Graecia Capta: The Landscapes of Roman Greece*, Cambridge, 1993

—— (ed.), *The Early Roman Empire in the East*, Oxford, 1997

Alföldy, G., *Römische Sozialgeschichte*, 4th edn, Stuttgart, 2011

Allen, R. E., *The Attalid Kingdom, a Constitutional History*, Oxford, 1983

Austin, M. M., *The Hellenistic World from Alexander to the Roman Conquest: A Selection of Ancient Sources in Translation*, 2nd edn, Cambridge, 2006

Bagnall, R. S., *The Administration of the Ptolemaic Possessions Outside Egypt*, Leiden, 1976

Bagnall, R., and P. Derow, *Historical Sources in Translation: The Hellenistic Period*, 2nd edn, Oxford, 2004

Beck, H., and P. Funke (eds.), *Federalism in Greek Antiquity*, Cambridge, 2015

Bekker-Nielsen, T., *Urban Life and Local Politics in Roman Bithynia: The Small World of Dion Chrysostomos*, Aarhus, 2008

Bernhard, R., *Polis und römische Herrschaft in der späten Republik (149–31 v.Chr.)*, Berlin, 1985

——, *Rom und die Städte des hellenistischen Ostens (3.–1. Jahrhundert v. Chr.)*, Munich, 1998

Berthold, R. M., *Rhodes in the Hellenistic Age*, Ithaca, NY, 1984

Bikerman, E. J., *Institutions des Séleucides*, Paris, 1938

Billows, R. A., *Kings and Colonists: Aspects of Macedonian Imperialism*, Leiden, 1995

Birley, A. R., *Hadrian, the Restless Emperor*, London, 1997

Borg, B. (ed.), *Paideia: The World of the Second Sophistic*, Berlin and New York, 2004

Bosworth, A. B., *Conquest and Empire: The Reign of Alexander the Great*, Cambridge, 1988

Bouché-Leclercq, A., *Histoire des Séleucides (323–64 avant J.-C.)*, Paris, 1913–14

Boulay, T., *Arès dans la cité: Les poleis et la guerre dans l'Asie Mineure hellénistique*, Pisa and Rome, 2014

Bowersock, G. W., *Augustus and the Greek World*, Oxford, 1965

——, *Greek Sophists in the Roman Empire*, Oxford, 1969

Bowman, A. K., *Egypt After the Pharaohs: 332 BC–AD 642, from Alexander to the Arab Conquest*, 2nd edition. London, 1996

Braund, D., *Rome and the Friendly King: The Character of Client Kingship*, London, 1984

Brélaz, C., *La sécurité publique en Asie Mineure sous le Principat (Ier–IIIème s. ap. J.-C.): Institutions municipales et institutions impériales dans l'Orient romain*, Basel, 2005

Bresson, A. (ed.), *Approches de l'écomonie hellénistique*, Saint-Bertrand-de-Comminges, 2006

Bresson, A., and R. Descat (eds.), *Les cités d'Asie Mineure occidentale au IIe siècle a.C.*, Paris, 2001

Bricault, L., *Recueil des inscriptions concernant les cultes isiaques*, Paris, 2005

Brun, P., *Les archipels égéens dans l'antiquité grecque (Ve–IIe siècles av. notre ère)*, Paris, 1996

Bugh, G. R. (ed.), *The Cambridge Companion to the Hellenistic World*, Cambridge, 2006

Buraselis, K., *Kos between Hellenism and Rome: Studies on the Political, Institutional and Social History of Kos from ca. the Middle Second Century BC until Late Antiquity*, Philadelphia, 2000

Camia, F., *Rome e le poleis. L'intervento di Roma nelle controversie territoriali tra le comunità greche di Grecia e d'Asia Minore nel secondo secolo a.C.: Le testimonianze epigrafiche*, Athens, 2009

Capdetrey, L., *Le pouvoir séleucide: Territoire, administration, finances d'un royaume hellénistique (312–129 avant J.-C.)*, Rennes, 2009

Cartledge, P., and A. Spawforth, *Hellenistic and Roman Sparta: A Tale of Two Cities*, London, 1989

Champlin, E., *Nero*, Cambridge, MA, 2003

Chaniotis, A., *War in the Hellenistic World: A Social and Cultural History*, Malden, MA, 2005

——, 'Festivals and Contests in the Greek World', in *Thesaurus Cultus et Rituum Antiquorum*, VII, Los Angeles, 2011, 1–43

Chauveau, M., *Egypt in the Age of Cleopatra: History and Society under the Ptolemies*, translated by D. Lorton, Ithaca, NY, 2000

Cohen, G. M., *The Seleucid Colonies: Studies in Founding, Administration, and Organisation*, Wiesbaden, 1978

——, *The Hellenistic Settlements in Europe, the Islands, and Asia Minor*, Berkeley, 1995

——, *The Hellenistic Settlements in Syria, the Red Sea Basin, and North Africa*, Berkeley, 2006

Coloru, O., *Da Alessandro a Menandro: Il regno greco di Battriana*, Pisa, 2009

Cotton, H. M., R. G. Hoyland, J. J. Price and D. J. Wasserstein (eds.), *From Hellenism to Islam: Cultural and Linguistic Change in the Roman Near East*, Cambridge, 2009

Couvenhes, J.-C., and H.-L. Fernoux (eds.), *Les cités grecques et la guerre en Asie Mineure à l'époque hellénistique*, Tours, 2004

Crook, J. A., A. Lintott and E. Rawson (eds.), *The Cambridge Ancient History. Volume IX, Part 1: The Last Age of the Roman Republic, 146–43 BC*, 2nd edn, Cambridge, 1994

De Souza, P., *Piracy in the Graeco-Roman World*, Cambridge, 1999

Dignas, B., *Economy of the Sacred in Hellenistic and Roman Asia Minor*, Oxford, 2002

Dmitriev, S., *City Government in Hellenistic and Roman Asia Minor*, Oxford, 2005

Drexhage, H.-W., *Wirtschaftspolitik und Wirtschaft in der römischen Provinz Asia in der Zeit von Augustus bis zum Regierungsantritt Diokletians*, Bonn, 2007

Eck, W., *The Age of Augustus*, translated by D. L. Schneider, with new material by S. A. Takács, Oxford, 2003

—— (ed.), *Lokale Autonomie und römische Ordnungsmacht in den kaiserzeitlichen Provinzen*, Munich, 1999

Eckstein, A. M., *Mediterranean Anarchy, Interstate War, and the Rise of Rome*, Berkeley, 2006

Eddy, S. K., *The King is Dead: Studies in the Near Eastern Resistance to Hellenism, 334–31 BC*, Lincoln, NB, 1961

Ehling, K., *Untersuchungen zur Geschichte der späten Seleukiden (164–63 v. Chr.): Vom Tode des Antiochos IV. bis zur Einrichtung der Provinz Syria unter Pompeius*, Stuttgart, 2008

Errington, R. M., *A History of Macedonia*, translated by C. Errington, Berkeley, 1992

——, *A History of the Hellenistic World, 323–30 BC*, Malden, MA, 2008

Erskine, A. (ed.), *A Companion to the Hellenistic World*, Malden, MA, 2003

Erskine, A., and L. Llewellyn-Jones (eds.), *Creating a Hellenistic World*, Swansea, 2011

Fernoux, H.-L., *Notables et élites des cités de Bithynie aux époques hellénistiques et romaine (IIIe siècle av. J.-C.–IIIe siècle ap. J.-C.): Essai d'histoire sociale*, Lyon, 2004

——, *Le demos et la cite: Communautés populaires en Asie Mineure à l'époque impériale*, Rennes, 2011

Ferrary, J.-L., *Philhellénisme et impérialisme: Aspects idéologiques de la conquête romaine du monde hellénistique, de la seconde guerre de Macédoine à la guerre contre Mithridate*, 2nd edn, Paris, 2014

Fischer-Bovet, C., *Army and Society in Ptolemaic Egypt*, Cambridge, 2014

Fraser, P. M., *Ptolemaic Alexandria*, Oxford, 1972

Freeth, T., and A. Jones, 'The Cosmos of the Antikythera Mechanism', ISAW Papers 4. http://dlib.nyu.edu/awdl/isaw/isaw-papers/4/.

Fröhlich, P., *Les cités grecques et le contrôle des magistrats (IVe–Ier siècle avant J.-C.)*, Geneva, 2004

Fröhlich, P., and P. Hamon (eds.), *Groupes et associations dans les cités grecques (IIe siècle a. J.-C.–IIe siècle apr. J.-C.)*, Geneva, 2013

Fröhlich, P., and C. Müller (eds.), *Citoyenneté et participation à la basse époque hellénistique*, Geneva, 2005

Gabrielsen, V., *The Naval Aristocracy of Hellenistic Rhodes*, Aarhus, 1997

Galinsky, K., *Augustus: Introduction to the Life of an Emperor*, Cambridge, 2012

—— (ed.), *The Cambridge Companion to the Age of Augustus*, Cambridge, 2005

Gauthier, P., *Symbola: Les étrangers et la justice dans les cités grecques*, Nancy, 1972

——, *Les cités grecques et leurs bienfaiteurs (IVe–Ier siècle avant J.-C.): Contribution à l'histoire des institutions*, Paris, 1985

Gehrke, H.-J., *Geschichte des Hellenismus*, 4th edn, Munich, 2008

Goldhill, S. (ed.), *Being Greek under Rome: Cultural Identity, the Second Sophistic and the Development of Empire*, Cambridge, 2001

Goldsworthy, A., *Augustus: First Emperor of Rome*, New Haven, 2014

Grainger, J. D., *The League of the Aitolians*, Leiden, 1999

——, *The Syrian Wars*, Leiden, 2010

——, *The Seleukid Empire of Antiochos III, 223–187 BC*, Barnsley, 2015

——, *Great Power Diplomacy in the Hellenistic World*, London, 2017

Grajetzki, W., *Greeks and Parthians in Mesopotamia and Beyond, 331 BC–224 AD*, Bristol, 2011

Gray, B., *Stasis and Stability: Exile, the Polis, and Political Thought, c. 404–146 BC*, Oxford, 2015

Green, P., *Alexander to Actium: The Historical Evolution of the Hellenistic Age*, Berkeley, 1990

Gruen, E. S., *The Hellenistic World and the Coming of Rome*, Berkeley, 1984

Gutzwiller, K., *A Guide to Hellenistic Literature*, Malden, MA, 2007

Habicht, C., *Athens from Alexander to Antony*, translated by D. L. Schneider, Cambridge, MA, 1997

Halfmann, H., *Itinera primcipum: Geschichte und Typologie der Kaiserreisen im Römischen Reich*, Wiesbaden, 1986

——, *Die Senatoren aus dem östlichen Teil des Imperium Romanum bis zum Ende des 2. Jahrhunderts n. Chr.*, Göttingen, 1979

Hammond, N. G. L., and F. W. Walbank, *A History of Macedonia. Volume III: 336–167 BC*, Oxford, 1988

Hamon, P., 'Élites dirigeantes et processus d'aristocratisation à l'époque hellénistique', in H.-L. Fernoux and C. Stein (eds.), *Aristocratie antique: Modèles et exemplarité sociale*, Dijon, 2007, 79–100

Hansen, E. V., *The Attalids of Pergamon*, 2nd edn, Ithaca, NY, 1971

Harding, P. E., *Athens Transformed, 404–262 BC: From Popular Sovereignty to the Dominion of the Elite*, New York and London, 2015

Harris, W. V., *War and Imperialism in Republican Rome, 327–70 BC*, Oxford, 1979

——, *Roman Power: A Thousand Years of Empire*, Cambridge, 2016

——, and G. Ruffini (eds.), *Ancient Alexandria between Egypt and Greece*, Leiden, 2004

Hatzopoulos, M. B., *Macedonian Institutions Under the Kings: A Historical and Epigraphic Study*, Athens and Paris, 1996

Hauben, H., and A. Meeus (eds.), *The Age of the Successors and the Creation of the Hellenistic Kingdoms (323–276 BC)*, Leuven, 2014

Hekster, O., S. Schmidt-Hofner and C. Witschel (eds.), *Ritual Dynamics and Religious Change in the Roman Empire*, Leiden, 2009

Hoelbl, G., *A History of the Ptolemaic Empire*, translated by T. Saavedra, London, 2000

Holleaux, M., *Études d'épigraphie et d'histoire grecques*, Volumes I–III, Paris, 1938–42

Hoyos, D. (ed.), *A Companion to Roman Imperialism*, Leiden, 2013

Jones, A. H. M., *The Cities of the Eastern Roman Provinces*, Oxford, 1971

Jones, C. P., *The Roman World of Dio Chrysostome*, Cambridge, MA, 1978

Kallet-Marx, R. M., *Hegemony to Empire: The Development of the Roman Imperium in the East from 148 to 62 BC*, Berkeley, 1995

Koehn, C., *Krieg – Diplomatie – Ideologie: Zur Außenpolitik hellenistischer Mittelstaaten*, Stuttgart, 2007

Kosmin, P. J., *The Land of the Elephant Kings: Space, Territory, and Ideology in the Seleucid Empire*, Cambridge, 2014

Kuhn, A., 'Herodes Atticus and the Quintilii of Alexandria Troas: Elite Competition and Status Relations in the Graeco-Roman East', *Chiron*, 42, 2012, 421–58

Labarre, G., *Les cités de Lesbos aux époques hellénistique et impériale*, Paris, 1996

Lane Fox, R., *Pagans and Christians*, London, 1986

—— (ed.), *Brill's Companion to Ancient Macedon*, Leiden, 2011

Launey, M., *Recherches sur les armées hellénistiques*, new edition with addenda and postscript by Y. Garlan, P. Gauthier and C. Orrieux, Paris, 1987

Levick, B. M., *Roman Colonies in Southern Asia Minor*, Oxford, 1967

——, *Augustus: Image and Substance*, London, 2010

Lewis, N., *Greeks in Ptolemaic Egypt: Case Studies in the Social History of the Hellenistic World*, Oxford, 1986

Lintott, A. W., *Imperium Romanum: Politics and Administration*, London, 1993

Ma, J., *Antiochos III and the Cities of Western Asia Minor*, 2nd edn, Oxford, 2002

——, *Statues and Cities: Honorific Portraits and Civic Identity in the Hellenistic World*, Oxford, 2013

McKechnie, P., and P. Guillaume (eds.), *Ptolemy II Philadelphus and His World*, Leiden, 2008

MacMullen, R., *Paganism in the Roman Empire*, New Haven and London, 1981

——, *Christianizing the Roman Empire (AD 100–400)*, New Haven, 1984

Magie, D., *Roman Rule in Asia Minor to the End of the Third Century after Christ*, Princeton, 1950

Manning, J. G., *Land and Power in Ptolemaic Egypt: The Structure of Land Tenure*, Cambridge, 2003

——, *The Last Pharaohs: Egypt under the Ptolemies, 305–30 BC*, Princeton, 2010

Martinez-Sève, L., *Atlas du monde hellénistique (336–31 av. J.-C.): Pouvoirs et territoires après Alexandre le Grand*, Paris, 2011

Matthaei, A., and M. Zimmermann (eds.), *Urbane Strukturen und bürgerliche Identität im Hellenismus*, Heidelberg, 2015

Migeotte, L., *L'emprunt public dans les cités grecques: Recueil des documents et analyse critique*, Québec, 1984

Migeotte, L., *Les souscriptions publiques dans les cités grecques*, Geneva, 1992

Millar, F., *The Emperor in the Roman World (31 BC–AD 337)*, 2nd edn, London, 1992

——, *The Roman Near East (31 BC–AD 337)*, Cambridge, MA, 1993

Mitchell, S., *Anatolia: Land, Men, and Gods in Asia Minor*, Oxford, 1993

Monson, A. *From the Ptolemies to the Romans: Political and Economic Change in Egypt*, Cambridge, 2012

Nock, A. D., *Conversion: The Old and the New in Religion from Alexander the Great to Augustine of Hippo*, Oxford, 1933

Oliver, J. H., *Greek Constitutions of Early Roman Emperors from Inscriptions and Papyri*, Philadelphia, 1989

Oliver, G. J., *War, Food, and Politics in Early Hellenistic Athens*, Oxford, 2007

Papazoglou, F., *Laoi et paroikoi: Recherches sur la structure de la société hellénistique*, Belgrade, 1997

Peachin, M. (ed.), *The Oxford Handbook of Social Relations in the Roman World*, Oxford, 2011

Perrin-Saminadayar, É., *Éducation, culture et société à Athènes: Les acteurs de la vue culturelle athénienne (299–88): un tout petit monde*, Paris, 2007

Pomeroy, S. B., *Women in Hellenistic Egypt from Alexander to Cleopatra*, New York, 1984

Prag, J. R. W., and J. C. Quinn (eds.), *The Hellenistic West: Rethinking the Ancient Mediterranean*, Cambridge, 2013

Préaux, C., *L'économie royale des Lagides*, Brussels, 1939

——, *Le monde hellénistique: La Grèce et l'Orient de la mort d'Alexandre à la conquête romaine de la Grèce (323–146 av. J.-C.)*, Paris, 1978

Price, S. R. F., *Rituals and Power: The Roman Imperial Cult in Asia Minor*, Cambridge, 1984

Puech, B., *Orateurs et sophistes grecs dans les inscriptions d'époque impériale*, Paris, 2002

Quass, F., *Die Honoratiorenschicht in den Städten des griechischen Ostens: Untersuchungen zur politischen und sozialen Entwicklung in hellenistischer und römischer Zeit*, Stuttgart, 1993

Raaflaub, K. A., and M. Toher (eds.), *Between Republic and Empire: Interpretations of Augustus and His Principate*, Berkeley, 1993

Reynolds, J., *Aphrodisias and Rome*, London, 1982

Rizakis, A. D., and E. S. Lepeniotis (eds.), *Roman Peloponnese. Volume 3: Society, Economy, and Culture under Roman Rule*, Athens and Paris, 2010

Rizakis, A. D., and I. P. Touratsoglou (eds.), *Villae rusticae: Family and Market-oriented Farms in Greece under Roman Rule*, Athens and Paris, 2013

Robert, L., *Les gladiateurs dans l'orient grec*, Paris, 1940

——, *Choix d'écrits*, edited by D. Rousset, Paris, 2007

Rostovtzeff, M., *The Social and Economic History of the Hellenistic World*, Oxford, 1941

Roubineau, J.-M., *Les cités grecques (VIe–IIe siècle avant J.-C.): Essai d'histoire sociale*, Paris, 2015

Sartre, M., *L'Asie Mineure et l'Anatolie d'Alexandre à Dioclétien, IVe siècle av. J.-C./ IIIe siècle ap. J.-C.* Paris, 1995

——, *D'Alexandre à Zénobie: Histoire du Levant antique, IVe siècle av. J.-C.–IIIe siècle ap. J.-C.*, Paris, 2001

Scheidel, W., I. Morris and R.P. Saller (eds.), *The Cambridge Economic History of the Greco-Roman World*, Cambridge, 2007

Schneider, C., *Kulturgeschichte des Hellenismus*, Munich, 1967–9

Scholz, P., *Der Hellenismus: Der Hof und die Welt*, Munich, 2015

Schwartz, S., *Imperialisn and Jewish Society: 200 BCE–640 CE*, Princeton, 2001

——, *The Ancient Jews from Alexander to Muhammad*, Cambridge, 2014

Sherk, R. K., *Roman Documents from the Greek East: Senatus consulta and epistulae to the Age of Augustus*, Baltimore, 1969

——, *Rome and the Greek East to the Death of Augustus*, Cambridge, 1984

Sherwin-White, A. N., *Roman Foreign Policy in the East 168 BC to AD 1*, London, 1984

Sherwin-White, S. M., *Ancient Cos: An Historical Study from the Dorian Settlement to the Imperial Period*, Göttingen, 1978

Sherwin-White, S. M., and A. Kuhrt, *From Samarkhand to Sardis: A New Approach to the Seleucid Empire*, Berkeley, 1993

Shipley, G., *The Greek World after Alexander 323–30 BC*, London, 2000

Stavrianopoulou E. (ed.), *Shifting Social Imaginaries in the Hellenistic Period: Narrations, Practices, and Images,* Leiden, 2013

Strootman, R., *Courts and Elites in the Hellenistic Empires: The Near East after the Achaemenids, c. 330 to 30 BCE*, Edinburgh, 2014

Syme, R., *The Roman Revolution*, Oxford, 1939

Thompson, D. J., *Memphis under the Ptolemies*, Princeton, 1988

Thonemann, P., *The Maeander Valley: A Historical Geography from Antiquity to Byzantium*, Cambridge, 2011

——, *The Hellenistic World: Using Coins as Sources*, Cambridge, 2015

—— (ed.), *Attalid Asia Minor: Money, International Relations, and the State*, Cambridge, 2013

van Bremen, R., *The Limits of Participation: Women and Civic Life in the Greek East in the Hellenistic and Roman Periods*, Amsterdam, 1996

van Nijf, O., and R. Alston (eds.), *Political Culture in the Greek City after the Classical Age*, Leuven, 2011

Varga, R., and V. Rusu-Bolindeț (eds.), *Official Power and Local Elites in the Roman Provinces*, London, 2016

Vatin, C., *Recherches sur le mariage et la condition de la femme mariée à l'époque hellénistique*, Paris, 1970

Velissaropoulos-Karakostas, J., *Droit grec d'Alexandre à Augustue (323 av. J.-C.–14 ap. J.-C.): Personnes, biens, justice*, Athens, 2011

Versnel, H. S., *Coping with the Gods: Wayward Readings in Greek Theology*, Leiden, 2011

Veyne, P., 'L'identité grecque devant Rome et l'empereur', *REG*, 112, 1999, 510–67

Walbank, F. W., *A Historical Commentary on Polybius. Volume I: Commentary on Books I–VI. Volume II: Commentary on Books VII–XVIII. Volume III: Commentary on Books XIX–XL*, Oxford, 1957–79

Walbank, F. W., A. E. Astin, M. W. Frederiksen and R. M. Ogilvie (eds.), *The Cambridge Ancient History. Volume VII, Part 1: The Hellenistic World*, 2nd edn, Cambridge, 1994

Walbank, F. W., A. E. Astin, M. W. Frederiksen and R. M. Ogilvie (eds.), *The Cambridge Ancient History. Volume VIII: Rome and the Mediterranean to 133 BC*, 2nd edn, Cambridge, 1989

Weber, G., *Dichtung und höfishe Gesellschaft: Die Rezeption von Zeitgeschichte am Hof der ersten drei Ptolemäer*, Stuttgart, 1991

—— (ed.), *Kulturgeschichte des Hellenismus von Alexander bis Kleopatra*, Stuttgart, 2007

Welles, C. B., *Royal Correspondence in the Hellenistic Period: A Study in Greek Epigraphy*, New Haven, 1934

Whitmarsh, T. (ed.), *Local Knowledge and Microidenities in the Imperial Greek World*, Cambridge, 2010

Wiemer, H.-U., *Krieg, Handel und Piraterie: Untersuchungen zur Geschichte des hellenistischen Rhodos*, Berlin, 2002

Wilhelm, A., *Kleine Schriften*, Berlin, 1974

Will, É., *Histoire politique du monde hellénistique, 323–30 av. J.-C.*, 3rd edn, Paris, 2003

Wörrle, M., *Stadt und Fest im kaiserzeitlichen Kleinasien: Studien zu einer agonistischen Stiftung aus Oinoanda*, Munich, 1988

Wörrle, M., and P. Zanker (eds.), *Stadtbild und Bürgerbild im Hellenismus*, Munich, 1995

Worthington, I., *By the Spear: Philip II, Alexander the Great and the Rise and Fall of the Macedonian Empire*, Oxford, 2014

Zuiderhoek, A., *The Politics of Munificence in the Roman Empire: Citizens, Elites, and Benefactors in Asia Minor*, Cambridge, 2009

CHRONOLOGY

336 BC	Assassination of Philip II of Macedonia; Alexander becomes king
335	Destruction of Thebes
334–325	Alexander's campaign in Asia
334	Alexander's victory at Granikos
333	Alexander defeats Darius III in Issos
332–331	Alexander in Egypt; foundation of Alexandria
331	Alexander defeats Darius III in Gaugamela
330	Burning of the palace in Persepolis; assassination of Darius III
330–327	Alexander conquers north-east Iran
327–325	Alexander's campaign in Punjab
326	Alexander's battles in Hydaspes; victory over Poros
325	Alexander's return from India; Nearchos explores the Indian Ocean and the Persian Gulf
324	Alexander's edict concerning the return of exiles; mutiny of Alexander's army in Opis; death of Hephaistion
323	Death of Alexander; Philip III Arrhidaios and Alexander IV are proclaimed kings under the guardianship of Karteros; division of satrapies among Alexander's generals
323/22	The Hellenic or Lamian War (revolt of Greek cities against the Macedonian supremacy); defeat of Athens
321–281	Wars of the Successors for the division of Alexander's empire
321/320	Perdikkas and Eumenes against Antipatros, Krateros, Antigonos Monophthalmos and Ptolemy; division of Alexander's empire in the settlement at Triparadeisos
319–315	Kassandros against Polyperchon and Olympias; Antigonos against Eumenes
319–288	Autocratic rule of Agathokles of Syracuse in Sicily
317	Olympias orders the murder of Philip III
315	Defeat and death of Eumenes

314	Coalition of Kassandros, Lysimachos, Ptolemy and Seleukos against Antigonos Monophthalmos and his son Demetrios Poliorketes; Antigonos and Demetrios declare the freedom of the Greek cities
312	Seleukos returns to his satrapy in Babylon
311	Peace agreement among the Successors
310	Kassandros orders the murder of Alexander IV, the last member of the Argead dynasty
308–306	Campaign of Agathokles of Syracuse in North Africa
307	Liberation of Athens from Macedonian occupation by Demetrios Poliorketes
306	Victory of Demetrios Poliorketes over Ptolemy near Salamis in Cyprus; the 'Year of the Kings'; Antigonos Monophthalmos and Demetrios assume the title of king; their example is followed by Ptolemy, Kassandros, Lysimachos and Seleukos
305–304	Siege of Rhodes by Demetrios Poliorketes
304	Agathokles is proclaimed king in Sicily
303–301	War of Ptolemy, Kassandros, Lysimachos and Seleukos against Antigonos and Demetrios; Antigonos and Demetrios found a Hellenic Alliance
301	Antigonos is killed at the Battle of Ipsos; Ariarathes II founds the kingdom of Kappadokia
297	Death of Kassandros, king of Macedonia; he is succeeded by Philip IV; Zipoetes is proclaimed king of Bithynia; Pyrrhos is proclaimed king of Epirus
296	Death of Philip IV, king of Macedonia; dynastic conflict between Kassandros' sons Alexander and Antipatros
295	Demetrios Poliorketes occupies Athens
294	Demetrios is proclaimed king of Macedonia
288	Lysimachos and Pyrrhos expel Demetrios from Macedonia; Lysimachos expels Pyrrhos and reigns alone in Macedonia and Thrace; his wife is Arsinoe, daughter of Ptolemy I
287–285	Unsuccessful campaign of Demetrios in Asia Minor; Demetrios is captured by Seleukos and dies in captivity in 283
283	Death of Ptolemy I, king of Egypt; Arsinoe makes Lysimachos order the murder of his son Agathokles; Agathokles' widow, Lysandra, and her brother Ptolemy Keraunos seek refuge in the court of Seleukos I
283–246	Ptolemy II, king of Egypt (281–c. 268 together with Arsinoe II)
281	War between Seleukos and Lysimachos; Lysimachos is killed in the Battle of Kouropedion; Seleukos is murdered by his ally Ptolemy Keraunos, who becomes king in Macedonia
281–261	Antiochos I, king of the Seleucid kingdom
280–275	Campaigns of Pyrrhos of Epirus in Italy and Sicily

279–278	Invasion of the Gauls (Galatians); death of Ptolemy Keraunos; anarchy in Macedonia; victory of the Aetolians over the Gauls at Delphi; rise of the Aetolian League
278	The Gauls cross over to Asia Minor and begin their raids against the Greek cities
277	Victory of Antigonos Gonatas over the Gauls in Lysimacheia; Antigonos is proclaimed king
275/4–271	First Syrian War between Antiochos I and Ptolemy II for the control of Koile Syria
274–272	Pyrrhos regains part of Macedonia; war of Pyrrhos against Antigonos Gonatas; Pyrrhos is killed in Argos (272)
272–239	Antigonos Gonatas, sole king of Macedonia
268–261	Chremonidean War: Antigonos Gonatas against Ptolemy II, Athens, Sparta and their allies; Gonatas prevails; Macedonian occupation of Athens (until 229)
264–241	First Punic War between Rome and Carthage
261–246	Antiochos II, king of the Seleucid kingdom
260–253	Second Syrian War: Antiochos II, Rhodes and Antigonos Gonatas against Ptolemy II
255–254	Bithynian Succession War
251	Aratos liberates Sikyon; Sikyon joins the Achaean League
250–245	Secession of Alexander, commander of the Macedonian garrison in Corinth, from Antigonos Gonatas
247	Creation of the Parthian kingdom
246	Death of Ptolemy II (January) and Antiochos II (summer)
246–221	Ptolemy III, king in Egypt
246	Beginning of the Third Syrian War or War of Laodike; victorious campaign of Ptolemy III in the Seleucid kingdom (Syria and Mesopotamia)
246–225	Seleukos II, king of the Seleucid kingdom
245	Victory of Antigonos Gonatas over the Ptolemaic fleet in Andros; Seleukos II reconquers territories in northern Syria and Mesopotamia
243	Aratos liberates Corinth from the Macedonian garrison
241	End of the Third Syrian War; Ptolemy III gains territories in Syria
241–197	Attalos I, ruler of Pergamon; he is proclaimed king in 238
240	Sessession of Antiochos Hierax from the Seleucid kingdom; rule in Asia Minor
239	Death of Antigonos Gonatas; alliance of the Aetolian and Achaean Leagues
239–229	Demetrios II, king of Macedonia
239–233	War of Demetrios against the Aetolian and Achaean Leagues

238	Victories of Attalos I of Pergamon in wars against the Gauls in Asia Minor
231–229	Invasion of Dardanians in Macedonia
230–227	Victorious war of Attalos I of Pergamon against Antiochos Hierax; death of Antiochos Hierax in 226
229–221	Antigonos Doson, king of Macedonia
229	Liberation of Athens from Macedonian garrison
229–228	First Illyrian War: the Romans defeat Queen Teuta
229–222	Kleomenes' War (Sparta against the Achaean League)
229–220	Aetolian raids on the Peloponnese and in central Greece
227	Military operations of Antigonos Doson of Macedonia in Caria (Asia Minor)
225–222	Seleukos III, king of the Seleucid kingdom
224–222	Hellenic Alliance under the leadership of Antigonos Doson; war against Kleomenes of Sparta; defeat of Kleomenes in the Battle of Sellasia (222)
222–187	Antiochos III, king of the Seleucid kingdom
222–213	War of Antiochos III against Molon, who controls parts of Asia Minor; victory of Antiochos
221	Death of Ptolemy III and Antigonos Doson; the Carthaginian commander Hasdrubal is murdered in Spain and is succeeded by Hannibal
221–179	Philip V, king in Macedonia
221–204	Ptolemy IV, king in Egypt
221–219	War of Lyttos on Crete (Knossos and Gortyn with their allies against Lyttos, civil war in Gortyn); military operations of Hannibal in Spain
220	War of Rhodes against Byzantion for the abolishment of duties on vessels passing through the straits
220–217	'Social War': the Hellenic Alliance under Philip V of Macedonia against the Aetolian League; Dardanian invasions in Macedonia (220–219, 217)
219–218	Second Illyrian War: Rome defeats Demetrios of Pharos
219–217	Fourth Syrian War between Ptolemy IV and Antiochos III
218	Hannibal begins his campaign against Rome; the start of the Second Punic War
217	22 June: Ptolemy IV defeats Antiochos III in the Battle of Rhaphia; late June: Hannibal defeats the Romans near the Lake Trasimene; August: peace conference in Naupaktos between Philip V and the Aetolians
216	Hannibal defeats the Romans in Cannae
216–213	War between Antiochos III and the usurper Achaios in Asia Minor
215	Treaty of alliance between Philip V and Hannibal
215–205	First Macedonian War: Philip V against Rome
214	Death of Aratos

212	The Romans capture Syracuse; alliance between the Aetolian League and Rome against Philip V
212–205	Reconquest of the eastern provinces by Antiochos III
206	Peace treaty between the Aetolians and Philip V
205	Peace of Phoinike ends the First Macedonian War; revolt of the native Egyptians in south Egypt
205–185	South Egypt is ruled by native pharaohs
205–201	First Cretan War: Cretan cities, allied with Philip V, against Rhodes, Kos and other islands
204	Death of Ptolemy IV
204–180	Ptolemy V, king of Egypt
203/202	Secret treaty between Philip V and Antiochos III to divide the Ptolemaic kingdom
202	Defeat of Hannibal in the Second Punic War; Fifth Syrian War: Antiochos III against Ptolemy V
202–200	Military operations of Philip V in south Asia Minor; war of Philip V against Rhodes
201	Attalos I and Rhodes request the help of Rome against Philip V
200–197	Second Macedonian War: Philip V against Rome and her allies Pergamon, Rhodes and Athens
197	Victory of Titus Quintius Flamininus over Philip V at Kynos Kephalai; Antiochos III occupies Macedonian and Ptolemaic possessions in Asia Minor and Thrace; death of Attalos I
197–158	Eumenes II, king of Pergamon
196	Flamininus declares the freedom of the Greek cities
195	War of the Romans against King Nabis of Sparta
194	The Roman troops withdraw from Greece; 'Cold War' between Antiochos III and Rome
192–188	Antiochos' War: Antiochos III and the Aetolians against Rome and her allies, Pergamon and Macedonia
191	Defeat of Antiochos III in Thermopylai; return to Asia Minor
189	Defeat of Antiochos III at Magnesia
188	Peace of Apameia: Antiochos loses his possesions in Asia Minor; Eumenes II of Pergamon and Rhodes gain territories
185	Death of Antiochos III in Iran; creation of an autonomous Graeco-Bactrian kingdom under Euthydemos
187–175	Seleukos IV, king in the Seleucid kingdom
180–175	Creation of separate Graeco-Bactrian and Graeco-Indian kingdoms
180	Death of Ptolemy V
180–170	First reign of Ptolemy VI
179	Death of Philip V
179–168	Perseus, king of Macedonia

175	Seleukos V is murdered by his chief minister Heliodoros
175–164	Antiochos IV seizes power in the Seleucid kingdom
171–168	Third Macedonian War: Rome and her allies against Perseus of Macedonia
170	Sixth Syrian War; Antiochos IV invades Egypt; Ptolemy VI is replaced as king by his brother Ptolemy VIII
170–118	Dynastic conflicts and civil wars in Egypt between Ptolemy VI (170–145), Ptolemy VIII (170–163, 145–116), Cleopatra II (145–127, 124–116) and Cleopatra III (139–101)
168	Victory of Aemilius Paullus over Perseus in the Battle of Pydna; the end of the Antigonid monarchy; the Macedonian kingdom is divided into four states; 1,000 Greek hostages in Rome; Rhodes loses its possession in Asia Minor; Delos is declared a free harbour; Antiochos IV is forced by the Romans to retreat from Egypt; he recalls the privileges of the Jews in Jerusalem; beginning of the revolt of the Maccabees
164	Death of Antiochos IV; usurpations and civil wars between various branches of the Seleucids begin; Judah Maccabee occupies Jerusalem
159–154	War between Pergamon and Prusias II, king of Bithynia; victory of Pergamon
158	Death of Eumenes II
158–138	Attalos II, king of Pergamon
153–145	Usurpation of the Seleucid throne by Alexandros Balas
149–148	Andriskos seizes power in Macedonia and re-establishes the Macedonian kingdom; he is defeated by the Romans; Macedonia becomes the first Roman province in Greece
146	Achaean War: the Achaean League against Rome; the Achaeans are defeated, Corinth is destroyed and Greece is placed under direct Roman administration
145–139	Demetrios II, king in the Seleucid kingdom
143/142	The Seleucid Demetrios II recognises the independence of Judaea
142–138	Usurpation of the Seleucid throne by Diodotos Tryphon
141	The Parthians occupy Seleukeia on the Tigris, a Seleucid capital
139	Demetrios II is defeated by the Parthians and spends ten years in captivity
138	Death of Attalos II
138–133	Attalos III, king of Pergamon
133	Death of Attalos III of Pergamon, who bequeaths his kingdom to the Romans
133–129	Aristonikos' War: Aristonikos, illegitimate son of Attalos II of Pergamon, fights against the Romans supported by lower social strata
130	The Seleukids lose Mesopotamia to the Parthians
129	Aristonikos is defeated; creation of the Roman province of Asia

123–122	The reforms of Caius Gracchus in Rome; measures concerning the collection of tribute in Asia
c. 105–96	Ptolemy Apion, king in Cyrenaica
96	Ptolemy Apion bequeaths his kingdom to the Romans; Cyrenaica becomes a province in 74
88–86	First Mithridatic War: Mithridates VI, king of Pontos, and his Greek allies against Rome; victorious campaign of Sulla in Greece
85	Peace of Dardanos between Sulla and Mithridates VI
83	The population of Antioch invites the king of Armenia Tigranes II to take over the Seleucid kingdom
83–81	Second Mithridatic War: Mithridates VI against Rome
74	Cyrenaica and Bithynia become Roman provinces
74–64	Third Mithridatic War: Mithridates VI against Rome
74–67	Campaigns of Lucullus against Mithridates
69–67	Conquest of Crete by the Romans
67	Lex Gabinia: Pompey receives an extraordinary command in the war against the pirates and Mithridates
64	Mithridates VI commits suicide; the kingdom of Pontos is abolished; Pompey reorganises the East; creation of the province of Bithynia and Pontos; Pompey founds cities in Asia Minor
63	The Seleukid kingdom becomes a Roman province
59	Rome annexes Cyprus
55	Ptolemy XII regains his throne in Egypt with Roman help
49–48	Civil war between Pompey and Caesar
48	Caesar defeats Pompey at Pharsalos; Pompey is murdered in Alexandria
47	Caesar is appointed dictator in Rome; Bellum Alexandrinum: Caesar subdues an uprising in Alexandria and establishes Cleopatra VII as queen
44	Caesar is murdered; Cleopatra returns from Rome to Alexandria with her son Kaisarion
43	Triumvirate in Rome: Octavian, Mark Antony and Lepidus; Antony controls the Roman East
40	Antony allies himself with Cleopatra
37–36	Antony reorganises the Roman East, creating client kingdoms and enlarging the kingdom of Cleopatra
31	Rome declares war on Antony and Cleopatra; victory of Octavian at Actium
30	Antony and Cleopatra commit suicide; Kaisarion is put to death by Octavian; Egypt is annexed by Rome
27	Octavian, now under the name Imperator Caesar Augustus, establishes a monarchical regime in Rome
27–AD 14	Reign of Augustus

25	Galatia becomes a Roman province
6	The kingdom of Paphlagonia is abolished and attached to the province of Galatia
c. 10	The last Graeco-Indian kingdom in northern India is abolished
AD 6	Part of the kingdom of Judaea becomes a Roman province
14–37	Reign of Tiberius
18	The kingdom of Kappadokia become a Roman province
37–41	Reign of Caligula
41–54	Reign of Claudius
43	Lycia becomes a Roman province
44	The realm of King Herod Agrippa in Judaea becomes a Roman province
46	The kingdom of Thrace becomes a Roman province
54–68	Reign of Nero
63	Nero annexes the kingdom of Pontos and Colchis
64	Fire destroyes parts of Rome; prosecution of Christians
66–70	Jewish revolt
66–7	Nero visits Greece; he declares the Greek cities free
68	Opposition to Nero in Rome; Nero commits suicide; end of the Julio-Claudian dynasty
69	Civil war in the Roman Empire (the 'Year of the Four Emperors'); Vespasian seizes power and founds the Flavian dynasty
69–79	Reign of Vespasian
70	Jerusalem is captured by Titus, Vespasian's son
70–73	Last resistance of Jews in Masada
c. 71	Lycia and Pamphylia are joined in one province
c. 73	The kingdom of Kommagene is annexed and becomes part of the province of Syria
79–81	Reign of Titus
81–96	Reign of Domitian
96	Domitian is murdered; end of the Flavian dynasty
96–8	Reign of Nerva, who establishes the dynasty of the adopted emperors (Antonine dynasty)
98–117	Reign of Trajan
101–6	Conquest of Dacia
107	Conquest of the Nabatean kingdom in Arabia
113–15	Conquest of Mesopotamia; the Roman Empire reaches its greatest extent
115–17	Jewish revolts in Syria, Egypt and Cyrenaica
117–38	Reign of Hadrian
123–5	Hadrian visits Greece and Asia Minor
128–32	Second trip of Hadrian to the East (Syria, Egypt, Asia Minor, Greece)
130	Death of Antinoos in Egypt

INDEX